Cambridge International AS and A Level

Biology

Revision Guide

John Adds and Phil Bradfield

CAMBRIDGE
UNIVERSITY PRESS

CAMBRIDGE
UNIVERSITY PRESS

University Printing House, Cambridge CB2 8BS, United Kingdom

One Liberty Plaza, 20th Floor, New York, NY 10006, USA

477 Williamstown Road, Port Melbourne, VIC 3207, Australia

4843/24, 2nd Floor, Ansari Road, Daryaganj, Delhi – 110002, India

79 Anson Road, #06–04/06, Singapore 079906

Cambridge University Press is part of the University of Cambridge.

It furthers the University's mission by disseminating knowledge in the pursuit of education, learning and research at the highest international levels of excellence.

www.cambridge.org
Information on this title: www.cambridge.org/9781316600467

© Cambridge University Press 2017

First published 2017

20 19 18 17 16 15 14 13 12 11 10 9 8 7 6 5 4 3 2

Printed in Spain by GraphyCems

A catalogue record for this publication is available from the British Library

ISBN 978-1-316-60046-7 Paperback

....

NOTICE TO TEACHERS IN THE UK

It is illegal to reproduce any part of this work in material form (including photocopying and electronic storage) except under the following circumstances:

(i)   where you are abiding by a licence granted to your school or institution by the Copyright Licensing Agency;

(ii) where no such licence exists, or where you wish to exceed the terms of a license, and you have gained the written permission of Cambridge University Press;

(iii) where you are allowed to reproduce without permission under the provisions of Chapter 3 of the Copyright, Designs and Patents Act 1988, which covers, for example, the reproduction of short passages within certain types of educational anthology and reproduction for the purposes of setting examination questions.

....

The exam-style questions and sample answers in this title were written by the author and have not been produced by Cambridge International Examinations.

Table of contents

How to use this book

Learning outcomes set the scene of each chapter, help with navigation through the book and give a reminder of what's important about each topic.

Worked example 2.01

Question

The diagram shows the structure of two molecules of α-glucose:

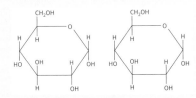

1 Copy the diagram and show how these two molecules are linked together to form a molecule of maltose.

2 Name the type of reaction involved in this process.

3 Name the type of bond formed.

Answers

1 It is important to be careful when copying the structure of the glucose molecules (e.g. by showing the positions of the –OH and –H correctly on each carbon atom). When these two molecules of glucose join to form maltose, water is lost by the removal of –OH and –H from each molecule, so you should carefully draw a circle round these on carbon atom number 1 of the first glucose molecule and carbon atom number 4 of the second glucose molecule, with water (H_2O) given off as a product. The two glucose molecules are now linked by a –O– bond between carbon atom 1 and carbon atom 4.

2 This is an example of a condensation reaction.

3 The type of bond formed is known as a glycosidic bond. (Be careful to spell this correctly!)

Worked examples provide a step-by-step approach to answering questions, guiding you through from start to finish.

Sample question 8.01

The llama is a mammal that lives in the high Andes of South America, often at an altitude of over 5000 metres above sea level. The oxygen dissociation curve for llama haemoglobin is to the left of the dissociation curves for most other mammals. Suggest why this is an important adaptation for llamas. [4 marks]

[Mark points are shown in square brackets – to a maximum of 4 marks]

At high altitudes, the partial pressure of oxygen in the air is low. [1] Because the dissociation curve is to the left of other mammals, llamas' haemoglobin will have a relatively high affinity for oxygen. This means that it will be fully saturated with oxygen [1] at low partial pressures [1]. Haemoglobin from other mammals would only be partly saturated with oxygen at high altitudes [1]. This is how llamas are adapted to life at high altitudes.

This is a good explanation of the importance of this effect. Remember that as the dissociation curve moves to the left, it implies that the haemoglobin has an increased affinity for oxygen. In other words, it will pick up oxygen and become saturated at lower partial pressures. As altitude increases, the air pressure drops which is why the partial pressure of oxygen decreases. At an altitude of 5000 metres, the partial pressure of oxygen in air is only about 50% of its value at sea level.

Sample questions contain an example of an excellent answer and an explanation of how the answer achieves this.

Progress check 5.01

Explain the difference between:

1 A chromosome and a chromatid.

2 A centromere and a telomere.

Progress check questions allow you to check your own knowledge and see how well you're getting on.

TIP

Remember the letters **PMAT**:

Prophase = **P**ro means first, or 'before'

Metaphase = chromosomes in **M**iddle

Anaphase = chromosomes move **A**part

Telophase = **T**wo nuclei

Tips contain quick suggestions to remind you about key facts and highlight important points.

Revision checklist

Check that you know:

- [ ] the structure of nucleotides, including ATP
- [ ] the structures of RNA and DNA
- [ ] the importance of base pairing between complementary bases
- [ ] semi-conservative replication of DNA
- [ ] polypeptides are coded for by genes and genes form part of a DNA molecule
- [ ] gene mutations and how a gene mutation may result in a changed polypeptide
- [ ] how the sequence of nucleotides codes for the amino acid sequence and sickle cell anaemia
- [ ] how the information in DNA is used during protein synthesis, including the roles of mRNA, tRNA and ribosomes.

Revision checklist occur at the end of each chapter so you can check off the topics as you revise them.

Exam-style questions

1 Figure 1.10 is a drawing made from an electron micrograph of an animal cell.

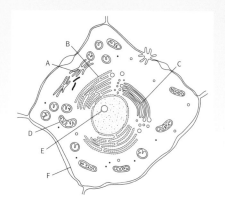

Figure 1.10 A drawing made from an electron micrograph of an animal cell.

a Copy and complete Table 1.03, name the organelles A to F and state one function of each. [6]

b Explain why an electron micrograph of this cell shows more detail than a light micrograph taken at the same magnification. [2]

c Name three other structures, not visible in Figure 1.10, which could be seen in an electron micrograph of a plant leaf cell. [3]

2 Table 1.04 lists some features of animal, plant and bacterial (prokaryotic) cells. Copy and complete Table 1.04, placing a tick (✔) in the appropriate box if the statement is correct and a cross (✗) if it is not. [8]

3 a Briefly describe the structure of a virus particle. [3]

b 'All viruses are parasitic'. Explain this statement. [2]

Exam-style questions help you to thoroughly prepare for examinations . Complete these questions and check your answers against those provided at the back of the book.

Acknowledgements

Thanks to the following for permission to reproduce photos:

Cover Colin Varndell/SPL; Fig 1.4 STEVE GSCHMEISSNER/Getty Images; Fig 3.7 LAGUNA DESIGN/SPL; Fig 5.4 STEVE GSCHMEISSNER/SPL; Fig 5.5a SCIENCE PICTURES LIMITED/SPL; Fig 5.5b SCIENCE PHOTO LIBRARY; Fig 5.6 ARTURO LONDONO, ISM/SPL; Fig 7.4 Ed Reschke/Getty Images; Fig 7.7, 7.11, 7.13, 14.5, P1 Q4 © John Adds; Fig 7.9 DR KEITH WHEELER/SPL; Fig 8.1a-d Dr. Gladden Willis/Getty Images; Fig 9.4, 9.5, 11.1, 13.16 BIOPHOTO ASSOCIATES/SPL; Fig 11.4 Cheryl Tyron/CDC/Getty Images; Fig 11.5 DR M.A. ANSARY/SPL; Fig 12.6 Bengal at a glance/Getty Images; Fig 13.10 JEFF CARROLL/AGSTOCKUSA/SPL; Fig 14.4 DR P. MARAZZI/SPL; Fig 15.6 Panel Rey/EyeEm/Getty Images; Fig 16.1a, b Alila Medical Media/Shutterstock; Fig 16.8 SCIEPRO/Getty Images; Fig 16.9 SIA KAMBOU/AFP/Getty Images; Fig 17.3 Axel Bueckert/Getty Images; Fig 17.6 JEFF LEPORE/SPL; Fig 17.8 PAUL D STEWART/SPL; Fig 17.9 Science VU/Getty Images; Fig 17.12a Watcha/Getty Images; Fig 17.12b randimal/Getty Images; Fig 18.1 MICHAEL MARTEN/SPL; Fig 18.2 ephotocorp/Alamy Stock Photo; Fig 18.4 JOHN SHAW/SPL; Fig 18.8 EYE OF SCIENCE/SPL; Fig 18.9 LOUISE MURRAY/SPL; Fig 18.10 RICHARD R. HANSEN/SPL; Fig 18.11 M.H. SHARP/ SPL; Fig 18.12, 18.13 FRANS LANTING, MINT IMAGES/SPL; Fig 18.14 imageBROKER/Alamy Stock Photo; P2.6 Nigel Cattlin/Alamy Stock Photo; P2.8 Jennifer Booher/Alamy Stock Photo

SPL = Science Photo Library

Cell structure

Learning outcomes

When you have finished this unit, you should be able to:

- ☐ compare the structure of animal and plant cells as seen through a light microscope

- ☐ measure cells using an eyepiece graticule and stage micrometer scale

- ☐ use the units of length needed in cell studies (millimetre, micrometre and nanometre)

- ☐ calculate the magnifications of drawings and micrographs

- ☐ calculate the sizes of specimens from drawings and micrographs

- ☐ understand the difference between magnification and resolution

- ☐ interpret electron micrographs of animal and plant cells

- ☐ recognise these cell structures and know their functions:

- cell surface membrane
- nucleus, nuclear envelope and nucleolus
- rough endoplasmic reticulum
- smooth endoplasmic reticulum
- Golgi body
- mitochondria
- ribosomes
- lysosomes
- microtubules
- centrioles
- chloroplasts
- cell wall
- plasmodesmata
- large permanent vacuole and tonoplast of plant cells

- ☐ outline the role of ATP in cells

- ☐ compare the structure of a bacterial cell with that of animal and plant cells

- ☐ outline the main features of viruses.

The **cell** is the basic 'unit' of living organisms. There are thousands of different types of cell. Each type is adapted for a different function, but they are all recognisable as cells by the structures they contain.

1.01 The structure of animal and plant cells

You should have the opportunity to make temporary slides of suitable animal and plant cells, such as human cheek cells or cells from the leaf of a plant. Stains such as iodine solution or methylene blue are often used to show the cell contents more clearly. For example, iodine stains starch in plant cells blue-black, and colours the nuclei, cytoplasm and cell walls pale yellow. Using a light microscope only enables you to see the larger structures present in cells. From slides you can make drawings of the cells. Alternatively, a photograph

of a cell as seen through a light microscope can be taken. A photograph of an image seen through a light microscope is called a light micrograph.

Using a school microscope, you can identify the structures shown in Figure 1.01.

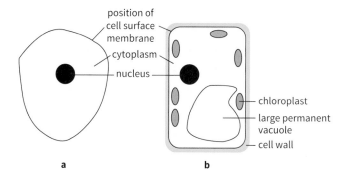

Figure 1.01 The main structures of typical animal and plant cells visible with a school microscope: **a** animal cell and **b** plant cell.

It is possible to see one or two other cell structures through a light microscope, such as **mitochondria** and **Golgi bodies**. However, this needs a very high quality microscope and often involves special staining procedures.

Progress check 1.01

1   What structures can you see in *both* an animal cell *and* a plant cell through a light microscope?

2   What structures are visible in a plant cell but not in an animal cell?

3   Explain why stains are used when making microscope slides of cells.

1.02 Measuring cells

Ideally, to measure a cell you would place a scale or ruler on the slide alongside the specimen. This is not physically possible, but you can use a separate slide with a 'ruler' called a stage micrometer. This has a scale a millimetre in length, divided into 100 divisions (each division = 0.01 mm or 10 μm). The stage micrometer is used together with a scale in the eyepiece lens, called an eyepiece graticule. The eyepiece graticule has no measureable units such as millimetres, because the divisions will represent different lengths depending on the magnification you are using. We say that the eyepiece scale is in arbitrary units. This means that the divisions on the scale are all the same size and can be used for comparison, but if you want to know the actual length of an image, you have to calibrate the eyepiece graticule divisions using the stage micrometer.

Worked example 1.01

Question

A student placed a stage micrometer slide on the stage of his microscope and observed it using a medium power objective lens. He lined up the micrometer scale with the eyepiece graticule and noted that 100 divisions on the graticule scale measured 25 divisions on the stage micrometer (Figure 1.02).

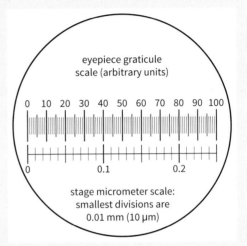

Figure 1.02 Image of a stage micrometer scale aligned alongside an eyepiece graticule scale.

The student removed the stage micrometer from the microscope and replaced it with a slide of some plant tissue. He focused on a cell using the same medium power objective lens. He noted that the cell measured 48 divisions on the eyepiece scale.

Calculate the length of the plant cell in micrometres (μm).

Answer

Step 1:

The length of 25 divisions on the stage micrometer = $25 \times 10 \, \mu m = 250 \, \mu m$

Therefore each eyepiece division is equivalent to:

$$\frac{250 \, \mu m}{100} = 2.5 \, \mu m$$

Step 2:

Using the *same magnification*, 48 divisions on the eyepiece scale are equivalent to:

$48 \times 2.5 \, \mu m = 120 \, \mu m$

Therefore the length of the plant cell is 120 μm.

Units of length used in cell studies

- 1 millimetre (mm) = 1/1000 of a metre, or 10^{-3} m
- 1 micrometre (µm) = 1/1000 of a mm, or 10^{-6} m
- 1 nanometre (nm) = 1/1000 of a µm, or 10^{-9} m.

Cells vary a great deal in size, but on average they are a fraction of a millimetre in diameter or length, with plant cells tending to be larger than animal ones. The plant cell in Worked example 1.01 was 120 µm in length. There are 1000 µm in a millimetre; so 120 µm is equal to 0.12 mm.

The structures within a cell are called organelles. Large organelles such as the nucleus and mitochondria are normally measured in micrometres. A typical nucleus is about 5–10 µm in diameter, while a mitochondrion is about 1 µm in diameter and up to 10 µm in length. Smaller organelles are measured in nanometres. For example, a **ribosome** is about 25 nm in diameter, while the cell surface membrane has a thickness of around 7 nm.

Progress check 1.02

1 The student in Worked example 1.01 measured the size of the nucleus of the plant cell and found it to be three divisions on his eyepiece scale, using the same medium power objective lens. What is the diameter of the nucleus in micrometres?

2 A chloroplast is 7 µm in length. What is this length in:

   a millimetres

   b nanometres?

1.03 Magnification

The **magnification** of a drawing or photomicrograph is the number of times larger the drawing or photomicrograph is, when compared with the actual size of the specimen. For example, the formula for the magnification of a drawing is:

$$\text{magnification} = \frac{\text{size of drawing}}{\text{size of specimen}}$$

The measurement of the drawing and that of the specimen must be in the *same units* in the formula.

A magnification is written like this: ×200 (meaning 'times 200').

Worked example 1.02

Question

A student looked at a plant cell through a microscope and measured its diameter. She found it to be 38 µm. She made a drawing of this cell and measured the diameter of the drawing with a ruler (Figure 1.03). What is the magnification of her drawing?

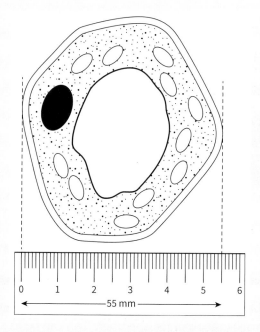

Figure 1.03 A student's drawing of a cell, with a ruler marked in millimetres alongside the drawing.

→

Step 1:

The width of the drawing measures 55 mm on the ruler. The drawing and the specimen must be measured in the same units. The specimen is 38 μm and the drawing is 55 mm. It is easiest to convert 55 mm into μm:

size of drawing in μm = (55 mm × 1000 μm/mm) = 55 000 μm

Step 2:

Actual size of specimen = 38 μm

$$\text{magnification} = \frac{\text{size of drawing}}{\text{size of specimen}}$$

$$= \frac{55\ 000\ \text{μm}}{38\ \text{μm}}$$

$$= \times 1447$$

$$= \times 1400 \text{ (to two significant figures)}$$

(i.e. the student's drawing is 1400 times larger than the actual cell on the slide.)

The magnification of a microscope can be found by multiplying the power of the eyepiece by the power of the objective lens. For example, a ×10 eyepiece and a ×40 objective gives the microscope an overall magnification of 10 × 40 = ×400.

> **TIP**
>
> When putting a magnification on a drawing, do not be tempted to use the microscope magnification. This only tells you how much bigger the image seen through the microscope is in comparison with the specimen. The magnification of a drawing will depend on how big you make your drawing!

Drawings or photomicrographs should always show the magnification of the specimen. This can be as a number (e.g. ×800) or by using a scale bar. A scale bar is a line drawn alongside the specimen, with the length of the line labelled (Figure 1.04).

Figure 1.04 Photomicrograph of red blood cell, with a scale bar.

The scale bar can be used to find the magnification. In Figure 1.04 the scale bar is 40 mm in length, which is 40 000 μm, so:

$$\text{magnification of the scale bar (and the specimen)} = \frac{\text{size of scale bar on the photomicrograph}}{\text{real size of scale bar}}$$

$$= \frac{40\ 000\ \text{μm}}{5\ \text{μm}}$$

$$= \times 8000$$

Magnification and resolution

A good quality light microscope can magnify objects about 2000 times (×2000), allowing us to view structures down to about 1 μm in length. However, at this magnification the 'detail' that is visible is very limited. The amount of detail is called the **resolution**. It is defined as the shortest distance between two points that can be distinguished as being separate. In a light microscope this is about 0.2 μm (200 nm). Through this microscope, two points that are closer than 200 nm will appeared blurred together and not visible as separate points.

We could take a photomicrograph and increase its magnification, 'blowing it up' so that it was the size of a poster, but this would not improve its resolution. To increase the magnification and improve the resolution of an image we have to use an electron microscope. The wavelength of a beam of electrons is much less than that of visible light, so an electron microscope can achieve a much better magnification and resolution than a light microscope. The useful limit of a modern **transmission electron microscope (TEM)** is over a million times magnification, with a resolution of less than 1 nm.

1.04 Electron micrographs of cells

A photograph of a specimen seen through an electron microscope is called an electron micrograph. Whereas a light microscope is normally used to look at cells at a magnification of a few hundred times, most electron micrographs are taken in the approximate range ×10 000 to ×200 000. Using higher magnifications and the improved resolution, much more can be seen of the structure within a cell and within the individual organelles. This fine detail is called the ultrastructure

of the cell. Figure 1.05 shows a diagram of a typical plant cell from a leaf, as seen through the electron microscope.

Much of the mass of a cell consists of membranes. As well as the cell surface membrane, the cytoplasm contains an extensive membrane system called **rough endoplasmic reticulum** (rough ER) covered with tiny organelles called **ribosomes**. There is also **smooth endoplasmic reticulum** (smooth ER), which lacks ribosomes. Other organelles such as the **nucleus, mitochondria** and **chloroplasts** are also surrounded by their own membranes. Membranes serve to isolate the processes and chemical reactions going on within the organelles. This is called **compartmentalisation**. All the membranes in a cell have a similar structure (see Unit 4). Table 1.01 shows a summary of the main organelles found in cells.

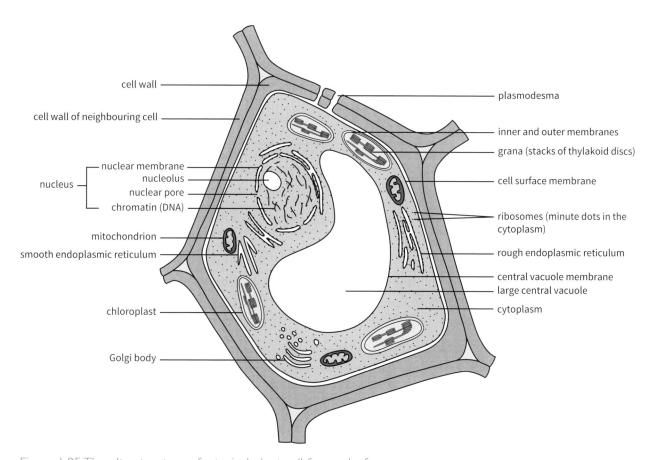

Figure 1.05 The ultrastructure of a typical plant cell from a leaf.

Organelle	Location and size	Structure and function(s)
cell surface membrane	surrounds cell (about 7 nm thick)	composed of phospholipids and protein (see Unit 4); partially permeable and controls the movement of substances into and out of the cell; allows cells to interact with each other and to respond to signals from outside the cell
nucleus	in cytoplasm, usually one per cell (about 5–10 µm in diameter)	contains the hereditary material (**deoxyribonucleic acid (DNA)**) coding for the synthesis of proteins in the cytoplasm. Surrounded by a double membrane called the **nuclear envelope**
nucleolus	one to several in nucleus (1–2 µm in diameter)	synthesises ribosomal RNA and makes ribosomes
rough ER	throughout cytoplasm (membranes about 4 nm thick)	'rough' because covered with ribosomes; membranes enclose compartments (sacs) that transport proteins synthesised on the ribosomes
smooth ER	in cytoplasm; extent depends on type of cell (membranes about 4 nm thick)	similar to rough ER but no ribosomes; synthesises and transports lipid molecules
Golgi body	in cytoplasm (variable in size and number)	synthesises glycoproteins (proteins with carbohydrate groups attached); packages proteins for export from the cell
mitochondria (singular = mitochondrion)	in cytoplasm; can be many thousands in some cells (around 1 µm diameter, up to 10 µm in length)	produce **adenosine triphosphate (ATP)** by aerobic respiration (see below and Unit 12)
ribosomes	attached to rough ER or free in cytoplasm (20–25 nm in size)	site of protein synthesis
lysosomes	in cytoplasm; variable in number (0.1–0.5 µm in diameter)	digests unwanted materials and worn-out organelles
microtubules	throughout cytoplasm (long hollow protein tubes 25 nm in diameter)	along with thinner protein filaments form the **cytoskeleton**; involved in movement of organelles
centrioles	two hollow cylinders about 0.5 µm long, present in animal cells; lie next to the nucleus in a region called the centrosome	made of protein microtubules; the centrosome is a microtubule organising centre (MTOC) and is involved with the formation of the spindle during nuclear division (see Unit 5), but the exact function of the centrioles is unknown; plant cells do not have a centrosome or centrioles, but can still form a spindle
chloroplasts	in cytoplasm of some plant cells (up to 10 µm in length)	contain **chlorophyll** and are the site of photosynthesis (see Unit 13)
cell wall	layer surrounding plant cells, variable thickness	made of the carbohydrate **cellulose** (see Unit 2); supports the plant cell and maintains its shape
plasmodesmata (singular = plasmodesma)	pores in plant cell wall (about 50 nm in diameter)	contain fine strands of cytoplasm linking a plant cell with its neighbouring cells and allowing movement of materials between cells
vacuole	large central space in plant cells (variable in size)	contains various solutes such as sugars, mineral salts and pigments; surrounded by a membrane called the **tonoplast**, which controls exchange of materials between the vacuole and the cytoplasm (note that animal cells have vacuoles, but these are small temporary structures)

Table 1.01 Summary of the main organelles present in cells.

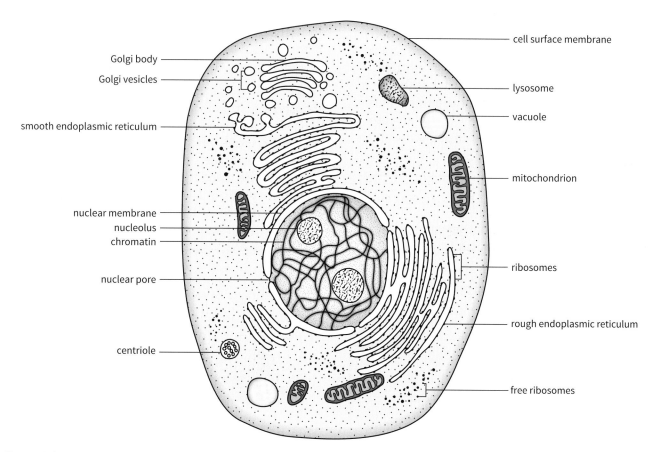

Many of the structures in Table 1.01 will be described in more detail in later units of this book (see references in Table 1.01). For now all you need to be able to do is recognise the organelles and give an *outline* of their functions.

Figure 1.06 is a diagram of the structure of a typical animal cell, as seen through an electron microscope.

With reference to Figures 1.05 and 1.06, note these extra points:

- The nucleus is surrounded by a double membrane called the nuclear envelope. The outer membrane of the nuclear envelope is continuous with the endoplasmic reticulum.

- The nuclear envelope contains 'holes' called **nuclear pores**. These allow movement of materials between the nucleus and the cytoplasm. For example, messenger RNA (mRNA) made in the nucleus can exit to the cytoplasm, carrying the instructions for protein synthesis encoded in the DNA (see Unit 6). Substances made in the cytoplasm can enter the nucleus through the pores (e.g. ATP).

- The nucleus contains the hereditary material (DNA) within structures called **chromosomes**. These are only visible when the nucleus divides (see Unit 5). Between cell divisions the chromosomes form a loosely coiled material called **chromatin**.

- The endoplasmic reticulum forms a complex three-dimensional system of sheet-like membranes and tubes enclosing fluid-filled sacs. Rough ER is 'studded' with ribosomes. Smooth ER lacks ribosomes, and is more tubular in appearance than rough ER. Ribosomes are also found 'loose' in the cytoplasm, where they are known as free ribosomes.

- Ribosomes are the site of protein synthesis. They are composed of protein and RNA. The 'instructions' for protein synthesis are encoded in the DNA and carried out to the ribosomes by mRNA.

- Ribosomes in the cytoplasm are large (known as 80S ribosomes). There are also smaller ribosomes (70S) in mitochondria and chloroplasts.

- The Golgi body (also known as the Golgi apparatus) consists of a stack of flattened membranes enclosing hollow sacs, called **cisternae**. Small spherical membrane vesicles containing protein are continually 'pinched off' the rough ER and fuse together to

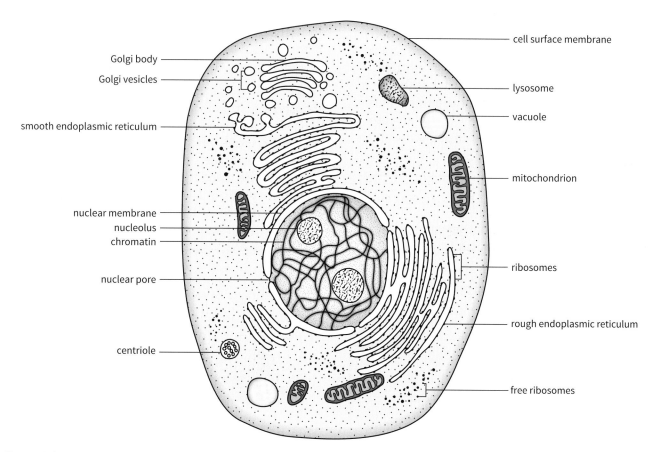

Figure 1.06 The ultrastructure of a typical animal cell.

form the Golgi body, on its side closest to the nucleus. Inside the cisternae the protein is chemically modified, such as by addition of carbohydrate to form **glycoproteins**. At the side furthest from the nucleus, vesicles containing the modified protein bud off from the cisternae and are transported to other parts of the cell. Some vesicles may fuse with the cell membrane, releasing their contents out of the cell. This secretion process is called **exocytosis** (see Unit 4). The Golgi body is also involved in making lysosomes.

- Lysosomes are found in most animal and plant cells. They are membrane-bound sacs formed when digestive enzymes are incorporated into vesicles from the Golgi body. The single membrane surrounding the lysosome keeps the digestive enzymes separate from the rest of the cell. Lysosomes can fuse with vacuoles containing unwanted structures such as old organelles. The enzymes in the lysosome then break down (digest) the unwanted material. Lysosomes are especially common in animal cells that carry out a process called phagocytosis, such as some white blood cells (see Unit 8), where they are used to digest pathogenic organisms such as bacteria.

- Chloroplasts are found in cells from the green parts of plants such as leaves and green stems. They are surrounded by a membrane and contain a complex internal system of membranes called **thylakoids**, arranged in stacks called **grana**. The membranes contain photosynthetic pigments such as chlorophyll, which absorb light energy and use it to make organic molecules such as glucose and starch (see Unit 13).

Progress check 1.03

1 Explain the difference between the magnification and the resolution of a microscope.

2 Briefly describe the location of these organelles and their functions:

  a nucleolus

  b lysosomes

  c plasmodesmata.

3 Arrange theses organelles in increasing order of size: nucleus, chloroplast, ribosome, centriole.

1.05 Mitochondria and the role of ATP

Mitochondria are present in nearly all animal and plant cells. The number of mitochondria in a cell is directly related to its energy demands. Cells that require a lot of energy, such as a muscle cell, contain many thousands of mitochondria, whereas less active cells have fewer of these organelles. Aerobic respiration takes place inside mitochondria. This releases energy, which is used to make a substance called adenosine triphosphate (ATP). ATP is the universal energy 'currency' in cells.

During respiration, energy-rich molecules such as glucose are broken down in a series of reactions. The chemical energy contained within these molecules is used to make ATP, which is in turn used to drive all the energy-requiring processes in a cell. To extract the energy from ATP, the molecule is broken down by a hydrolysis reaction, to form adenosine diphosphate (ADP) and phosphate. A simplified equation for this is:

ATP + water → ADP + phosphate + energy

The details of the formation of ATP during respiration are described in full in Unit 12, but at this stage all you need to know is that most ATP is formed during the last stages of respiration, which take place in the mitochondria. To carry out these stages a cell needs oxygen, which is why this is called *aerobic* respiration.

Figure 1.07 shows the internal structure of a mitochondrion. It has a smooth outer membrane and an inner membrane that is folded into a number of shelf-like **cristae**, which increases the surface area of the inner membrane. The last two stages of aerobic respiration are called the **Krebs cycle** and **oxidative phosphorylation**. The Krebs cycle takes place in the fluid-filled **matrix** of the mitochondrion and oxidative phosphorylation (where most ATP is produced) occurs on the inner membrane.

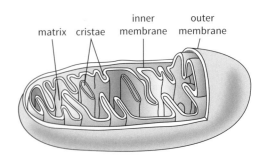

Figure 1.07 The internal structure of a mitochondrion.

Sample question 1.01

Explain the involvement of the nucleus, rough endoplasmic reticulum and Golgi body in the synthesis of glycoproteins in a cell. [10 marks]

[Mark points are shown in square brackets – to a maximum of 10 marks]

The nucleus contains the genetic material within the chromosomes, in the form of deoxyribonucleic acid (DNA) **[1]**. DNA carries the instructions (genetic code) needed for the synthesis of proteins **[1]** in the cytoplasm. These instructions are carried out to the cytoplasm by messenger RNA (mRNA) **[1]** through pores in the nuclear envelope **[1]**, and enter the sacs of the rough endoplasmic reticulum (rough ER) **[1]**, which are continuous with the nuclear envelope **[1]**. The rough ER is covered in small organelles called ribosomes **[1]**, where proteins are synthesised **[1]**. Small vesicles containing protein are pinched off the rough ER **[1]** and fuse together to form the cisternae of the Golgi body **[1]**, on its side closest to the nucleus. Inside the cisternae the protein is chemically modified by addition of carbohydrate to form glycoproteins **[1]**. At the side furthest from the nucleus, vesicles containing the modified protein bud off from the cisternae **[1]** and are transported to other parts of the cell.

This question requires you to know the location, structure and function of each of the three named organelles, and to put this information together as an account of the sequence of events taking place that result in production of glycoproteins in the cytoplasm.

The sample answer is laid out in the correct sequence and summarises the steps clearly, without including any irrelevant information.

Note that it is best to give the full names of biological terms when they are first used, such as deoxyribonucleic acid (DNA). The abbreviations can then be used in the rest of the answer.

1.06 Prokaryotic cells

The cells described so far in this unit are examples of **eukaryotic** cells. Eukaryotic means 'having a true nucleus'. Bacteria are also composed of cells, but they are much smaller than eukaryotic cells and simpler in structure. They are called **prokaryotic** cells (meaning 'before nucleus'). Bacterial cells have no nucleus or nuclear membrane. Their DNA is loose in the cytoplasm, forming a single circular loop, which is sometimes called a **bacterial chromosome**. Some bacteria also have smaller loops of DNA in the cytoplasm, called **plasmids**. Their cells lack endoplasmic reticulum and membrane-bound organelles such as mitochondria and chloroplasts.

The structure of a generalised bacterial cell is shown in Figure 1.08.

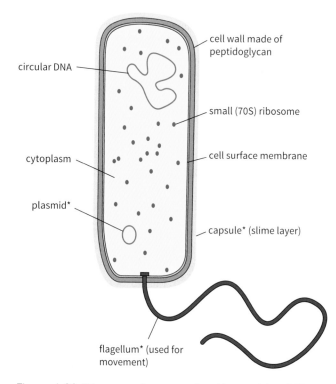

Figure 1.08 Diagram of a generalised bacterial cell. The structures marked with an asterisk are not found in all bacteria.

Eukaryotic cells	Prokaryotic cells
large (typically 10–100 μm in diameter)	small (typically 0.5–3 μm in diameter); volume as little as 1/10 000 of a eukaryotic cell
true nucleus surrounded by a nuclear membrane	no nucleus
linear DNA associated with protein, forming true chromosomes	circular DNA, not associated with proteins; may contain separate loops of DNA called plasmids
if present, cell wall made of cellulose (in plants) or chitin (in fungi)	cell wall made of **peptidoglycan** (a polysaccharide with some amino acid groups)
endoplasmic reticulum present	no endoplasmic reticulum or associated organelles such as the Golgi body
membrane-bound organelles such as mitochondria and chloroplasts present	no membrane-bound organelles (infolds of the cell surface membrane may be involved in photosynthesis and other processes)
large (80S) ribosomes attached to the rough ER and free in the cytoplasm	small (70S) ribosomes free in the cytoplasm
flagella present in some cells; they have a complex structure containing several microtubules	if present, flagella are made of a single microtubule

Table 1.02 Differences between eukaryotic and prokaryotic cells.

A comparison of the structure of eukaryotic and prokaryotic cells is given in Table 1.02.

1.07 Viruses

Viruses are tiny particles that are much smaller than bacteria. They do not consist of cells, and in many ways can be thought of as being intermediate between a chemical and a living organism. Viruses are not free-living and can only reproduce inside a host cell (i.e. they are parasites).

Viruses cause many diseases in plants and animals. For example, the tobacco mosaic virus produces brown blotches on the leaves of tobacco plants and the human influenza virus causes the symptoms we know as 'flu'. The **human immunodeficiency virus (HIV)** is the virus responsible for causing acquired immune deficiency syndrome (AIDS).

A virus particle is very simple in structure. It has no nucleus or cytoplasm, and consists of genetic material contained within a protein coat (Figure 1.09). The protein coat or **capsid** is made up of many individual protein molecules called **capsomeres**. The genetic material can be either DNA or RNA and makes up just a few genes. The genetic material, along with one or two enzymes, is all that the virus needs in order to reproduce within the host cell. The virus takes over the host cell, instructing it to make more virus particles. This normally causes the death of the host

cell. Some viruses are surrounded by a membrane called an envelope. This is not part of the virus itself – it is derived from the host cell. During the life cycle of the virus, the virus particles burst out of the host cell, taking part of the surface membrane of the host cell with them.

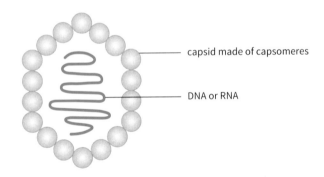

Figure 1.09 The structure of HIV.

Progress check 1.04

1   Briefly describe (in one paragraph) the main differences between a eukaryotic and a prokaryotic cell.

2   Explain why some biologists do not regard viruses as living organisms.

Revision checklist

Check that you know:

- [ ] the similarities and differences between an animal and a plant cell as seen through the light microscope

- [ ] the units of length used in cell studies (millimetre, micrometre and nanometre)

- [ ] how to calculate the magnifications of drawings, photomicrographs or electron micrographs

- [ ] how to calculate the sizes of specimens from drawings, photomicrographs or electron micrographs

- [ ] the difference between magnification and resolution

- [ ] how to describe and interpret electron micrographs of animal and plant cells

- [ ] how to recognise the following cell structures and knowing their functions:

- cell surface membrane
- nucleus, nuclear envelope and nucleolus
- rough endoplasmic reticulum
- smooth endoplasmic reticulum
- Golgi body
- mitochondria
- ribosomes
- lysosomes
- microtubules
- centrioles
- chloroplasts
- cell wall
- plasmodesmata
- large permanent vacuole and tonoplast of plant cells

- [ ] an outline of the role of ATP in cells

- [ ] how to compare the structure of a bacterial cell with the structure of animal and plant cells

- [ ] an outline of the main features of viruses.

Exam-style questions

1 Figure 1.10 is a drawing made from an electron micrograph of an animal cell.

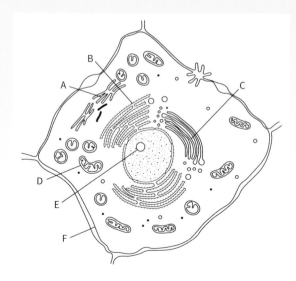

Figure 1.10 A drawing made from an electron micrograph of an animal cell.

a Copy and complete Table 1.03, name the organelles A to F and state one function of each. [6]

b Explain why an electron micrograph of this cell shows more detail than a light micrograph taken at the same magnification. [2]

c Name three other structures, not visible in Figure 1.10, which could be seen in an electron micrograph of a plant leaf cell. [3]

2 Table 1.04 lists some features of animal, plant and bacterial (prokaryotic) cells. Copy and complete Table 1.04, placing a tick (✓) in the appropriate box if the statement is correct and a cross (✗) if it is not. [8]

3 a Briefly describe the structure of a virus particle. [3]

b 'All viruses are parasitic'. Explain this statement. [2]

	Name of organelle	Function
A		
B		
C		
D		
E		
F		

Table 1.03

Feature	Animal cell	Plant cell	Bacterial cell
cell wall made of cellulose			
cell surface membrane			
rough endoplasmic reticulum			
ribosomes			
cytoskeleton			
Golgi apparatus			
chloroplasts			
mitochondria			

Table 1.04

Biological molecules

Learning outcomes

When you have finished this unit, you should be able to:

- describe how to carry out chemical tests for reducing sugars, non-reducing sugars, starch and lipids, including a semi-quantitative test for reducing sugars

- describe the ring structures of α-glucose and β-glucose

- understand what is meant by the terms monomer, polymer, macromolecule, monosaccharide, disaccharide and polysaccharide

- understand the formation of a glycosidic bond in the formation of disaccharides and polysaccharides

- describe how glycosidic bonds in disaccharides and polysaccharides may be broken

- know the structure of the polysaccharides starch, glycogen and cellulose and how the structures are related to their functions

- know the structure and formation of a triglyceride and how the structure of triglycerides is related to their functions

- know the structure of a phospholipid and understand how the structure of phospholipids is related to their functions in living organisms

- know the structure of an amino acid and how peptide bonds are formed and broken

- explain the different types of structures in proteins and the types of bonds that hold protein molecules in shape

- describe the structure of haemoglobin as an example of a globular protein and the structure of collagen as an example of a fibrous protein and relate their structures to their function

- explain how the structure and properties of water molecules are related to the roles of water in living organisms.

2.01 Testing for biological molecules

Biological molecules are organic substances found in living organisms and include **reducing sugars**, **non-reducing sugars**, **starch**, **proteins** and **lipids**. These molecules can be identified using simple chemical tests which are summarised in Table 2.01.

Biological molecule	Reagent used	Description of test
reducing sugars	Benedict's reagent	Benedict's regent contains copper (II) ions. When heated with reducing sugars, the copper (II) ions are reduced to copper (I) compounds, changing colour from blue to form a range of coloured precipitates, from green, to yellow, orange, red or brown. This test can be used semi-quantitatively, using a range of concentrations of a reducing sugar.
non-reducing sugars	Benedict's reagent, following acid hydrolysis	Sucrose is a commonly occurring non-reducing sugar. When heated with dilute acid, such as hydrochloric acid, sucrose is hydrolysed into its constituent monosaccharides, glucose and fructose, which are both reducing sugars. Excess acid is then neutralised by the addition of sodium hydrogen carbonate and the mixture is then tested with Benedict's reagent. This will show the production of reducing sugars.
starch	iodine in potassium iodide solution	Iodine solution is initially brown, but turns blue to black in the presence of starch. This test can be used quantitatively, using standard starch solutions and a colorimeter to measure the intensity of the blue colour produced.

→

Biological molecule	Reagent used	Description of test
proteins	biuret reagent	Biuret reagent is initially blue, but forms a violet colour when added to a solution containing proteins. This test can also be used quantitatively, using standard protein solutions and a colorimeter to measure the intensity of the violet colour produced.
lipids	ethanol	This test relies on the solubility of lipids in different solvents. A sample containing lipids is first shaken with ethanol. Lipids will dissolve in the ethanol, but when water is added, a milky emulsion is formed.

Table 2.01 Tests for biological molecules.

2.02 Carbohydrates

Carbohydrates are compounds containing the elements carbon, hydrogen and oxygen, usually in the ratio of 1 : 2 : 1. Single molecules, or simple sugars, known as **monosaccharides**, include glucose, fructose and galactose. These simple sugars each have six carbon atoms in their structure and are therefore sometimes referred to as hexoses, derived from the Greek word 'hex' meaning six. Simple sugars with five carbon atoms are known as pentoses, those with three carbon atoms are known as trioses.

Glucose exists in two forms, α-**glucose** and β-**glucose**, as shown in Figure 2.01.

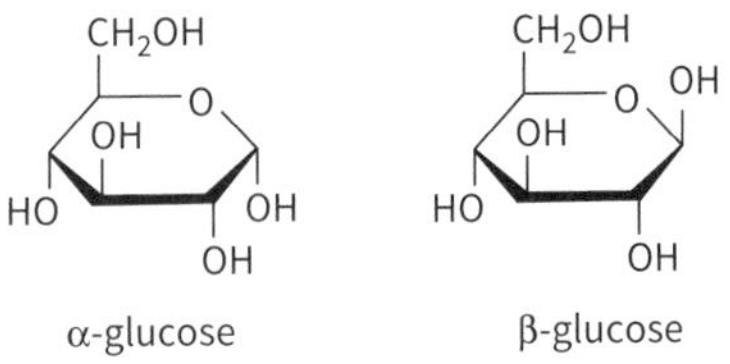

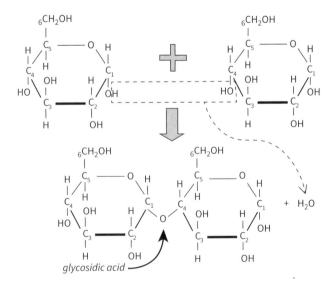

Figure 2.01 The structure of α-glucose and β-glucose.

Notice that the only difference between these two forms of glucose is the position of the –OH group on carbon atom number 1 in the ring. This small difference changes the properties of these two molecules.

Many large molecules are made up of large numbers of smaller molecules joined together in long chains. The smaller molecules are referred to as **monomers**, which join together forming **polymers**. For example, many thousands of glucose molecules can join together to form large molecules of starch or cellulose. Glucose molecules are the monomers, starch and cellulose are polymers. These polymers are sometimes referred to as **macromolecules** (very large molecules). Starch, cellulose, proteins and nucleic acids (see Unit 6) are macromolecules.

The polymers formed by many monosaccharides joining together are called **polysaccharides**.

Two monosaccharide monomers can also join together to form a **disaccharide** – a sugar consisting of two monosaccharides joined by a chemical bond. **Sucrose** is an example of a disaccharide. Three examples of disaccharides are shown in Table 2.02.

Disaccharides	Constituent monosaccharides
maltose (malt sugar)	two molecules of α-glucose joined together
sucrose (cane sugar)	α-glucose joined to fructose
lactose (milk sugar)	β-glucose joined to galactose

Table 2.02 Examples of disaccharides and their constituent monosaccharides.

Monosaccharides join together to form disaccharides and polysaccharides by the formation of **glycosidic bonds**, in a **condensation reaction** between two –OH groups on adjacent monosaccharides. Water is a product of this reaction.

Figure 2.02 shows how two molecules of α-glucose join together to form a molecule of maltose.

Figure 2.02 Formation of maltose.

The glycosidic bonds in disaccharides and in polysaccharides can be broken by the process of **hydrolysis**. In living organisms, disaccharides and polysaccharides are broken down to monosaccharides in the process of digestion. The chemical test for non-reducing sugars involves acid hydrolysis of glycosidic bonds.

The two forms of glucose, α-glucose and β-glucose, form different polysaccharides. **Starch** is a polymer of α-glucose and exists in two forms, known as **amylose** and **amylopectin**.

Amylose consists of many thousands of α-glucose monomers, joined by 1,4 glycosidic bonds only. The numbers 1 and 4 refer to the positions of the carbon atoms in the glucose molecules. The long chain coils to form a helix (Figure 2.03).

Amylopectin also consists of many thousands of α-glucose monomers, but it is a branched molecule. Branching occurs as a result of the formation of 1,6 glycosidic bonds (i.e. between carbon atoms 1 and 6), as illustrated in Figure 2.03. Amylose and amylopectin molecules form starch grains in many plant cells.

Glycogen is similar in structure to amylopectin, but is more highly branched because the 1,6 glycosidic bonds between the α-glucose monomers form more frequently. Glycogen molecules clump together to form glycogen granules in many animal cells, including liver cells.

Starch and glycogen are energy storage molecules, starch in plants and glycogen in animals. Starch and glycogen are both large, insoluble molecules and therefore do not affect the osmotic properties of cells, but they can be rapidly broken down to form glucose, which is used as an energy source.

Cellulose is a polymer of β-glucose, joined by 1,4 glycosidic bonds. The properties of cellulose are different from those of starch and cellulose is a structural polysaccharide, found in plant cell walls. Long, straight chains of cellulose molecules form bundles known as microfibrils, which in turn form cellulose fibres (Figure 2.05). The chains of cellulose fibres are held together by hydrogen bonding between projecting –OH groups. Cellulose fibres have a high tensile strength and the way in which they are arranged imparts considerable strength to plant cell walls.

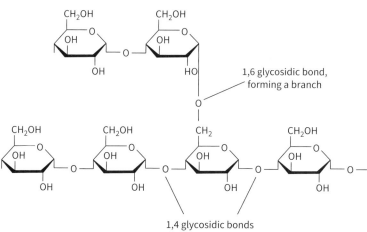

Figure 2.03 Glycosidic bonds in the structure of amylopectin

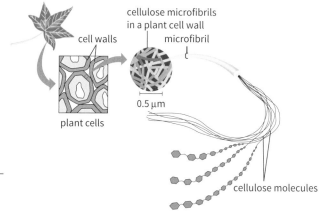

Figure 2.05 The structure of cellulose molecules, microfibrils and fibres.

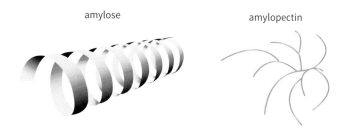

Figure 2.04 The structure of amylose and amylopectin.

Worked example 2.01

Question

The diagram shows the structure of two molecules of α-glucose:

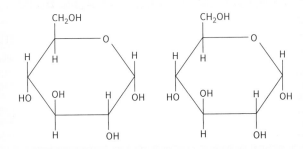

1   Copy the diagram and show how these two molecules are linked together to form a molecule of maltose.

2   Name the type of reaction involved in this process.

3   Name the type of bond formed.

Answers

1   It is important to be careful when copying the structure of the glucose molecules (e.g. by showing the positions of the −OH and −H correctly on each carbon atom). When these two molecules of glucose join to form maltose, water is lost by the removal of −OH and −H from each molecule, so you should carefully draw a circle round these on carbon atom number 1 of the first glucose molecule and carbon atom number 4 of the second glucose molecule, with water (H_2O) given off as a product. The two glucose molecules are now linked by a −O− bond between carbon atom 1 and carbon atom 4.

2   This is an example of a condensation reaction.

3   The type of bond formed is known as a glycosidic bond. (Be careful to spell this correctly!)

TIP

Be careful to distinguish between the different forms of glucose, α-glucose and β-glucose, particularly when describing the structure and functions of the polysaccharides starch, glycogen and cellulose.

Spelling is important in words such as 'amylose', which could be confused with 'amylase'.

2.03 Lipids

Lipids, like carbohydrates, also consist of the elements carbon, hydrogen and oxygen, but in different proportions. Lipids include a variety of different compounds, such as fats, oils, steroids and phospholipids which all have the property of insolubility in water (oil and water do not mix!), but they are soluble in organic solvents such as ethanol. This forms the basis of the simple emulsion test for lipids.

Fats and oils belong to a type of lipid known as **triglycerides**. A triglyceride molecule consists of glycerol (a type of alcohol) joined to three fatty acids ('tri' means three). Each fatty acid joins to

one of the −OH groups of glycerol, by means of a condensation reaction forming an **ester bond** and water. This is illustrated in Figure 2.06.

glycerol

a free fatty acid

triglyceride

Figure 2.06 The formation of a triglyceride from glycerol and fatty acids.

Triglycerides have a number of functions in living organisms, including energy storage, insulation and they can act as a source of metabolic water. This is important in some desert mammals, such as kangaroo rats, which obtain most of their water from the oxidation of food.

The yield of energy from the metabolism of triglycerides is about twice that of the metabolism of the same mass of carbohydrates, due to the presence of more C–H bonds in triglycerides.

Phospholipids are a special type of lipid in which one of the fatty acids is replaced with a phosphate group. This phosphate group is strongly polar and will attract water molecules, but the fatty acid hydrocarbon chains are non-polar. The phosphate part of the phospholipid molecule is said to be hydrophilic, because it has an affinity for water, but the hydrocarbon chains are hydrophobic.

This property of phospholipids is important because the molecules form membranes around cells, consisting of a double layer of phospholipids, with the polar parts of the molecules on the outside and the non-polar parts on the inside (Figure 2.07). The structure and properties of the cell membrane is described in Unit 4.

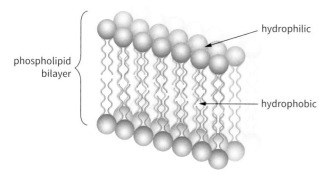

Figure 2.07 The arrangement of phospholipids in a bilayer forming the cell membrane.

Progress check 2.01

Explain how the properties of phospholipid molecules are related to the formation of a double layer in cell membranes.

2.04 Proteins

Proteins have many functions in living organisms, including structural proteins such as collagen and keratin, muscle contraction, defence against disease, transport and storage of oxygen and acting as receptors on cell surface membranes. Some hormones, including insulin and glucagon, are proteins and all enzymes are proteins.

All proteins are made of one type of monomer, **amino acids**, which join together by the formation of **peptide bonds**. This is another example of a condensation reaction and the reverse reaction, in which peptide bonds are broken, is hydrolysis. Digestion of proteins in the stomach and small intestine involves hydrolysis by enzymes.

Twenty different amino acids occur in proteins, but amino acids all have the same general structure, as shown in Figure 2.08. The R group is the variable part of the molecule.

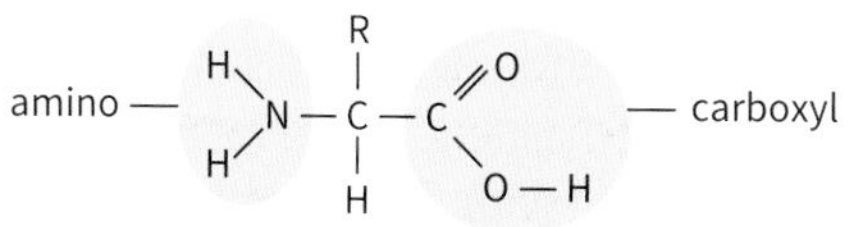

Figure 2.08 The general structure of an amino acid.

Figure 2.09 shows how two amino acids join together, in a condensation reaction, to form a peptide bond. Addition of further amino acids eventually forms a long chain, referred to as a polypeptide.

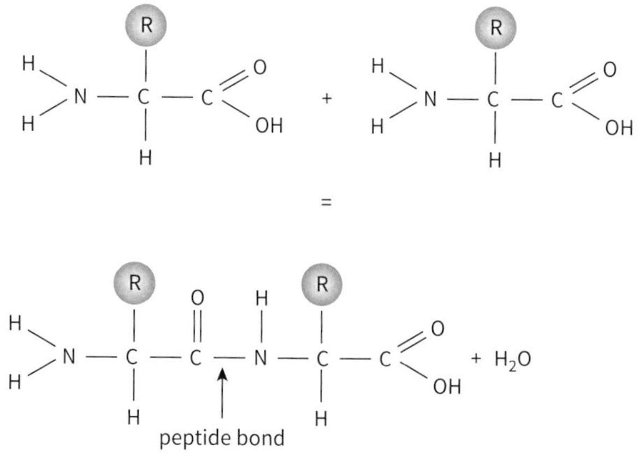

Figure 2.09 The formation of a peptide bond between two amino acids.

Once formed in the process of protein synthesis, the polypeptide chain folds in a very specific way, to form the functional protein.

We use the terms **primary structure, secondary structure**, **tertiary structure** and **quaternary structure** when describing structural features of protein molecules.

The sequence of amino acids in the polypeptide chain is referred to as the primary structure. A change is this sequence can have significant effects on the structure and function of the final protein, as illustrated by haemoglobin A and haemoglobin S. Haemoglobin S is the type of haemoglobin which results in sickle cell anaemia.

The polypeptide chain may then coil or fold to form the secondary structure, either in the form of a coil, known as an α-helix, or a folded structure known as a β-pleated sheet. The secondary structure is held in shape by hydrogen bonds between –OH and –NH groups in the amino acids within the polypeptide.

Further folding of the polypeptide chain may then form a compact shape, referred to as the tertiary structure. This structure is held in shape by the formation of several different types of bonds between the R groups of amino acids in the polypeptide chain. These bonds include ionic bonds and covalent disulfide bonds. Some R groups are non-polar (e.g. those in the amino acids phenylalanine and leucine) and form hydrophobic interactions within the molecule. Hydrogen bonding is also present within the tertiary structure.

Some proteins consist of two or more polypeptide subunits and have a quaternary structure. For example, one haemoglobin molecule consists of four polypeptide chains, two α chains and two β chains. Each of these polypeptide chains is associated with a haem group, containing iron. The structure of a molecule of haemoglobin is shown in Figure 2.10.

A molecule of haemoglobin is a compact, almost spherical shape and is an example of a **globular protein**. The iron in the haem group is able to combine reversibly with oxygen, so when fully saturated with oxygen, each molecule of haemoglobin carries four molecules of oxygen.

Collagen, a structural protein found in skin, tendons and other connective tissues, is an example of a fibrous protein. Collagen consists of long polypeptide chains, often with many glycine and proline amino acids. Each of these polypeptide chains associates with two others, forming a triple helix structure, illustrated in Figure 2.11.

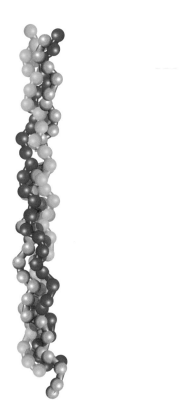

Figure 2.11 A triple helix of polypeptides forming a molecule of collagen.

Many of these collagen molecules are arranged side by side and covalently bonded to each other, forming collagen fibrils. Many collagen fibrils form larger bundles, referred to as collagen **fibres**. Collagen is flexible, but has a very tensile strength and is able to resist pulling forces without stretching.

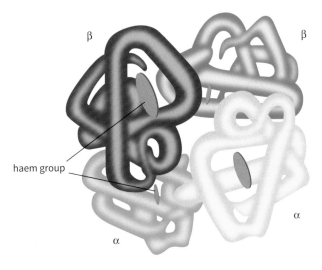

Figure 2.10 The essential structure of a molecule of haemoglobin, with two α chains and two β chains.

Progress check 2.02

Table 2.03 refers to the structures of some biological molecules. If the statement is correct, place a tick (✓) in the box and if the statement is incorrect, place a cross (✗) in the box.

Statement	Starch	Cellulose	Triglyceride	Protein
contains the elements carbon, hydrogen and oxygen only				
is a polymer of β-glucose				
components are joined by ester bonds				
contains the elements carbon, hydrogen, oxygen and nitrogen				

Table 2.03

2.05 Water

Water is essential for life and water molecules have a number of special properties related to the roles of water in living organisms. Water is described as a dipolar molecule, because it has slight charges associated with the oxygen and hydrogen atoms. The oxygen atom has a slight negative charge and the hydrogen atoms have a slight positive charge. These slight positive and negative charges form weak forces of attraction between adjacent water molecules. These forces of attraction are known as **hydrogen bonding**, as illustrated in Figure 2.12.

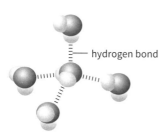
— hydrogen bond

Figure 2.12 Hydrogen bonding between water molecules.

Hydrogen bonding in water is responsible for many of the properties of water that are important for living organisms.

Water acts a **solvent** because substances will dissolve in water to form solutions. Such substances are said to be hydrophilic and include polar solutes such as simple sugars and ions, including sodium ions and chloride ions. Substances that do not dissolve in water are said to be hydrophobic. These substances are non-polar and include fats and oils.

Water has a **high specific heat capacity**. This means that a relatively large amount of energy is required to increase the temperature of water and the temperature of water tends to remain about the same if the environmental temperature changes. As a result, the temperature of an organism's body tends to stay stable. Also, the temperature of large bodies of water, including lakes and ponds, stays relatively constant when the environmental temperature changes.

Water has a **high latent heat of vapourisation**. It takes a relatively large amount of energy to break the hydrogen bonds and to change water from a liquid to a gas. As a result, when water evaporates it has a cooling effect. This helps to maintain body temperature of animals that rely on sweating as a means of temperature regulation and it also has a cooling effect on leaves in transpiration.

TIP

Practise drawing the structures of glucose, an amino acid and a triglyceride and naming the characteristic bonds associated when these molecules join together or are formed.

Much of the information in this section can be summarised in the form of tables, listing the essential facts.

Sample question 2.01

You are provided with two solutions: A and B. One of these contains a reducing sugar only and the other contains a mixture of a reducing sugar and a non-reducing sugar. Giving experimental details, explain how you would identify each of the two solutions A and B. [10 marks]

[Mark points are shown in square brackets – to a maximum of 10 marks]

Put equal volumes of the solutions into two separate test-tubes and label these A and B [1]. Then add the same volume of Benedict's reagent to each test-tube and heat them in a water bath [1]. The blue Benedict's reagent will change colour in both tubes, because they both contain reducing sugar [1].

Next, put the same volume of solutions A and B into another two test-tubes and add dilute hydrochloric acid to each tube [1]. After heating, the tubes will be allowed to cool then add sodium hydrogen carbonate to both tubes [1] to neutralise any remaining acid [1]. Heating with dilute acid will hydrolyse the non-reducing sugar and produce more reducing sugars [1].

Finally, add Benedict's reagent to both tubes and heat them again [1]. By comparing the colour produced in the tubes [1], it should be possible to determine which solution contained the mixture of reducing sugar and non-reducing sugar, because this solution will produce a deeper coloured precipitate [1], or will change colour more quickly than the solution originally containing reducing sugar only [1].

This is a detailed account of the experimental method and clearly explains the steps that should be taken to identify these two solutions. The answer is also set out in the correct sequence, showing good understanding of the method required to carry out a semi-quantitative Benedict's test to estimate the concentration of reducing sugars. The answer includes details of the tests for both reducing and non-reducing sugars.

Notice that the answer includes references to using the same volume of solutions A and B and the same volume of Benedict's reagent, which is necessary to make suitable comparisons and to draw valid conclusions from this experiment.

Revision checklist

Check that you know:

- [ ] chemical tests for reducing sugars, non-reducing sugars and starch

- [ ] the emulsion test for lipids and the biuret test for proteins

- [ ] the semi-quantitative test for reducing sugars using Benedict's reagent

- [ ] the structure of α-glucose and β-glucose

- [ ] how to define the terms monomer, polymer, macromolecule, monosaccharide, disaccharide and polysaccharide

- [ ] the formation of glycosidic bonds by condensation reactions

- [ ] the breakage of glycosidic bonds by hydrolysis

- [ ] the structures of starch, glycogen and cellulose

- [ ] how the structures of polysaccharides are related to their functions in living organisms

- [ ] the structure of a triglyceride and the formation of ester bonds

- [ ] how the structure of triglycerides is related to their functions in living organisms

- [ ] the structure and functions of phospholipids in living organisms

→

- ☐ the structure of an amino acid
- ☐ the formation and breakage of peptide bonds
- ☐ primary, secondary, tertiary and quaternary structure in proteins
- ☐ the types of bonding that hold protein molecules in shape
- ☐ haemoglobin as an example of a globular protein and collagen as an example of a fibrous protein
- ☐ how the structures of haemoglobin and collagen are related to their functions
- ☐ how hydrogen bonding occurs between water molecules
- ☐ how the properties of water are related to its roles in living organisms.

Exam-style questions

1 a Describe the structure of cellulose. [3]

  b Explain how the structure of cellulose is related to its functions. [3]

Total: 6

2 a Explain what is meant by each of the following terms relating to protein structure:

  i primary structure [2]

  ii secondary structure. [2]

b Give <u>three</u> differences between the structure of haemoglobin and the structure of collagen. [3]

Total: 7

Enzymes

Enzymes are protein molecules that act as biological catalysts. They take part in metabolic reactions in cells, speeding them up. When a reaction is over, each enzyme molecule is available to be used again. The substance (or substances) that the enzyme acts upon is called its **substrate**. The substance (or substances) formed is called the product.

> **TIP**
> Avoid saying 'an enzyme catalyses its substrate'. It is not possible to catalyse a *substance*. Enzymes catalyse *reactions*.

There are many different enzymes, each catalysing a different reaction. Most of them are inside cells. These are called intracellular enzymes. Some types of enzyme are released by cells, for example the enzymes secreted into the gut to digest food. These are known as extracellular enzymes.

3.01 How enzymes work

Enzymes are globular proteins (see Unit 2). There is a small region on the surface of the enzyme called the **active site**. The substrate binds to the enzyme at the active site, forming an enzyme–substrate complex. A reaction then occurs, and the product(s) leave the active site. The idea that the substrate fits exactly into the active site of the enzyme is known as the **lock and key hypothesis** (Figure 3.01).

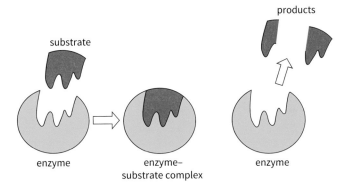

Figure 3.01 The lock and key hypothesis.

The substrate forms temporary bonds with the R groups of amino acids in the active site to form the enzyme–substrate complex. The bonds are weak interactions such as ionic and hydrogen bonds. In this model of enzyme action the substrate is the 'key', which fits into the enzyme's 'lock'.

A more recently developed model is called the **induced fit hypothesis** (Figure 3.02). This suggests that, before it enters, the substrate is not a perfect fit in the active site. When it does enter, the shape of the active site changes slightly to accommodate the substrate. This is rather like the way a glove changes shape when you put your hand in it. The induced fit hypothesis is really a modified version of the lock and key mechanism, and is now known to be a better model of what actually takes place.

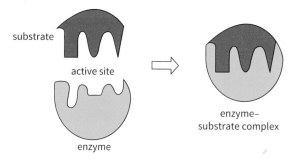

Figure 3.02 The induced fit hypothesis.

In either model, a particular substrate will only fit into the active site of a particular enzyme. We say that the shape of the active site is 'complementary' to the shape of the substrate. This means that an enzyme will only work with one substrate – it is *specific* to its substrate, so that it will only catalyse one reaction.

Specificity is important, because there are thousands of different metabolic reactions happening in cells. Which ones can take place depends on which enzymes the cell makes. In this way a cell exercises control over its metabolism.

Progress check 3.01

1   From your knowledge of protein structure (see Unit 2), explain briefly why proteins are suitable molecules to produce the specificity needed by enzymes.

2   Explain the main difference between the lock and key and the induced fit models of enzyme action.

Enzymes and activation energy

When a chemical reaction takes place, bonds in the reactants are broken and then new bonds are made in forming the products. Breaking bonds requires energy, and forming bonds gives out energy. The energy needed to break bonds in the reactants is called the **activation energy** of the reaction. In a test-tube this energy may be provided by heat, but in cells this is not possible. The temperature in cells is relatively low, so that without enzymes most metabolic reactions would take place very slowly, or not at all.

All catalysts, including enzymes, speed up reactions by lowering the activation energy of a reaction. This is easiest to show as a graph (Figure 3.03).

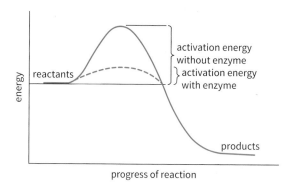

Figure 3.03 Enzymes speed up a reaction by lowering the activation energy needed to start the reaction.

Enzymes do this by forming the enzyme–substrate complex. The complex changes the shape of the substrate slightly, which reduces the energy needed to break its bonds.

3.02 Following the progress of an enzyme-catalysed reaction

You can monitor the progress of an enzyme-catalysed reaction by either:

• measuring the rate of formation of a product

• measuring the rate at which a substrate is used up.

a Measuring the rate of formation of a product

An enzyme called catalase speeds up the breakdown of hydrogen peroxide, which is a waste product of metabolism. Hydrogen peroxide is toxic and would be harmful if it built up in cells. Catalase breaks it down into water and oxygen, which are both harmless:

$$\text{hydrogen peroxide} \xrightarrow{\text{catalase}} \text{water} + \text{oxygen}$$

The activity of catalase can be followed by measuring the rate of formation of oxygen gas.

Catalase is present in all living tissues. High concentrations of catalase can be obtained from readily available sources, such as a suspension of yeast cells or a potato tuber that has been macerated with water in a food blender. If hydrogen peroxide solution is added to one of these, the reaction mixture will produce oxygen, which you can collect in a gas syringe (Figure 3.04).

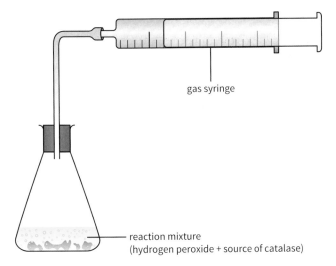

gas syringe

reaction mixture
(hydrogen peroxide + source of catalase)

Figure 3.04 Collecting oxygen from the breakdown of hydrogen peroxide.

A graph of the volume of gas collected against time will look like Figure 3.05. Note that the rate is fastest at the start. This is called the initial rate of reaction. Over time the reaction slows. After 3 minutes the reaction stops and the curve levels off.

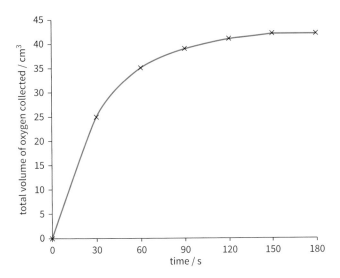

Figure 3.05 The progress of the breakdown of hydrogen peroxide, catalysed by the enzyme catalase.

The rate is fastest at the start because it depends on random collisions between enzyme and substrate molecules. As the reaction proceeds, the substrate is used up, so there are fewer collisions and the rate slows. For this reason, when we want to compare enzyme activity under different conditions, we always measure the *initial* rate of reaction.

b Measuring the rate at which a substrate is used up

The enzyme amylase catalyses the hydrolysis of starch into the reducing sugar maltose:

$$\text{starch} + \text{water} \xrightarrow{\text{amylase}} \text{maltose}$$

This reaction can be monitored by recording the disappearance of the starch, by testing for it using a solution of iodine in potassium iodide. You take samples of the reaction mixture (starch suspension + amylase) every 10 seconds and test it for starch. At first, when starch is present, the iodine solution will turn blue-black. When the starch has been broken down into maltose the iodine solution will remain yellow-brown.

To obtain continuous results over a period of time you can monitor the disappearance of the blue colour in a colorimeter. Figure 3.06 shows the expected results.

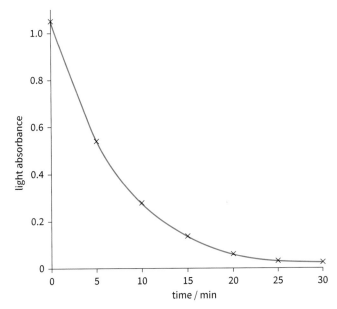

Figure 3.06 The progress of the breakdown of starch, catalysed by the enzyme amylase.

Progress check 3.02

1 Briefly explain the meaning of activation energy (of a reaction).

2 The enzyme invertase catalyses the hydrolysis of sucrose to glucose and fructose:

$$\text{sucrose} + \text{water} \xrightarrow{\text{invertase}} \text{glucose} + \text{fructose}$$

Suggest how you could monitor this reaction in order to measure the activity of invertase.

Sample question 3.01

Figure 3.07 shows a computer model of the enzyme carbonic anhydrase. This enzyme catalyses the conversion of carbon dioxide and water to carbonic acid (H_2CO_3). The carbonic acid then dissociates into hydrogen ions (H^+) and hydrogencarbonate ions (HCO_3^-):

$$CO_2 + H_2O \xrightarrow{\text{carbonic anhydrase}} \underset{\substack{\text{carbonic} \\ \text{acid}}}{H_2CO_3} \longrightarrow H^+ + HCO_3^-$$

The arrow shows the position of the enzyme's active site.

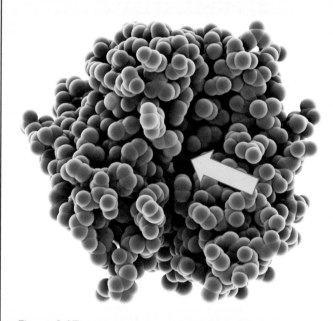

Figure 3.07

1   Suggest how you could monitor this reaction in order to measure the activity of carbonic anhydrase. [2]

2   Explain why the shape of the active site is important in the way that the enzyme works. [3]

3   Figure 3.08 shows the energy changes during the progress of an uncatalysed reaction.

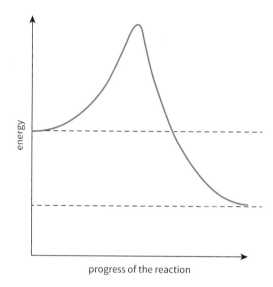

Figure 3.08

Label the activation energy of this reaction on Figure 3.08. [1]

4   On Figure 3.08, draw a curve to show the changes in energy taking place during the progress of the same reaction when it is catalysed by an enzyme. [2]

[Mark points are shown in square brackets – to a maximum of 8 marks]

1 Measure the change in concentration of a reactant / a product [1].

Measure the change in pH (because H^+ ions are formed) [1].

Use an indicator / monitor changes in colour of an indicator in a colorimeter [1].

Use a pH meter [1].

[Maximum 2]

2 Substrates / carbon dioxide and water, fit into / bind to / enter, active site [1].

(Substrates have) complementary shape [1].

Reference to specificity (of the enzyme) [1].

Lock and key / induced fit hypothesis [1].

Temporary bonds form with active site / with R groups (of amino acid residues) [1].

[Maximum 3]

3 Label and arrow or bracket clearly indicating height of peak above the upper dashed line [1].

4 Line with one peak, below that of uncatalysed curve [1].

Curve starts and finishes at the dashed lines [1].

The most obvious substance to measure here is the concentration of hydrogen ions (i.e. the pH). The concentration of H^+ should increase as the reaction proceeds, so the pH will fall.

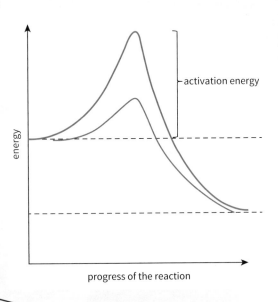

If you have to label on a diagram, use a label line or bracket. Make sure the labels are clear and unambiguous, like this:

3.03 Factors affecting the rate of enzyme-catalysed reactions

There are a number of factors that affect the rate of an enzyme-catalysed reaction. These include:

• temperature
• pH
• enzyme concentration
• substrate concentration
• the presence of inhibitors.

a Temperature

An increase in temperature increases the kinetic energy of molecules. As the temperature rises, both enzyme and substrate molecules move more quickly and collide with each other more often, with higher energies. There are a greater number of successful collisions leading to conversion of substrate into product. So at first, as the temperature rises, the rate of reaction increases.

However, beyond a certain point, higher temperatures start to change the shape of the enzyme molecule. Enzymes are globular proteins with a tertiary structure that is maintained by bonds between the R groups of polypeptide chains. High temperatures cause these bonds to break, damaging the tertiary structure of the protein. This process is called **denaturation** – the protein becomes denatured.

Denaturing changes the shape of the active site, so that substrate molecules are unable to form an enzyme–substrate complex and the rate of reaction decreases.

The rate at any temperature depends on the balance between these two factors (kinetic energy and denaturation), which produces an optimum temperature, where the reaction occurs most rapidly (Figure 3.09).

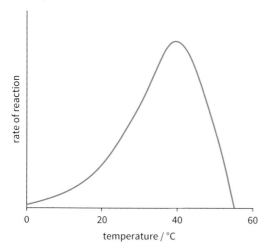

Figure 3.09 The effect of temperature on the activity of an enzyme.

Organisms have evolved enzymes that are adapted to the temperature of their surroundings. For example, human enzymes have an optimum at about body temperature (37 °C), while some bacteria that live in hot springs have evolved 'heat-resistant' enzymes, which are not denatured by temperatures as high as 100 °C.

b pH

Enzymes also have an optimum pH at which they work best (Figure 3.10). A change in pH affects the concentration of hydrogen ions (H^+) around the enzyme molecule. This affects the ionisation of R groups on the amino acids of the protein. In turn this affects the shape of the active site, and the ease of formation of an enzyme–substrate complex. At the optimum pH, the shape of the active site is complementary to the shape of the substrate.

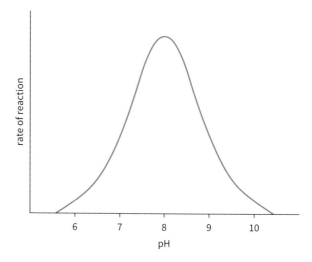

Figure 3.10 The effect of pH on the activity of an enzyme.

Most enzymes have an optimum pH near neutral (pH 7) but there are exceptions. The enzyme pepsin is found in the human stomach, and has evolved to work under the acid conditions present there. It has an optimum pH of about 2.

If the pH around an enzyme is very different from its optimum, this will result in permanent denaturing.

c Enzyme concentration

Enzyme molecules are not used up during the reactions they catalyse, so they can be used over and over again. As a result, enzymes work efficiently in very low concentrations. Usually there is an excess of substrate molecules, so the rate of reaction is limited by the concentration of the enzyme. Because of this, if the concentration of enzyme is increased it will result in an increase in collisions between enzyme and substrate molecules, and a faster rate of reaction (Figure 3.11). In theory, at high concentrations of enzyme, the concentration of substrate would become limiting and the rate level off, but this does not normally happen if there is plenty of substrate available.

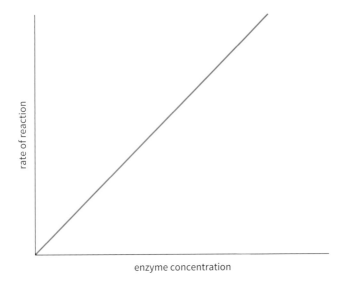

Figure 3.11 The effect of enzyme concentration on the activity of an enzyme.

d Substrate concentration

If the concentration of substrate is low, some of the active sites of the enzyme molecules will be unoccupied, and the rate of reaction will be low. If the concentration of substrate is increased, there will be more frequent collisions between enzyme and substrate molecules, more enzyme–substrate complexes are formed, producing a faster rate of reaction. However, at high substrate concentrations, the concentration of the enzyme becomes limiting – at this point the curve levels off (Figure 3.12).

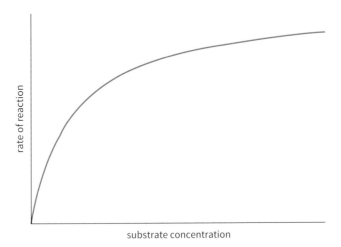

Figure 3.12 The effect of substrate concentration on the activity of an enzyme.

e The presence of inhibitors

Inhibitors are substances that reduce the rate of an enzyme-catalysed reaction. They do so by altering the shape of the active site, either directly or indirectly.

Some substances are permanent inhibitors. They cause denaturation of the enzyme and their effects are non-reversible. For example, heavy metal ions such as lead (Pb^{2+}) and mercury (Hg^+) fall into this category.

Other inhibitors are reversible. These only bind to the enzyme temporarily, so that their effect is not permanent. They fall into two categories: competitive and non-competitive.

Competitive inhibitors are molecules that have a shape that is similar to that of the substrate. They can fit temporarily into the active site, preventing the substrate from entering. This reduces the number of enzyme–substrate complexes and slows the reaction (Figure 3.13a). The greater the concentration of inhibitor relative to substrate in a mixture, the more effect the inhibitor will have in reducing the activity of the enzyme.

Non-competitive inhibitors do not have a shape like that of the substrate. They do not attach to the active site, but bind to other parts of the enzyme, altering the overall shape of the enzyme molecule, including the active site. This does not prevent the substrate entering the active site, but the site is no longer the correct shape to catalyse the reaction, so the enzyme–substrate complex is inactive (Figure 3.13b). However, if the concentration of substrate is increased, the enzyme will still not be able to catalyse the reaction – so the relative concentrations of inhibitor and substrate do not affect the rate. Figure 3.14 compares the effects of these two types of inhibitors as a graph.

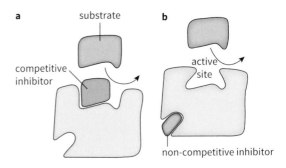

Figure 3.13 Competitive and non-competitive enzyme inhibitors.

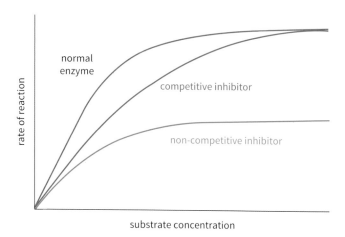

Figure 3.14 The effects of competitive and non-competitive inhibitors on the activity of an enzyme.

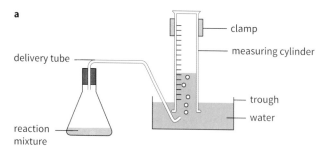

a

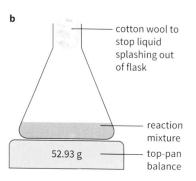

b

Figure 3.15 Some other ways to measure the rate of oxygen production from the breakdown of hydrogen peroxide by catalase.

Progress check 3.03

1 Describe what happens to a protein when it is denatured by heat.

2 Assuming all other factors are kept constant, explain why increasing the concentration of substrate does not always increase the rate of an enzyme-catalysed reaction.

3.04 Investigating factors affecting the rate of enzyme-catalysed reactions

Many different enzymes are suitable for investigation in a school laboratory. Here we will look at the breakdown of hydrogen peroxide by catalase, which can be monitored by collecting the oxygen produced during the reaction.

Figure 3.04 shows one way this can be done using a gas syringe, but there are other methods. If you do not have a gas syringe, the oxygen can be collected over water in a measuring cylinder. You can even connect a delivery tube to the reaction vessel and count the number of bubbles of gas produced per minute from a delivery tube, although this method is not very precise, and only works if the rate of reaction is slow. Alternatively you can measure the weight decrease as the oxygen is lost, by placing the flask on a top-pan balance (Figure 3.15).

A good source of catalase is a 1% suspension of yeast, which consists of living fungal cells. You can place a set volume (e.g. $100\,cm^3$) of 3% hydrogen peroxide solution in the flask and add a set volume (e.g. $10\,cm^3$) of the yeast suspension. Immediately insert the bung and delivery tube in the flask and collect the oxygen in the gas syringe, recording the volume collected at suitable intervals.

> **TIP**
> You will need to experiment to find suitable volumes to use – it will depend on the activity of the yeast, temperature used and so on.

Having decided upon a suitable method, you can select a factor to change. It is important that only one factor is changed at a time, and that any other variables that might affect the results are kept constant (controlled). This is called a 'controlled experiment'. For example, if you want to know the effect of temperature on the rate of reaction, you must keep variables such as pH, volumes of solutions, and enzyme and substrate concentration, constant.

a Temperature

A fixed temperature is achieved by placing the reaction flask or tube in a water bath. The best type to use is an electric thermostatically controlled water bath, which will maintain a temperature to within ±1 °C. Alternatively you can use a beaker of water heated over a Bunsen burner. You should try six or more temperatures over a suitable range (e.g. 20 °C to 80 °C), which might be expected to cover the optimum for catalase.

You must leave the reaction flask to reach the correct temperature (this is called 'equilibrating to temperature'). The yeast should be maintained at this temperature too. Then start the reaction as described above and measure the initial rate of production of oxygen. Repeat the procedure with the flask at the other temperatures. If you have time it is best to carry out replicate measurements at each temperature, to identify any anomalous results.

Plot a graph of the initial rate of reaction (= enzyme activity) against temperature. Your graph should look something like Figure 3.09, but note that yeast enzymes may have a relatively high optimum temperature.

b pH

Buffer solutions are solutions of salts that resist changes in pH. They can be added to a reaction mixture to maintain the pH of the mixture. You can adapt the catalase experiment by changing the pH of the mixture. Add an equal volume of buffer solution to the hydrogen peroxide solution in the flask, before adding the yeast to start the reaction. Here again, all other factors must be kept constant. This time they include temperature, which should be maintained at a constant value, close to the optimum for the enzyme (e.g. 40 °C). Various buffer solutions are available – assuming the optimum pH of catalase is likely to be near neutral (pH 7) you could use a range between pH 5 and pH 9.

When you have your results, plot a graph of the initial rate of reaction (= enzyme activity) against pH. It should look similar to Figure 3.10.

c Enzyme concentration

Make a number of dilutions of the yeast suspension that you used in the last two experiments (Table 3.01).

Volume of yeast suspension / cm³	Volume of distilled water / cm³	Concentration of catalase / % of original
100	0	100
80	20	80
60	40	60
40	60	40
20	80	20
0	100	0

Table 3.01 Dilutions of the yeast suspension used in the temperature and pH experiments.

You can now adapt the catalase experiment by using these different concentrations of the enzyme. Add an equal volume of the optimum pH buffer solution to the hydrogen peroxide solution in the flask. Now add the most concentrated yeast suspension to start the reaction. All other factors must be controlled. Repeat with the other concentrations of enzyme. You should be able to plot a graph of the initial rate of reaction against concentration of enzyme that looks like Figure 3.11.

d Substrate concentration

This is very similar to the way you investigate enzyme concentration, but instead of changing the concentration of catalase, keep that constant and change the concentration of hydrogen peroxide.

Sample question 3.02

The enzyme trypsin will hydrolyse the protein in a suspension of powdered milk, turning it clear. A student carried out an experiment to investigate the effect of temperature on the activity of trypsin. She incubated 10 cm³ of trypsin solution and 10 cm³ of a suspension of powdered milk separately in a water bath at 30 °C. After the tubes had equilibrated to temperature, she mixed the contents of the tubes and recorded the time taken for the mixture to clear. She repeated the measurements at different temperatures. Her results are shown in Table 3.02.

Temperature / °C	Time for hydrolysis of protein / min	Rate of reaction / cm³ min⁻¹
22	5.12	
30	2.28	
41	1.34	
45	1.20	
52	1.24	
57	1.41	
61	1.67	
66	3.72	
69	10.04	

Table 3.02

1 Calculate the rates of reaction by dividing the volume of milk by the times taken for hydrolysis. Write your answers in the last column of Table 3.02. Express your answer in cm³ min⁻¹. [3]

2 Plot a graph of rate of reaction against temperature. [4]

3 Explain the effects of temperature on the rate of reaction. [5]

1

Temperature / °C	Time for hydrolysis of protein / min	Rate of reaction / cm³ min⁻¹
22	5.12	1.95
30	2.28	4.39
41	1.34	7.46
45	1.20	8.33
52	1.24	8.06
57	1.41	7.09
61	1.67	5.99
66	3.72	2.69
69	10.04	1.00

The rates of reaction are rounded to three significant figures (the same number of significant figures as for the time in Table 3.02).

2

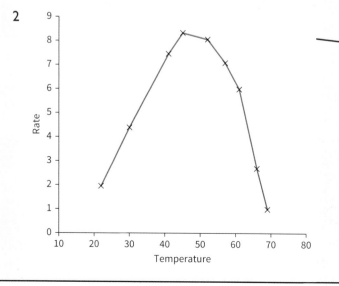

Choose a suitable scale for each axis, slightly bigger than the range of the values. Do not forget to label each axis and include units.

Axes right way round, labelled, with correct units [1].

Axes drawn to a suitable scale, sensible increments [1].

All points plotted correctly with suitable symbol (cross, or dot in a circle) [1].

Lines joined point-to-point, with a ruler [1].

3 Between 22 °C and 45 °C the rate increases due to the increased kinetic energy of the molecules/increased collisions of enzyme and substrate [1] resulting in more enzyme–substrate complexes forming [1]. Above 52 °C the rate decreases due to denaturing of the enzyme [1], changing the shape of the active site [1], so fewer enzyme–substrate complexes formed [1]. The optimum temperature is between 45 °C and 52 °C [1].

It is sensible to answer part 3 by explaining the results from low through to high temperatures. Note that you do not know where the optimum is exactly – it must lie somewhere between 45 °C and 52 °C.

3.05 Enzyme affinities and the Michaelis–Menten constant

If you draw a graph of the rate of an enzyme-catalysed reaction against concentration of substrate (Figure 3.12), the curve is a parabola. There is a mathematical equation called the Michaelis–Menten equation that describes this hyperbolic curve. The rate (velocity) is given the symbol v and the concentration of substrate $[S]$ – the square brackets mean 'concentration of'. The equation fits the results that are obtained experimentally, and predicts that at high concentrations of substrate the rate will level off and approach a theoretical maximum limit, called **V_{max}**.

The equation also uses another mathematical term called the **Michaelis–Menten constant, K_m**. K_m is the value of $[S]$ at which the reaction rate is equal to half that of V_{max} ($\frac{1}{2}V_{max}$). This is shown in Figure 3.16.

The problem with trying to calculate K_m from Figure 3.16 is that you cannot tell for certain when V_{max} has been reached – the dotted line is only an estimate drawn by eye. However it is possible to draw another graph, from which the exact values of V_{max} and K_m can be found. This is a 'double reciprocal plot' where the values of $1/v$ are plotted against $1/[S]$. This graph produces a straight line, where the intercept on the y-axis is $1/V_{max}$, and the intercept on the x-axis is $-1/K_m$ (Figure 3.17). From these values we can calculate V_{max} and K_m.

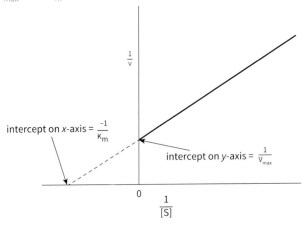

Figure 3.17 A double reciprocal plot of $1/v$ against $1/[S]$ for an enzyme-catalysed reaction.

K_m is a very useful value in enzyme kinetics. At $\frac{1}{2}V_{max}$ half the active sites of the enzyme are occupied by substrate, so K_m is a measure of how tightly the substrate is bound to the enzyme, which is called the affinity of the enzyme for its substrate. The lower the

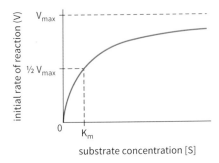

Figure 3.16 Graph of initial reaction rate V against initial substrate concentration [S] for an enzyme-catalysed reaction.

value of K_m, the greater the enzyme affinity and vice versa. Different enzymes have widely different K_m values (Table 3.03).

Enzyme	Substrate	K_m / μmol dm⁻³
catalase	hydrogen peroxide	1 100 000
carbonic anhydrase	carbon dioxide	8 000
chymotrypsin	protein	5 000
pyruvate carboxylase	pyruvate	400
lactate dehydrogenase	lactate	60
fumarase	fumarate	5

Table 3.03 K_m values for selected enzymes (note that the unit for K_m is a concentration).

The value of K_m depends on the reaction conditions. Factors such as pH, temperature and the presence of inhibitors cause changes to the K_m of an enzyme, and give biochemists valuable information about the way enzymes work.

Progress check 3.04

A competitive inhibitor binds reversibly to the active site of an enzyme, temporarily preventing the formation of an enzyme–substrate complex.

1   How does the inhibitor change the affinity of the enzyme for its substrate?

2   What effect will this have on the enzyme's K_m?

3   What effect will the inhibitor have on the enzyme's V_{max}?

3.06 Immobilised enzymes

Enzymes have a wide range of commercial uses, including food manufacture, production of pharmaceuticals, and in medicine. Enzymes isolated from cells or tissues may be more useful in a commercial process if they are **immobilised**. This is where molecules of the enzyme are attached to, or trapped within, an insoluble material. Immobilisation makes enzymes more stable and resistant to changes in temperature or pH. It also means that the enzymes can be retained and used again – they are not lost during the industrial process.

One method of immobilising enzymes is within alginate beads. The enzyme is mixed with a solution of sodium alginate, which is then added drop by drop into a beaker of calcium chloride solution. When the drops fall into the calcium chloride the sodium alginate is converted into insoluble calcium alginate, which forms jelly-like beads. The beads contain the enzyme, immobilised in a matrix of the calcium alginate.

You can load the alginate beads into the barrel of a syringe. This apparatus can now be used to conduct experiments on the immobilised enzyme (Figure 3.18). The substrate is added through the open end of the syringe barrel. The reaction takes place as the substrate passes through the alginate beads, and the product, uncontaminated by enzyme, is collected at the bottom.

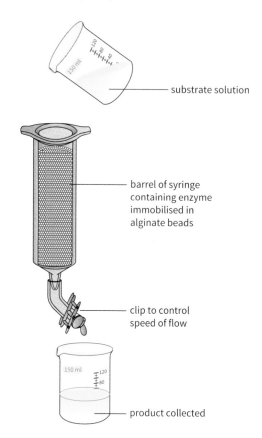

Figure 3.18 Using an enzyme immobilised in alginate beads.

Immobilised enzymes are thought to be more stable than enzymes free in solution because the enzyme molecules are held in place by the alginate, and are not so easily denatured. However it is possible that immobilisation may sometimes lower the activity of an enzyme, because the enzyme molecules are unable to move about. You can test this hypothesis by comparing the activity of the immobilised enzyme with that of a solution of the same enzyme, with all other conditions controlled.

Revision checklist

Check that you know:

- ☐ the nature of enzymes as globular proteins that catalyse reactions

- ☐ the difference between intracellular enzymes and extracellular enzymes

- ☐ enzymes work by forming an enzyme–substrate complex at the active site

- ☐ the lock and key hypothesis and the induced fit hypothesis

- ☐ catalysis reduces the activation energy of a reaction

- ☐ an enzyme-catalysed reaction can be followed by measuring the rate of formation of a product or the rate of disappearance of a substrate

- ☐ the effects of the following factors on the rate of enzyme-catalysed reactions and how to investigate them:

  - temperature
  - pH
  - enzyme concentration
  - substrate concentration
  - inhibitor concentration

- ☐ the effects of competitive and non-competitive reversible inhibitors on enzyme activity

- ☐ the use of the maximum rate of reaction (V_{max}) to derive the Michaelis–Menten constant (K_m) to compare the affinity of enzymes for their substrates

- ☐ the effect of immobilising an enzyme in alginate on its activity and how to investigate this.

Exam-style questions

1 Which of these statements describes some properties of enzymes?

   1 They are globular proteins

   2 They catalyse the breakdown of large molecules into smaller ones

   3 They increase the numbers of collisions between molecules

   4 They supply the activation energy needed to start a reaction

   A: 1 and 2 / B: 1 and 3 / C: 2 and 3 / D: 3 and 4 [1]

   Total: 1

2 The activity of an enzyme was measured at different values of pH. The temperature was maintained at 40 °C. The results are shown in Figure 3.19.

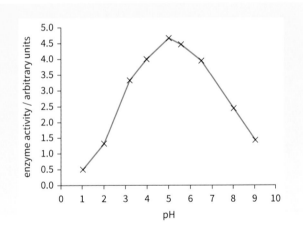

Figure 3.19 The activity of an enzyme at different pH values.

a If you carried out this experiment, how would you change the pH of the reaction mixture? [1]

b Describe the effect of pH on this enzyme. [2]

c Explain why the activity of the enzyme is low at pH 2. [3]

   Total: 6

3   If a fruit or vegetable such as apple or sweet potato is cut with a knife, the cut surface turns brown on exposure to the air. The browning is due to the action of an enzyme in the plant tissue, called catechol oxidase. This enzyme catalyses the oxidation of a colourless substance called catechol into a pale yellow compound called benzoquinone:

$$\underset{\text{(colourless)}}{\text{catechol + oxygen}} \xrightarrow{\text{catechol oxidase}} \underset{\text{(pale yellow)}}{\text{benzoquinone + water}}$$

Benzoquinone is rapidly oxidised by the air to form a dark brown pigment called melanin. Catechol is present in low concentrations in the vacuoles of the plant cells. Catechol oxidase is present in the cytoplasm of the cells.

a   State two reasons why browning does not occur in uncut tissues. [2]

b   Suggest a method you could use to monitor the course of the enzyme-catalysed reaction. [1]

c   Draw a sketch graph to show how the initial rate of reaction would vary with increasing concentrations of the substrate catechol. Explain the reasons for the shape of the curve. [6]

d   A substance called 4-hydroxybenzoic acid is a competitive inhibitor of catechol oxidase. On your sketch graph, add a second curve to show how the initial rate of reaction will be affected by the presence of this inhibitor. Explain the reasons for these effects. [4]

Total: 13

Cell membranes and transport

4.01 Fluid mosaic membranes

The **fluid mosaic model** of membrane structure proposes that the cell surface membrane consists of a double layer of **phospholipids**, known as a bilayer, in which there are other components, including **proteins**, **glycoproteins**, **glycolipids** and **cholesterol**. This model of membrane structure is illustrated in Figure 4.01.

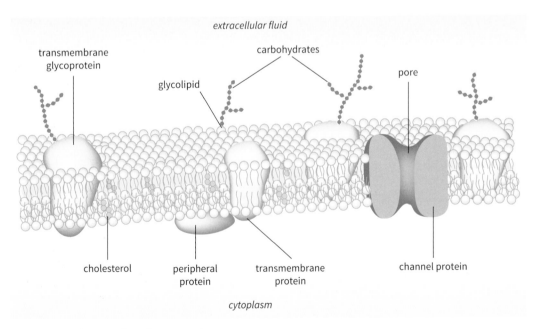

Figure 4.01 The structure of the cell surface membrane.

Remember that phospholipid molecules have hydrophilic heads and hydrophobic tails, and the molecules orientate themselves with their heads on the outside of the membrane.

TIP
The fatty acids tails of phospholipids consist of carbon and hydrogen only, making them non-polar and therefore hydrophobic.

The cell surface membrane has important roles in controlling the movement of substances into and out of the cell and in communication with other cells through the process of **cell signalling**.

Table 4.01 summarises the components of the cell surface membrane and their functions.

Components	Functions
phospholipids	form a bilayer, with polar (hydrophilic) phosphate groups on the outside and non-polar (hydrophobic) hydrocarbon chains on the inside
glycolipids	these are lipids with short carbohydrate chains attached; these chains project on the outside of the membrane and attract water molecules; they also act as receptors for signalling molecules, including hormones
proteins	membrane proteins form specific channels or carriers for substances into and out of the cell; some membrane proteins are enzymes
glycoproteins	these are proteins with short, branched carbohydrates attached; these carbohydrates project on the outside of the cell and have various functions, including acting as receptors
cholesterol	cholesterol molecules fit between the phospholipids of the bilayer and help to regulate fluidity of the membrane; cholesterol is also important for maintaining the stability of cell membranes

Table 4.01 Functions of the components of the cell surface membrane.

The cell surface membrane forms a selective barrier between the cell contents and the environment of the cell, regulating the movement of substances into and out of the cell and responding to various signals, including hormones.

Cell signalling involves the ways in which cells respond to various signals, coordinating the activities of the cells.

Cell signalling molecules are very diverse; some are lipid soluble and are able to pass through the phospholipid bilayer, directly into the cell cytoplasm where they bind with a receptor molecule. Other signalling molecules are water soluble and attached to a specific receptor on the cell surface membrane of a target cell. This starts a chain of events, resulting in a response in the target cell, such as a change in metabolism, or cell secretion.

TIP
Steroids, such as oestrogen, are able to pass through the cell surface membrane because these molecules are hydrophobic. They interact with receptors in the cytoplasm or in the nucleus.

4.02 Cell transport mechanisms

Substances move through the cell membrane in a variety of different ways including:

- diffusion
- facilitated diffusion
- osmosis
- active transport
- endocytosis
- exocytosis.

These transport processes are summarised in Table 4.02

Process	Description
diffusion	this is a passive process in which there is a net movement of molecules or ions from a region of high concentration to a region of low concentration, down a concentration gradient; small molecules, such as water, oxygen and carbon dioxide, are able to diffuse directly through the phospholipid bilayer
facilitated diffusion	this involves the movement of larger modules and ions, such as glucose and sodium ions, through specific transport proteins in the cell membrane; facilitated diffusion is also a passive process and substances tend to move down their concentration gradient
osmosis	osmosis is a special type of diffusion, in which water molecules move through a partially permeable membrane; we say that water moves down a water potential gradient – from a region of high water potential to a region of low water potential through a partially permeable membrane

→

Process	Description
active transport	active transport involves the movement of molecules or ions against their concentration gradient (from low to high) by means of specific carrier proteins; this process requires an input of energy, which is supplied by ATP (adenosine triphosphate) (e.g. the movement of sodium ions and potassium ions by means of a sodium–potassium pump
endocytosis	this is a form of 'bulk transport' of materials into a cell; phagocytosis (e.g. a white blood cell engulfing a bacterial cell) is a type of endocytosis. Endocytosis is an active process.
exocytosis	this is the reverse process of endocytosis and is the way in which substances are secreted by a cell (e.g. digestive enzymes are secreted by secretory cells in the pancreas by the process of exocytosis). Exocytosis is an active process.

Table 4.02 Membrane transport processes.

4.03 Investigating diffusion using plant tissue and non-living materials

Some plant cells, such as beetroot, contain pigments (coloured substances). If samples of beetroot tissue are immersed in water and exposed to a range of temperatures, it will be found that at higher temperatures, the beetroot cell membranes are damaged and the coloured pigment diffuses out of the cells into the surrounding water.

Diffusion can also be demonstrated by filling a test-tube with a gel made with gelatine. When the gel has set, the tube is inverted into a shallow container of food dye, or another coloured substance such as copper sulfate. The coloured substance will be seen to diffuse up the gel. You could also add a few drops of universal pH indicator to the gelatine. When the gelatine sets, invert the test-tube into a shallow container of dilute hydrochloric acid.

Sample question 4.01

Beetroot cells contain a red pigment (betalain) in their vacuoles. Giving experimental details, explain how you would investigate the effect of temperature on the permeability of beetroot cells. [10 marks]

[Mark points are shown in square brackets – to a maximum of 10 marks]

Small pieces of beetroot tissue would be cut carefully to ensure that they are the same size. These pieces of tissue are then rinsed with distilled water to remove pigment that escapes from cells damaged by cutting [3].

Water baths are set up at a range of temperatures, such as 20 °C, 30 °C, 40 °C, 50 °C and 60 °C. There is a test-tube, containing 10 cm³ of distilled water in each water bath. Sufficient time is left for the water in the test-tubes to reach the temperature of the water bath and then one piece of beetroot tissue is placed in each test-tube. The test-tubes are then left for 30 minutes [4].

After 30 minutes, the test-tubes are shaken carefully and the colours of the liquid in the test-tubes are compared. The intensity of the colour of the liquid can be measured with a colorimeter, to give quantitative results [3].

This answer carefully sets out the stages in this experiment, with references to the control of variables, such as the size of the pieces of tissue and the volume of distilled water in each test-tube. It is essential to control these variables, as they would affect the results. It is also important to rinse the pieces of tissue at the start of the experiment, otherwise pigment that leaks from damaged cells would affect the results.

At high temperatures, the membrane surrounding the vacuole and the cell surface membrane are damaged, allowing pigment to diffuse out of the cells. The pigment is water soluble and, as more pigment is lost from the cells, the solution becomes darker in colour. If a colorimeter is used, it is possible to plot a graph of absorbance (on the y-axis) against temperature (on the x-axis).

4.04 Calculating surface areas and volumes of simple shapes and investigating surface area to volume ratios

You should know how to calculate the surface areas and volumes of simple shapes, such as cubes. As three-dimensional objects increase in size, the surface area to volume ratio decreases. This is significant because cells rely on diffusion for the uptake of oxygen, which is required for aerobic respiration. Diffusion is only effective over a short distance, so this limits the size of organisms that rely only on diffusion for the uptake of substances. As organisms become larger and more complex, diffusion is insufficient and transport systems are needed to overcome the limitations of diffusion.

As the surface area of a cube increases, the surface area to volume ratio decreases. As organisms increase in size, there is a corresponding decrease in their surface area to volume ratio. This means that the distance over which diffusion occurs increases and, as a result, the rate of diffusion decreases.

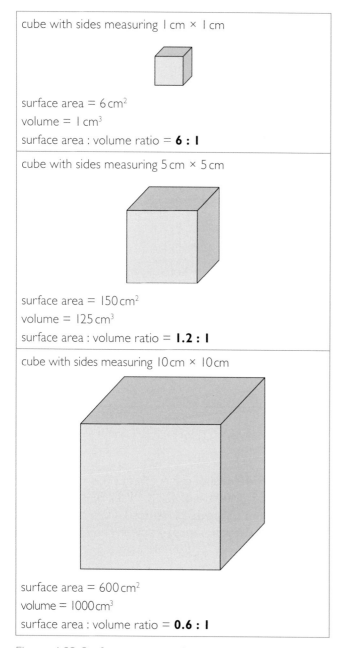

cube with sides measuring 1 cm × 1 cm

surface area = 6 cm²
volume = 1 cm³
surface area : volume ratio = **6 : 1**

cube with sides measuring 5 cm × 5 cm

surface area = 150 cm²
volume = 125 cm³
surface area : volume ratio = **1.2 : 1**

cube with sides measuring 10 cm × 10 cm

surface area = 600 cm²
volume = 1000 cm³
surface area : volume ratio = **0.6 : 1**

Figure 4.02 Surface area to volume ratios

Progress check 4.01

Copy and complete Table 4.03 below by calculating the surface areas and volumes of the shapes.

Shape	Surface area / cm²	Volume / cm³
a cube with sides measuring 3 cm		
a sphere with a radius of 4 cm		

Table 4.03

4.05 Investigating the effect of different surface area to volume ratios on diffusion using agar blocks

Cubes of solid agar, containing universal indicator solution, can be cut to different sizes. For example, with sides measuring 0.5 cm, 1.0 cm and 2.0 cm. These blocks are then placed in dilute hydrochloric acid and the time taken for each block to completely change colour is recorded. The time taken can then be related to the surface area and volume of each block.

4.06 Estimating water potential of plant tissues by immersing plant tissue in solutions with different water potentials

Plant tissue placed in a solution with the same water potential as the tissue will be in equilibrium with the solution and will have no overall uptake or loss in water. This can be investigated by cutting discs or strips of a suitable tissue such as potato tubers. These are weighed and then placed separately in a range of sucrose solutions of different concentrations. After a period of time, the tissues are removed, carefully blotted and reweighed. The percentage change is mass is calculated and plotted against the concentration of the sucrose solutions. The concentration of sucrose corresponding to a 0% change in mass can be read from the graph. At this point, the water potential of the solution is equal to the water potential of the tissue.

Worked example 4.01

Question

Discs of potato tissue were placed in sucrose solutions of different concentrations. The discs were weighed before immersion in the sucrose solutions. After 1 hour, the discs were removed, blotted carefully and weighed again. The results are shown in table 4.04:

Concen-tration of sucrose solution / mol dm⁻³	Initial mass of potato discs / g	Mass of potato discs after 1 h / g	Percentage change in mass / %
0.0	8.2	8.5	
0.2	7.9	8.0	
0.4	8.5	8.4	
0.6	8.6	8.3	
0.8	8.3	7.9	

Table 4.04

Copy and complete the table by calculating the percentage change in mass for each set of potato discs.

Answer

To calculate the percentage change, work out the difference in mass for each set of discs, then divide this by the original mass. Multiply the answer by 100 to express as a percentage.

So for the first set of discs, the calculation is:

8.5 − 8.2 = 0.3

0.3 ÷ 8.2 = 0.037 (rounded up)

0.037 × 100 = 3.7%

Notice that some of the changes are positive, indicating that these discs increased in mass and some of the changes are negative, showing a decrease in mass.

4.07 Explaining the movement of water between cells and solutions and the effects on plant and animal cells

Water always tends to move down a water potential gradient. However, in a fully turgid plant cell, the cell wall resists any further uptake of water by the cell (the overall water potential of the cell is zero when the cell is turgid). If plant cells are placed in a solution with a low water potential (e.g. 0.8 mol dm⁻³ sucrose solution), water will leave the cells and the cell contents shrink. Eventually, the cells will become plasmolysed, when the cell contents shrink away from the cell wall. Animal cells do not have a cell wall and, if placed in pure water, will take up water until the cell membrane ruptures and the cell lyses. If animal cells are placed in a solution with a lower water potential than the cell contents, the cells lose water and shrink.

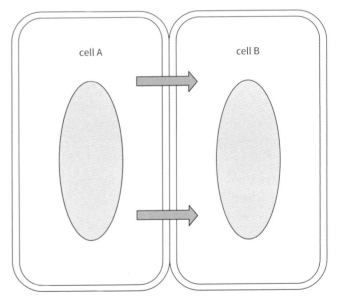

Figure 4.03 Water moving from one plant cell to another, by osmosis

If the water potential of cell A (Ψcell A) is −425 kPa and the water potential of cell B (Ψcell B) is −550 kPa, water will tend to move, by osmosis, from cell A to cell B, down the water potential gradient.

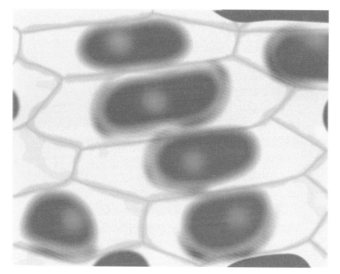

Figure 4.04 Plasmolysed plant cells

If plant cells are placed in a solution with a lower water potential than the cells, the cells will lose water and the contents shrink. These cells have a pigment in the cytoplasm and the cell contents have shrunk away from the cell wall. The cells are said to be **plasmolysed**.

Progress check 4.02

Explain what would happen to red blood cells if placed in:

1   1.0% sodium chloride solution.

2   Distilled water.

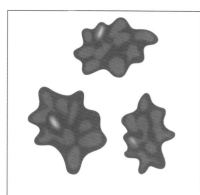

red blood cells placed in a solution with a high concentration of solute molecules lose water and the cells shrink.

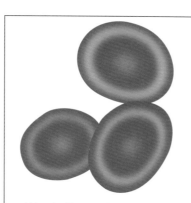

red blood cells in a solution with the same solute concentration as the cell contents remain their normal, biconcave shape.

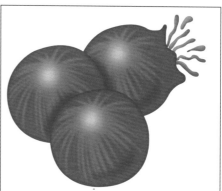

red blood cells placed in a solution with a low solute concentration, or in distilled water, swell and burst (cell lysis).

Figure 4.05 Osmosis in red blood cells

Exam-style questions

1   *Nitella* is a species of alga that grows in fresh water. *Nitella* has large cells and it is possible to measure the concentrations of ions in the vacuole. Table 4.05 shows the concentrations of potassium ions (K^+) and chloride ions (Cl^-) in the vacuole of *Nitella* and in fresh water:

Ion	Concentration in vacuole / mmol dm^{-3}	Concentration in freshwater / mmol dm^{-3}
potassium	76	0.1
chloride	170	1.3

Table 4.05

a   Compare the concentrations of these ions in the vacuole and in fresh water. [2]

b   Suggest an explanation for the difference. [2]

c   Suggest what effect a metabolic inhibitor would have on the concentrations of these ions in the vacuole of *Nitella*. [3]

Total: 7

2   a   Explain how the properties of phospholipids are related to their role in the formation the cell surface membrane. [4]

b   Some drugs pass through the cell membrane. Suggest what properties these drugs should have to enable them to pass through the cell membrane. [2]

Total: 6

Revision checklist

Check that you know:

- [ ] the fluid mosaic model of membrane structure

- [ ] the roles of cell surface membranes

- [ ] the process of cell signalling

- [ ] membrane transport processes, including diffusion, facilitated diffusion, osmosis, active transport, endocytosis and exocytosis

- [ ] diffusion using plant tissue and non-living materials

- [ ] surface areas and volumes of simple shapes and surface area to volume ratios

- [ ] the effect of different surface area to volume ratios on diffusion using agar blocks

- [ ] how to find the water potential of plant tissues by immersing plant tissue in solutions with different water potentials

- [ ] the movement of water between cells and solutions and the effects on plant and animal cells.

The mitotic cell cycle

Mitosis is a type of nuclear division that produces two daughter nuclei that are genetically identical. They contain the same number of chromosomes as each other and the parent nucleus. Mitosis is one stage of a sequence of events called the mitotic cell cycle.

> **TIP**
> It is a common mistake to describe mitosis as 'cell division'. The process of mitosis is part of cell division, but refers specifically to the division of the nucleus.

5.01 The structure of chromosomes

The nucleus contains thread-like structures called **chromosomes**. Different species of organisms have a characteristic number of chromosomes (e.g. in humans there are 46). They only become visible during cell division, when each chromosome can be seen to be made up of two identical structures called **chromatids** (Figure 5.01).

Each chromatid contains identical copies of DNA, which is produced by the process of DNA replication (see Unit 6). This takes place during the cell cycle, before the nucleus divides. The chromatids are joined at a region called the **centromere**, which can be at any point along the length of the chromosome, but is in a characteristic position for a particular chromosome. Each chromatid contains one DNA molecule, which is composed of a series of **genes**. The genes are the 'units' of inheritance. There are no genes at the centromere.

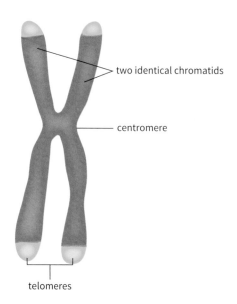

two identical chromatids

centromere

telomeres

Figure 5.01 The structure of a chromosome.

In each chromatid, the DNA is wrapped around globular protein molecules called **histones**. The histone proteins act as 'spools' around which the DNA winds. This holds the long DNA molecule in position and prevents it from becoming tangled up. Together, the DNA and histones are known as chromatin.

At both ends of each chromatid are regions of special DNA called **telomeres**. Telomeres act as 'caps' on the end of the chromosomes, preventing loss of DNA during DNA replication (see below).

5.02 The cell cycle

When an organism grows from a fertilised egg, cells divide repeatedly. During development, some cells become specialised and divide less frequently and others stop dividing altogether. However, even in an adult organism some cells continue to divide and replace cells that die. The sequence of events between cell divisions is known as the **cell cycle** (Figure 5.02).

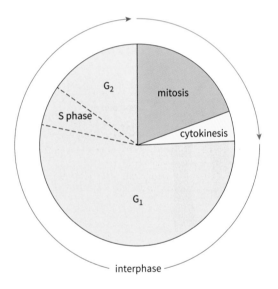

Figure 5.02 The cell cycle.

The cell cycle is divided into three stages: interphase, mitosis and cytokinesis.

1   **Interphase** is the non-dividing stage that takes up most of the cycle. It consists of three phases:

- G_1 (the first growth phase), when much protein synthesis occurs, organelles are produced and the amount of cytoplasm increases. If the cell is not going to divide again, it remains in this phase.

- S phase, when the DNA replicates (S stands for synthesis of DNA). This produces the two identical copies of DNA needed to form the chromatids. The cell only enters this phase if it is to undergo a further division.

- G_2 (the second growth phase). This is a shorter period of growth when proteins needed for cell division are synthesised, such as the microtubules that form the spindle fibres during mitosis (see below).

2   **Mitosis** is the process where a nucleus divides to produce two daughter nuclei that are genetically identical to each other and with the parent cell. Mitosis is described in greater detail below.

3   **Cytokinesis** is the division of the cytoplasm and the formation of the two daughter cells. In animal cells this involves a constriction of the cytoplasm, while in plant cells a new cell wall forms between the two daughter nuclei.

5.03 Mitosis

Mitosis is a continuous process that follows the G_2 stage of interphase. For convenience, it is considered to occur in four stages, called **prophase**, **metaphase**, **anaphase** and **telophase**. Most cells contain many chromosomes, but to make the process easier to understand, Figure 5.03 shows these stages as they would be seen in an animal cell containing just four chromosomes.

A key point to remember is that the copying of the DNA molecules in the chromosomes has taken place before mitosis, in the S phase. The chromatids contain exact copies of the DNA, so when they separate they are equivalent to chromosomes once more. The DNA will replicate again during interphase, before the next division.

Remember the letters **PMAT**:

Prophase = **P**ro means first, or 'before'

Metaphase = chromosomes in **M**iddle

Anaphase = chromosomes move **A**part

Telophase = **T**wo nuclei

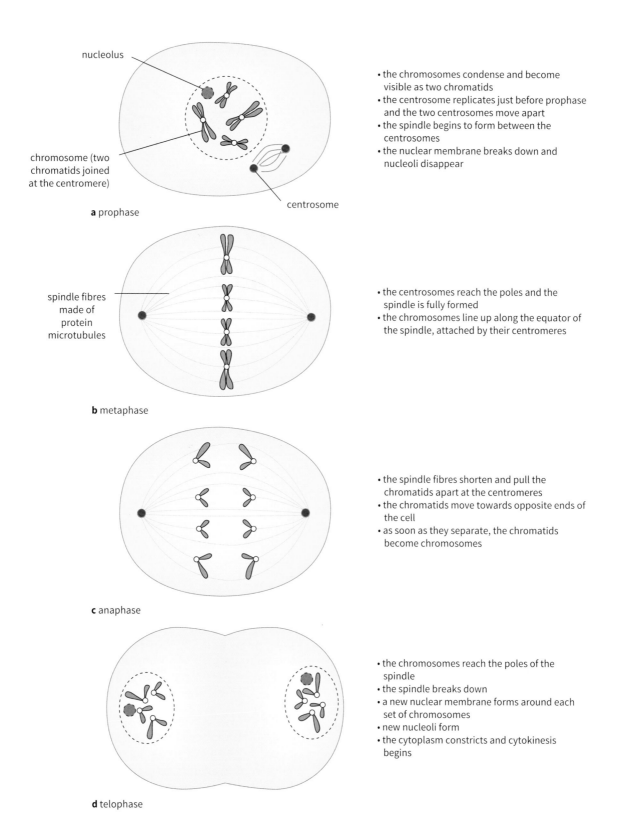

- the chromosomes condense and become visible as two chromatids
- the centrosome replicates just before prophase and the two centrosomes move apart
- the spindle begins to form between the centrosomes
- the nuclear membrane breaks down and nucleoli disappear

a prophase

- the centrosomes reach the poles and the spindle is fully formed
- the chromosomes line up along the equator of the spindle, attached by their centromeres

b metaphase

- the spindle fibres shorten and pull the chromatids apart at the centromeres
- the chromatids move towards opposite ends of the cell
- as soon as they separate, the chromatids become chromosomes

c anaphase

- the chromosomes reach the poles of the spindle
- the spindle breaks down
- a new nuclear membrane forms around each set of chromosomes
- new nucleoli form
- the cytoplasm constricts and cytokinesis begins

d telophase

Figure 5.03 The stages of mitosis.

5.04 Observing mitosis in root tips

To see cells undergoing mitosis you need to select a tissue that is actively dividing. One tissue that is suitable is a region known as the root tip meristem. This is found just behind the tip of a growing root. The best method is to make a 'root tip squash' preparation. This involves staining the root and then gently squashing it to spread out the cells.

Suitable roots can be obtained from onions, garlic or broad bean plants. The following method uses broad beans. Bean seeds are first germinated and grown in compost until the roots are about 10–20 cm in length.

Procedure

1 About 10 cm³ of acetic orcein stain is placed in a boiling tube. Three drops of dilute hydrochloric acid are added, and the tube covered with a cap of aluminium foil. (Acetic orcein has a strong vinegar-like smell that can be an irritant. The foil reduces the escape of fumes from the tube.)

2 A bean plant is removed from its compost and the roots rinsed under the tap. A few undamaged roots a few centimetres in length are cut off.

3 The roots are placed tip down in the stain and the foil replaced. The tube is heated in a water bath at 70 °C for 30 minutes. The acid and heat helps to separate the cells so that they squash easily.

4 A stained root tip is transferred to a microscope slide and a scalpel used to trim off and discard all but the last few millimetres of the tip.

5 Two drops of acidified acetic orcein stain is added to the root tip on the slide and a coverslip placed on top. A piece of filter paper is placed over the coverslip and the coverslip pressed down using the wooden handle of a mounted needle. This spreads out the root cells, so that they can be observed under the microscope.

With a little practice (repeating steps 4 and 5), cells from the meristem tissue just behind the tip can be located, and different stages of mitosis identified. The chromosomes are stained dark red by the acetic orcein. Alternatively, prepared slides of root tips can be used (Figure 5.04).

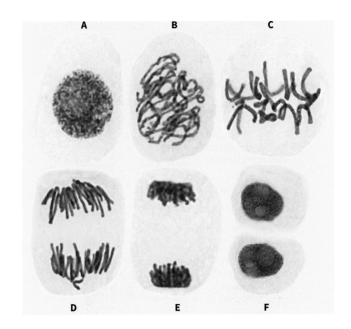

Figure 5.04 Photomicrograph of cells from onion root tip stained with acetic orcein.

Progress check 5.02

Some of the cells in Figure 5.04 are undergoing mitosis, and some are from other stages in the cell cycle. Identify as precisely as possible which stage is shown by each of cells A to F. Explain your reasoning, using only information you can see in this photomicrograph.

5.05 The significance of mitosis

Mitosis results in the formation of daughter cells with the same number of chromosomes as each other and as the parent cell. They are genetically identical (clones). This is important for several reasons:

- *Growth.* Multicellular organisms grow from unicellular zygotes. Each cell must have the same genes as in the zygote. Growth can take place throughout the body, as in animals, or in specialised meristems as in plants. Mitosis gives rise to many cells, which then differentiate to form tissues and organs.

- *Repair and replacement of tissues.* Mitosis is needed to renew certain tissues or replace worn-out cells. For example, cells in the epidermis of the skin and the lining of the gut are constantly replaced. A human red blood cell only lasts a few months in the body before it is broken down – over 2 million new red blood cells are made in the bone marrow every second.

- *Asexual reproduction.* Some organisms can produce new individuals from a single parent, without the formation and fusion of gametes. For example, unicellular organisms such as *Amoeba* reproduce by dividing into two cells. More complex animals such as *Hydra* forms new individuals by budding. Many plants carry out vegetative propagation, where part of the parent plant forms new individuals (Figure 5.05).

a

b

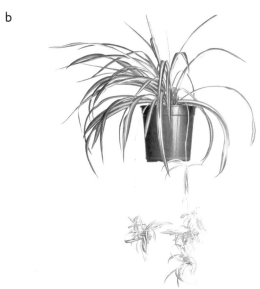

Figure 5.05 **a** *Hydra* is a small freshwater relative of sea anemones. Here it is producing a bud, which will eventually drop off and form a new individual. **b** The spider plant *Chlorophytum* produces plantlets from shoots emerging near the base of the plant. The plantlets detach and grow into new plants.

5.06 Telomeres

You have seen that telomeres are short regions of special DNA at the ends of chromosomes (Figure 5.01). They have been likened to the plastic tips on the end of shoelaces (Figure 5.06).

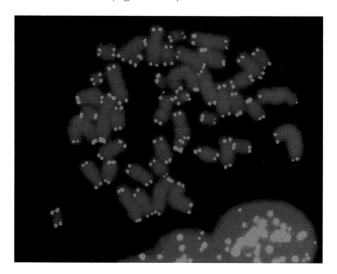

Figure 5.06 Light micrograph of human chromosomes (blue) showing telomeres stained with a fluorescent dye (pink).

A telomere consists of a region of non-coding, repeated base sequences. It protects the end of the chromosome from deterioration.

During DNA replication, the enzyme that copies the DNA cannot continue all the way to the end of the DNA molecule. This means that each time a cell divides, the end of the chromosome becomes shorter. Without the telomeres, the genes at the end of the coding DNA would be lost. To prevent this happening, part of the telomere is used up instead, allowing the cells to divide without losing genes. When the telomeres are too short, genes are activated which prevent the cell dividing any more (Figure 5.07).

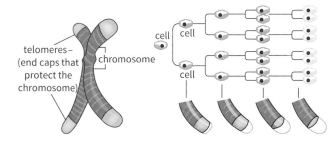

Figure 5.07 As cells divide the telomeres become shorter.

Telomeres act as a protection against uncontrolled cell division. However, there are some cells in the body that need to divide repeatedly, such as those that produce blood cells. These cells produce an enzyme called telomerase, which rebuilds the telomeres. If other cells in the body mutate and produce telomerase, these cells can divide without limit. This is a cause of some cancers (see below).

Loss of telomeres is associated with the aging process. Cells can normally divide only about 50–70 times, with telomeres becoming progressively shorter until the cell becomes inactive, or dies. Each time a cell divides it loses between 30 and 200 DNA base pairs. A baby has about 8000 DNA base pairs in its telomeres, while there are about 3000 in adult humans and 1500 in elderly people. This seems to be one of the factors responsible for the way the body ages.

5.07 Stem cells

A **stem cell** is a cell that retains the ability to divide many times by mitosis while remaining undifferentiated, but following this can differentiate into specialised cells such as muscle or nerve cells. In humans there are two types:

* embryonic stem cells, which are found in an early stage of development of the embryo, called the blastocyst. Embryonic stem cells can differentiate into any type of cell

* adult stem cells, which are found in various tissues in adults, such as bone marrow, skin, and the lining of the intestine

Stem cell therapy is the use of adult stem cells to regenerate tissues damaged by disease or injury. The most successful example of this therapy is bone marrow transplantation, which is a highly developed and widely used medical practice.

5.08 Cancer

It is important that growth and repair of tissues is *controlled*, so that it only happens at the right time and place in the body. Mitosis and cell division are under the control of genes. If any of these genes mutate, cell division may not occur at all, or cells may divide over and over again, producing a mass of cells called a **tumour**.

Some tumours are benign, which means that they do not spread around the body. However there are also malignant tumours, where some of the tumour cells break away and travel around the body. They then invade other tissues, causing secondary tumours to grow. Malignant tumours are **cancers**.

Some faulty genes that cause cancers are inherited, such as the mutated genes that result in one type of breast cancer. Other genes may spontaneously mutate to produce cancerous tumours. Although this is a random event, the likelihood of mutation can be increased by certain factors, such as:

* ionising radiation (e.g. X-rays and gamma-rays)
* certain chemicals, including several present in the tar from tobacco smoke

Sample question 5.01

Bone marrow contains stem cells that divide by mitosis to produce blood cells. Each time a stem cell divides it produces a replacement stem cell and a cell that develops into a blood cell. Figure 5.08 shows the changes in the mass of DNA in a bone marrow stem cell over a period of time.

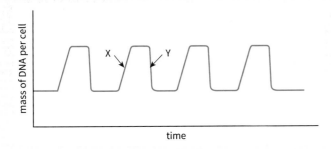

Figure 5.08 The changes in the mass of DNA in a bone marrow stem cell over time.

1 What happens in the cell to cause the changes in the mass of DNA at the points labelled X and Y on the graph? [2]

2 How many blood cells have been formed during the period shown in the graph? [1]

3 What happens to the number of chromosomes in the stem cell? [1]

[Mark points are shown in square brackets]

1 At X replication of the DNA takes place [1]. At Y cytokinesis (or cytoplasmic / cell division) takes place [1].

2 4 [1].

3 The chromosome number remains constant [1].

At X there is an increase in the amount of DNA, so this must represent the time in the cell cycle when DNA replication takes place. At Y the mass of DNA returns to what it was before replication, so this must be cytokinesis, when the cytoplasm constricts and divides the cell into two new cells.

The graph shows four complete cycles so it must have divided four times, each time producing one stem cell and one blood cell.

• ultraviolet (UV) radiation in sunlight, which causes a skin cancer called malignant melanoma

• some types of viruses, such as the human papilloma virus (HPV) – a virus that causes genital warts and can result in cervical cancer.

The factors that increase the probability of a person developing cancer are called carcinogens.

Progress check 5.03

Explain the meaning of the following terms:

1 Vegetative propagation.

2 Stem cell.

3 Carcinogen.

Revision checklist

Check that you know:

■ the structure of a chromosome

■ the events taking place during the cell cycle

■ the events taking place during the stages of mitosis

■ how to make a root tip squash preparation showing cells undergoing mitosis

■ the significance of mitosis in growth, repair and replacement of tissues, and asexual reproduction

■ the significance of telomeres in allowing continued cell division and preventing the loss of genes

■ the significance of mitosis in cell replacement and tissue repair by stem cells

■ how uncontrolled cell division can result in tumour formation and cancers.

Exam-style questions

1 a At what stage in the cell cycle do the following events take place?

   i Synthesis of proteins needed to form microtubules of the spindle.

   ii Replication of DNA.

   iii Separation of daughter chromatids. [3]

   b A cell in the G_1 stage of interphase contained 10 arbitrary units of DNA. If the cell divided by mitosis, how many units of DNA would be present in the following locations?

   i In the nucleus at the end of G_2.

   ii In the cell during anaphase.

   iii In each nucleus at the end of telophase. [3]

   Total: 6

2 a Why is a root tip particularly suitable material to use in preparing a slide to show mitosis? [1]

   b Name a suitable stain for staining chromosomes in a root tip squash preparation. [1]

   c What evidence would you see in a root tip squash preparation that metaphase takes longer than anaphase? [1]

   d State two functions of a centromere during mitosis. [2]

   Total: 5

3 a Describe the function of telomeres in protecting the ends of a chromosome during cell division. [4]

   b Explain how uncontrolled cell division can result in cancer. [3]

   Total: 7

Nucleic acids and protein synthesis

Learning outcomes

When you have finished this unit, you should be able to:

- ☐ describe the structure of nucleotides, including ATP

- ☐ describe the structures of RNA and DNA

- ☐ explain the importance of base pairing between complementary bases

- ☐ describe semi-conservative replication of DNA

- ☐ know that a polypeptide is coded for by a gene and that a gene forms part of a DNA molecule

- ☐ know that a gene mutation is a change in the sequence of nucleotides that may result in a changed polypeptide

- ☐ describe the way in which the sequence of nucleotides codes for the amino acid sequence with reference to sickle cell anaemia

- ☐ understand how the information in DNA is used during protein synthesis, including the roles of messenger RNA (mRNA), transfer RNA (tRNA) and ribosomes.

6.01 Nucleotides

Nucleotides consist of three main parts:

- a 5-carbon sugar

- a nitrogen-containing organic base

- an inorganic phosphate group.

These three parts are linked together, by covalent bonds, as shown in Figure 6.01

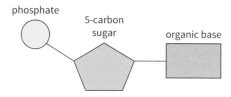

Figure 6.01 The essential structure of a nucleotide.

A molecule of glucose contains six carbon atoms, and is an example of a hexose. Sugars containing five carbon atoms are known as **pentoses**. Two different pentoses occur in nucleotides, these are known as **ribose** and **deoxyribose**.

There are five different organic bases that occur in DNA and RNA, and these bases are divided into two groups, called **purines** and **pyrimidines**. You do not need to know the structural formulae for the bases or the sugars, but you should recognise that purines have a double ring structure and that pyrimidines have a single ring structure, as shown in Figure 6.02.

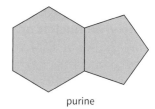

pyrimidine   purine

Figure 6.02 The essential structure of a pyrimidine base and a purine base.

Table 6.01 gives the names of the five bases, which are often abbreviated to their first letter. You should remember which of these bases are purines and which bases are pyrimidines.

Purines	Pyrimidines
adenine (**A**)	cytosine (**C**)
guanine (**G**)	thymine (**T**)
	uracil (**U**)

Table 6.01 The organic bases.

TIP Be careful not to confuse thymine (the base) with thiamine (vitamin B1). The spelling of these words should be clear and unambiguous.

6.02 ATP

ATP (adenosine triphosphate) is a phosphorylated nucleotide, consisting of adenine and ribose, joined to three phosphate groups, as shown in Figure 6.03.

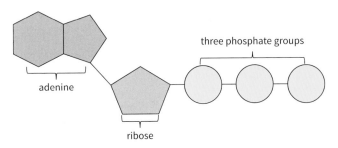

Figure 6.03 The essential structure of ATP.

Adenine joined to ribose in this way forms **adenosine**. Be careful not to confuse adenine with adenosine.

6.03 RNA and DNA

RNA (ribonucleic acid) and **DNA (deoxyribonucleic acid)** are both **polynucleotides** – they consist of many single nucleotides joined together to form long chains. You should remember from Unit 2 that large molecules, such as proteins and polysaccharides, can be built up by joining many small molecules together to form polymers.

Progress check 6.01

1 Name the monomers in proteins and in polysaccharides and the types of bond formed when these monomers join together.

2 Which of the following statements is not correct?

A: adenine is a purine base found in DNA and in ATP

B: ribose and deoxyribose are both pentose sugars

C: cytosine and thymine are both pyrimidine bases

D: adenosine consists of adenine joined to deoxyribose

Nucleotides join together by the formation of phosphodiester bonds to form polynucleotides, as illustrated in Figure 6.04.

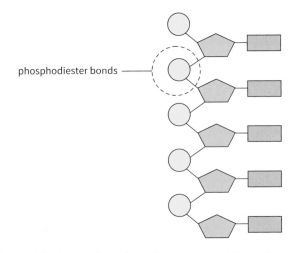

Figure 6.04 Part of a polynucleotide, consisting of nucleotides joined by phosphodiester bonds, shown in the dotted circle.

RNA is a **single-stranded polynucleotide**. Each nucleotide in RNA consists of a phosphate group, ribose and an organic base. The bases in RNA are adenine (A), cytosine (C), guanine (G) and uracil (U).

DNA is a **double-stranded polynucleotide**, consisting of two **complementary** polynucleotide strands, held together by hydrogen bonding between complementary pairs of bases. In DNA, each nucleotide consists of a phosphate group, deoxyribose and an organic base. The bases in DNA are adenine (A), thymine (T), guanine (G) and cytosine (C). In DNA, adenine always pairs with thymine and guanine always pairs with cytosine, forming **complementary base pairs**. Remember that adenine and guanine are both purine bases; thymine and cytosine are both pyrimidine bases, so one purine base pairs with its complementary pyrimidine base. There are two hydrogen bonds between adenine and thymine and three hydrogen bonds between guanine and cytosine.

The two polynucleotide strands in DNA are said to be antiparallel, because they run in opposite directions, one in the direction of carbon atom number 3 to carbon atom number 5 in deoxyribose and the other strand from carbon atom number 5 to carbon atom number 3 in the complementary strand. This is illustrated in Figure 6.05

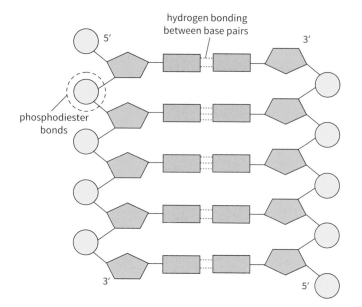

phosphodiester bonds

hydrogen bonding between base pairs

Figure 6.05 Two antiparallel strands in a molecule of DNA. The numbers refer to the positions of carbon atoms 3 and 5 in deoxyribose in each strand.

In DNA, the two polynucleotide chains twist around each other, forming the famous double helix, shown in Figure 6.06.

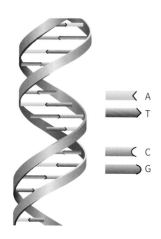

Figure 6.06 The double helix structure of DNA.

Molecules of DNA have the ability to make identical copies of themselves, through the process of **semi-conservative replication**. In outline, the two strands of DNA separate, by breaking the hydrogen bonds between complementary base pairs. Each strand of DNA acts as a template for the synthesis of a new, complementary strand alongside it. Complementary bases to those in the strand of DNA are joined together to form a strand of RNA. Remember that A (adenine) always pairs with T (thymine) and C (cytosine) always pairs with G (guanine) so, for

example, where there is a C in the original strand, there will be a G in the newly synthesised strand. The process of semi-conservative replication results in the formation of two identical DNA strands, each one consisting of one original strand and one newly synthesised strand. Semi-conservative replication occurs during the S phase of the cell cycle (described in Unit 5) and is controlled by a number of enzymes, including DNA helicase and DNA polymerase. DNA helicase separates the two strands of the DNA double helix by breaking the hydrogen bonds between the base pairs. DNA polymerase joins nucleotides together to form the new, complementary strands of DNA.

Worked example 6.01

Question

Analysis of a DNA molecule showed that it contained 18% thymine. Calculate the percentage of cytosine in this molecule.

Answer

To calculate the percentage of cytosine, we use the principle of complementary base pairing. If the percentage of thymine is 18%, then the percentage of adenine must also be 18%, so the total percentage of adenine and thymine is 36%. The remaining bases are cytosine and guanine, making up 100 − 36 = 64%. Half of this will be cytosine, so the percentage of cytosine is 32%.

6.04 The genetic code and protein synthesis

DNA contains genetic information and the sequence of bases on one of the strands specifies the sequence of amino acids joined together to form a polypeptide in the process of protein synthesis. Each part of a DNA molecule which codes for a particular polypeptide is referred to as a **gene**. Different forms of a gene are known as alleles.

Each sequence of three bases (e.g. CGA) is referred to as a **codon**. With four different bases, there are 64 possible codons, which is more than enough to specify the 20 different amino acids that occur in proteins. The genetic code is said to be **degenerate**, as it is possible for several different codons to specify the same amino acid.

Progress check 6.02

1 Explain why there are 64 codons and why just two bases would be insufficient.

2 The diagram shows the sequence of bases in part of a DNA molecule.

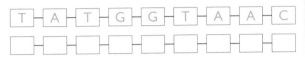

Copy and complete the diagram by writing the complementary bases in the boxes. How many amino acids are coded for by this part of the DNA molecule?

The process of protein synthesis essentially consists of two stages:

- **transcription**, in which a molecule of **messenger RNA (mRNA)** is synthesised

- **translation**, in which the sequence of bases on the mRNA molecule is used to specify the order in which amino acids are joined together to form a polypeptide.

Be careful not to confuse the terms *transcription* and *translation*.

In the process of transcription, one strand of part of a DNA molecule is used as a template for the synthesis of a complementary strand of mRNA, following the rules of complementary base pairing. You should remember that in RNA the base uracil (U) replaces the base thymine (T). Uracil is complementary to adenine, so where there is an A in the DNA strand, there will be a U in the mRNA strand. During transcription, the enzyme **RNA polymerase** joins free nucleotides to form complementary mRNA, which then separates from the DNA strand.

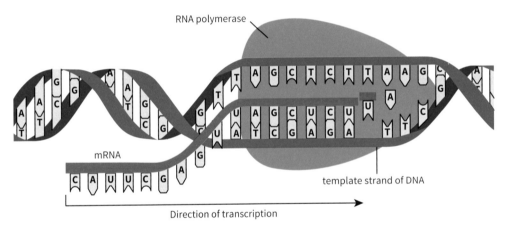

Figure 6.07 The process of transcription

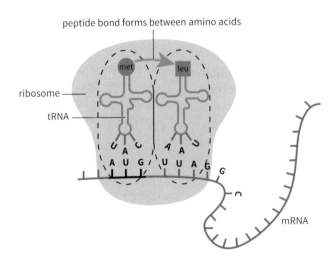

Figure 6.08 The process of translation

Sample question 6.01

The nucleotide base sequence in part of a gene is:

AACGTCTTCTCCTGCGGTTAT

1 Write the complementary sequence in the strand of mRNA after transcription.

2 How many codons are there in this strand of mRNA?

3 Explain what is meant by the term 'gene'.

[3 marks]

[Mark points are shown in square brackets – to a maximum of 3 marks]

1 UUGCAGAAGAGGACGCCAAUA [1]

2 There are seven codons. [1]

3 A gene is part of a DNA molecule in which the nucleotide base sequence codes for one polypeptide. [1]

The sequence of nucleotide bases is shown correctly. Remember that in RNA, the base uracil (U) replaces thymine (T). Uracil is complementary to adenine.

A codon is a triplet of bases. In this strand of mRNA there are 21 nucleotide bases, so there are seven codons (7 × 3 = 21). The answer is correct.

This is an accurate explanation of the term. You should remember that the sequence of nucleotide bases in DNA specifies the exact sequence of amino acids (the primary structure) of a polypeptide, after the mRNA has been translated in the process of protein synthesis. You could refer to a table showing all 64 codons and translate the mRNA in part 1 into a sequence of amino acids.

In a eukaryotic cell, mRNA leaves the nucleus and attaches to a ribosome in the cytoplasm. Ribosomes are the sites of protein synthesis, in which the genetic code, carried on the mRNA molecule, is translated into the appropriate sequence of amino acids.

Protein synthesis involves another type of RNA, called **transfer RNA (tRNA)**. Each molecule of tRNA has a region with three exposed bases, referred to as the **anticodon** and another part of the tRNA molecule is attached to a specific amino acid. The anticodon is complementary to a codon on mRNA and so the tRNA molecule brings the correct amino acid, as specified by the mRNA codon, to the ribosome. As an example, the mRNA codon GCA specifies the amino acid alanine. The anticodon, which is complementary to GCA, is CGU, so the tRNA with this anticodon will be attached to a molecule of the amino acid alanine. Each amino acid has its own, specific, tRNA molecule.

The ribosome moves along the mRNA and, as it does so, tRNA molecules bring the appropriate amino acids as specified by the sequence of codons on mRNA. The amino acids are joined by the formation of peptide bonds (see Unit 2), building up a polypeptide chain. This process continues until a stop codon (e.g. UAA) is reached.

Worked example 6.02

Question

The sequence of bases in part of a strand of DNA is:

GGCCTTATCGTACGT

How many codons are there in this part of the DNA strand? Write the complementary sequence of bases in mRNA formed from this strand of DNA

Answer

Remember that the genetic code is based on non-overlapping sequences of triplets of bases. There are 15 bases in this strand, so there are five codons:

GGC

CTT

ATC

GTA

CGT

The strand of mRNA has a complementary sequence of bases to the DNA strand, but do not forget that the base uracil (U) replaces thymine (T) in RNA! This is easy to forget.

So the complementary sequence will be: **CCGGAAUAGCAUGCA**.

You could decode this part of mRNA, by referring to a table showing the entire genetic code.

6.05 Mutations and sickle cell anaemia

A change in the nucleotide sequence in DNA is referred to as a mutation and this may result in a change in the amino acid sequence in the polypeptide coded for by the affected gene.

One example of this is illustrated by a mutation which results in the formation of a type of haemoglobin, known as haemoglobin S.

In this mutation, one of the codons in the gene for the β chain of haemoglobin is altered, from CTT to CAT. This mutation results in the substitution of the amino acid valine for glutamic acid in the sixth position in the β chain of the haemoglobin molecule and the synthesis of haemoglobin S. This small change has a considerable effect on the structure and properties of the haemoglobin molecule. Figure 6.07 shows how the mutation changes the amino acid sequence in part of the haemoglobin molecule.

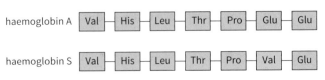

Figure 6.09 The amino acid sequences in part of the β globin chain of haemoglobin A and in haemoglobin S. The only difference is the substitution of valine in haemoglobin S for glutamic acid in haemoglobin A.

The allele for haemoglobin A is often written as **Hb^A** and the allele for haemoglobin S is indicated as **Hb^S**. People who are homozygous for the allele for haemoglobin S, in other words they have two copies of the mutated gene (**Hb^SHb^S**), develop a condition known as **sickle cell anaemia**. Sickle cell anaemia is an example of a genetic disease (see Units 16 and 17 for more details).

Revision checklist

Check that you know:

- [ ] the structure of nucleotides, including ATP

- [ ] the structures of RNA and DNA

- [ ] the importance of base pairing between complementary bases

- [ ] semi-conservative replication of DNA

- [ ] polypeptides are coded for by genes and genes form part of a DNA molecule

- [ ] gene mutations and how a gene mutation may result in a changed polypeptide

- [ ] how the sequence of nucleotides codes for the amino acid sequence and sickle cell anaemia

- [ ] how the information in DNA is used during protein synthesis, including the roles of mRNA, tRNA and ribosomes.

Exam-style questions

1 Explain what is meant by each of the following terms:

   a Gene. [2]

   b Transcription. [2]

   c Translation. [4]

   Total: 8

2 a Give <u>three</u> differences between the structure of a molecule of DNA and a molecule of RNA. [3]

   b With reference to an example, explain why a change in one base in DNA may result in the synthesis of a different polypeptide. [5]

   Total: 8

Transport in plants

Plants have two transport systems:

- **xylem**, which carries water and minerals from the roots to the leaves in a one-way flow

- **phloem**, which carries products of photosynthesis from the leaves to other parts of the plant.

Both are **mass flow** systems, which means that materials move through them in bulk, due to a difference in pressure – like water flowing through a pipe.

Note: in this unit you should have opportunities to draw and label plant tissues from prepared microscope slides. You should also draw and label individual cells from different tissues. You can use the diagrams in this unit to help you.

>
> **TIP** Use an eyepiece graticule to help you draw tissues in the correct proportions (see Unit 1).

7.01 Transport in the xylem

Water is absorbed by the roots of a plant and travels through the plant in the xylem. Loss of water from the leaves is called **transpiration** and is the driving force for water movement. The movement of water from roots to stem and leaves is called the transpiration stream.

> **TIP** Make sure that you can define transpiration and distinguish between transpiration and the transpiration stream.

a Transpiration

In a well-watered plant, about 98% of water entering a leaf is lost to the air in transpiration. The rest is used in photosynthesis and other metabolic processes, or for maintaining the turgidity of cells. Most water is lost through pores in the leaf called **stomata** (singular = stoma). There are more stomata on the underside of most leaves. This is because the underside of a leaf is shaded and cooler than the top of the leaf, so less evaporation will take place. Water travels down a gradient of water potential from the leaf cells to the air outside the leaf (see Unit 4 for an explanation of water potential).

A leaf contains many cells in contact with air spaces in the mesophyll tissue (Figure 7.01). Liquid water evaporates from the cell walls and diffuses into the air spaces between the mesophyll cells, then diffuses out through the stomata. Water in the leaf cells is replaced by osmosis from the xylem, passing out of the vessels through pits in their walls (see structure of xylem in Figure 7.01). The evaporation of water from the leaf maintains the water potential gradient and produces a suction force. This force is called 'transpiration pull' and drives the rest of the transpiration stream.

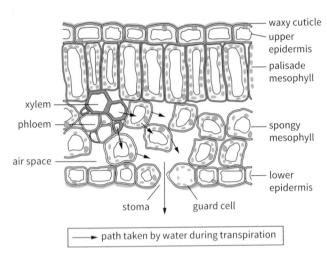

Figure 7.01 Transverse section of a leaf.

Each stoma is surrounded by a pair of **guard cells**, which can change shape to open and close the stoma. For photosynthesis to take place, the stomata must be open to exchange carbon dioxide and oxygen. Plants must photosynthesise, so they cannot avoid transpiration taking place – transpiration is an inevitable consequence of the need for photosynthesis.

Evaporation of water requires heat, so transpiration also functions to cool the leaf. This is a very important role – leaves are exposed to the direct rays of the Sun and would easily overheat, denaturing enzymes and halting the leaf's metabolism.

7.02 Uptake of water by roots

Soil water contains few solutes while cells of the root contain many dissolved substances, so soil water has a higher water potential than the cells. Because of this, water enters root hair cells from the soil by osmosis down the water potential gradient.

Root hair cells are modified epidermal cells that increase the surface area of the root to maximise water uptake. The water then moves across the

parenchyma cells of the root cortex, and into the xylem (Figure 7.02). Water is transported to all parts of the plant in the xylem, maintaining a continuous flow down a water potential gradient.

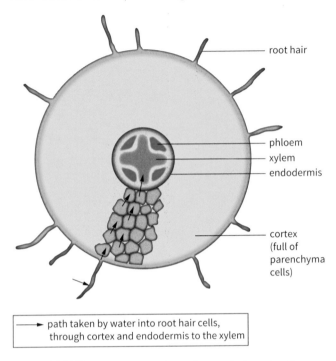

Figure 7.02 Transverse section of a root showing the pathway taken by water.

Water crosses the root in two ways (Figure 7.03):

- the **symplast** pathway, through the cytoplasm or vacuoles of the cells
- the **apoplast** pathway, along cell walls of the root cortex cells.

Some water enters the cortex cells through their partially permeable surface membranes, by osmosis. It then passes through the cytoplasm or vacuole of each cell and from cell to cell via plasmodesmata. This is the symplast pathway. It allows cells to have metabolic control over the movement of water and mineral ions.

When the rate of transpiration is high, most water travels through the apoplast pathway. The permeable, mesh-like structure of the cellulose fibres in the cell walls allows free movement of water molecules, rather like water soaking through filter paper. This means that water moves from cell to cell without ever having to enter the cytoplasm of the cortex cells. Water continues to pass along the cell walls until it reaches the innermost layer of cells of the cortex, called the **endodermis** (Figure 7.03). The walls of the

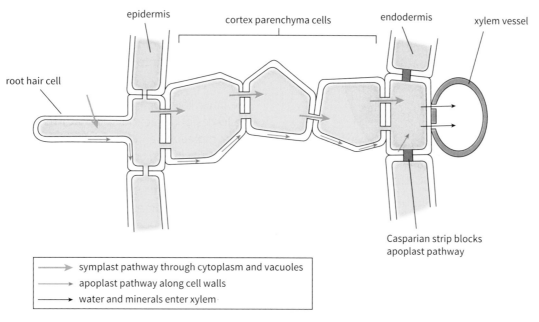

epidermis   cortex parenchyma cells   endodermis   xylem vessel

root hair cell

Casparian strip blocks
apoplast pathway

→ symplast pathway through cytoplasm and vacuoles
→ apoplast pathway along cell walls
→ water and minerals enter xylem

Figure 7.03 The pathways taken by water through the cells of the root.

endodermis cells contain a ring of waterproof material called suberin, known as the Casparian strip. Suberin in the Casparian strip blocks the apoplast pathway, so that the water is diverted into the cytoplasm and vacuoles of the cells (i.e. through the symplast pathway). This ensures that all water movement is controlled by the root cells.

Note that water also moves through the mesophyll cells of the leaves via the apoplast and symplast pathways. In the leaves there is no equivalent of the Casparian strip.

Uptake of mineral ions

Mineral ions such as nitrate, phosphate and potassium are absorbed by the root hairs. Some ions are absorbed by diffusion or facilitated diffusion. Others are taken up against a concentration gradient, by active transport. They then take the same pathways as water does, travelling through the root cortex and entering the xylem. Facilitated diffusion and active transport occur through specialised protein molecules in the surface membrane of any cells involved (see Unit 4). This means that their uptake and transport can be selectively controlled by the cells. The endodermis plays a key role in this.

Active transport of mineral ions from the endodermis into the xylem also helps to lower the water potential inside the xylem, causing more water to enter the

xylem by osmosis from the root cells. This results in a positive pressure called root pressure. However, root pressure is not large and does not play a significant role in driving the transpiration stream. It can only push water a few centimetres up the xylem. Most water movement is due to transpiration pull.

Progress check 7.01

1   Explain the difference between transpiration, transpiration pull and the transpiration stream.

2   Explain why transpiration is an inevitable consequence of gas exchange in plants.

3   In a root, water enters the root hair cells and passes across the cells of the root cortex, before entering the xylem vessels. Explain why water moves in this direction.

7.03 The structure of xylem

Xylem forms a continuous transport system throughout a plant. In young, non-woody stems the xylem and phloem are together arranged in strands called **vascular bundles**, located around the periphery of the stem (Figure 7.04).

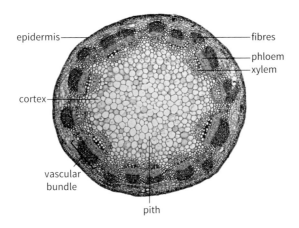

Figure 7.04 Light micrograph of a transverse section of a stem of *Helianthus* (sunflower).

Xylem tissue contains several types of cells. One type consists of dead, empty cells that lack end walls, called **xylem vessel elements**. They are arranged one on top of each other to form hollow tubes or vessels that transport water up the stem (Figure 7.05).

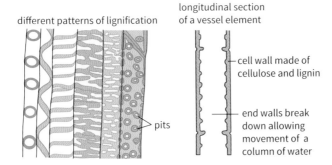

Figure 7.05 Xylem vessels.

Xylem vessels contain no cytoplasm, so there is no restriction to movement of water and minerals from the roots to the leaves. Their walls are made of cellulose and a material called **lignin**. Lignin provides strength, which prevents the vessels collapsing under the negative pressure caused by transpiration. Lignin is also waterproof. Non-lignified gaps in the cell walls called pits allow for lateral movement of water out of the vessels and into other vessels or into neighbouring cells. Lignin is deposited in the cell walls in a variety of patterns, such as rings and spirals.

Water movement through xylem vessels

Vessels are very narrow, with a lumen tens of micrometres in diameter. This narrow diameter is important in allowing water to pass up a vessel in a continuous column. If the vessels were wider, the columns would break up and the flow would stop. The narrowness of the vessel means that there is a large surface area to volume ratio, so lots of water is in contact with the xylem wall.

The inner lining of a vessel is made of cellulose. There are forces of attraction called **adhesion** between water molecules and this inner wall – the lining is hydrophilic. In addition there are attractive forces called **cohesion** between the water molecules, due to hydrogen bonds (see Unit 2). Together, these forces maintain the columns of water all the way up the stem of a plant – a height that can be over a hundred metres in the tallest species of trees. Transpiration at the leaves produces a negative pressure or **tension**, which pulls the molecules of water up through the xylem. You can imagine the water molecules arranged like a chain – transpiration pull at the leaves moves the whole chain through the plant, resulting in the transpiration stream (Figure 7.06). This explanation of the way that water moves through xylem is called the **cohesion–tension theory**.

Progress check 7.02

1   List four ways the structure of a xylem vessel is adapted for its function.

2   Describe the pathway taken by water from the cytoplasm of a root hair cell to a xylem vessel in the centre of the root.

7.04 Investigating transpiration

You should have the opportunity to carry out a number of investigations related to transpiration:

- taking peels of leaf epidermis to see stomata
- taking impressions of leaf epidermis
- measuring the rate of transpiration using a potometer
- measuring the surface area of leaves using grids.

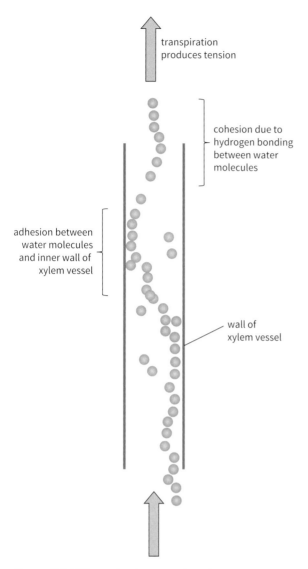

Figure 7.06 The cohesion–tension theory.

a Epidermal peels

It is possible to remove a piece of the epidermis from a leaf to view stomata through a microscope. A suitable leaf to use is lettuce.

1 Peel off a strip of epidermis using forceps, or tear the leaf like tearing a sheet of paper. The epidermis will be visible as a thin transparent layer along the tear.

2 Place a piece of epidermis from the lower surface of the leaf onto a microscope slide.

3 Add a drop of water and a cover slip.

The specimen in Figure 7.07 has epidermal cells with wavy interlocking margins, like the pieces of a jigsaw puzzle. Stomata and their pairs of guard cells are distributed irregularly between the epidermal cells.

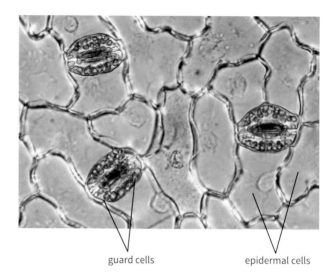

Figure 7.07 Epidermis of the surface of a leaf showing three stomata.

b Leaf impressions

Impressions (moulds) of the surface of leaf epidermis can be made using clear nail varnish.

1 Choose a suitable smooth, broad leaf that does not have leaf hairs.

2 Paint a thin layer of nail varnish about 1 cm square on the lower surface of the leaf.

3 Leave the nail varnish to dry for at least 30 minutes.

4 Peel off the dry square using forceps and place it on a microscope slide, with the side that was touching the leaf uppermost. There is no need to use a coverslip. Impressions of the epidermal cells and stomata will be visible under the microscope.

Both of the above methods can be used for counting the number of stomata per unit area of leaf.

c Potometers

Transpiration is water loss from the leaves of a plant, but this is difficult to measure. Potometers actually measure the rate of *uptake* by a plant or a leafy shoot. Since about 98% of the water taken up is lost by transpiration, we usually assume that a potometer measures the rate of transpiration.

Potometers are a variety of shapes and sizes. Figure 7.08 shows one version that has a reservoir for refilling the potometer tube and a scale for taking measurements. As the shoot takes up water, the water is drawn along the capillary tube. The rate of movement can be measured.

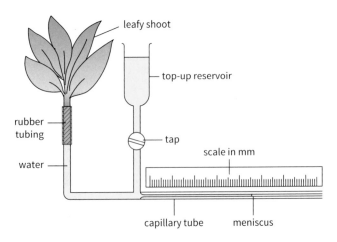

leafy shoot

top-up reservoir

rubber tubing

tap

water

scale in mm

capillary tube

meniscus

Figure 7.08 A potometer.

The main problem with setting up a potometer is to make sure that there are no leaks – if air bubbles get into the potometer it will not work.

1 Place a short piece of rubber tubing on the end of the glass tube and submerge the tube under water in a sink or large bowl. Squeeze the end of the rubber tubing to remove any air from the tubing and capillary.

2 Take a leafy shoot and place the cut end under water. Using a sharp blade, cut off a piece of the stem at an angle. Cutting the stem under water ensures there is no air in the end of the stem.

3 Insert the stem into the tubing, keeping both under water. The angled cut makes it easier to push the stem into the rubber tubing.

4 Remove the assembled potometer from the water and seal the ends of the rubber tubing with a little petroleum jelly.

5 Gently blot any excess water from the shoot with a paper towel and leave the apparatus to dry fully before taking measurements.

You can now use the potometer to measure the rate of transpiration under different conditions. The movement of water in the capillary tube is timed, and converted to a rate in millimetres per second (mm s^{-1}). If the internal radius of the capillary tube is known, the rate can be converted to a volume per second by using the formula $\pi r^2 L$ to find the volume, where r is the radius and L is the distance travelled by the meniscus in the tube.

Different environmental factors can be investigated, such as:

- using a fan to change the wind speed
- using a bench lamp to change light intensity

- removing leaves from the shoot to find the effect of changing leaf area.

d Measuring the surface area of a leaf

You can measure surface area of a leaf by placing it on graph paper, drawing around the leaf in pencil and counting the number of squares enclosed by the outline. You should count squares that are wholly inside the outline, plus squares that are more than half covered. Ignore squares that are less than half inside the leaf outline.

This method can be used to find the total leaf area of a shoot in a potometer experiment. This allows you to measure the rate of transpiration per unit area of leaf, enabling you to make meaningful comparisons between different plants, or between different species of plant.

Worked example 7.01

Question

A student sets up a leafy shoot in a potometer as shown in Figure 7.08. After allowing the shoot to equilibrate to the new conditions, she noted that the water in the capillary tube moved a distance of 18.7 cm in 5.00 minutes. The internal diameter of the capillary tube was 1.00 mm. The student then removed the shoot from the potometer and measured its total leaf area, which was 265 cm^2.

(Note that the values in the question are given to three significant figures. The same number of significant figures should be used in the answer.)

Calculate the rate of uptake of water by the shoot in cm^3 per minute per square centimetre of leaf area (cm^3 min^{-1} cm^{-2} leaf area).

Answer

Step 1:

The question asks for the answer to be given in cm^3 min^{-1} cm^{-2} leaf area. The internal diameter of the capillary tube is given in mm, so this value must be halved to find the radius, and converted to cm:

internal radius = 0.5 mm = 0.05 cm

Step 2:

The total volume of water taken up = $\pi r^2 L$, where $\pi = 3.142$ (to four significant figures), so:

volume of water = $(3.142 \times 0.05^2 \times 18.7)$ cm^3

Step 3:

This is the volume taken up in 5 minutes, so:

$$\text{volume of water taken up per minute} = \frac{3.14 \times 0.05^2 \times 18.7}{5}\ \text{cm}^3\ \text{min}^{-1}$$

$$= 0.02936\ \text{cm}^3\ \text{min}^{-1}$$

(Use at least the same number of significant figures for any constants (such as π), and for any answers to intermediate steps in the calculation – only round up at the end, to avoid rounding errors.)

Step 4:

The rate of water uptake per cm^2 of leaf area is calculated by dividing the water uptake per minute by the leaf area:

$$= 0.02936\ \text{cm}^3\ \text{min}^{-1} \div 265\ \text{cm}^2$$

$$= 0.000115\ \text{cm}^3\ \text{min}^{-1}\ \text{cm}^{-2}\ \text{leaf area}$$

Or in scientific notation:

rate $= 1.15 \times 10^{-4}\ \text{cm}^3\ \text{min}^{-1}\ \text{cm}^{-2}$ leaf area.

7.05 Factors affecting the rate of transpiration

a Temperature

High temperatures increase the rate of transpiration. This is because heat increases the rate of evaporation of water from the mesophyll cells of the leaf, and increases the rate of diffusion of water vapour out of the leaf.

b Humidity

Low humidity increases the rate of transpiration. If the air around a leaf is dry, this increases the gradient of water potential between the air spaces in the leaf and the outside of the leaf, so water vapour diffuses out through the stomata more rapidly.

c Wind speed

High wind speed increases the rate of transpiration. In windy conditions, air currents will remove any water vapour from around the surface of the leaves. This helps to maintain the water potential gradient between the air spaces in the leaf and the outside of the leaf.

d Light intensity

Transpiration is faster in the light than in the dark. This is because stomata open in the light to allow gas exchange for photosynthesis; so more water vapour is lost.

7.06 Xerophytic plants

Xerophytes are plants that are adapted to live in conditions of low water availability. This can be due to low rainfall (in a desert) or because they live in habitats such as sand dunes, where rainwater drains away before a plant can take advantage of it. These plants show xerophytic features, which are adaptations to increase water uptake, or to reduce water loss. These features include:

- extensive root systems to maximise water uptake
- swollen stems to store water (e.g. cacti)
- thick waxy cuticle on aerial parts of the plant to reduce evaporation
- specialised leaves to reduce water loss.

A good example of a xerophyte with leaves that are well adapted to reduce water loss is marram grass (*Ammophila* spp.). This plant grows on sand dunes in exposed coastal locations, where water is in short supply and the windy conditions increase the rate of transpiration. The leaves show a number of adaptations, including being rolled or curled along their length, and having thick waxy cuticle, leaf hairs and sunken stomata (Figure 7.09).

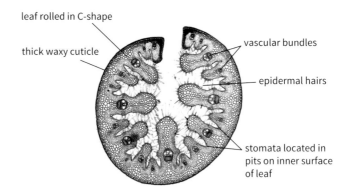

Figure 7.09 Transverse section of a leaf of marram grass (*Ammophila arenaria*).

The rolled leaf, presence of leaf hairs and location of the stomata all serve to trap humid air next to the inner surface of leaf. This helps to reduce the drying action of the wind. When water is available, the leaves uncurl and flatten to expose a greater surface area to the Sun for photosynthesis.

Progress check 7.03

1 Explain why high air humidity reduces the rate of transpiration.

2 Describe how the rate of transpiration at night will differ from the rate during the day. Explain your answer.

3 List three adaptations to reduce water loss shown by the leaves of xerophytic plants.

7.07 Transport in the phloem

Substances made by a plant during photosynthesis are called **assimilates**. Soluble assimilates are moved through the phloem in a process known as **translocation**. The main assimilate moved in this way is the disaccharide sucrose. The syrup-like sap in the phloem can contain up to 30% sucrose by mass. Phloem also contains amino acids, minerals and plant hormones.

Unlike xylem, phloem contains only living cells. These include **sieve tube elements** and **companion cells**. Sieve tube elements contain cytoplasm and some organelles, but no nuclei, ribosomes or vacuoles. Each sieve tube element has a companion cell lying alongside it (Figure 7.10).

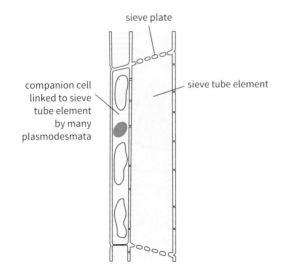

Figure 7.10 Phloem cells

Sieve tube elements are arranged end-to-end, forming continuous tubes. The ends of each cell are made of perforated cell walls called sieve plates, which allow mass flow of sap from one element to the next. In any single sieve tube, material flows in one direction, but some cells transport sap up and some down the plant – the movement is bidirectional. There are many plasmodesmata connecting the cytoplasm of each sieve tube element with its associated companion cell. Companion cells have nuclei and a normal complement of organelles, including many mitochondria. They control the activities of the sieve tube elements, so that the two cells act as a single functional unit.

TIP

Remember that the presence of many mitochondria in a cell shows that it is able to make much ATP from aerobic respiration.

Figure 7.11 shows a transverse section through a vascular bundle. Phloem sieve tubes can be seen in the middle of the bundle (stained blue). If you look carefully you can see a companion cells alongside some of the sieve tubes. Larger xylem vessels are visible below the area of phloem (the lignified walls of the vessels are stained red). The red tissue above the phloem consists of fibres. These also have lignified walls but their function is to support the stem and they do not transport water.

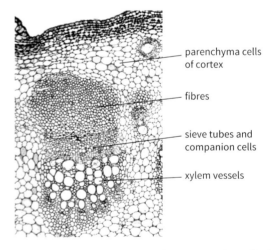

Figure 7.11 Transverse section of a vascular bundle in a stem of *Helanthus* (*sunflower*).

How assimilates move through the phloem

Phloem sap moves from places where sucrose is produced, to places where it is used up or stored. A part of the plant that is a net producer of sucrose is called a **source**. The main sources are the mature photosynthesising leaves, as well as storage organs such as potato tubers, where starch can be broken down to produce sugar. Sucrose enters the phloem at a source.

Any plant organ that is a net consumer of sucrose, such as roots, buds, flowers, young leaves, stems and fruits, is called a **sink**. A storage organ can be a source *or* a sink, depending on whether it is building up starch reserves in the summer, or breaking them down during a period of growth. Sucrose leaves the phloem at a sink.

Assimilates such as sucrose move through the phloem from sources to sinks. This mass flow requires metabolic energy, because sucrose has to be transported (or 'loaded') into phloem against a concentration gradient – sucrose is much more concentrated in sieve tubes and companion cells than in neighbouring cells. Loading of sucrose takes place by active transport:

- The surface membranes of companion cells contain **proton pumps**, which use energy from ATP to transport protons (hydrogen ions, H^+) out of the cell. This generates a H^+ gradient that drives sucrose uptake through a cotransport protein, also located in the membrane (Figure 7.12).

- The increase in concentration of sucrose inside the companion cell causes sucrose to move by diffusion down a concentration gradient into its associated sieve tube element.

- The increased concentration of sucrose lowers the water potential in the phloem, causing water to enter by osmosis from the surrounding mesophyll cells.

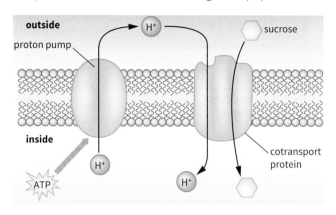

Figure 7.12 Cotransport of sucrose.

At a sink, sucrose is used up. Sucrose therefore diffuses down its concentration gradient, from the phloem sieve tubes to the tissue that is consuming the sucrose. This again generates a water potential gradient, so that water follows the sucrose, by osmosis.

Phloem sap moves from source to sink at rates of up to 1 metre per hour, which is much faster than can be explained by diffusion. This movement is driven by the mechanisms described above, which cause a build-up of fluid pressure at the source and a lowered fluid pressure at the sink. In other words there is a gradient of hydrostatic pressure between source and sink, which results in mass flow.

Sample question 7.01

Table 7.01 contains some comparisons between xylem vessels and phloem sieve tubes. Copy and complete the table. [7 marks]

Feature	Xylem vessels	Phloem sieve tubes
living or non-living		living
contain nuclei	no	
direction of flow of materials through plant	one direction. from roots to leaves	
substances transported		sucrose and amino acids
permeability of cell wall to water	not permeable	
components of cell wall		

Table 7.01

[Mark points are shown in square brackets – to a maximum of 7 marks]

Feature	Xylem vessels	Phloem sieve tubes
living or non-living	non-living [1]	
contain nuclei		no [1]
direction of flow of materials through plant		bidirectional. from sources to sinks [1]
substances transported	water and mineral ions [1]	
permeability of cell wall to water		permeable [1]
components of cell wall	cellulose and lignin [1]	cellulose [1]

Rows 1 and 2: these are simple choices – take the cue from the completed boxes. Note that sieve tubes contain cytoplasm but no nuclei.

Row 3: A complete answer requires two statements. The flow through the plant is bidirectional (alternatively you could say 'happens in both directions'). 'From sources to sinks' is the best answer to the second part, or you could give an example of a source and a sink.

Row 5: 'Permeable' or 'fully permeable' is correct. 'Semipermeable' or 'partially permeable' are incorrect – these terms apply to the cell surface membrane, not the cell wall.

Revision checklist

Check that you know:

- the location and arrangement of tissues in a transverse section of a leaf

- the meaning of transpiration and how it takes place in a leaf

- the location and arrangement of tissues in a transverse section of a root

- the uptake of water by roots – the symplast and apoplast pathways and the role of the Casparian strip

- the uptake of mineral ions by roots

- the location and arrangement of tissues in a transverse section of a stem

- the structure of xylem vessel elements and how their structure is related to their function

- movement of water through xylem vessels – the cohesion–tension theory

- how transpiration can be investigated using epidermal peels, leaf impressions, potometers and measuring the area of leaves

- explanations of the factors that affect the rate of transpiration

- the adaptations of the leaves of xerophytic plants to reduce water loss

- the structure of phloem sieve tube elements and companion cells and how their structures are related to their functions

- the movement of assimilates in the phloem from sources to sinks

- loading of sucrose into phloem using proton pumping and cotransport.

Exam-style questions

1 Figure 7.13 shows xylem tissue in a longitudinal section through the stem of a plant.

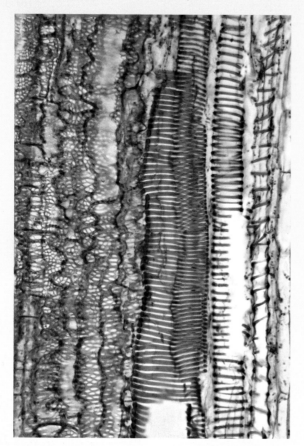

Figure 7.13 Xylem tissue in a longitudinal section through the stem of a plant.

a Describe the structure of xylem vessels. [4]

b Explain how water is moved through the xylem. [3]

c Describe and explain how water moves from the xylem vessels in the leaves to the atmosphere surrounding the leaves of a plant. [5]

Total: 12

2 Figure 7.14 shows an apparatus used to measure the rate of water uptake by a leafy shoot.

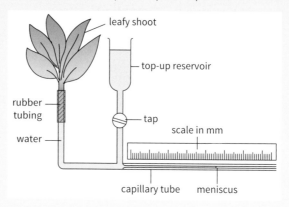

Figure 7.14 Apparatus used to measure the rate of water uptake by a leafy shoot.

a State the name of this apparatus. [1]

b Describe how you would set up this apparatus to measure the rate of water uptake. [4]

c Explain why the rate of water uptake by the shoot shown in Figure 7.14 will not be the same as the rate of transpiration. [2]

d Table 7.02 contains some factors that affect the rate of transpiration. Copy and complete Table 7.02. [6]

Total: 13

Factor	Increase or decrease in rate	Explanation
high temperature		increases the rate of evaporation of water from the mesophyll cells of the leaf / increases the rate of diffusion of water vapour out of the leaf
high humidity		
high light intensity	increase	
high wind speed		

Table 7.02

3 Assimilates are transported in phloem sieve tubes by a process called translocation. The main assimilate is the sugar sucrose.

a Name another major assimilate transported in the sieve tubes. [1]

b Describe how sucrose is loaded into the sieve tube elements from leaf mesophyll cells. [3]

c Explain how assimilates that enter the phloem sieve tubes are translocated to other parts of the plant. [4]

Total: 8

Transport in mammals

Learning outcomes

When you have finished this unit, you should be able to:

- [ ] state that the mammalian circulatory system is closed and a double system consisting of the heart, blood vessels and blood

- [ ] make diagrams of the structure of arteries, veins and capillaries, and be able to recognise these vessels using a light microscope

- [ ] explain the relationship between the structure and function of arteries, veins and capillaries

- [ ] draw the structure of red blood cells, monocytes, neutrophils and lymphocytes from stained slides and photomicrographs

- [ ] explain the differences between blood, tissue fluid and lymph

- [ ] describe the role of haemoglobin in the transport of oxygen and carbon dioxide, including the role of carbonic anhydrase, the formation of haemoglobinic acid and carbaminohaemoglobin

- [ ] understand oxygen dissociation curves of adult oxyhaemoglobin at different carbon dioxide concentrations (the Bohr effect)

- [ ] explain the effect of high altitude on the red blood cell count in humans

- [ ] describe the external and internal structure of the mammalian heart

- [ ] explain the differences in the thickness of the walls of the different chambers of the heart

- [ ] describe the cardiac cycle, including blood pressure changes

- [ ] explain how heart action is initiated and controlled.

8.01 The circulatory system

Mammals have a closed, double circulatory system. This means that blood travels in vessels, arteries, veins and capillaries. The term 'double' refers to the fact there are two circuits – one in which blood travels from the heart to the lungs and back to the heart and the other in which blood is pumped from the heart, around the rest of the body and back to the heart. The first circuit, to the lungs, is referred to as the **pulmonary circulation** and the second, around the rest of the body, is called the **systemic circulation**. The heart acts as a pump and provides the force needed for the circulation of the blood.

Blood consists of a fluid, known as **plasma**, in which the blood cells are suspended. Blood cells include:

- red blood cells
- white blood cells, such as monocytes, neutrophils and lymphocytes
- platelets.

The structure and functions of red blood cells and three types of white blood cells are summarised in Table 8.01.

Type of cell	Structure of cell	Function of cell
red blood cells	relatively small cells with no nucleus, they are described as 'biconcave discs' in shape	transport of oxygen and carbon dioxide
	red blood cells are packed with haemoglobin, which gives blood its colour	
monocytes	the largest of the white blood cells	monocytes are phagocytic and are able to engulf invading bacteria and other small particles

→

Type of cell	Structure of cell	Function of cell
	they have a clear cytoplasm and an indented or 'horseshoe'-shaped nucleus	
neutrophils	these are the most abundant type of white blood cell. They have a granular cytoplasm and a lobed, irregular-shaped nucleus	like monocytes, neutrophils are also phagocytic
lymphocytes	these cells have a relatively large, round nucleus and clear cytoplasm	there are several different types of lymphocytes; some develop into plasma cells that synthesise and secrete specific antibodies

Table 8.01 Structure and functions of blood cells.

These types of blood cells are illustrated in Figure 8.01.

Figure 8.01 shows a section through a red blood cell (top) and a surface view of a red blood cell (bottom). Red blood cells have no nucleus, mitochondria or endoplasmic reticulum. The diameter of a red blood cell is approximately 7m.

Progress check 8.01

Copy and complete table 8.02 to show the essential structural features of each type of blood cell.

Blood cell	Essential structural features
red blood cell	
neutrophil	
lymphocyte	
monocyte	

Table 8.02

There are three different types of blood vessels: **arteries**, **veins** and **capillaries**. Arteries carry blood, under relatively high pressure, away from the heart. Veins return blood, under low pressure, back to the heart. A network of capillaries connects arteries with veins. Capillaries are the main sites of exchange of materials, such as oxygen and carbon dioxide, between blood and body tissues.

Arteries have thick walls, containing collagen, elastic fibres and smooth muscles, which enables them to withstand the high pressure of blood. Smaller arteries can change their diameter, by contraction or relaxation of the smooth muscle. This alters blood flow; a decrease in diameter decreases the blood flow and an increase in diameter increases blood flow. As an example, blood flow to the skin can be altered in this way as a means of regulating body temperature.

Veins are relatively thin walled in relation to the diameter of their lumen, which offers little resistance to blood flow under low pressure.

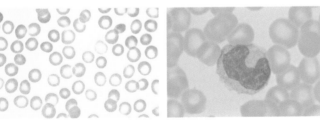
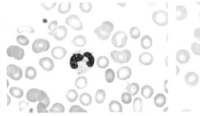
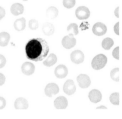

red blood cells   monocyte   neutrophil   lymphocyte

Figure 8.01 Blood cells as seen using a light microscope.

Capillaries have a wall consisting of just a single layer of flattened cells and have a diameter which is about the same as the diameter of a red blood cell. The capillary wall is quite permeable, allowing free exchange of water and solutes between blood and body tissues.

Figure 8.02 shows the structure of an artery, a vein and a capillary, as seen in section.

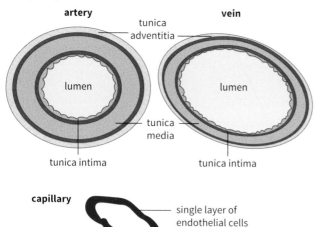

Figure 8.02 Artery, vein and capillary.

The walls of capillaries have small pores, which allow water and low molecular mass solutes, including glucose and ions, to pass out of the capillaries. This occurs because of the relatively high blood pressure within the capillaries and results in the formation of **tissue fluid**. Plasma proteins are too large to pass through the pores and stay in the capillaries. The blood pressure steadily drops in capillaries as blood passes from the arterial end towards the venous end. At the venous end of capillaries, the osmotic effect of the plasma proteins draws water back into the capillaries, so tissue fluid is reabsorbed. Not all of the tissue fluid is reabsorbed; some passes into lymphatic capillaries and forms **lymph**. Lymph is similar in composition to tissue fluid, but lymph contains proteins, derived from the lymphatic system. Lymph is eventually returned to the bloodstream, via ducts which connect the lymphatic system to veins near the neck.

Progress check 8.02

Copy and complete the table by naming the blood vessels from their description.

Description	Type of blood vessel
small vessels (usually about the same diameter as a red blood cell) with a wall consisting of one layer of flattened endothelial cells	
relatively thick-walled vessels which transport blood away from the heart	
thin-walled vessels, often containing valves, that transport blood back to the heart	

Blood has an essential role in the transport of oxygen and carbon dioxide. Oxygen attaches to haemoglobin forming oxyhaemoglobin. You should remember from Unit 2 that each haemoglobin molecule consists of four subunits; each subunit can carry one molecule of oxygen, so when a molecule of haemoglobin is fully saturated with oxygen, it carries four molecules of oxygen.

Carbon dioxide is carried in the blood in three different ways:

- in simple solution, dissolved in plasma
- combined with $-NH_2$ groups of haemoglobin, forming **carbaminohaemoglobin**
- in the form of **hydrogencarbonate (HCO_3^-) ions**.

In actively respiring tissues, such as working muscle, carbon dioxide diffuses from the tissue into the capillaries and dissolves in plasma. Some of the carbon dioxide then diffuses into red blood cells. Red blood cells contain the enzyme **carbonic anhydrase**, which rapidly combines carbon dioxide with water, forming carbonic acid. Carbonic acid dissociates, forming hydrogen ions and hydrogencarbonate ions. The hydrogen ions combine with haemoglobin, forming haemoglobinic acid and the hydrogencarbonate ions diffuse out of the red blood cells, into the plasma. The majority of carbon dioxide is transported in the form of hydrogencarbonate ions.

In the capillaries surrounding the alveoli, these reactions essentially go into reverse and carbon dioxide diffuses out of the blood and into the alveoli.

Progress check 8.03

List the ways in which carbon dioxide is transported in the blood.

An important property of haemoglobin is that it combines reversibly with oxygen, picking oxygen up in the lungs and releasing it to respiring tissues. As haemoglobin picks up oxygen, it becomes more saturated with oxygen, until fully saturated. A graph showing the relationship between the saturation of haemoglobin with oxygen and the partial pressure of oxygen to which the haemoglobin is exposed is an S-shaped curve, known as the oxygen dissociation curve. This is illustrated in Figure 8.03.

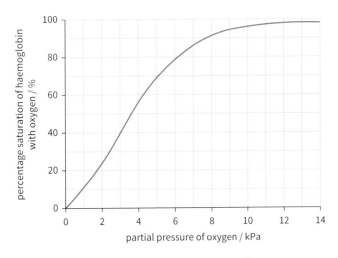

Figure 8.03 An oxygen dissociation curve for haemoglobin.

The position of the dissociation curve along the x-axis can vary. If the partial pressure of carbon dioxide increases (e.g. in respiring tissues), the dissociation curve moves to the right. This is known as the **Bohr effect** and the significance of this is that the affinity of haemoglobin for oxygen is reduced, so oxygen is released from the haemoglobin and the oxygen then diffuses from the blood to the tissues. This effect is illustrated in Figure 8.04.

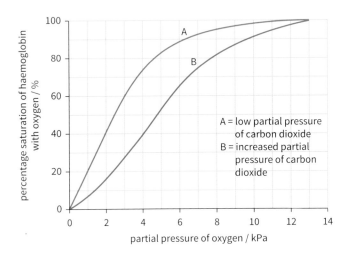

Figure 8.04 The Bohr effect.

You can see from Figure 8.05 that, at a given partial pressure of oxygen, the haemoglobin is less fully saturated with oxygen at a higher partial pressure of carbon dioxide.

Haemoglobin is essential for the transport of oxygen. One of the adaptations to life at high altitudes, where the partial pressure of oxygen in the air is lower than it is at sea level, is an increase in the number of red blood cells. This increases the carrying capacity of blood for oxygen. Table 8.03 shows the effect of high altitude on the mean number of red blood cells in a group of mountaineers.

Altitude	Mean numbers of red blood cells / dm^{-3}
sea level	5.0×10^{12}
mountaineers on Mt Everest at 5790 m	5.6×10^{12}

Table 8.03 The effect of altitude on the numbers of red blood cells.

Sample question 8.01

The llama is a mammal that lives in the high Andes of South America, often at an altitude of over 5000 metres above sea level. The oxygen dissociation curve for llama haemoglobin is to the left of the dissociation curves for most other mammals. Suggest why this is an important adaptation for llamas. [4 marks]

[Mark points are shown in square brackets – to a maximum of 4 marks]

At high altitudes, the partial pressure of oxygen in the air is low. [I] Because the dissociation curve is to the left of other mammals, llamas' haemoglobin will have a relatively high affinity for oxygen. This means that it will be fully saturated with oxygen [I] at low partial pressures [I]. Haemoglobin from other mammals would only be partly saturated with oxygen at high altitudes [I]. This is how llamas are adapted to life at high altitudes.

This is a good explanation of the importance of this effect. Remember that as the dissociation curve moves to the left, it implies that the haemoglobin has an increased affinity for oxygen. In other words, it will pick up oxygen and become saturated at lower partial pressures. As altitude increases, the air pressure drops which is why the partial pressure of oxygen decreases. At an altitude of 5000 metres, the partial pressure of oxygen in air is only about 50% of its value at sea level.

8.02 The heart

The mammalian heart has four chambers: two **atria** and two **ventricles**. The right side of the heart receives blood from the systemic circulation and pumps it to the lungs; the left side of the heart receives blood from the lungs and pumps it around the rest of the body.

The wall of the heart consists of cardiac muscle and the walls of the atria are thinner than those of the ventricles; the wall of the left ventricle is thicker and more muscular than the wall of the right ventricle. There are valves between the atria and the ventricles, the atrioventricular valves. The atrioventricular valve between the right atrium and the right ventricle is

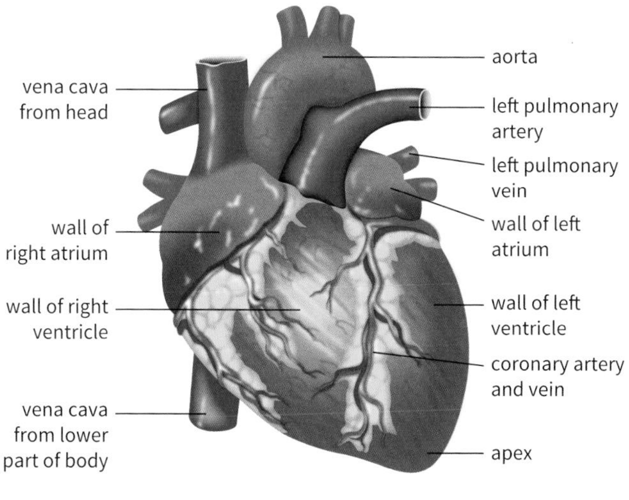

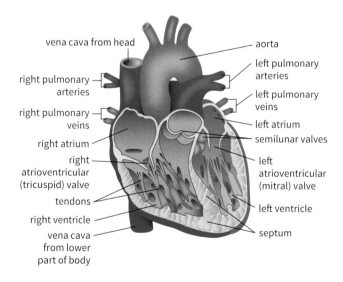

Figure 8.05 External appearance of a mammalian heart, as seen from the front

Figure 8.06 Internal structure of a mammalian heart

known as the **tricuspid valve**, and the valve between the left atrium and the left ventricle is referred to as the **mitral (or bicuspid) valve**. These valves close to prevent back flow of blood from the ventricles into the atria when the ventricles contract.

Contraction of the left ventricle generates a considerably higher pressure than contraction of the right ventricle. The left ventricle has to provide sufficient pressure to force blood around the entire systemic circulation, while the right ventricle pumps blood round the pulmonary circulation only which requires a lower pressure. The systemic circulation has a higher resistance to blood flow than the pulmonary circulation and the wall of the left ventricle is thicker than the wall of the right ventricle, to generate a higher pressure needed to drive blood around the systemic circulation.

At rest, the human heart beats about 72 times a minute, although there is considerable variation between individuals. The rhythmic sequence of events, each time the heart beats, is known as the **cardiac cycle**. Contraction of the heart is knows as **systole** and relaxation is referred to as **diastole**. There are three main stages in the cardiac cycle:

- atrial systole
- ventricular systole
- diastole.

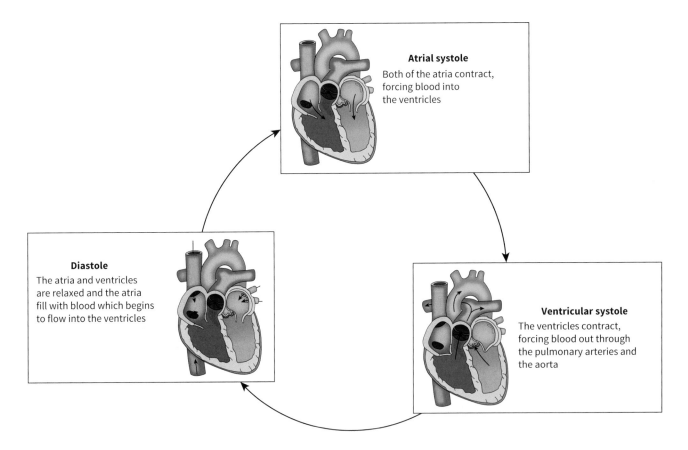

Figure 8.08 The cardiac cycle

Worked example 8.01

Question

The cardiac cycle of a person at rest was recorded and found to last for 0.8 seconds. Calculate the heart rate in beats per minute.

Answer

If one cardiac cycle has a duration of 0.8 seconds, the number of heart beats in 1 minute will be:

$60 \div 0.8 = 75$ beats per minute

The cardiac cycle is controlled and coordinated by special tissues within the heart itself. Cardiac muscle is myogenic – it contracts and relaxes on its own, without the need for nervous stimulation.

The heart has its own natural pacemaker, a group of specialised muscle cells in the wall of the right atrium, known as the **sinoatrial node** (SAN) or **pacemaker**. These cells regularly send out an electrical impulse that spreads over the wall of the atria, stimulating them to contract. This impulse does not spread directly to the ventricles because there is a layer of fibrous, non-conducting tissue between the atria and the ventricles. Instead, the impulse is picked up by a structure known as the **atrioventricular node** (AVN), situated inside the right atrium. The AVN is attached to specialised cardiac muscle tissue, forming **Purkyne tissue**, in the septum between the right ventricle and the left ventricle. The Purkyne tissue conducts the electrical impulse to the apex of the ventricle, ensuring that the ventricles contract in a coordinated way. The ventricles contract from the apex (the bottom of the heart) upwards, this ensures that blood is effectively forced upwards into the aorta and the pulmonary arteries. There is a slight delay at the AVN, which means that the impulse reaches the ventricles after the atria contract. This arrangement of the conducting tissues in the heart ensures that it contracts in a controlled way, with the atria contracting shortly before the ventricles contract. This allows the ventricles to fill with blood before they contract, forcing blood into the pulmonary arteries and the aorta.

TIP

Purkyne tissue is sometimes referred to as Purkinje tissue. The bundle of His, in the septum between the left and right ventricles, consists of Purkyne tissue, which is a form of modified heart muscle.

Revision checklist

Check that you know:

- ☐ the mammalian circulatory system as a closed double circulation consisting of a heart, blood vessels and blood

- ☐ how to observe and make plan diagrams of the structure of arteries, veins and capillaries, using prepared slides and recognising these vessels using the light microscope

- ☐ the relationship between the structure and function of arteries, veins and capillaries

- ☐ how to observe and draw the structure of red blood cells, monocytes, neutrophils and lymphocytes using prepared slides and photomicrographs

- ☐ the differences between blood, tissue fluid and lymph

- ☐ the role of haemoglobin in the transport of oxygen and carbon dioxide, including the role of carbonic anhydrase, the formation of haemoglobinic acid and carbaminohaemoglobin

- ☐ the significance of the oxygen dissociation curves of adult haemoglobin at different carbon dioxide concentrations (the Bohr effect)

- ☐ the significance of the increase in the red blood cell count of humans at high altitude

- ☐ the external and internal structure of the mammalian heart

- ☐ the differences between the thickness of the walls of the different chambers of the heart

- ☐ the cardiac cycle, including pressure changes during systole and diastole

- ☐ how heart action is initiated and controlled, with reference to the sinoatrial node, the atrioventricular node and the Purkyne tissue.

Exam-style questions

1 a Describe the role of carbonic anhydrase in the transport of carbon dioxide in the blood. [3]

   b Explain the importance of the Bohr effect. [3]

   c Explain how carbon dioxide is released from the blood in the alveolar capillaries. [4]

   Total: 10

2 Table 8.04 shows the mean numbers of red blood cells in a group of mountaineers as they ascended a mountain on the Nepal–Tibet border.

Day	Mean number of red blood cells / dm^{-3}
0 (altitude 0 km)	5.1×10^{12}
5	5.3×10^{12}
10	5.6×10^{12}
15	5.8×10^{12}
20 (altitude 4 km)	6.0×10^{12}

Table 8.04

a Calculate the percentage change in the mean number of red blood cells from 0 to 20 days. [2]

b Explain the importance of this change. [3]

   Total: 5

3 a Heart muscle is described as being myogenic. Explain what is meant by the term 'myogenic'. [2]

   b Explain how the cardiac cycle is controlled and coordinated. [6]

   Total: 8

Gas exchange and smoking

Animals take in oxygen for aerobic respiration and release carbon dioxide. In humans and other mammals, exchange of these gases with the environment takes place in the air sacs (**alveoli**) of the lungs. Exchange occurs by diffusion between the air in the alveoli and blood in capillaries surrounding each alveolus.

9.01 The human gas exchange system

Ventilation movements produce a tidal flow of air in and out of the lungs. Air passes through the **trachea**, **bronchi** and **bronchioles** before reaching the alveoli (Figure 9.01).

9.02 Cells and tissues of the gas exchange system

The trachea, bronchi and bronchioles contain a number of specialised tissues and cells (Figure 9.02):

- **Cartilage** gives support to the walls of the trachea and bronchi. During inhalation the pressure inside the airways falls, and the cartilage stops them collapsing. The wall of the trachea contains C-shaped rings of cartilage, while the outer wall of the bronchi and larger bronchioles has irregular blocks of cartilage rather than complete rings.

- A **ciliated epithelium** lines the trachea, bronchi and larger bronchioles. The epithelium of the trachea and bronchi also contains **goblet cells**,

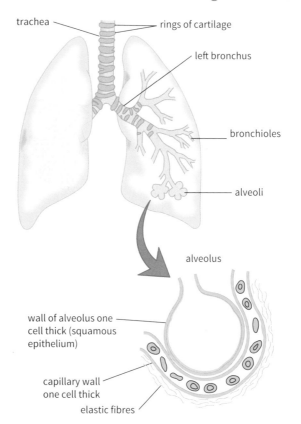

Figure 9.01 The human gas exchange system.

trachea — rings of cartilage

left bronchus

bronchioles

alveoli

alveolus

wall of alveolus one cell thick (squamous epithelium)

capillary wall one cell thick

elastic fibres

which secrete mucus to trap particles of dust and bacteria. The mucus is contained in secretory vesicles and released by exocytosis. The epithelial cells are covered with **cilia**, which beat back and forth to sweep the mucus and trapped particles up the airways towards the mouth, where they are swallowed. This action helps to prevent the particles entering the lungs and causing infection (Figure 9.03). Any bacteria that are swallowed will be destroyed by stomach acid. **Mucous glands** below the epithelium of the trachea and bronchus also produce mucus.

- **Smooth muscle** is present in the walls of the trachea, bronchi and bronchioles. Smooth muscle cells undergo slow, rhythmic contractions, which they can do for extended periods without tiring. Contraction and relaxation of smooth muscle alters the diameter of the bronchial tubes. This is particularly important in the bronchioles, which widen during exercise to allow more air to enter the alveoli.

- **Elastic fibres** are present in the walls of all the bronchial tubes and between the alveoli. During inhalation, the elastic fibres stretch to allow the

airways and alveoli to expand. During exhalation they recoil, helping to decrease the volume of the alveoli and push the air out of the lungs.

a part of the wall of the trachea

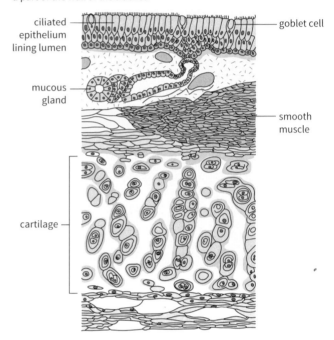

b Bronchus

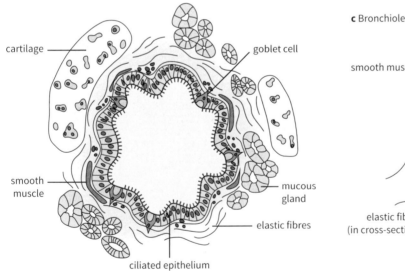

c Bronchiole

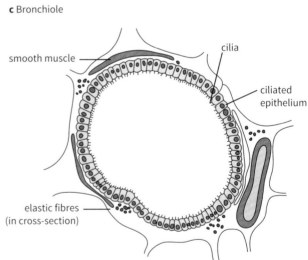

Figure 9.02 Transverse sections of parts of the bronchial airways (not drawn to the same scale). **a** Part of the wall of the trachea. **b** Bronchus. **c** Bronchiole.

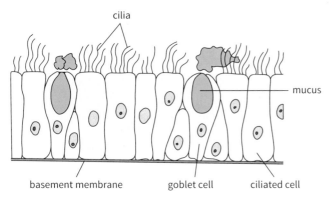

cilia

mucus

basement membrane   goblet cell   ciliated cell

Figure 9.03 Ciliated epithelium and goblet cells.

Progress check 9.01

1 Describe the arrangement and function of cartilage in the trachea.

2 Explain the role of goblet cells in the gas exchange system.

3 Explain the function of elastic fibres in the tissue between the alveoli.

9.03 Gas exchange in the alveoli

The walls of each alveolus are composed of a single layer of flat cells called a **squamous epithelium** (Figure 9.01). There is a network of blood capillaries in contact with the alveolus, and these also have walls made of a single layer of cells. The distance between the air in the alveolus and the blood inside the capillaries is very short (less than 1 μm). This short distance speeds up the rate of diffusion of gases.

TIP

Note that the alveolus has a 'thin wall of cells', not 'a thin cell wall'.

Compared with the blood in the capillaries, alveolar air has a higher concentration of oxygen and a lower concentration of carbon dioxide. Oxygen therefore

diffuses from the air in the alveolus, across the walls of the alveolus and capillary and enters the blood. Carbon dioxide diffuses in the opposite direction. The diffusion gradients are maintained by:

• blood flow past the alveolus, which brings deoxygenated blood from the pulmonary artery and takes away the oxygenated blood through the pulmonary vein

• ventilation of the lungs, which replaces alveolar air with air from outside the body.

Worked example 9.01

Question

Figure 9.04 is a light micrograph of a section through some alveoli (magnification ×450).

Calculate the diameter of the alveolus shown by the line X–Y. Give your answer in μm.

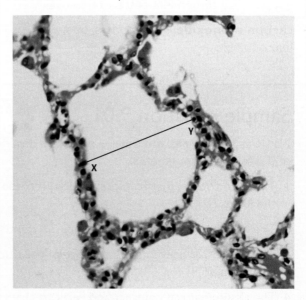

Figure 9.04 Light micrograph of a section through some alveoli (magnification ×450).

Answer

Step 1:

The length of line X–Y is 31 mm. (Some leeway is allowed here; 30 or 32 mm is acceptable.)

The question asks for the answer to be given in μm, so convert 31 mm into μm:

length of line X–Y = (31 mm × 1000 μm/mm) = 31 000 μm.

→

9 Gas exchange and smoking

79

Step 2:

The magnification of the light micrograph is ×450.

$$\text{magnification} = \frac{\text{size of micrograph}}{\text{size of real specimen}}$$

$$\begin{array}{l}\text{size of real}\\\text{specimen}\\(\text{line X–Y})\end{array} = \frac{\text{size of micrograph}}{\text{magnification}} = \frac{31\ 000\,\mu m}{450}$$

= 69 µm (to two significant figures).

9.04 Smoking and health

Tobacco smoke contains several substances that harm the gas exchange and cardiovascular systems. These include nicotine, carbon monoxide and tar:

- **nicotine** is a colourless, odourless chemical that is the addictive component of tobacco smoke

- **carbon monoxide** is a colourless, odourless gas that is highly toxic

- **tar** is the oily brown substance that is deposited in the filter of a smoked cigarette (and in the smoker's lungs); it contains a number of harmful chemicals, including many known to cause cancer.

a The short-term effects of nicotine and carbon monoxide on the cardiovascular system

i Nicotine

Nicotine is the addictive drug in tobacco smoke. In the lungs it is quickly absorbed by the blood and within seconds binds to receptors on neurones (nerve cells) in the brain and other parts of the nervous system. It stimulates nerve endings in the brain to release a transmitter substance called dopamine. This gives a smoker a feeling of pleasure.

When nicotine binds to nerves in the rest of the body this results in a number of short-term effects on the heart and blood vessels:

- the nerves stimulate smaller arteries and arterioles throughout the body to constrict (narrow); this causes an increase in the resistance to blood flow

Sample question 9.01

Name as precisely as you can the structure described in each of the following statements.

1 The blood vessel that transports deoxygenated blood to the lungs. [1]

2 The epithelial cell that secretes mucus in the trachea. [1]

3 The tissue that prevents the collapse of the trachea during inhalation. [1]

4 The tissue that can contract and relax to change the diameter of the bronchioles. [1]

[Mark points are shown in square brackets – to a maximum of 4 marks]

1 Pulmonary artery [1].

2 Goblet cell [1].

3 Cartilage [1].

4 Smooth muscle [1].

'Pulmonary' means to do with the lungs. An artery leads away from the heart, in this case to the lungs.

Just the name of the tissue is needed – you do not need to include details of the blocks or rings.

Muscle is the only tissue that actively contracts. In the bronchioles it is a particular type of muscle called smooth muscle.

- the nerves stimulate the release of the hormone adrenaline from the adrenal gland; adrenaline increases the heart rate.

The combination of increased heart rate and increased resistance to blood flow through the arteries results in high blood pressure. Nicotine also increases the risk of blood clots forming.

ii Carbon monoxide

Carbon monoxide in tobacco smoke enters the blood in the lungs. In the red blood cells it combines with haemoglobin, forming the stable compound carboxyhaemoglobin. Carbon monoxide binds to haemoglobin 200 times more tightly than oxygen – we say that haemoglobin has a higher *affinity* for carbon monoxide than for oxygen. This reduces the oxygen-carrying capacity of the blood, so that a smoker's blood may carry up to 15% less oxygen than the blood of a non-smoker. This means that the amount of oxygen transported to the heart, brain and other tissues is lower. Depriving the heart of oxygen reduces its ability to pump blood.

b The effects of smoking on the gas exchange system

Tobacco smoke has been shown to contain over 7000 different chemicals, hundreds of which are toxic. Several lung diseases are caused by smoking. These include chronic bronchitis, emphysema and lung cancer.

i Chronic bronchitis

Tar from cigarette smoke coats the lining of a smoker's airways, causing irritation and the production of excess mucus by the goblet cells. It destroys the cilia, as well as causing them to beat less strongly. Mucus and bacteria build up in the lungs, resulting in infections such as bronchitis. Smokers often develop chronic (long-term) bronchitis.

TIP People often think 'chronic' means 'very bad'. It does not – it refers to any medical condition that is *long lasting*.

Build up of mucus in the alveoli restricts gas exchange and causes a persistent cough. The 'smoker's cough' damages the lining of the bronchioles, forming scar tissue. This makes the airways narrower, causing breathing difficulties. Infections cause the lining to become inflamed, further narrowing the airways.

ii Emphysema

Irritation of the lungs by years of smoking causes the breakdown of lung tissue, a condition known as emphysema. Inflammation and infections of the airways stimulates white blood cells called macrophages to leave the blood and enter the airways. To do this, they secrete an enzyme that breaks down the elastic tissue between the walls of the alveoli. Coughing bursts the weakened alveoli, so that over several years the surface area for gas exchange is reduced. Decreased gas exchange means that insufficient oxygen reaches the cells for respiration. A person suffering from emphysema lacks energy and struggles to breathe, often having difficulty in walking a few paces.

A patient with chronic bronchitis, emphysema or both is said to have **chronic obstructive pulmonary disease (COPD)**. The key symptom of the disease is poor flow of air into and out of the airways. The condition gets worse over time. The prime cause of COPD is smoking – about 20% of smokers will develop COPD and about half of lifelong smokers will get the disease. Looking at the statistics the other way round, of those patients diagnosed with COPD, 80–95% are either smokers or ex-smokers.

iii Lung cancer

Over 70 of the chemicals in the tar from cigarettes are known to cause mutations to DNA. If these mutations affect the genes that control cell division they can cause cancer – they are **carcinogens**. Most cancers caused by smoking occur in the lungs, but they can develop in any part of the airways, and cancerous cells may spread to other parts of the body, producing secondary tumours (see Unit 5). The symptoms of lung cancer are shortness of breath, a persistent cough, chest pain and weight loss. However, lung cancer is a 'silent' disease – it takes many years before there are any noticeable signs of the cancer, by which time it may be difficult to treat.

Progress check 9.02

1 Nicotine and tar are two components of tobacco smoke. Explain the difference between these substances.

2 Describe how nicotine brings about changes to the heart rate and blood pressure.

3 Explain how smoking causes lung cancer.

Revision checklist

Check that you know:

- ☐ the structure of the human gas exchange system
- ☐ the structure of the walls of the trachea, bronchi, bronchioles and alveoli
- ☐ the structure and function of cartilage, cilia, goblet cells, mucous glands, smooth muscle and elastic fibres in the gas exchange system
- ☐ how gas exchange takes place in the alveoli
- ☐ the short-term effects of nicotine and carbon monoxide on the cardiovascular system
- ☐ the cause and effects of chronic obstructive pulmonary disease (COPD)
- ☐ the cause and effects of lung cancer.

Exam-style questions

1 Figure 9.05 is a light micrograph of a section through part of the gas exchange system.

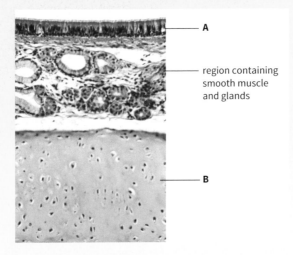

Figure 9.05

- a Name two types of cell found in tissue A. [2]
- b Describe how the two types of cell in tissue A work together to maintain the health of the gas exchange system. [3]
- c Name tissue B. [1]
- d Describe the function of tissue B. [2]

Total: 8

2 Alveoli form the gas exchange surface in human lungs.

- a Explain how alveoli are adapted for efficient gas exchange. [4]
- b Explain how smoking increases the risk of pathogens entering the alveoli. [3]
- c Describe how the alveoli of a person with emphysema are affected by the disease. [2]

Total: 9

3 Table 9.01 compares the structure of different parts of the gas exchange system. Copy and complete the table. Use a tick (✓) if the structure is present or a cross (✗) if it is absent. [5]

Total: 5

	Trachea	Bronchus	Bronchiole	Alveoli
ciliated epithelium				
squamous epithelium				
cartilage				
elastic fibres				
smooth muscle				

Table 9.01

Infectious disease

Learning outcomes

When you have finished this unit, you should be able to:

- [ ] define the term disease

- [ ] explain the difference between an infectious disease and a non-infectious disease

- [ ] name and state the type of causative organisms of cholera, malaria, tuberculosis (TB), HIV/acquired immune deficiency syndrome (AIDS), smallpox and measles

- [ ] explain how cholera, measles, malaria, TB and HIV/AIDS are transmitted

- [ ] discuss the biological, social and economic factors that need to be considered in the prevention and control of some infectious diseases

- [ ] discuss the factors that influence global patterns of distribution of malaria, TB and HIV/AIDS and assess the importance of these diseases worldwide

- [ ] outline how penicillin acts on bacteria and why antibiotics have no effect on viruses

- [ ] outline how bacteria become resistant to antibiotics

- [ ] discuss the consequences of antibiotic resistance and the steps that can be taken to reduce its impact.

10.01 Infectious diseases

A **disease** is a type of disorder of an organism which is characterised by particular symptoms. Infectious diseases are caused by organisms known as **pathogens**, and can be transmitted from one organism to another. Non-infectious diseases include disorders such as emphysema and lung cancer, described in Unit 9, and genetic disorders, such as sickle cell anaemia and haemophilia, described in Unit 16.

A pathogen is an organism that can cause disease and these include viruses, bacteria, fungi and protoctists. The names and types of pathogens associated with some infectious diseases are summarised in Table 10.01.

> **TIP**
>
> Protoctists are single-celled eukaryotic organisms. Be careful not to confuse protoctists with prokaryotes.

Infectious disease	Causative organism (pathogen)	Type of causative organism
malaria	*Plasmodium* spp.	protoctist
cholera	*Vibrio cholerae*	bacterium
tuberculosis (TB)	*Mycobacterium tuberculosis* and *Mycobacterium bovis*	bacterium
HIV/acquired immune deficiency syndrome (AIDS)	human immunodeficiency virus (HIV)	virus
smallpox	*Variola*	virus
measles	*Morbillivirus*	virus

Table 10.01 Some infectious diseases and their causative organisms.

Progress check 10.1

Copy and complete Table 10.02 by naming the type of causative organism for each infectious disease.

Infectious disease	Type of causative organism
HIV/AIDS	
cholera	
smallpox	
malaria	
TB	
measles	

Table 10.02

Progress check 10.02

Copy and complete Table 10.04 by describing the way in which each infectious disease is transmitted.

Infectious disease	How the disease is transmitted
HIV/AIDS	
cholera	
malaria	
TB	
measles	

Table 10.04

The spread of a pathogen from one person to another is referred to as **transmission**. This can occur in a variety of ways, such as eating contaminated food, or breathing droplets of moisture containing the pathogen.

Table 10.03 summarises the ways in which cholera, measles, malaria, TB and HIV/AIDS are transmitted.

Infectious disease	Causative organism	Mode of transmission
cholera	*Vibrio cholerae*	contaminated food and drinking water
measles	*Morbillivirus*	infected droplets via the respiratory system
malaria	*Plasmodium*	bite of a female *Anopheles* mosquito
TB	*M. tuberculosis* and *M. bovis*	inhalation of infected droplets or can be spread to humans via milk from infected cattle
HIV/AIDS	HIV	contaminated blood, semen or across the placenta

Table 10.03 Transmission of some infectious diseases.

Understanding the ways infectious diseases are transmitted is important in developing strategies for controlling their spread and preventing infection. In the case of malaria, where the pathogen is spread by mosquitoes, taking steps to control mosquito populations, or to prevent humans from being bitten by mosquitoes, can control the spread of malaria. This may involve the use of insecticides or reducing areas of stagnant water which are needed for the life cycle of mosquitoes. Infectious diseases that are spread directly from person to person are often more prevalent in areas of poverty, with poor sanitation and overcrowded living conditions. Sewage contamination of water supplies is one way in which cholera is spread. Close contact with infected people helps to ensure the spread of disease by droplet inhalation. People who are poorly nourished are also usually more susceptible to infection. The HIV is spread only via contaminated body fluids, blood and semen, so factors such as having multiple sexual partners increase the risk of transmission. HIV can be spread via contaminated blood, so drug users, who inject drugs intravenously and share needles, are at an increased risk of infection.

Progress check 10.03

List three ways in which the transmission of malaria may be reduced.

Table 10.05 gives some information about the global pattern of distribution and mortality of malaria, TB and HIV/AIDS. The World Health Organization (WHO) estimates that about 3.2 billion people (approximately half the population of the world) are at risk of malaria. Prevention and control measures for malaria have led to a decrease in the mortality rates by 47%. However, people living in poor countries are the most susceptible to malaria. It was estimated by the WHO that 90% of all deaths from malaria in 2013 occurred in the African region and most of these were children under the age of 5 years.

Infectious disease	Global distribution	Annual mortality worldwide
malaria	*most of the tropics, in particular Africa, India, the far East and South America*	about 438 000 in 2015, of which 90% were in Africa
TB	*worldwide, with a high incidence in Southeast Asia and Africa*	an estimated 1.5 million people died from TB in 2014
HIV/AIDS	*worldwide, particularly prevalent in sub-Saharan Africa, South and Southeast Asia*	between 940 000 and 1.1 million people died from HIV related causes in 2015

Table 10.05 Global distribution and mortality of some infectious diseases

10.02 Antibiotics

Antibiotics are drugs that kill or inhibit the growth of bacteria, without harming the cells of an infected organism.

TIP

Be careful not to confuse antibiotics with antibodies.

Antibiotics work by exploiting differences between the bacterial cells and the cells of the infected organism.

Progress check 10.04

Make a table to summarise the differences between the structure of a bacterial cell and the structure of a mammalian cell.

Antibiotics have a number of specific targets in bacterial cells, including the bacterial cell wall, the cell membrane, protein synthesis and DNA replication.

Penicillin is a well-known example of an antibiotic and was first used to treat bacterial infections in the 1940s. Penicillin inhibits the action of an enzyme which is responsible for the formation of cross-links in the bacterial cell wall. This results in weakening of the cell wall and death of the bacterial cells as they take up water by osmosis and burst, or lyse.

Penicillin has no effect on mammalian cells, as they do not have a cell wall, nor does penicillin (and other antibiotics) have any effect on viruses. There are, however, a number of antiviral drugs which inhibit the replication of viruses.

One problem associated with the use of antibiotics is the development of resistance in bacteria that were previously susceptible to the antibiotic. This can arise as a consequence of a mutation in a bacterial cell, meaning that the bacterium is no longer inhibited by the antibiotic. Continued use of this antibiotic selects those bacterial cells that are unaffected by the antibiotic. As a consequence, treatment of that infection becomes more difficult.

In 2013, there were an estimated 480 000 new cases of multidrug-resistant tuberculosis (MDR-TB) worldwide. Antibiotic resistance is a global concern and threatens the ability to treat common infectious diseases.

TIP

Be careful not to confuse resistance with immunity.

Steps can be taken to reduce the impact of antibiotic resistance, including:

- hand-washing and avoiding contact with infected people
- using antibiotics only when properly prescribed by health-care professionals
- completing the full course of antibiotic treatment
- never sharing antibiotics with other people
- avoiding the use of broad-spectrum antibiotics
- prescribing antibiotics only when they are needed and not for viral infections.

Sample question 10.01

Explain how resistance to antibiotics can arise in bacteria. Distinguish between vertical transmission and horizontal transmission of resistance. [8 marks]

[Mark points are shown in square brackets – to a maximum of 8 marks]

Bacteria can become resistant to antibiotics by mutation [1]. These bacteria carry a gene which confers resistance to an antibiotic [1]. Continued use of the antibiotic selects those bacteria that are resistant [1]; susceptible bacteria will be killed or are unable to divide in the presence of the antibiotic [1]. As the resistant bacteria divide, a large population of resistant bacterial cells is built up [1]. This is **vertical transmission** of resistance [1].

Bacteria can conjugate and plasmids, containing a gene for resistance, are passed from one cell to another [1]. This is known as **horizontal transmission** of resistance [1].

This answer correctly outlines the process by which populations of bacteria with resistance to antibiotics occur and distinguishes clearly between vertical and horizontal transmission of resistance. It is important to remember that mutations, which confer resistance to an antibiotic, arise spontaneously in bacteria; they are not caused by the antibiotic.

Revision checklist

Check that you know:

- ☐ the differences between an infectious disease and a non-infectious disease

- ☐ the causative organism of cholera, malaria, TB, HIV/AIDS, smallpox and measles

- ☐ how cholera, measles, malaria, TB and HIV/AIDS are transmitted

- ☐ the biological, social and economic factors that need to be considered in the prevention and control of cholera, measles, malaria, TB and HIV/AIDS

- ☐ the factors that influence the global patterns of distribution of malaria, TB and HIV/AIDS and the importance of these diseases worldwide

- ☐ how penicillin acts on bacteria and why antibiotics do not affect viruses

- ☐ how bacteria become resistant to antibiotics with reference to mutation and selection

- ☐ the consequences of antibiotic resistance and the steps that can be taken to reduce its impact.

Exam-style questions

1 a Explain what is meant by each of the following terms:

   i   pathogen [1]

   ii antibiotic. [2]

   b Explain why penicillin has no effect on viruses. [3]

   c Give three steps that can be taken to reduce the impact of antibiotic resistance. [3]

   Total: 9

2 a Name the causative organism of each of the following diseases:

   i   cholera [1]

   ii malaria [1]

   iii tuberculosis. [1]

   b Explain how malaria is transmitted. [2]

   c Suggest why some areas, such as Florida in the USA, are free from malaria, although they have the right climatic conditions for this disease. [3]

   Total: 8

Immunity

Immunity is the body's ability to prevent disease-causing microorganisms (pathogens) from entering it, and to destroy the pathogens if they do manage to enter. There are two types of response of the body – general and specific.

A person is born with a general immunity, involving a wide range of physical, cellular and chemical mechanisms, such as:

- physical barriers such as the epidermis of the skin and the epithelia of the airways

- hydrochloric acid in the stomach to kill bacteria

- an antibacterial enzyme called lysozyme in tears and saliva

- blood clotting at a wound to prevent the entry of pathogens

- phagocytosis by white blood cells.

These responses are a general defence against all pathogens – they are non-specific. Humans also show *adaptive* immunity. This is where cells of the immune system react to the presence of a particular pathogen, destroying it and at the same time providing future protection against that pathogen. For example, someone who recovers from measles will be protected against that disease for the rest of their life. Unlike general immunity, adaptive immunity is highly specific. There is one response to the tuberculosis bacterium, another response to the common cold virus and so on.

11.01 Phagocytes

Phagocytes are white blood cells that are produced by mitotic division of stem cells in the bone marrow. Two types of cell that are formed are **neutrophils** and **monocytes** (Figure 11.01).

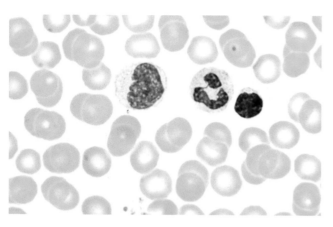

Figure 11.01 A blood smear, showing three types of white blood cells, surrounded by many red cells. The cell on the left is a monocyte, the largest type of white blood cell. The middle cell is a neutrophil, with its distinctive lobed nucleus. On the right is a lymphocyte, which produces antibodies.

TIP

Note that a phagocyte is not a particular type of white blood cell. It is any cell that can carry out phagocytosis.

Neutrophils are very abundant in the blood, making up between 50% and 70% of the white cells. They travel around the body in the bloodstream. At the site of an infection they are attracted by chemical signals from bacterial cells and damaged body cells. They leave the blood by squeezing through the walls of capillaries, where they destroy these cells by **phagocytosis**. Phagocytosis is a process where a cell engulfs solid particles to form a vacuole called a phagosome. It takes place by endocytosis (see Unit 4). The phagosome fuses with lysosomes containing digestive enzymes such as proteases. These digest and destroy the pathogen.

The lifespan of a neutrophil is short – it has been calculated that they last for a few days in the blood and a similar time in the tissues, so that an enormous number (about 10^{11}) have to be produced in the bone marrow every day.

Monocytes are fewer in number than neutrophils, making up about 5% of white blood cells. They remain in the blood for a few days and then migrate through capillary walls into various organs, such as the lungs, liver, spleen, kidney and lymph nodes. Here they mature into large cells called **macrophages**. Macrophages perform phagocytosis on any bacteria that have entered these organs.

11.02 The immune response

The **immune response** is the reaction of the body to 'foreign' substances, especially disease-causing microorganisms. The term should include general immunity, but it is often just applied to the specific immune response that leads to adaptive immunity.

White blood cells recognise bacteria and viruses by the presence of **antigens** on the surface of the pathogen. Antigens are chemicals that act as labels or markers. They are various types of molecule, including proteins, glycoproteins and polysaccharides, as well as certain waste materials and toxins produced by pathogens. The immune system recognises these as 'foreign' to the body, or **non-self**. At the same time, each of us has our own unique set of antigens on our cells, which the immune system recognises as belonging to the body, or **self**. The immune system can therefore distinguish between self and non-self. The specific immune response depends on this ability and is the role of another type of white blood cell, the **lymphocyte**.

Progress check 11.01

1   Describe what happens when a neutrophil destroys a bacterium by phagocytosis.

2   What are antigens? Explain the difference between self and non-self antigens.

11.03 Lymphocytes

On average, about 30% of white blood cells are lymphocytes. They have a large nucleus filling most of the cell, surrounded by a little cytoplasm (Figure 11.01). There are several kinds of lymphocyte, but the two main types are **B-lymphocytes** and **T-lymphocytes**. Both of these cells are produced in the bone marrow before birth.

- B-lymphocytes (or **B cells**) stay in the bone marrow until they are mature. They then circulate around the body. Some remain in the blood, while others accumulate in the lymph nodes and spleen.

- T-lymphocytes (**T cells**) leave the bone marrow and mature in the thymus gland, which is located under the sternum just above the heart. The thymus is most active before birth and during childhood, but shrinks and disappears after puberty. When they are mature, the T cells accumulate in the same areas of the body as the B cells.

Lymphocytes have receptor proteins on their surface that bind with antigens. One important difference between B cells and T cells is that B cells can bind to antigens on the surface of an invading virus or bacterium itself, whereas T cells can only bind to antigens on the outside of *infected cells* (see below). Additionally, B cells respond to antigens only found in body fluids, whilst T cells respond to antigens which are part of a cell (e.g. in the cell surface membrane of an APC). The body contains many thousands (probably millions) of different varieties of B and T cells. Each has specific receptor sites on its surface, whose shape matches the shape of a particular antigen. In this way, the lymphocytes can recognise and respond to a massive range of different antigens. As the lymphocytes mature, lymphocytes with receptors for self antigens are destroyed, so that only non-self antigens are recognised.

a The action of B-lymphocytes

When receptors on a B cell bind with an antigen, the B cell becomes activated and starts to divide rapidly by mitosis, producing millions of genetically identical **plasma cells**.

> **TIP**
>
> Recall that a group of genetically identical cells is known as a clone.

Plasma cells secrete proteins called **antibodies** into the blood plasma. The antibodies are similar in structure to the receptors in the B cell surface membrane and have the same binding sites specific to the antigens on the surface of the pathogen.

The antibodies now bind to the antigens. Some antibodies destroy the pathogen directly, such as by causing bacterial cells to burst open. Some antibodies neutralise toxins. Other antibodies indirectly destroy pathogens by causing them to clump together. In this state they are inactive and can be easily recognised and dealt with by phagocytes. Antibodies can also deal with viruses in a number of ways, such as by preventing them from infecting their host cells.

Some of the clone of B cells do not produce antibodies but instead become **memory cells**. Memory cells allow us to become immune to a disease. They remain in the blood for many years. If the person becomes re-infected by the same pathogen, the memory B cells start to divide and produce more antibodies. This secondary immune response is faster, longer lasting and

more effective than the first (primary) response, so that the pathogen is killed before it has time to multiply and cause symptoms of the disease (Figure 11.02).

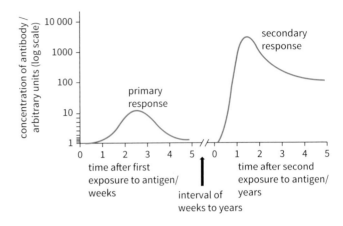

Figure 11.02 The levels of antibody production in the primary and secondary immune responses. The secondary response may happen many years after exposure to the pathogen produced the primary response.

b The action of T-lymphocytes

T cells do not make antibodies. Activated T cells are able to recognise body cells that have non-self antigens on them. These are known as **antigen-presenting cells**. They include:

* cells that are infected with virus particles

* macrophages that have taken up virus particles by phagocytosis and broken them down, in doing so exposing molecules of the virus on their surface

* cancer cells that have mutations that resulted in tumours.

T cells target these different antigen-presenting cells and destroy them.

There are several different types of T cell. Two of the most important kinds are:

* **Helper T cells**, which release hormone-like chemicals called **cytokines**. These substances stimulate the appropriate B cells to divide into a clone of antibody-producing plasma cells and memory cells. Some cytokines stimulate macrophages to carry out phagocytosis, while others activate killer T cells.

* **Killer T cells**, which roam the body searching for virus-infected cells, tumour cells or cells that are damaged in some other way. They attach to infected cells and destroy them, killing the host cell and the pathogen. Some killer T cells punch holes in the surface membrane of infected cells and secrete toxic

chemicals into them. Others activate a programmed cell death process that is part of the genetic code of every cell. The remains of the destroyed cells are 'mopped up' by macrophages.

Memory helper T cells and memory killer T cells are produced in the same way as memory B cells. They remain in the body, ready to be activated during a secondary response to antigens.

Progress check 11.02

1 Where are T-lymphocytes (T cells) produced?

2 Describe how B-lymphocytes (B cells) produce antibodies against a particular antigen.

3 B-lymphocytes produce memory cells. What is their role?

4 Name two types of T cells.

11.04 White blood cell counts

There is a great deal of variation in the numbers of white blood cells between individuals (Table 11.01).

Cell type	Normal range / mm⁻³ of blood
all white blood cells	4500–10 000
neutrophils	3000–6000
B-lymphocytes	70–600
T-lymphocytes	500–2500

Table 11.01 The normal ranges of numbers of white blood cells; the values are commonly measured per mm³ (mm⁻³) of blood.

During an infection the numbers of each type of white cell may increase above this range, so blood tests are routinely performed to count the cells in order to diagnose a disease and monitor its progress, as well as assess the effectiveness of any treatment.

Neutrophils increase in number as a result of infections by bacteria or viruses, or by other pathogenic organisms such as fungi or protoctist parasites. The number may rise in patients with injured tissues, such as a broken bone or a burn. Inflammatory disorders, including **autoimmune diseases** such as rheumatoid arthritis also increase the number of neutrophils in the blood (see below). Lymphocytes also increase in number as a consequence of a number of medical problems. These

include viral infections, as well as infections by some species of bacteria and parasitic protoctists.

Cell counts can also be elevated by cancer of the white blood cells, called **leukaemia**. There are various types of leukaemia. Chronic lymphocytic leukaemia is the most common form of leukaemia. It is a cancer of the bone marrow stem cells that produce B cells. Lymphoblastic leukaemia is a cancer of the lymphoid stem cells that give rise to lymphocytes. Neutrophils and monocytes originate from cells in bone marrow called myeloid stem cells. Myeloid leukaemia is a cancer of these cells. It results in uncontrolled mitosis and an increased number of immature and mature neutrophils in the blood.

11.05 Antibodies

Antibodies are secreted by plasma cells in response to antigens. They are globular glycoproteins with a quaternary structure, called **immunoglobulins**. Antibodies consist of four polypeptide chains: two long ('heavy') chains and two short ('light') chains. Disulfide bonds (–S–S–) hold the chains together and maintain the tertiary structure of the protein (Figure 11.03).

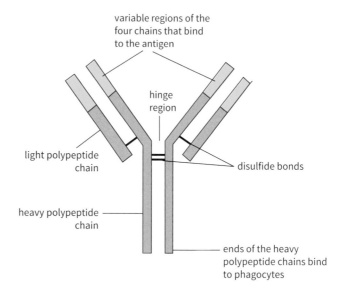

Figure 11.03 The structure of an immunoglobulin.

The molecule has two identical antigen-binding sites formed by the variable regions of the heavy and light polypeptide chains. These regions are specific to the particular clone of plasma cells that produced them. Each forms a three-dimensional shape that will only bind with one antigen. The hinge region allows the molecule some flexibility, for easier binding. The rest of the heavy and light chains are constant regions – they are identical in all antibodies with this structure.

11.06 Types of immunity

There are two types of immunity, active and passive. Both types may be acquired naturally or artificially:

- **Active immunity** occurs when the body produces its own antibodies to a particular antigen. It is **natural** when it happens as the result of an infection and **artificial** if it is the result of **vaccination**.

- **Passive immunity** is when the body does not make its own antibodies, but receives them from somewhere else. It is **natural** when the antibodies are received by a baby in its mother's milk or by a fetus across the placenta during pregnancy. It is **artificial** as the result of an injection of antibodies from another person (Table 11.02).

	Active (body makes antibodies)	Passive (body receives antibodies)
natural	natural active immunity – the result of an infection	natural passive immunity – antibodies pass from the mother to her offspring across the placenta or in breast milk
artificial	artificial active immunity – by injection of antigens (vaccination)	artificial passive immunity – by injection of antibodies

Table 11.02 Types of immunity.

Each type of immunity has its advantages. Active immunity is much longer lasting than passive immunity, because active immunity results in the production of memory cells that remain in the blood and respond quickly to a secondary infection. Natural passive immunity gives a baby protection against diseases until its immune system is fully functional. Artificial passive immunity can give immediate protection (e.g. injecting tetanus antibodies can prevent tetanus from developing after a person has suffered a wound).

11.07 Vaccination

A **vaccine** is a preparation of antigens from a pathogen, which is given to a person in order to stimulate the primary immune response and the production of memory cells. The memory cells provide immunity against the pathogen, so that a second exposure should not result in the person getting the disease. The procedure is called **vaccination**.

There are several types of vaccine:

- living pathogens (with surface antigens) that have been treated to make them safe; these are known as attenuated organisms (e.g. the measles vaccine)

- dead pathogens (e.g. typhoid)

- harmless forms of toxins called toxoids (e.g. tetanus)

- antigens extracted from the pathogen, or made by genetic engineering (e.g. hepatitis B).

The vaccine may be injected into a vein or muscle, or taken by mouth (orally). Sometimes it may be effective for many years or even a lifetime. Other vaccines are less effective and further 'booster' vaccinations may be required after a number of years. Vaccines made from living (attenuated) pathogens tend to be more effective in promoting an immune response. Because they are living they slowly reproduce, so that the immune system is continually presented with antigen to stimulate the response.

Vaccination programmes have been very successful in eliminating some diseases. The most well-known case is smallpox, caused by a virus called variola. In 1967 this highly contagious disease affected 10 million people in 30 countries around the world (Figure 11.04).

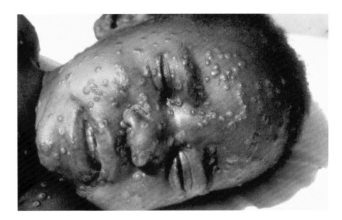

Figure 11.04 A boy with smallpox. His face is covered with the characteristic pustules and lesions.

The World Health Organization (WHO) launched a programme that aimed to eradicate smallpox from the world's population. The programme included vaccination, isolation of patients to prevent transmission of the disease and observation to detect cases of infection. The last case of smallpox was identified in 1977 and the WHO declared the world officially free of smallpox in 1980.

There are a number of reasons why eradication was possible with smallpox, but has not been possible with other diseases such as measles, tuberculosis (TB), malaria and cholera:

- The variola virus is transmitted directly from person to person by direct contact or droplet infection. It needs to be in the human body and cannot survive for long in air, water or soil. Contrast this with the bacterium that causes cholera (*Vibrio cholerae*), which survives for long periods in water.

- There is no intermediate host that transmits the disease (as with, for example, the malaria mosquito), so no need to take measures to deal with a vector of the disease.

- Smallpox does not infect other species, so humans cannot be infected from domestic animals. There is no 'animal reservoir'. Compare this with TB, which can be passed to humans from infected cattle.

- The antigens on the variola virus are stable, so the smallpox vaccine is very effective and gives long-term protection against the virus. This is not the case with many pathogens. For example, the protoctist that causes malaria (*Plasmodium*) mutates and frequently changes its surface antigens, and a successful vaccine for malaria has not yet been developed. The two vaccines that have been developed against the cholera pathogen are not 100% effective and only produce short-term immunity lasting up to a few years.

- The smallpox vaccine is made from a live strain of a similar but harmless virus, so it mimics a natural infection, multiplying and presenting the immune system with antigens. This makes it particularly effective.

- The vaccine is very simple to administer, using a steel two-pronged (bifurcated) needle to penetrate the skin. The needle can be sterilised and reused.

- Smallpox spreads slowly and appears in clusters of cases. It has a long incubation period, during which the people at risk can be isolated. This contrasts with the short incubation period and rapid spread of diseases such as measles or cholera.

- People that develop smallpox do not become infectious until they develop the characteristic skin rash, which is easily recognised. With some diseases (e.g. TB) carriers can show no symptoms of the disease but still be infectious.

Progress check 11.03

1   State three reasons why a person might have a white blood cell count that is higher than normal.

2   Explain the difference between active and passive immunity.

3   How does vaccination work?

4   Why is it difficult to develop effective vaccines against malaria?

Sample question 11.01

Effective vaccines have been developed against measles. The commonly used vaccine consists of a weakened (attenuated) strain of the virus. The vaccine is normally given to children when they are about 1 year old, followed by a booster injection when they are about 4 years old.

This question requires you to bring together several areas of the topic of immunity – vaccination, the primary immune response, the role of memory cells and the secondary immune response.

Explain how this vaccine gives a child long-term immunity. [5 marks]

The attenuated virus in the vaccine has surface antigens that promote a primary immune response in the child being vaccinated. Macrophages take up the virus particles by phagocytosis and display the antigen on their surface. These are known as antigen-presenting cells. B-lymphocytes (B cells) that have receptors complementary to the antigens divide repeatedly by mitosis, producing a clone of B cells. The same occurs with T-lymphocytes to form a clone of T cells. The cells are specific to the antigen from the attenuated virus. Activated B cells produce plasma cells that form antibodies against the virus. Activated T cells produce helper T cells and killer T cells, which have various roles in the immune response. Both types of lymphocyte also produce memory cells, which remain in the blood for many years. If the same antigen enters the body in future, the memory cells are able to divide rapidly and produce antibodies against the virus. This secondary response is faster and produces higher levels of antibodies so that the person is unlikely to develop measles. The booster injection is given to increase the formation of memory cells and give further protection against the pathogen.

Notice that there are more marks available than the 5 marks given for the question – you can miss some points but still gain full marks.

There are a number of facts that could be included in this account. Go through the sample answer and identify the following mark points:

- *the vaccine / attenuated virus has antigens which stimulates the immune response (alternatively a description of the primary immune response is fine).*
- *macrophages take up the virus (by phagocytosis) and act as antigen-presenting cells.*
- *reference to T lymphocytes / T cells (or named T cells – helper T cells / killer T cells).*
- *B/T-lymphocytes have appropriate receptors / recognise antigens*
- *lymphocytes divide by mitosis / rapidly form a clone*
- *reference to lymphocyte specificity*
- *formation of memory cells.*
- *booster injection further stimulates memory cell formation / is used in case first vaccination does not work*
- *second infection by virus causes faster response / higher levels of antibodies / produces no symptoms of the disease.*

11.08 Autoimmune diseases

An autoimmune disease occurs when the body mounts an immune response against its own (self) antigens. When T cells mature in the thymus, many have receptors that are complementary to self antigens. Normally these T cells are destroyed, but sometimes they escape destruction and can stimulate an immune response against the body's own proteins. The T cells release cytokines that stimulate B cells to divide and produce 'autoantibodies'.

Over 80 autoimmune diseases have been identified, and they are caused by both genetic and environmental factors. Some well-known examples are rheumatoid arthritis, multiple sclerosis and type 1 diabetes. A less well-known example is **myasthenia gravis (MG)**.

MG is a disease that causes weakness in the voluntary muscles of the body. The ends of motor neurones release a chemical called acetylcholine, which diffuses across the gap between a motor neurone and the muscle fibres (see Unit 15). Acetylcholine binds with receptors on the cell surface membrane of the muscle fibres, bringing about a sequence of events that leads to muscle contraction.

A person with MG has helper T cells that are specific to the acetylcholine receptors. These T cells release cytokines that stimulate B cells to divide into a clone of plasma cells, all making antibodies against the receptors. The antibodies bind to the acetylcholine receptors and block them. With the receptors blocked, the muscle cells are unable to respond to nerve impulses and are not stimulated to contract.

The symptoms and severity of MG varies widely between individuals. It typically begins with the patient having trouble with eye and eyelid movement, facial expression and swallowing (Figure 11.05) but can progress to affect other muscles in the body.

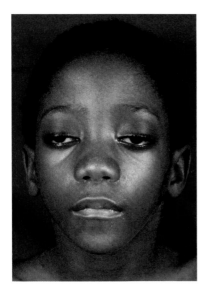

Figure 11.05 Person with myasthenia gravis, showing the drooping eyelids typical of the condition.

The condition gets worse with activity and better with rest. It can be treated very effectively by using drugs to improve transmission across the neuromuscular junction or to decrease the production of abnormal antibodies. There are also treatments that filter abnormal antibodies from the blood. Sometimes surgical removal of the thyroid gland is performed. Some patients with MG go into remission, when the symptoms disappear and they do not require further treatment.

11.09 Monoclonal antibodies

Monoclonal antibodies are antibodies that are made on a large scale in the laboratory. They are prepared from a single clone of cells, so that each is specific to a particular antigen. They have a wide range of uses in biological and medical research, as well as in the diagnosis and treatment of disease.

a Producing monoclonal antibodies

Monoclonal antibodies are produced by specially prepared cells called **hybridomas**. A hybridoma is a cell formed by fusing together an antibody-producing plasma cell with a cancer cell. The plasma cells secrete antibodies but cannot divide, while the cancer cells divide indefinitely. Putting the two features together in a hybridoma produces a cell that divides repeatedly by mitosis and produces antibodies.

A summary of the method is shown in Figure 11.06. An antigen for which the antibody is required is injected into a mouse. The mouse B cells respond to the antigen by producing antibody-forming plasma cells. Spleen cells are taken from the mouse and placed with cancer cells in a special medium that fuses together the cell surface membranes of the two types of cell. The composition of the medium only allows the hybridoma cells to grow. Single hybridoma cells are then selected and placed in wells on a tray, where they grow into clones.

The clones in the wells produce different antibodies, so the one secreting the required antibody has to be identified. This is done by assaying for its ability to bind with the antigen. Once isolated, the clone will divide indefinitely to produce the antibody, which can be extracted and purified.

b Using monoclonal antibodies in the diagnosis of disease

> **TIP**
> You only need to know an *outline* of the uses of monoclonal antibodies in diagnosis and treatment of disease.

Once a monoclonal antibody against a particular antigen has been produced, it can be used to detect the presence of that antigen and to measure how much is present. If the antigen is on a disease-causing organism or infected cells, it can be used for diagnosis of the disease. Hundreds of different monoclonal antibodies have been produced for this purpose. The antibody needs to be 'labelled', so that it shows up in the assay procedure. This is done in a number of ways, such as by binding the antibody to a coloured dye, to a fluorescent substance or to a radioactive chemical. Some methods use an enzyme attached to the antibody. The enzyme's substrate is added and then an assay carried out for a product of the enzyme-catalysed reaction. The activity of the enzyme gives a

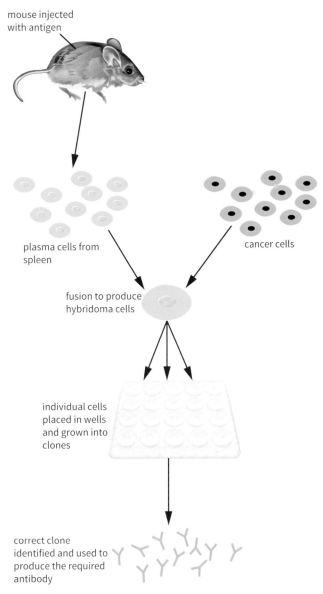

mouse injected with antigen

plasma cells from spleen

cancer cells

fusion to produce hybridoma cells

individual cells placed in wells and grown into clones

correct clone identified and used to produce the required antibody

Figure 11.06 Making monoclonal antibodies.

measure of the quantity of antigen present.

Examples of diagnostic uses include:

- Establishing the presence of pathogens. For example, one test for HIV/AIDS detects the presence of a protein present in the capsid of the virus.

- Diagnosing cancers by testing for abnormal proteins on the surface membrane of cancer cells. A blood test for prostate cancer uses monoclonal antibodies to bind to prostate-specific antigens in the blood. Monoclonal antibodies are routinely used to detect leukaemias.

- Identifying the particular strain of a pathogen that is causing an infection, so the most appropriate treatment can be carried out.

- Detecting the presence of autoantibodies in a person with an autoimmune disease.

- Detecting and measuring the levels of hormones in the blood.

- Tissue typing – detecting the antigens of both donor and patient before an organ transplant.

c Using monoclonal antibodies in the treatment of disease

Monoclonal antibodies are also used to treat a number of diseases. The main types of disease that are targeted are inflammatory conditions such as ulcerative colitis and Crohn's disease, autoimmune disorders such as multiple sclerosis and rheumatoid arthritis, and many different cancers. Monoclonal antibodies are also used to prevent rejection of organ transplants.

The monoclonal antibodies bind to specific antigens associated with these diseases. They work in various ways, often inducing death of the cells showing the target molecule. Alternatively, if the target molecule is a receptor in the surface membrane, the antibody may prevent it from binding with its signal molecule, disrupting the cell's signalling pathway (see Unit 4).

To take one well-documented example, the drug Herceptin™ is a monoclonal antibody that is highly effective in treating some kinds of breast cancer. In the cell surface membrane of many cells is a receptor protein called HER2 (human epidermal growth factor receptor 2). HER2 responds to protein growth factors (cytokines) in the blood, switching on genes in the cell and stimulating mitosis. Some cells have too many HER2 receptors, resulting in uncontrolled cell division that leads to breast cancer. Herceptin™ binds to the HER2 receptors on these cells and interferes with their action, as well as marking the receptors for destruction by cells of the immune system.

There are problems with monoclonal antibodies, however. If the antibodies are raised in mice (or other laboratory animals) and introduced into humans, they will be recognised as non-self and cause an immune response. The patient develops human anti-mouse antibodies (HAMAs), which cause adverse reactions and destroy the monoclonal antibodies. This is a particular problem if a person has to undergo extended and repeated treatments. To overcome this, mouse antibodies are altered to make their protein structure more like that of human antibodies. The two main ways of achieving this are:

- Making chimaeric antibodies (a chimaera is a mythical animal combining the bodies of two different species). A chimaeric antibody is made by combining genetic material from a mouse with genetic material from a human, and then introducing this into mouse cancer cells to generate antibodies. The chimaeric antibody is usually about one-third mouse and two-thirds human, with the variable regions of the heavy and light chains being mouse while the constant regions are human (see Figure 11.03).

- Making humanised antibodies. Humanised antibodies contain a greater proportion of human protein (typically over 90%). They are made by taking

segments of mouse DNA coding for the variable region of the antibody and inserting them into the DNA for a human antibody. Again this DNA is expressed in cultures of mammalian cells such as mouse cancer cells in order to produce the required antibodies.

Progress check 11.04

1 Briefly describe how monoclonal antibodies are produced.

2 How can a monoclonal antibody be used to detect the presence of a pathogen?

3 If a monoclonal antibody is used to treat a disease, why might it be rejected by the patient's body?

Revision checklist

Check that you know:

- [ ] phagocytes and phagocytosis
- [ ] the immune response, antigens, self and non-self
- [ ] the mode of action of B-lymphocytes
- [ ] the mode of action of T-lymphocytes
- [ ] the function of memory cells
- [ ] the effects of infections and leukaemias on white blood cell counts
- [ ] the structure of an antibody molecule and how it relates to its function
- [ ] active and passive immunity, natural and artificial immunity
- [ ] how vaccination can control some diseases
- [ ] why vaccination has eradicated smallpox but not measles, TB, malaria or cholera
- [ ] autoimmune diseases
- [ ] the hybridoma method for producing monoclonal antibodies
- [ ] the use of monoclonal antibodies in the diagnosis of disease
- [ ] the use of monoclonal antibodies in the treatment of disease.

Exam-style questions

1 Macrophages are phagocytic cells that are found in many tissues, including the alveoli of the lungs. Explain how macrophages help to protect the alveoli from becoming infected by bacteria. [4]

Total: 4

2 Figure 11.07 is a diagram of an antibody molecule. Antibodies are proteins.

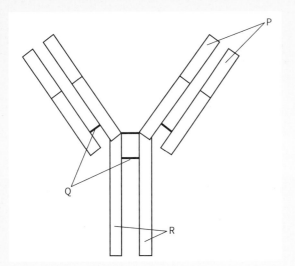

Figure 11.07

a What level of protein structure is shown by an antibody molecule? Explain your answer. [2]

b Identify the parts of the molecule labelled P, Q and R and state one function of each of these features. [3]

c The region labelled R is hydrophilic in antibodies that are secreted by plasma cells, whereas in antibodies found on the surface of B-lymphocytes, region R is hydrophobic. Suggest reasons for this difference. [2]

d Monoclonal antibodies can be produced commercially for use in the diagnosis of infectious diseases. Name the type of cell used to produce monoclonal antibodies. [1]

Total: 8

3 B-lymphocytes respond to the presence of non-self antigens by dividing by mitosis to produce a clone of plasma cells that produce antigens, along with a clone of memory cells, which are involved in the secondary immune response.

a Explain what is meant by a *non-self antigen*. [2]

b Briefly explain how B-lymphocytes recognise non-self antigens. [2]

c Describe how B-lymphocyte memory cells are involved in the secondary immune response. [3]

Total: 7

4 a There are four different ways that a person can become immune to an infectious disease. Copy and complete Table 11.03 to identify these types of immunity. [4]

Source of antigen	Type of immunity
non-self antigen is present on a pathogen that invades the body	
non-self antigen is given by vaccination	
antibody enters the body of a baby in breast milk	
antibody enters the body by injection	

Table 11.03

b In 1980 the World Health Organization declared that the world was free of smallpox. Outline why it was possible to eradicate smallpox, while this has not been possible with other diseases such as measles and malaria. [4]

c The protoctist organism that causes malaria undergoes frequent mutations, changing its surface antigens and making the disease difficult to control by vaccination. Explain why a vaccine may not be effective when the surface antigens change. [2]

Total: 10

Practical skills for AS

Learning outcomes

When you have finished this unit, you should be able to:

- ☐ understand how to carry out an experiment

- ☐ identify the dependent and the independent variable

- ☐ describe how to change the independent variable within a suitable range

- ☐ describe an appropriate control which removes the effect of the independent variable

- ☐ describe which variables to standardise to provide accurate results

- ☐ choose a suitable technique to measure the dependent variable

- ☐ record your results in a suitable table, with appropriate headings and units

- ☐ present your results in the form of an appropriate graph

- ☐ interpret your results and identify sources of error

- ☐ draw conclusions and make scientific explanations

- ☐ suggest improvements or modifications to extend an investigation

- ☐ use a microscope to make measurements and observations of cells and tissues, including drawing plan diagrams.

Your practical skills for AS will be assessed by means of a written exam (Paper 3), which will focus on the following skills:

- manipulation, measurement and observations

- presentation of data and observations

- analysis, conclusions and evaluation.

Paper 3 is a 2-hour question paper and carries a total of 40 marks. The paper has two or more questions and you will be assessed on your ability to:

- carry out an investigation or investigations

- carry out an activity using a light microscope.

Table P1.01 shows how the marks for Paper 3 are awarded.

Skill	Total marks	Breakdown of marks	
manipulation of apparatus, measurement and observation	16 marks	making decisions about measurements or observations	8 marks
		successfully collecting data and observations	8 marks
presentation of data and observations	12 marks	recording data and observations	4 marks
		displaying calculations and reasoning	2 marks
		data or observations layout	6 marks
analysis, conclusions and evaluation	12 marks	interpreting data or observations and identifying sources of error	6 marks
		drawing conclusions	3 marks
		suggesting improvements to a procedure or modifications to extend investigation	3 marks

Table P1.01 Skills and marks for Paper 3.

Paper 3 includes questions relating to different areas of AS biology and may include material from an unfamiliar context. You will be expected to show evidence of skills in the handling of familiar and unfamiliar biological materials. You will be given full instructions if you are asked about unfamiliar materials or techniques.

To cope successfully with the questions on Paper 3, it is essential that you are familiar with the practical activities included in the AS part of the syllabus. There are details of these in the relevant units and they are summarised in Table P1.02.

P1.01 Carrying out an experiment

You may be asked to carry out an experiment to investigate one of the following:

- the effect of a factor, such as temperature or concentration, on enzyme activity

- osmosis and plant tissues

- transpiration.

a Independent and dependent variables

When carrying out an experiment, it is important to distinguish between the **independent variable** and the **dependent variable**. The independent variable is the factor that you might change in an experiment; for example, if you were investigating the effect of temperature on enzyme activity, you might carry out the experiment at a range of different temperatures, such as 20 °C, 30 °C, 40 °C, 50 °C and 60 °C. These temperatures are set by the experimenter, so in this case temperature is the independent variable.

The dependent variable is the variable that changes as a result of changing the independent variable and are the results you might take during an experiment. For example, in the example above, investigating the effect

Syllabus section	Practical activities
1 Cell structure	• comparing the structure of typical animal and plant cells • calculating magnifications • using a graticule to measure cells • calculating the actual size of specimens
2 Biological molecules	• carrying out tests for reducing sugars, non-reducing sugars, starch, lipids and proteins • carrying out a semi-quantitative Benedict's test on a reducing sugar
3 Enzymes	• investigating the effect of factors on enzyme activity • investigating the effect of immobilising an enzyme on its activity
4 Cell membranes and transport	• investigating diffusion and the effect of changing the surface area to volume ratio on diffusion • estimating the water potential of tissues by immersing plant tissues in solutions of different water potential
5 The mitotic cell cycle	• observing and drawing stages of mitosis in root tip preparations
6 Nucleic acids and protein synthesis	• no practical activities included
7 Transport in plants	• drawing and labelling low power plans and details of cells and tissues in sections of roots, stems and leaves • using an eyepiece graticule to show tissues in correct proportions • investigating transpiration • making annotated drawings of sections through leaves of xerophytic plants
8 Transport in mammals	• observing and drawing sections through arteries, veins and capillaries using prepared slides • observing and drawing blood cells using prepared slides and photographs
9 Gas exchange and smoking	• observing and making plan diagrams to show the structure of the trachea, bronchi, bronchioles and alveoli
10 Infectious disease	• no practical activities included
11 Immunity	• no practical activities included

Table P1.02 Practical activities included in the AS syllabus.

of temperature on enzyme activity, the enzyme activity is the dependent variable. This might be recorded by noting the time taken to reach an end-point.

To illustrate the difference between these two variables, consider an experiment to investigate the effect of pH on the activity of the enzyme trypsin. Trypsin is a protease and will hydrolyse a cloudy suspension of casein, resulting in a clear solution. In this example, pH is the independent variable and you might choose to carry out the experiment at a range of pH values, such as 4.0, 5.0, 6.0, 7.0 and 8.0.

You would record the time taken for the cloudy suspension of casein to become clear (i.e. to reach an end-point), so the time taken to reach the end-point is the dependent variable. Remember that enzyme activity depends on a number of different factors, including temperature and substrate concentration, so it is important that all other factors, known as control variables, are kept constant and that only the independent variable is the one you change.

> **TIP**
> Remember to use **SI units** in your work. Do not use imperial units!

If you are required to vary the concentration of an enzyme (for example) on activity, it may be necessary to make dilutions of a standard solution. Suppose you were provided with a 1% standard solution of an enzyme and that you wanted to investigate the effect of enzyme concentration on activity. Table P1.03 shows how you would prepare a suitable range of enzyme concentrations, by adding measured volumes of distilled water.

Volume of standard 1% enzyme solution / cm³	Volume of distilled water added / cm³	Final concentration of enzyme / %
10.0	0.0	1.0
8.0	2.0	0.8
6.0	4.0	0.6
4.0	6.0	0.4
2.0	8.0	0.2
0.0	10.0	0.0

Table P1.03 Preparing a range of dilutions from a standard enzyme solution.

Notice that in each case, the total volume of solution is 10.0 cm³. One of the solutions contains no enzyme at all (0%). This is a **control** solution, to ensure that any changes are due to the presence of the enzyme itself and not any other factor. Another control solution could be an enzyme solution that has been boiled, to denature the enzyme, and then allowed to cool. These control solutions remove the effect of the independent variable.

Another method for producing a dilution series results in solutions in which each one is one tenth the concentration of the previous solution. This is sometimes called an exponential dilution series and results in concentrations of 1.0, 0.1, 0.01, 0.001, 0.0001 and so on. To prepare this dilution series, you start by adding 1.0 cm³ of the standard 1% enzyme solution to 9.0 cm³ of distilled water. This results in a 0.1% dilution. After mixing carefully, you then transfer 1.0 cm³ of this dilution to a further 9.0 cm³ of distilled water, producing a 0.01% dilution. The procedure is repeated, each time transferring 1.0 cm³ of the dilution to 9.0 cm³ of distilled water. At each stage, the solution is diluted by a factor of 10.

b Keeping variables constant

It is important that you are able to identify variables and to explain how to keep them constant. Some of these variables are included in Table P1.04.

Variable	How the variable is kept constant
temperature	Ideally, to keep temperature constant or to control temperature, you would use a thermostatically controlled water bath and check the temperature regularly using a thermometer. A beaker of water may also be used, carefully heated, for example by adding hot water or cooled with ice and again monitoring the temperature carefully with a thermometer.
pH	The pH is controlled using a buffer solution at a known pH value. The pH can be measured using indicator paper or indicator solution and a colour chart, or with an electronic pH meter.
light intensity	In a photosynthesis experiment, light intensity can be controlled by keeping the light at a set distance. Moving the light changes the light intensity, which is proportional to $1 \div (distance)^2$. An electric light gives off a significant amount of heat and it is important to ensure that this does not also change the temperature (e.g. by using a glass heat-shield).

Table P1.04 Some variables and how to keep them constant.

c Measuring the dependent variable and recording the results

The exact details of how to measure the dependent variable will be different for each type of measurement you are going to make. In the enzyme example described above, you could record the time taken for the mixture to become clear (the end-point of the reaction). If you were investigating the activity of an enzyme such as rennin, which causes milk to clot, you could record the time taken for small clots to appear in the mixture.

Catalase is an enzyme that breaks down hydrogen peroxide, forming oxygen gas and water. One way to measure the activity of catalase would be to record the volume of oxygen produced in a given time (e.g. $cm^3 min^{-1}$).

Figure P1.01 shows how the activity of catalase could be investigated.

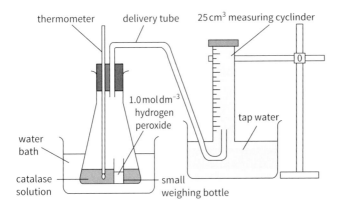

Figure P1.01 Investigating the activity of catalase.

Notice that in this experiment the hydrogen peroxide (substrate) is shown in a separate container in the conical flask. It is good experimental practice to allow the enzyme and the substrate to reach the temperature of the water bath separately before they are mixed together. When the substrate is mixed with the enzyme solution, the oxygen produced will collect in the measuring cylinder and the volume is recorded.

When carrying out experiments with quantitative results, it is important to record and display the results in a suitable form. You may be required to design a table to record your results.

Table P1.05 shows the results of an experiment to investigate the effect of trypsin concentration on the hydrolysis of a casein suspension.

Notice that the times taken to reach the end-point are recorded to the nearest second. The end-point is partly subjective, because it is not easy to find the exact time taken for the casein suspension to become completely clear. The mean times are expressed to the same number of decimal places as the individual readings, rounded up or down appropriately.

> **TIP**
>
> **Tabulating results**
>
> - Draw the table with neat, ruled lines.
> - Give each column a suitable heading, including the units.
> - By convention, the units are separated from what was measured using a solidus (/). You should always use SI units.
> - Do not repeat the units in the columns alongside the data.
> - The first column should be the independent variable, the next column(s) are your recordings of the results (dependent variable). Any derived values, such as the means as shown here, are in the last column.
> - Arrange the values for the independent variable in ascending order, from lowest to highest value.

Trypsin concentration / %	Time taken to reach the end-point / s			
	Reading 1	**Reading 2**	**Reading 3**	**Mean**
0.0	suspension remained cloudy	suspension remained cloudy	suspension remained cloudy	suspension remained cloudy
0.2	141	138	142	140
0.4	65	64	67	65
0.6	42	43	38	41
0.8	24	28	25	26
1.0	9	13	12	11

Table P1.05 The effect of enzyme concentration on the activity of trypsin.

d Plotting a graph of your results

Quantitative results, such as those shown in Table P1.05, can be presented in the form of a graph to show the relationship between the two variables.

> ### TIP
>
> ### Plotting a graph
>
> - Decide what type of graph is appropriate for the data: should it be a line graph, histogram or bar chart?
> - When plotting a line graph, be careful to orientate the axes correctly. The x-axis should be the independent variable and the y-axis should be the dependent variable.
> - Choose a suitable scale for the axes, making good use of the graph paper. Use a linear scale, so that the values on each axis go up in equal intervals. The scale should be chosen with care. The axes do not necessarily have to start at zero, but if they do, a break should be indicated if the values are, for example, 0, then 50, 60, 70, 80 and 100, as shown in Figure P1.02.
> - Label each axis fully, including the units. The label will usually be the same as the column headings for the variables.
> - Plot the points carefully, using either a cross (×) or a dot with a circle drawn round it (⊙).
> - Join the points carefully. If there is a clear relationship, it may be appropriate to draw a smooth curve through the points. For example, a graph showing the relationship between light intensity and the rate of photosynthesis. Otherwise, join successive points with ruled, straight lines.
> - Do not extrapolate your line (i.e. do not extend it beyond the plotted points).

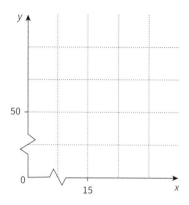

Figure P1.02 How to show a break in the values on the axes of a graph.

Figure P1.03 shows a graph of the results in Table P1.05.

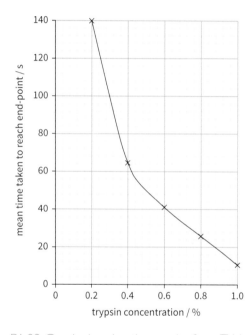

Figure P1.03 Graph showing the results from Table P1.05.

e Types of graph

You are likely to encounter three different types of graph in biology:

- line graph
- bar chart
- histogram.

Line graphs are used to show the relationship between one variable and another. For example, a graph to show the relationship between enzyme activity and temperature, or to show the relationship between the rate of transpiration and the time of day.

In a line graph, the independent variable is plotted on the x-axis (horizontal axis) and the dependent variable is plotted on the y-axis (vertical axis).

Points must be plotted carefully, using either neat, small crosses (**×**) or encircled dots (⊙). You need to think carefully about whether to join successive points with a ruled, straight line, or to draw a line of best fit. If you are unsure, it is usually safer to join successive points with ruled, straight lines. You should draw a smooth curve through the points **only** if you have a good reason to do so (e.g. a graph showing the relationship between the rate of photosynthesis and light intensity).

If there is no clear relationship do not draw a line, but leave as a **scattergram**. This can be useful to show whether or not there is a correlation between two variables.

Bar charts are used to display data where one of the variables is not numerical.

For example, if you wish to draw a graph to show the vitamin C content of a range of different fruits. In this case, you would plot the concentration of vitamin C on the y-axis and put the names of the different types of fruit on the x-axis.

By convention, the bars are drawn separately (i.e. not touching) and of equal width. The bars can be arranged in any order, but it is easier to make comparisons if they are arranged in descending order of size (highest to lowest).

A bar chart may also be used to show the difference between the two means, or two medians, of two sets of data.

Histograms are used when the independent variable is numerical and the data are continuous. The data are **grouped** into classes. The number of classes will depend on the nature of the data obtained. The y-axis represents the frequency (or number) in each class. In a histogram the bars should be drawn touching.

f Making measurements, accuracy and precision

When carrying out an experiment, it is likely that you will have to take readings and record quantitative results. You might take readings of temperature, mass, length, volume and time.

We use terms such as accuracy, precision, reliability and validity in relation to the results of an experiment which give an indication of the confidence you can have in your results. It is important to have an

understanding of these terms and they are explained in Table P1.07.

Term	Explanation
accuracy	a measurement is accurate if it is close to its true value, so accuracy relates to the closeness of a reading and its true value
precision	this relates to the closeness of agreement between a series of repeated readings; there may be some variation between readings, if there is a lot of variation, your results may be less precise
reliability	this indicates how much confidence you can place in your results; if results are reliable, you would expect to get the same readings each time you repeated the measurement
validity	a reading is valid if it really measures what it is intended to measure, this is why it is important to identify the dependent and independent variables carefully and to keep all other variables constant

Table P1.07 Terms used in measurements.

Progress check P1.01

A student carried out an experiment to investigate the effect of pH on the activity of the enzyme amylase. The experiment was repeated at each pH value. The student's record of the results is shown in table P1.06.

pH	amylase activity / arbitrary units
7.0	13, 12, 14
8.0	14, 16, 15
6.0	0, 0, 0
6.5	4, 2, 3

table P1.06

1 Name the independent variable and the dependent variable in this experiment.

2 State three control variables that should have been kept constant in this experiment.

3 Prepare a suitable table of the results. In your table, include a column to show the mean amylase activity at each pH value.

Progress check P1.02

State which type of graph (line, bar chart or histogram) would be appropriate to display each of the following.

1 The blood glucose concentration of a person, measured every 15 minutes for 3 hours after eating.
2 The relationship between the height of a plant and the number of flowers.
3 The number of different species of insects collected from each of five different species of trees.
4 The frequency of lengths of a sample of 100 leaves.
5 The mean widths of sun and shade leaves.
6 The relationship between wind speed and the rate of transpiration.

Worked example P1.01

Question

In an estuary, the salinity (salt concentration) of the water varies. An investigation was carried out into the relationship between the salinity of the water and the concentration of nitrate ions in the water. The results are shown in Table P1.07.

Salinity of water / parts per thousand	Concentration of nitrate ions / $\mu g\,dm^{-3}$
27.2	40
27.4	36
27.8	34
28.0	33
28.2	32
28.4	26
28.6	28
28.7	22
29.1	21
29.4	16
29.6	14
29.9	11

Table P1.07

1 Plot a suitable graph of the data in Table P1.07.
2 Draw a line of best fit through the points.
3 What conclusion can you draw from these results?

Answer

1 A line graph is appropriate here, showing the relationship between these two variables, with the concentration of nitrate ions and the units on the y-axis and salinity, again with units, on the x-axis.

Note that the scale for salinity does not need to start at zero, because the lowest value is 27.2. You could, therefore, start this axis at a value of 27.0. Your graph should look like this:

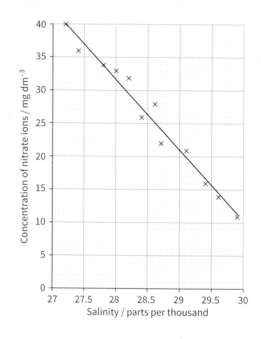

2 The line of best fit is a neat straight line, drawn with about the same number of points and approximately the same distance above and below the line. The line of best fit does not necessarily need to go through the first and last plotted points. Remember not to extrapolate your line!

3 The results show that as the salinity increases, the concentration of nitrate ions decreases. In other words, there is an inverse relationship between these two variables. As the salinity changes from 27.2 to 29.9 parts per thousand, the concentration of nitrate ions decreases by 29 $\mu g\,dm^{-3}$.

i Estimating errors in measurements

No matter how much care you might take to read a scale, there may be some uncertainty in your reading. For example, a measuring cylinder may have been graduated in units of 1 cm^3 and unless the meniscus of a liquid is *exactly* on a graduated line, you may have to estimate the value to the nearest cubic centimetre. As a general rule, the uncertainty of a reading is expressed as ± half of the smallest scale division, so if you are reading a volume in the measuring cylinder to the nearest cm^3, it could be expressed as 35 ± 0.5 cm^3. If you measured a *change* in volume, by taking two readings, the total error will be ±1 cm^3.

You may be asked to calculate the percentage error. This is the error in the measurement divided by the measurement itself, multiplied by 100.

In the example above, if the difference in volumes is 5.0 ± 1 cm^3, the percentage error is (1 ÷ 5.0) × 100 = 5%.

ii Drawing conclusions from experimental results and describing data

You may be asked to draw conclusions from your experiment. If you have plotted a suitable graph of the data, this should show the relationship between the dependent variable and the independent variable. When interpreting the results from such a graph you should:

- describe the overall trend, such as that as the independent variable increases, the dependent variable decreases

- comment on any changes in gradient in the graph

- use data from your graph, such as to illustrate when there is a change in gradient, quoting values from both the x-axis and the y-axis

- be careful not to use phrases such as 'the concentration of substrate decreased quickly at first' unless the independent variable is time.

You may be asked to calculate the mean of a set of data or to calculate the rate of change, possibly by using the gradient of the curve on a graph.

When calculating a mean value, set out the steps in your calculation clearly and ensure that you quote the answer to an appropriate number of decimal places, that is, no more than in the original set of data. For example, suppose you collected six leaves from a plant growing in a shady place and measured the maximum width of each leaf.

The results are: 2.8 cm, 3.6 cm, 2.5 cm, 3.9 cm, 4.4 cm and 3.1 cm.

Calculating the mean:

(2.8 + 3.6 + 2.5 + 3.9 + 4.4 + 3.1) ÷ 6

= 20.3 ÷ 6

= 3.4 cm

Remember to give appropriate units with your answer. Your calculator may show a result of 3.3833333, which is rounded up to 3.4 to be consistent with the original data.

Always show the steps in your calculations and quote the answer to the same number of decimal places as in the original data.

To calculate the gradient of a straight line, select two points on the line and draw a right angle triangle using these points. Measure the values x_1 and y_1 and then calculate the gradient as $y_1 ÷ x_1$. This is illustrated in Figure P1.04.

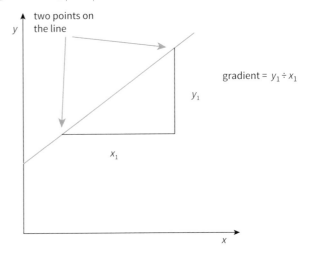

Figure P1.04 Calculating the gradient of a straight line.

To calculate the gradient of a curve, you first need to draw a tangent to the curve and then draw a right angle triangle. Find the values x_1 and y_1, and then divide y_1 by x_1 to find the rate. This is illustrated in Figure P1.05.

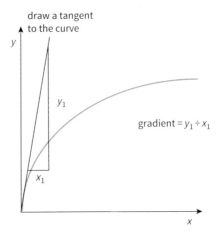

Figure P1.05 Calculating the gradient of a curve.

Worked example P1.02

In an experiment using catalase and the substrate hydrogen peroxide, the total volume of oxygen produced each minute for 10 minutes was recorded. The results of this experiment are shown in Table P1.08.

Time / min	Total volume of oxygen produced / cm³
0	0
1	1.6
2	3.3
3	4.6
4	5.7
5	6.7
6	7.3
7	7.9
8	8.2
9	8.5
10	8.5

Table P1.08

1   Plot a suitable graph of these results.

2   Draw a smooth curve through the plotted points.

3   Find the initial rate of reaction.

Answer

1   Your graph should look like this:

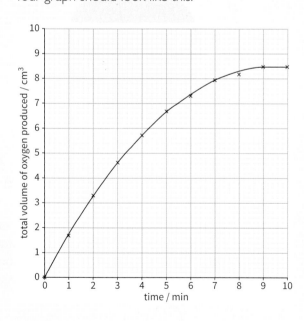

The dependent variable is the volume of oxygen and the independent variable is time. Both of the axes are labelled and units are included. Both of the axes have a linear scale and the points are plotted carefully.

2   Your curve should be similar to the curve shown above. In this instance it is acceptable to draw a smooth curve, as asked by the question. A straight line of best fit is not appropriate.

3   To find the initial rate of reaction, you need to draw a tangent to the first part of the curve:

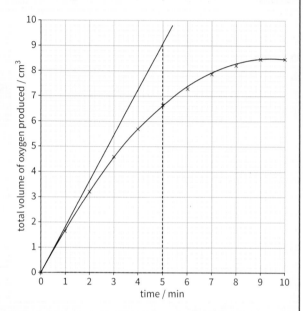

Take two readings from the line, e.g. 9.0 cm³ and 5 minutes, gives an initial rate of

$9.0 \div 5$

$= 1.8 \, \text{cm}^3 \, \text{min}^{-1}$

Notice that although the volume of oxygen produced increases during the experiment, the rate of reaction steadily decreases. You could compare the initial rate with the rate at, say, 5 minutes, by drawing another tangent to the curve at 5 minutes and finding the rate. The rate decreases because the concentration of the substrate decreases.

iii Sources of error and suggestions for improvements

It is important to distinguish between genuine errors and mistakes that you might have made in, for example, taking a reading from a thermometer and reading the scale incorrectly. Errors arise because of uncertainty in the accuracy of measuring equipment, or because of variables that are difficult to control.

> **TIP**
>
> Do not confuse mistakes in taking readings with experimental errors!

We recognise two different types of errors: **systematic** and **random**. Systematic errors arise if a measuring instrument is incorrectly calibrated, for example. The value read from the scale will always differ from the 'true' value by the same amount. Random errors arise as a result of difficulties in controlling variables or in measurement of the dependent variable. For example, it is difficult to maintain the temperature of a water bath at an exactly constant value, or to determine the end-point of a reaction by eye, as there will always be a certain amount of variability. This is why it is important to replicate your readings and to obtain a mean value. For example, if you are investigating the effect of temperature on enzyme activity, it is better to take at least three readings at each temperature and then find the mean value at each temperature. This gives a better indication of the 'true' value and will help you to spot any anomalies. An anomaly is a result that is clearly out of line with the others. If you have time, you should repeat this reading to check, but if not, do not include it in the calculation of the mean value.

When making suggestions for improvement, think about the following possibilities:

- Are there any variables that were not controlled?
- How can these variables be effectively controlled?
- Is there a better way of measuring the dependent variable?
- Could I have used apparatus that is more accurate?

P1.02 Making a biological drawing

You should be familiar with the use of a microscope to make observations of cells and tissues in a prepared slide. You may also be asked to stain and make a temporary slide of cells, using a stain such as methylene blue.

Microscopes have an eyepiece lens, usually with a magnification of ×10, and two or more objective lenses. These usually have magnifications of ×4, ×10 and ×40. The eyepiece lens may contain a graticule, a scale divided into 100 arbitrary units, which can be used to make measurements of cells. The graticule needs to be calibrated, using a stage micrometer, so that we know the actual dimensions of the eyepiece scale. The eyepiece graticule needs to be calibrated for each of the objective lenses.

The **magnification** of an image is the number of times larger the image is compared with the actual size. You may be asked to calculate the magnification of a cell or of an organelle from a photograph. If we know the **actual** size of the cell or organelle, we can calculate the magnification using the formula:

magnification = measured size of image ÷ actual size

Remember to use the same units for the measured size and the actual size. For example, the actual size may be given in micrometres (μm). You would probably measure the size of the image in millimetres (mm). There are 1000 μm in 1 mm.

Here is an example to illustrate how to calculate magnification. The image shows a red blood cell. The red blood cell has an actual diameter of 7.0 μm. Measure the diameter of the image and then calculate the magnification.

First measure the diameter carefully, suppose this is 37 mm:

37 mm = 37 000 μm, so the magnification is 37 000 ÷ 7 = ×5285.7

You may also be asked to calculate the actual size of an image, given the magnification. In this case, you divide the measured size of the image by the magnification. You may find it helpful to remember the formula shown by the triangle:

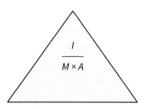

where I is the image size, M is magnification and A is the actual size.

In the exam, one of the questions is likely to require you to make a drawing of a specimen on a slide and viewed using a microscope or of a photograph taken through a microscope (known as a photomicrograph).

We recognise two different types of drawings make using a microscope: **a low power plan** and a **high power drawing**. A low power plan is used to show the distribution of tissues, such as in a transverse section through a plant stem or a leaf. Individual cells should not be shown in a low power plan. When making a low power plan, you should use the low magnification objective lens of the microscope (e.g. ×4).

A high power drawing shows the details of individual cells. This could be a small group of palisade mesophyll cells or cells from a root tip showing stages of mitosis. You should use the high magnification objective lenses of the microscope for a high power drawing, these are typically ×10 or ×40.

TIP

Making a drawing

- Make the drawing large enough to show essential features. Use most of the space available in the question paper.
- Ensure that the proportions are correct, such as the relative lengths and widths of a group of palisade cells.
- Use clear outlines for your drawings, rather than 'sketchy' lines, with a sharp pencil, usually HB.
- Use a clean eraser to rub out any mistakes.
- Do not shade or colour in your drawing.
- If you are asked to label your drawing, use straight label lines, drawn using a ruler. Label lines must not cross each other and should precisely touch the structure being labelled. Do not include arrow heads on the label lines.

TIP

If you have to make a drawing from a prepared microscope slide, you will not be expected to be familiar with the specimen, but you should be able to identify tissues, such as xylem in a section of plant tissue.

P1.03 Making a temporary slide of cells

Specimens such as a moss leaf or a leaf from an aquatic plant (e.g. *Elodea*) can be used to make a temporary slide to view using a microscope. The specimen should be mounted in a small drop of distilled water on a microscope slide and a coverslip applied carefully, to avoid trapping air bubbles. You may be asked to add a stain, such as methylene blue or iodine solution, to the specimen. Figure P1.06 shows how to lower the coverslip onto a microscope slide, using a mounted needle.

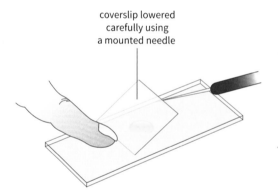

coverslip lowered carefully using a mounted needle

Figure P1.06 Making a temporary slide to view cells with a microscope, using a mounted needle.

Revision checklist

Check that you know how to:

- [ ] carry out an experiment
- [ ] identify the dependent and the independent variable
- [ ] change the independent variable within a suitable range
- [ ] use appropriate controls which remove the effect of the independent variable
- [ ] identify which variables to standardise to provide accurate results
- [ ] use a suitable technique to measure the dependent variable

- [ ] record the results in a suitable table, with appropriate headings and units
- [ ] present the results in the form of a suitable graph
- [ ] interpret the results and identify sources of error
- [ ] draw conclusions and make scientific explanations
- [ ] suggest improvements or modifications to extend an investigation
- [ ] use a microscope to make measurements and observations of cells and tissues, including drawing plan diagrams.

Exam-style questions

1   An experiment was carried out to investigate the effect of wind speed on the rate of transpiration of a leafy shoot, using a potometer.

 a   Name the independent variable and the dependent variable in this experiment. [2]

 b   State two variables other than wind speed, that affect the rate of transpiration. [2]

 c   In this experiment, the bubble in the potometer capillary tube moved 2.5 cm in 20 minutes, in still air. The diameter of the capillary tube was 0.5 mm. The volume of a cylinder (V) is given by the formula $V = \pi r^2 \times d$, where d is the distance moved by the bubble. Calculate the mean rate of uptake of water by the shoot, expressing your answer in mm^3 min^{-1}. [3]

Total: 7

2   Living yeast cells contain enzymes called dehydrogenases. These enzymes remove hydrogen from substrates. Artificial hydrogen acceptors, such as methylene blue, can be used to investigate the activity of dehydrogenases. Methylene blue is blue in the oxidised state, but turns colourless when it is reduced. A solution of

methylene blue is added to the yeast suspension and will turn colourless when the methylene blue is reduced.

You are provided with a suspension of living yeast cells and a solution of methylene blue. Plan an experiment you could carry out to investigate the effect of temperature on the activity of dehydrogenases.

 a   State the independent variable and the dependent variable in this experiment. [2]

 b   Describe the method you would use, including the control of variables and collection of quantitative results. [6]

 c   Explain how your results would be presented and analysed. [6]

Total: 14

3   A student investigated the effect of the concentration of sucrose solutions on plasmolysis in plant cells. Small pieces of onion epidermis were immersed in sucrose solutions at a range of concentrations. The pieces of epidermis were then examined using a microscope and the numbers of plasmolysed cells were counted. This was then expressed as a percentage of the total number of cells observed at each sucrose

concentration. The results of this investigation are shown in Table P1.08

Concentration of sucrose solution / mol dm^{-3}	Percentage of cells plasmolysed / %
0.0	0.0
0.2	12
0.4	31
0.6	84
0.8	100

Table P1.08

a Plot a graph of these results. Join the points on your graph with ruled, straight lines. [4]

b Use your graph to find the concentration of sucrose solution in which 50% of the cells would be plasmolysed. [1]

c Suggest how the student should ensure that the results of this investigation are as reliable as possible. [2]

Total: 7

4 The photograph shows a section through a leaf as seen using a light microscope. [Photograph: © John Adds.]

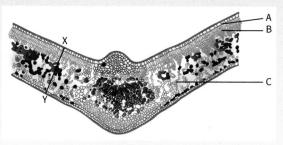

a Name the tissues labelled A, B and C. [3]

b i Measure the thickness of this leaf (in mm), as shown by the line X–Y. [1]

   ii The actual thickness of the leaf is 0.95 mm. Use your measurement from part **i** to calculate the magnification of this photograph [2].

c Make a low power plan to show the distribution of tissues in this leaf. You do not need to label your drawing. [5]

Total: 11

Energy and respiration

Learning outcomes

When you have finished this unit, you should be able to:

- ☐ explain why living organisms need energy, with reference to anabolic reactions, active transport, movement and maintenance of body temperature

- ☐ describe the features of ATP as the universal energy currency

- ☐ explain that ATP is synthesised in reactions in glycolysis and the Krebs cycle

- ☐ describe the roles of the coenzymes nicotinamide adenine dinucleotide (NAD), flavin adenine dinucleotide (FAD) and coenzyme A (CoA) in respiration

- ☐ explain that the synthesis of ATP is associated with the electron transport chain

- ☐ explain the relative energy values of carbohydrates, lipid and protein as respiratory substrates

- ☐ define the term respiratory quotient (RQ) and determine RQs from equations for respiration

- ☐ carry out investigations using simple respirometers to determine RQ values

- ☐ list the four stages in aerobic respiration and state where each occurs in eukaryotic cells

- ☐ outline the process of glycolysis

- ☐ explain that, in the presence of oxygen, pyruvate is converted to acetyl CoA in the link reaction

- ☐ outline the main steps of the Krebs cycle

- ☐ explain that some of the reactions in the Krebs cycle involve decarboxylation and dehydrogenation and the reduction of coenzymes

- ☐ outline the process of oxidative phosphorylation

- ☐ carry out investigations to determine the effect of factors such as temperature and substrate concentration on the rate of respiration of yeast using an indicator

- ☐ describe the relationship between structure and function of mitochondria

- ☐ distinguish between aerobic and anaerobic respiration in mammalian tissue and in yeast

- ☐ explain the small yield of ATP from anaerobic respiration and the concept of an oxygen debt

- ☐ explain how rice is adapted to grow with its roots submerged in water

- ☐ carry out investigations to measure the effect of temperature on the respiration rate of germinating seeds or small invertebrates.

12.01 Energy and living organisms

All living organisms require a source of energy, which is used for a number of purposes including:

- anabolic reactions – the synthesis of large molecules from smaller molecules such as protein synthesis and DNA replication
- active transport
- movement
- maintenance of body temperature.

The structure of ATP (adenosine triphosphate) is described in Unit 6. ATP is often described as 'the universal energy currency' in living organisms, because it supplies the energy for these processes. You should remember that a molecule of ATP consists of adenosine attached to three phosphate groups.

Hydrolysis of the bonds between the phosphate group yields energy that can be used for processes requiring an input of energy, such as active transport.

The most important reaction for supplying energy in cells is the conversion of ATP to ADP (adenosine diphosphate) by the hydrolysis of the bond between the last two phosphate groups. This reaction yields 30.5 kJ per mole of ATP.

ATP is used rapidly in cells and the supply of ATP is replenished quickly by the phosphorylation of ADP to form ATP. This reaction requires an input of energy, and is associated with the reactions of **respiration** and the capture of light energy in **photosynthesis**.

One of the ways in which ATP is synthesised is by **substrate level phosphorylation**, reactions occurring in **glycolysis** and in the **Krebs cycle**. Glycolysis and the Krebs cycle are explained later in this unit; substrate level phosphorylation involves the transfer of a phosphate group from one molecule to ADP, resulting in the formation of ATP.

Some of the reactions in respiration (and photosynthesis) require the presence of **coenzymes**, which help with the catalytic reaction of an enzyme. Coenzymes involved with respiration are:

- coenzyme A (CoA)
- nicotinamide adenine dinucleotide (NAD)
- flavin adenine dinucleotide (FAD).

CoA transfers acetyl groups, formed in the link reaction from pyruvate, to the Krebs cycle.

NAD and FAD are also known as hydrogen carriers (or electron carriers), since they can combine with hydrogen, formed in some of the reactions of respiration:

NAD + 2H → reduced NAD

and

FAD + 2H → reduced FAD

Reduced hydrogen carriers have an important role in the final process of aerobic respiration, **oxidative phosphorylation**, in which significant amounts of ATP are produced. The process of oxidative phosphorylation occurs across the inner membrane of mitochondria. In this process, hydrogen is removed from reduced hydrogen carriers, and split into protons (H^+) and electrons.

It will be helpful at this stage to revise the structure of mitochondria (see Unit 1). Electrons pass from one carrier to another in the inner mitochondrial membrane and, as they do, protons are pumped into the space between the inner and the outer mitochondrial membrane. Protons accumulate in this space, setting up a higher concentration here than in the mitochondrial matrix. Protons flow back into the matrix, down their concentration gradient, through a channel in the enzyme ATP synthase. As the protons pass through, their energy is used to phosphorylate ADP to form ATP. Finally, the protons and electrons are combined with oxygen to form water.

A similar process occurs in the thylakoid membranes of chloroplasts, to produce ATP in the light-dependent reactions of photosynthesis. This is described in Unit 13.

In heterotrophic organisms, such as mammals, energy is derived from organic substances including carbohydrates, lipids and proteins. Carbohydrates and proteins yield about $17 kJ g^{-1}$, but using lipids as an energy source yields much more, about $37 kJ g^{-1}$.

The energy yield is related to the number of hydrogen atoms in the molecule. These hydrogens will be used to form reduced NAD and reduced FAD and, ultimately, ATP in the **electron transport chain**. Look again at the structure of a fatty acid and the structure of glucose to remind you of the numbers of carbon and hydrogen atoms in these molecules (see Unit 2).

The term **respiratory quotient (RQ)** means the ratio of the volume of carbon dioxide produced to the volume of oxygen used, in a given time, in respiration.

Consider glucose as a substrate in aerobic respiration, complete oxidation of glucose is shown by the equation:

$$C_6H_{12}O_6 + 6O_2 \rightarrow 6CO_2 + 6H_2O$$

This equation shows that, for each mole of glucose, 6 moles of oxygen are used and 6 moles of carbon dioxide are produced. The RQ value for glucose is, therefore, $6 \div 6 = 1$.

The RQ values for proteins and lipids are different, because of the proportions of oxygen used and carbon dioxide produced. Table 12.01 shows some typical RQ values.

Substrate	RQ value
carbohydrate	1.0
protein	0.8–0.9
lipid	0.7

Table 12.01 Some typical RQ values.

Worked example 12.01

Question

Calculate the RQ value for the complete oxidation of a fatty acid with the formula $CH_3(CH_2)_{14}COOH$.

Answer

To calculate the RQ value, you first need to write a balanced equation for the complete oxidation of this fatty acid:

$$CH_3(CH_2)_{14}COOH + 23O_2 \rightarrow 16CO_2 + 16H_2O$$

You can see from this equation that 23 moles of oxygen are used and 16 moles of carbon dioxide are produced. One mole of oxygen occupies the same volume as 1 mole of carbon dioxide (under standard conditions).

The RQ value is, therefore:

$16 \div 23 = 0.7$ (to one decimal place).

RQ values for living organisms can be determined using a simple respirometer, such as the one shown in Figure 12.01.

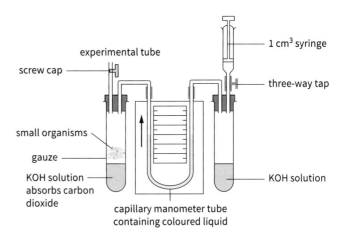

Figure 12.01 A simple respirometer.

This type of respirometer allows you to find both the volume of oxygen used and the volume of carbon dioxide produced by the living organisms.

12.02 Respiration

We can now put together the overall process of respiration, with the individual stages outlined already.

Essentially, aerobic respiration consists of four main stages, as shown in Figure 12.02.

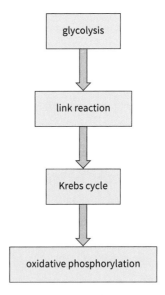

Figure 12.02 The main stages of aerobic respiration.

These stages occur in different parts of a eukaryotic cell, as summarised in Table 12.02.

Stage	Location
glycolysis	cytoplasm
link reaction	mitochondrial matrix
Krebs cycle	mitochondrial matrix
oxidative phosphorylation	inner mitochondrial membrane

Table 12.02 The locations of the stages of aerobic respiration.

Glycolysis is the first main stage of respiration. Glucose is first phosphorylated, using ATP, to form glucose 6-phosphate. Glucose 6-phosphate is then converted into fructose 6-phosphate and, using another molecule of ATP, this is converted into fructose 1,6-bisphosphate.

Fructose 1,6-bisphosphate is then split into two molecules of triose phosphate (glyceraldehyde 3-phosphate). Triose phosphate undergoes a sequence of further reactions, finally forming pyruvate, which is the end product of glycolysis. One of these reactions results in the formation of reduced NAD.

Two of the reactions also result in the synthesis of ATP, from the process of substrate level phosphorylation. Substrate level phosphorylation results in the direct synthesis of ATP, by the transfer of a phosphate group to ADP, which does not involve the electron transport chain. In glycolysis, for every molecule of glucose, two molecules of ATP are used in the first stages but four molecules of ATP are produced by substrate level phosphorylation. There is, therefore, a net gain of two molecules of ATP in glycolysis.

The products of glycolysis are, therefore, **pyruvate**, **ATP** and reduced **NAD**.

Progress check 12.01

In glycolysis, how many molecules of pyruvate are produced from two molecules of glucose?

In the presence of oxygen (i.e. in aerobic conditions) pyruvate enters a mitochondrion and, via the **link reaction**, is converted into an acetyl group. The link reaction involves several steps, but can be summarised by the equation:

pyruvate + CoA + NAD → acetyl CoA + CO_2 + reduced NAD

Notice that carbon dioxide is produced in the link reaction. Pyruvate contains three carbon atoms, but

the acetyl group contains two.

The next main stage of aerobic respiration is the **Krebs cycle**. In the Krebs cycle, a four-carbon compound, oxaloacetate, reacts with the acetyl group from acetyl CoA, forming a six-carbon compound, citrate. Citrate is then converted, in series of reactions, back into oxaloacetate.

You do not need to know all of the individual steps in the Krebs cycle, but you should know the main stages, illustrated Figure 12.03, and the products of the Krebs cycle.

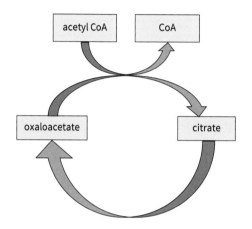

Figure 12.03 The essential steps of the Krebs cycle.

Reactions occurring in the Krebs cycle include decarboxylation, with the removal of carbon dioxide, and dehydrogenation of intermediate substrates resulting in the formation of reduced NAD and reduced FAD. Substrate level phosphorylation also occurs at one stage of the Krebs cycle, resulting in the production of ATP.

In summary, each turn of the Krebs cycle results in the production of:

- two molecules of carbon dioxide
- one molecule of reduced FAD
- three molecules of reduced NAD
- one molecule of ATP.

The final stage of aerobic respiration, oxidative phosphorylation, occurs in the inner mitochondrial membrane. In this process, the reduced hydrogen carriers are oxidised by passing their electrons to a series of carriers, forming the electron transport chain. The protons (H^+), derived from the reduced hydrogen carriers, move into the space between the inner and the outer membranes on the mitochondrion.

Worked example 12.02

Question

In oxidative phosphorylation, each molecule of reduced NAD yields three molecules of ATP and each molecule of reduced FAD yields two molecules of ATP.

Aerobic respiration of one molecule of a fatty acid yields eight molecules of ATP in the Krebs cycle, 31 molecules of reduced NAD and 15 molecules of reduced FAD. Calculate the total number of molecules of ATP produced.

Answer

From the information given, we know that each molecule of reduced NAD yields three molecules of ATP and that each molecule of reduced FAD yields two molecules of ATP in oxidative phosphorylation.

Therefore the total yield of ATP is:

31 × 3 = 93 (from reduced NAD)

and

15 × 2 = 30 (from reduced FAD)

Do not forget that a further eight molecules of ATP are produced in the Krebs cycle, so the total yield of ATP is:

93 + 30 + 8 = 131 molecules

Finally, the protons move back into the mitochondrial matrix, by facilitated diffusion, through a channel in the enzyme ATP synthase, resulting in the phosphorylation of ADP to produce ATP. The protons and electrons combine with oxygen to form water, which is the final product of aerobic respiration.

Most of the ATP produced in aerobic respiration is generated by the process of oxidative phosphorylation, in which the reduced hydrogen carriers are regenerated.

The effect of factors such as temperature on the rate of respiration can be investigated experimentally using redox indicators (artificial hydrogen acceptors). Redox indicators, such as dichlorophenolindophenol (DCPIP) and methylene blue, change colour when they are reduced.

A redox indicator can be added to a suspension of actively respiring yeast cells. The time taken for the indicator to change colour gives an indication of the rate of respiration of the cells.

Sample question 12.01

Tetrazolium chloride (TTC) is a redox indicator. TTC is colourless in the oxidised state, but forms a red compound when it is reduced.

Giving experimental details, explain how you would use a solution of TTC to investigate the effect of temperature on the rate of respiration of yeast cells. Name the independent variable and the dependent variable in this investigation. [10 marks]

[Mark points are shown in square brackets – to a maximum of 10 marks]

The independent variable is temperature and the dependent variable is the time taken for the TTC to change colour. **[2]**

First of all, it would be necessary to set up a set of water baths at a suitable range of temperatures, such as 10 °C, 20 °C, 30 °C, 40 °C and 50 °C. Temperatures can be adjusted by careful heating or use of ice **[2]**.

This answer correctly identifies the independent and the dependent variables. It is important to consider other variables that could affect the results, such as the volumes of TTC solution and yeast suspension. Note the use of the word 'equilibrate', which means that both the TTC solution and the yeast suspension are allowed to reach the temperature of the water bath before they are mixed together. A suitable range of temperatures (minimum five) is suggested.

Test-tubes containing yeast suspension and TTC solution are then placed separately in each water bath and left for the contents to equilibrate to the temperature of the water bath. It is essential that the same volume of TTC solution and of yeast suspension are used at each temperature [2].

The TTC solution and yeast suspensions are then mixed together and the test-tubes containing the mixture are returned to the water baths. As soon as they are mixed, the time is noted [2]. The contents of the test-tubes are then observed and the time taken for each to turn to a red colour is recorded [1]. This gives an indication of the rate of respiration [1]. The longer the time taken for the mixture to turn a red colour, the slower the rate of respiration. The time taken can be converted to a relative rate of reaction by finding the reciprocal of the time (i.e. 1 ÷ time) [1]. The experiment should be repeated at each temperature and the mean times calculated, to ensure that the results are repeatable [1].

Recording the time taken to reach a red colour gives a measure of the rate of respiration, as TTC functions as an artificial hydrogen acceptor, or redox indicator, in respiration. To display the results of this investigation, you could use a table as shown and plot a graph of the results, with the rate of respiration on the y-axis and temperature on the x-axis.

Temperature / °C	Time taken for TTC to turn red / s				Rate of reaction / s⁻¹
	Trial 1	Trial 2	Trial 3	Mean	
10					
20					
30					
40					
50					

Table 12.03

12.03 Anaerobic respiration

So far, we have described **aerobic respiration** – respiration in the presence of oxygen. Anaerobic respiration can also occur in cells if oxygen is unavailable. If there is no oxygen, oxidative phosphorylation cannot occur, so the reduced hydrogen carriers are regenerated in other ways.

In yeast cells and in some plant cells, in the absence of oxygen, pyruvate formed in glycolysis is first converted to ethanal and then into ethanol. The conversion of ethanal into ethanol is a reduction reaction and uses the hydrogens carried by reduced NAD, formed in glycolysis. This regenerates the oxidised form of NAD and allows glycolysis to continue. This process is referred to as **alcoholic fermentation** and is illustrated in Figure 12.04.

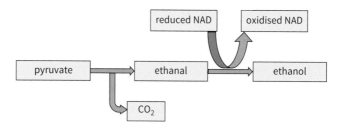

Figure 12.04 Alcoholic fermentation.

No further ATP is produced in alcoholic fermentation, so the net yield of ATP is the same as that from substrate level phosphorylation in glycolysis (i.e. two molecules of ATP per molecule of glucose). This is much less than that produced under aerobic conditions.

To summarise, the products of alcoholic fermentation are:

- ethanol
- carbon dioxide
- ATP.

A different form of anaerobic respiration occurs in muscle tissue and some types of microorganisms, when there is a shortage of oxygen, resulting in the production of lactate. This is known as lactic fermentation and is illustrated in Figure 12.05.

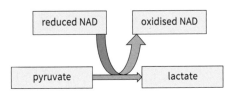

Figure 12.05 Lactic fermentation.

The conversion of pyruvate (from glycolysis) to lactate regenerates the oxidised form of NAD so that glycolysis can continue. Lactate is a 3-carbon compound and no carbon dioxide is produced. As with alcoholic fermentation, no further ATP is produced, so the net yield of ATP is two molecules per molecule of glucose.

Lactic fermentation occurs in muscle during short bursts of vigorous contraction, such as a sprint. Accumulation of lactate in muscle tissue results in an 'oxygen debt' in which extra oxygen is required to remove the lactate.

Progress check 12.02

Explain the fate of lactate after vigorous activity.

12.04 Adaptations of rice to anaerobic conditions

Rice plants are often grown in flooded fields, known as paddies (Figure 12.06).

The roots of the rice plants, growing in silt under water, receive little oxygen and respire anaerobically, producing ethanol. Ethanol is toxic to tissues and rice plants have a number of adaptations to growing in these conditions:

- the plants grow taller so the leaves have access to oxygen in the atmosphere
- stems and roots have loosely packed cells, forming aerenchyma, with large air spaces that allow diffusion of oxygen from aerial parts to the submerged roots
- rice plants contain high levels of the enzyme alcohol dehydrogenase; when oxygen is available, this enzyme rapidly converts ethanol back to ethanal
- rice tissues are relatively tolerant to ethanol, much of which is lost via adventitious roots.

Figure 12.06 A rice paddy.

Progress check 12.03

List three ways in which rice plants are adapted to living in waterlogged conditions.

12.05 Effect of temperature on respiration

A simple respirometer, such as that shown in Figure 12.01, can be used to investigate the effect of temperature on the respiration rate of germinating seeds or small invertebrates. To maintain the respirometer at a constant temperature, the experimental tube and the compensating tube should be immersed in a water bath. Sufficient time must be allowed for the apparatus to equilibrate to the temperature and for the organisms to adjust.

Revision checklist

Check that you know:

- [ ] why living organisms need energy, with reference to anabolic reactions, active transport, movement and the maintenance of body temperature

- [ ] the features of ATP as the universal energy currency

- [ ] ATP is synthesised in reactions in glycolysis and the Krebs cycle

- [ ] the roles of the coenzymes NAD, FAD and coenzyme A in respiration

- [ ] the synthesis of ATP is associated with the electron transport chain

- [ ] the relative energy values of carbohydrates, lipid and protein as respiratory substrates

- [ ] the term respiratory quotient (RQ) and how to determine RQs from equations for respiration

- [ ] how to carry out investigations using simple respirometers to determine RQ values

- [ ] the four stages in aerobic respiration and where each occurs in eukaryotic cells

- [ ] the process of glycolysis, in outline

- [ ] in the presence of oxygen, pyruvate is converted to acetyl CoA in the link reaction

- [ ] the main steps of the Krebs cycle

- [ ] the reactions in the Krebs cycle that involve decarboxylation and dehydrogenation and the reduction of coenzymes

- [ ] the process of oxidative phosphorylation

- [ ] investigations to determine the effect of factors such as temperature and substrate concentration on the rate of respiration of yeast using an indicator

- [ ] the relationship between structure and function of mitochondria

- [ ] the differences between aerobic and anaerobic respiration in mammalian tissue and in yeast

- [ ] the yield of ATP from anaerobic respiration and the concept of an oxygen debt

- [ ] how rice is adapted to grow with its roots submerged in water

- [ ] how to carry out investigations to measure the effect of temperature on the respiration rate of germinating seeds or small invertebrates.

Exam-style questions

1 Giving experimental details, explain how you would use a respirometer to make a valid comparison between the respiration rate of germinating barley with the respiration rate of germinating peas. [10]

Total: 10

2 With reference to the link reaction, explain what is meant by each of the following terms.

a Decarboxylation [3]

b Dehydrogenation [3]

Total: 6

3 a Define the term respiratory quotient (RQ). [1]

b Name the parts of a eukaryotic cell in which the following stages of respiration take place:

i glycolysis

ii the link reaction

iii the Krebs cycle

iv oxidative phosphorylation

v anaerobic respiration. [5]

Total: 6

Photosynthesis

Photosynthesis converts the simple inorganic substances carbon dioxide and water into complex organic compounds and releases oxygen as a waste product. During the process light energy is absorbed by chloroplast pigments and converted into the chemical energy of the products.

13.01 An overview of photosynthesis

Photosynthesis consists of two stages (Figure 13.01).

Because the reactions in the first stage use light energy, they are known as the **light-dependent reactions**. In this stage light is used to split water molecules into hydrogen and oxygen. Hydrogen atoms from the water are eventually used in the second stage to reduce carbon dioxide to carbohydrate. Because the reactions of the second stage do not use light energy directly, they are called the **light-independent reactions**.

The light-independent reactions use chemical energy in the form of ATP, which is generated by the

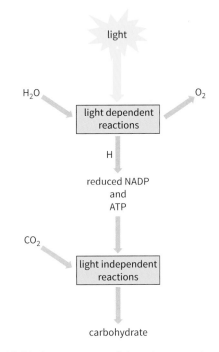

Figure 13.01 A summary of the photosynthesis reactions.

light-dependent reactions. The hydrogen atoms from the light-dependent stage are also not used directly, but transferred to carbon dioxide via a coenzyme called nicotinamide adenine dinucleotide phosphate (NADP). This carrier molecule transfers hydrogen as reduced NADP (sometimes called NADPH).

Both the light-dependent reactions and the light-independent reactions take place inside chloroplasts.

13.02 Chloroplasts

Chloroplasts are organelles found within the green parts of plants, particularly leaf mesophyll cells (Figure 13.02). They are surrounded by a double membrane or envelope and contain many internal membranes called lamellae. The membranes contain a number of different pigments, including **chlorophyll**, which gives the chloroplasts their green colour. The membrane proteins are associated with chlorophyll molecules, forming complexes called **photosystems**. There are two types of photosystem, called photosystem I (PSI) and photosystem II (PSII), containing different photosynthetic pigments.

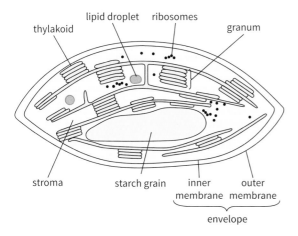

Figure 13.02 The structure of a chloroplast.

The lamellae form membrane-bound sacs called **thylakoids**. In places the thylakoids are arranged in stacks called **grana** (singular = granum). The thylakoids are the site of the light-dependent reactions. Surrounding the thylakoids is the fluid-filled matrix of the chloroplast called the **stroma**, where the light-independent reactions take place.

Chloroplasts often contain stores of energy-containing compounds that have been made by photosynthesis, such as starch grains and lipid droplets.

Progress check 13.01

1   Name the two stages of photosynthesis.

2   State where in the chloroplast the following take place:

   a   The light-dependent reactions.

   b   The light-independent reactions.

13.03 The light-dependent reactions

Four key things happen during the light-dependent reactions:

- light energy excites electrons in chlorophyll molecules, raising their energy level

- energy from the excited electrons is used to make ATP

- light is used to split water molecules into oxygen and hydrogen

- the hydrogen is used to reduce NADP

The processes can be summarised as a diagram called the 'Z-scheme' (Figure 13.03). The events taking place in Figure 13.03 have been numbered to make them easier to identify in the description below.

Chlorophyll molecules in PSI and PSII absorb light energy, raising them to a higher energy level (1). The excited electrons are emitted by the chlorophyll and taken up by acceptor molecules (2). This is effectively the point at which light energy is converted into chemical energy. Both photosystems lose electrons in this way, leaving the chlorophyll oxidised and the acceptor molecule reduced. So that photosynthesis can continue, the chlorophyll must be reduced again by replacement of the missing electrons. This takes place in a different way in the two photosystems.

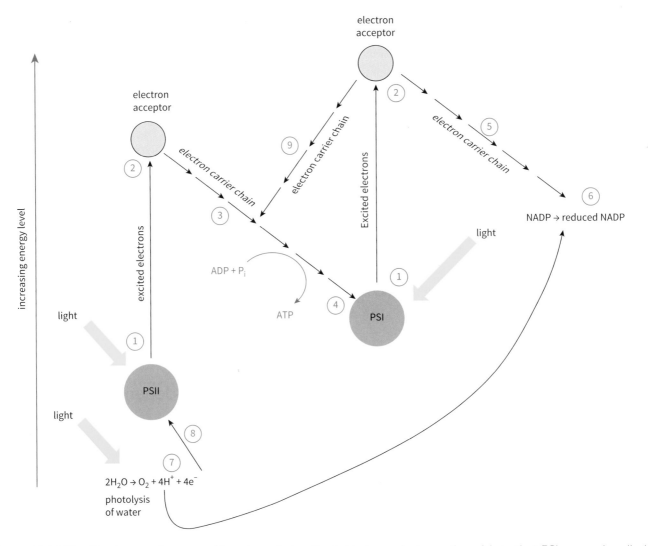

electron
acceptor

electron
acceptor

②

electron carrier chain

⑨

electron carrier chain

⑤

electron carrier chain

②

③

increasing energy level

excited electrons

Excited electrons

NADP → reduced NADP

⑥

light

ADP + Pᵢ

light

ATP

④

①

①

PSI

light

PSII

⑧

⑦

$2H_2O \rightarrow O_2 + 4H^+ + 4e^-$

photolysis
of water

Figure 13.03 The Z-scheme of events taking place during the light-dependent reactions. Note that PSI was only called this because it was discovered first – the process really starts with PSII.

The electrons emitted from PSII are passed along a chain of electron carriers ③. As they move from one carrier to the next, each carrier becomes reduced and then re-oxidised in a series of redox reactions. Each carrier in the chain has a lower energy level than the previous one, so that as the electrons are passed along, energy is released and used to synthesise ATP from ADP and inorganic phosphate (Pᵢ). This process is driven by light energy, so it is called **photophosphorylation**. The coupling of electron transport through the chain to ATP synthesis involves a mechanism very similar to that of ATP synthesis in mitochondria. Energy is used to pump protons into the space inside each thylakoid. This forms a proton gradient. Protons move out through the thylakoid membrane again through an ATP synthase, generating ATP.

At the end of the carrier chain, electrons are taken up by PSI, replacing those lost by that photosystem ④.

Note that photophosphorylation is similar to the oxidative phosphorylation that occurs during respiration, but uses light energy rather than chemical energy.

Electrons emitted from PSI are taken up by a different acceptor molecule and passed along a different chain of electron carriers ⑤. At the end of this chain they combine with hydrogen ions and NADP to form reduced NADP ⑥. The hydrogen ions for this reaction are supplied by the **photolysis** of water ⑦. PSII contains an enzyme that is activated by light, splitting water into oxygen and hydrogen atoms. Each hydrogen atom loses an electron, forming hydrogen ions (protons), H^+:

$$2H_2O \xrightarrow{\text{light}} O_2 + 4H^+ + 4e^-$$

The oxygen atoms combine to form molecular oxygen, which diffuses out of the chloroplast into the air around the leaf. The electrons are used to replace those emitted from chlorophyll in PSII ⑧.

a Cyclic and non-cyclic photophosphorylation

The formation of ATP by the Z-scheme is called *non-cyclic* photophosphorylation, because electrons lost from the chlorophyll pigments in PSI and PSII are not returned to these pigments to reduce them again. The end products of this process are ATP and reduced NADP.

Electrons from PSI may also be passed straight back to that photosystem through a chain of carriers linked to those from PSII ⑨. This is called *cyclic* photophosphorylation, and results in ATP synthesis, but no production of NADP.

Progress check 13.02

1   Write an equation for the photolysis of water.

2   What is photophosphorylation ?

3   What are the products of:

    a   non-cyclic photophosphorylation

    b   cyclic photophosphorylation ?

13.04 The light-independent reactions

The light-independent reactions take place in the stroma of the chloroplast. Using ATP for energy and reduced NADP to supply reducing power, carbon dioxide is converted into carbohydrate via a metabolic pathway called the **Calvin cycle** (Figure 13.04).

Carbon dioxide diffuses from air spaces in the leaf and dissolves in the watery layer around the

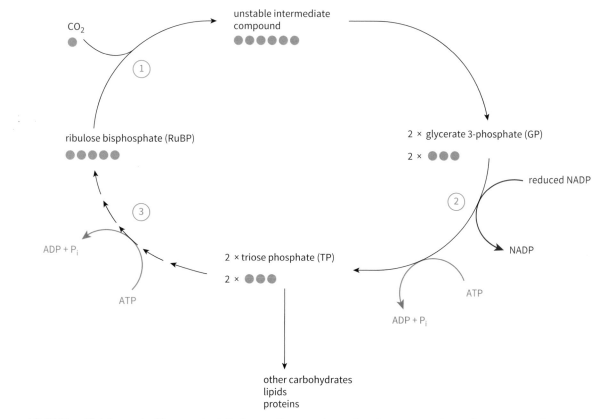

Figure 13.04 The Calvin cycle. The symbol ● shows the number of carbon atoms in each compound.

Unit 13 Photosynthesis

123

mesophyll cells. It diffuses into the cells and into the stroma of a chloroplast. Here it combines with a 5-carbon compound called **ribulose bisphosphate** (RuBP). The reaction is catalysed by an enzyme called ribulose bisphosphate carboxylase, known as **rubisco**. This step, when carbon dioxide is incorporated into an organic compound, is called carbon dioxide fixation ①.

TIP

You may see RuBP referred to as the carbon dioxide acceptor molecule.

The product of this reaction is an unstable 6-carbon compound, which immediately breaks down into two molecules of a 3-carbon compound called glycerate 3-phosphate. Both molecules of glycerate 3-phosphate are then phosphorylated and reduced, using ATP and reduced NADP from the light-dependent reaction ②. The product is a 3-carbon compound called **triose phosphate**. Triose phosphate is the first carbohydrate to be produced by photosynthesis.

Most of the triose phosphate is used to regenerate RuBP, allowing the Calvin cycle to continue ③. For every six molecules of triose phosphate made (i.e. three 'turns' of the cycle) only one is used to make products of photosynthesis, while the other five are recycled to make more RuBP. It requires six turns of the cycle to make one molecule of glucose.

Conversion of triose phosphate into other organic compounds

By reversing some of the reactions of respiration, a plant can convert triose phosphate into 6-carbon sugars such as glucose and fructose (Figure 13.05). Monosaccharides can be combined to form disaccharides such as sucrose, which is the main sugar transported in the phloem. They can also be turned into polysaccharides such as starch for storage and cellulose for making cell walls.

Triose phosphate can be converted into glycerol and also into pyruvate, from which fatty acids can be formed. Glycerol and fatty acids provide the building blocks of the lipids used in cell membranes and for energy storage.

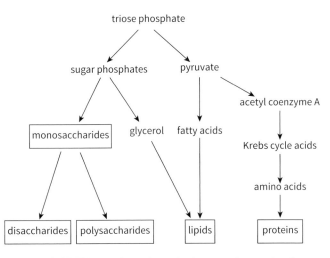

Figure 13.05 Triose phosphate is the starting point for making many organic compounds.

Triose phosphate can also be converted into acetyl coenzyme A, which is used in respiration. Acetyl groups from this compound enter the Krebs cycle, where they form organic acids. These can be combined with nitrogen to make amino acids, the building blocks of proteins.

Progress check 13.03

Copy and complete the following paragraph:

The enzyme rubisco catalyses the fixation of .... by ribulose bisphosphate (RuBP). The resulting 6-carbon compound immediately breaks down into two molecules of .... This compound is converted into triose phosphate (TP) using .... and .... produced by the light-dependent stage of photosynthesis. Some triose phosphate is used to regenerate ribulose bisphosphate so that the Calvin cycle can continue. The remaining triose phosphate is used to synthesise other compounds, including .... which can pass directly into the Krebs cycle.

13.05 Chloroplast pigments

A pigment is a coloured substance that absorbs light of certain wavelengths. The colour of a pigment depends on which light wavelength the pigment reflects (e.g. a green pigment reflects mainly green light). Chloroplasts contain several different pigments. There are two main groups: chlorophylls and carotenoids (Table 13.01).

Group	Name of pigment	Colour of pigment
chlorophylls	chlorophyll *a*	blue-green
	chlorophyll *b*	yellow-green
carotenoids	β-carotene	orange
	xanthophyll	yellow

Table 13.01 The main types of chloroplast pigments.

Chlorophyll *a* is the most abundant photosynthetic pigment. Its light absorption peaks are at wavelengths 430 nm (blue) and 662 nm (red). When it absorbs light it emits excited electrons that are taken up by acceptor molecules in the light-dependent reactions (Figure 13.03). For this reason, chlorophyll *a* is known as the **primary pigment**. Chlorophyll *b* and the carotenoids are **accessory pigments**. They absorb different wavelengths and transfer energy from the light to chlorophyll *a* in the two photosystems.

The wavelengths of light absorbed by each pigment can be shown by a graph called an **absorption spectrum** (Figure 13.06).

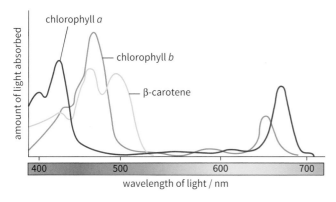

Figure 13.06 Absorption spectra for different chloroplast pigments.

The pigments absorb light mainly in the blue and red ends of the spectrum, while there is little absorption of green light. The absorption spectra of the chlorophylls and carotenoids are somewhat different, which increases the range of wavelengths that can be absorbed.

The absorption spectra suggest that blue and red light will work best for photosynthesis, while green is less effective. This is confirmed by an **action spectrum**, which shows the rate of photosynthesis against wavelength (Figure 13.07). The shape of the action spectrum is similar to that of the absorption spectrum for the combined chloroplast pigments, as you might expect.

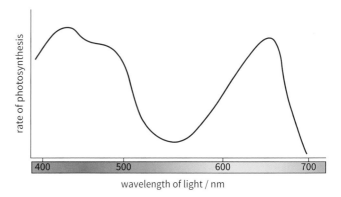

Figure 13.07 An action spectrum. The rate of photosynthesis can be found by measuring the release of oxygen from a suspension of isolated chloroplasts.

Separating chloroplast pigments using paper chromatography

Chromatography is a method of separating a mixture of substances on the basis of their solubility in a solvent. The simplest method is paper chromatography. To extract the pigments, some leaves are ground up with propanone using a pestle and mortar. A small concentrated spot of the extract is placed on a pencil line at one end of a strip of filter paper. The paper is then dipped in a suitable solvent, such as a mixture of 10% propanone to 90% hexane. The solvent rises up the paper, taking the pigments with it. Pigments that are more soluble in the solvent travel further up the paper, closer to the solvent front (Figure 13.08).

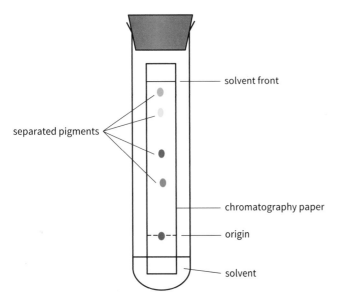

Figure 13.08 Chromatography of chloroplast pigments.

The relative positions of the different pigments will always be the same for a particular solvent. The pigments can be identified by their R_f **values**:

R_f value = distance travelled by the pigment from the origin/distance travelled by the solvent front from the origin

The R_f value is a decimal fraction between 0 and 1. For example, the orange pigment β-carotene is very soluble in the solvent described above and has an R_f value of 0.95. Chlorophyll *a* is less soluble in this solvent and has an R_f value of 0.65. Measurements are taken from the origin to the centre of each spot.

Worked example 13.01

Question

Chloroplast pigments were separated by paper chromatography. The distance from the origin to the solvent front was 76 mm. One of the separated pigments was found to be 32 mm from the origin. Calculate the R_f value for this pigment.

Answer

R_f value = distance travelled by the pigment from the origin/distance travelled by the solvent front from the origin

= 32 mm/76 mm

= 0.42 (to two significant figures)

(Note that the R_f value is a ratio and has no units – the mm cancel out.)

Progress check 13.04

1   Name the primary pigment of photosynthesis.

2   What is the function of accessory chloroplast pigments?

3   Explain the difference between an absorption spectrum and an action spectrum.

13.06 Limiting factors in photosynthesis

A number of environmental factors affect the rate of photosynthesis:

* *Light intensity.* Light is needed as the energy source for the light-dependent reactions, so light intensity affects the rate.

* *Temperature.* The light-independent reactions are affected by temperature. A higher temperature increases the kinetic energy of molecules. They collide more frequently and with higher energy, so that the enzyme-catalysed reactions are more likely to take place (temperature does not affect the light-dependent reactions).

* *Concentration of carbon dioxide.* Carbon dioxide is fixed in the light-independent reactions. Atmospheric air contains less than 0.04% carbon dioxide, which can limit the rate of photosynthesis if other factors such as light intensity are not a problem.

* *Availability of water.* Water is required for the light-dependent reactions. Usually there is enough water available for photosynthesis. However, a lack of water may affect the rate indirectly, by causing a plant to close its stomata and reduce the uptake of carbon dioxide.

The rate at which photosynthesis proceeds depends on the slowest step in the process. For example, if the concentration of carbon dioxide in the air was very low, its fixation by RuBP would slow down the rest of the process. In this situation carbon dioxide concentration restricts or limits the rate. Similarly, low light intensity (e.g. at night) can limit the rate. We call the factor which 'holds back' the rate the

limiting factor. In any particular set of environmental conditions only one factor can be the limiting factor. You can understand this better from Figure 13.09.

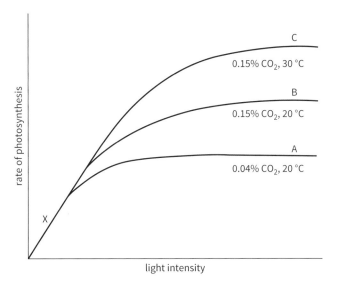

Figure 13.09 Light intensity, carbon dioxide concentration and temperature can all act as limiting factors in photosynthesis.

At point X on the graph, light intensity is the limiting factor, because an increase in light intensity increases the rate of photosynthesis. At point A, the limiting factor is the concentration of carbon dioxide, and neither temperature nor light intensity are limiting. If the concentration of carbon dioxide is raised (point B) carbon dioxide is no longer the limiting factor, and another factor becomes limiting, in this case temperature. Raising the temperature (point C) raises the rate even more.

Remember that above about 40 °C enzymes are denatured, causing the rate to fall again at higher temperatures.

a Limiting factors and crop yields

An understanding of limiting factors is used to increase crop yields of plants grown in glasshouses, where environmental conditions can be controlled (Figure 13.10).

- artificial lighting increases the light intensity for photosynthesis (the lights can also be left on to extend the day length)

- the glasshouse reduces heat losses and increases the temperature in which the plants grow; heating systems can also be employed

- heating systems that burn fossil fuels such as gas increase the concentration of carbon dioxide in the air around the plants.

These methods make sure that photosynthesis is less restricted by natural limiting factors. Growth of the plants is increased, increasing crop yield. (Growing plants in glasshouses also makes it easier to control pests, weeds and supply of minerals.)

Figure 13.10 Tomato plants growing in a glasshouse under controlled conditions.

13.07 Investigating the rate of photosynthesis using an aquatic plant

The simplest way to investigate the effect of environmental factors on the rate of photosynthesis is to measure the rate of production of oxygen in an aquatic plant. There are a number of ways this can be done, such as using the apparatus shown in Figure 13.11

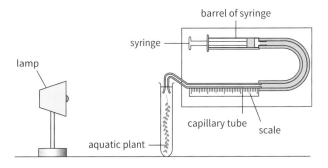

Figure 13.11 Apparatus for measuring the rate of photosynthesis in an aquatic plant.

1 A fresh piece of an aquatic plant is cut and placed upside down in the test-tube of water.

2 Bubbles of oxygen are collected in the flared end of the capillary tube.

3 After a measured period of time the oxygen is drawn into the capillary tube using the syringe.

4 The length of gas bubble in the syringe is measured. The length of the bubble per unit time is a measure of the rate of photosynthesis.

Using this method, you can investigate the effects of changing factors such as light intensity, carbon dioxide concentration and temperature.

- Light intensity is changed by changing the distance of the lamp from the plant. The closer the lamp, the higher the light intensity.

- Aquatic plants obtain their carbon dioxide as hydrogencarbonate ions from the water. The concentration of these ions can be varied by adding small amounts of sodium hydrogencarbonate to the water in the test-tube.

- Temperature can be maintained by placing the test-tube in a beaker of water to act as a water bath. The temperature of the water is monitored using a thermometer. The temperature can be varied over a suitable physiological range (e.g. 10–30 °C).

Whichever factor you investigate, you should aim to maintain the other factors constant. For example, if you vary the concentration of carbon dioxide, you should keep the lamp at a fixed distance from the plant and use a water bath at a constant temperature.

13.08 Investigating the rate of photosynthesis using a suspension of chloroplasts

A suspension of chloroplasts can be isolated from leaves of a plant such as spinach by liquidising the leaves in ice-cold buffer solution, then filtering or centrifuging the mixture to remove unwanted cell debris. When exposed to light, the chloroplasts carry out photolysis, splitting water into hydrogen ions, electrons and oxygen gas. This was discovered by the biochemist Robert Hill, and is known as the Hill reaction. In the plant cell the Hill reaction generates the 'reducing power' which is used to reduce NADP.

In this investigation a redox indicator such as dichlorophenolindophenol (DCPIP) is added, which changes colour when reduced:

oxidised DCPIP → reduced DCPIP
(blue)   (colourless)

This colour change is used to monitor the Hill reaction. The suspension is kept cold (0–4 °C) throughout the procedure to reduce the activity of proteolytic enzymes, which could damage the chloroplasts.

1 A freshly made suspension of chloroplasts in buffer is placed in a small cold tube and kept in the dark until used.

2 DCPIP solution is added to the tube, the tube shaken and the time noted.

3 The tube is placed at a fixed distance from a bright light from a bench lamp.

4 At suitable intervals, the tube is placed in a colorimeter with a red filter and the absorbance of the contents recorded.

Figure 13.12 shows a typical set of results. The rate of loss of blue colour (the slope of the curve) is proportional to the rate of production of reducing power by the chloroplasts in the Hill reaction.

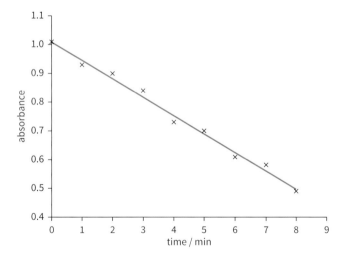

Figure 13.12 Colorimeter readings showing the loss of colour of DCPIP due to the Hill reaction in isolated chloroplasts illuminated by white light.

This method can be adapted to investigate the effect of light intensity on the rate, by moving the lamp to change the light intensity. The effects of different light wavelengths can be found by placing coloured filters in front of the lamp (Figure 13.13).

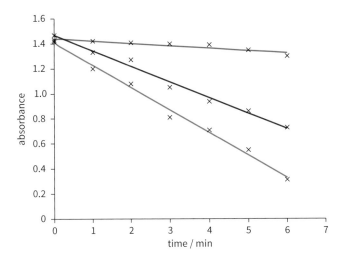

Figure 13.13 Colorimeter readings showing the loss of colour of DCPIP due to the Hill reaction in isolated chloroplasts illuminated by different wavelengths (colours) of light.

Progress check 13.05

1   On a bright, hot summer day, what environmental factor is most likely to limit the rate of photosynthesis in a plant ?

2   An understanding of limiting factors can be used to increase crop yields in a glasshouse. Describe three ways glasshouses can be adapted to reduce the effects of limiting factors.

3   a   Name a redox indicator that can be used to investigate photosynthesis in a suspension of chloroplasts.

    b   State the colour of this indicator in its oxidised and reduced forms.

13.09 C4 plants

In most plants, fixation of carbon dioxide happens via the enzyme rubisco, which combines the carbon dioxide with RuBP. These plants are called **C3 plants**, because the first stable product of the Calvin cycle is the 3-carbon compound glycerate 3-phosphate.

In certain environmental conditions, C3 plants have problems fixing carbon dioxide:

- On hot, dry days, stomata close. This reduces the concentration of carbon dioxide in the air spaces of the leaves, so that less is available to enter the Calvin cycle, limiting the rate of photosynthesis.

- At high temperatures and high light intensity, rubisco binds oxygen to RuBP in place of carbon dioxide. This reaction is called **photorespiration**. It results in RuBP being broken down into carbon dioxide and water. Like true respiration, photorespiration is an oxidative process, but it does not produce any ATP, and again means that less carbon dioxide is fixed.

Some plants have evolved a way of avoiding these problems. They use an alternative method of fixing carbon dioxide that produces a 4-carbon compound in the light-independent reaction. For this reason, they are called **C4 plants**. There are thousands of species of C4 plants. They are adapted to live in environments with a high light intensity and hot, dry conditions. Many are tropical grasses, and include important cultivated species, such as maize, sugar cane and sorghum.

Combined with this mechanism of C4 photosynthesis, C4 plants have a distinctive leaf anatomy. In their leaves they have two types of photosynthetic cells called **bundle sheath cells** and **mesophyll cells**, arranged in two rings around the vascular bundles (Figure 13.14).

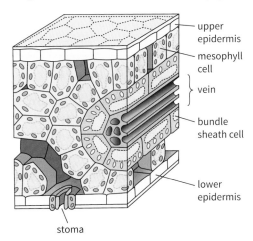

Figure 13.14 The arrangement of photosynthetic tissues in the leaf of a C4 plant.

Carbon dioxide is absorbed by the ring of mesophyll cells. Here, an enzyme called PEP carboxylase catalyses the combination of carbon dioxide from the air with a 3-carbon compound called phosphoenolpyruvate (PEP). This produces a 4-carbon compound called oxaloacetate (Figure 13.15). This uses reduced NADP and ATP from the light-dependent reactions.

The oxaloacetate is converted into another 4-carbon compound called malate, which enters the bundle sheath cells through plasmodesmata. In these cells carbon dioxide is removed from malate, passed to RuBP and enters the Calvin cycle, generating carbohydrates in the normal way. This decarboxylation generates the 3-carbon compound pyruvate, which is used to regenerate PEP in the bundle sheath cells.

The location of the bundle sheath cells isolates them from the air spaces in the outer part of the leaf, keeping them away from oxygen and preventing photorespiration. C4 plants have other adaptations, such as enzymes with a higher than normal optimum temperature.

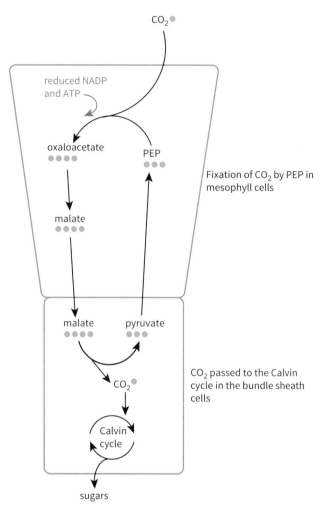

Fixation of CO_2 by PEP in mesophyll cells

CO_2 passed to the Calvin cycle in the bundle sheath cells

Figure 13.15 Photosynthesis in a C4 plant. The symbol ● shows the number of carbon atoms in each compound.

Sample question 13.01

Explain how the leaves of a C4 plant such as maize or sorghum is adapted to carry out efficient carbon fixation at high temperatures. [8]

In the light-independent reactions, C3 plants fix carbon dioxide by combining it with ribulose bisphosphate (RuBP). This reaction is catalysed by the enzyme ribulose bisphosphate carboxylase (rubisco). However, at high temperatures rubisco binds to oxygen, meaning there is less rubisco available to catalyse the reaction with carbon dioxide. This unwanted reaction with oxygen is called photorespiration. C4 plants have evolved physiological and structural adaptations to avoid photorespiration.

This question requires a longer written answer summarising the adaptation of C4 plants in a logical sequence.

This is a very complete and detailed answer. Hopefully you will be able to cover all this information, but there will be more mark points available than the 8 marks given for the question – you can afford to miss some points but still gain full marks.

In the leaf of a C4 plant there are two types of photosynthetic cells called bundle sheath cells and mesophyll cells, arranged in rings around vascular bundles. The light-dependent stage takes place in the outer ring of mesophyll cells, producing reduced NADP and ATP. Instead of fixing carbon dioxide to RuBP in these cells, C4 plants combine CO_2 with a 3-carbon compound called phosphoenolpyruvate (PEP), employing an enzyme called PEP carboxylase. This produces a 4-carbon compound called oxaloacetate. The oxaloacetate is converted into another 4-carbon compound called malate, which enters the bundle sheath cells. In these cells carbon dioxide is removed from malate, combines with RuBP and enters the Calvin cycle, generating carbohydrates in the normal way. This decarboxylation generates the 3-carbon compound pyruvate, which is used to regenerate PEP in the bundle sheath cells.

These adaptations mean that rubisco and fixation of CO_2 to RuBP is located away from oxygen in the outer mesophyll cells, preventing photorespiration and allowing the Calvin cycle to continue. The biochemical pathways also benefit from enzymes that have high optimum temperatures.

Go through the sample answer and tick off the following mark points:
In C3 plants:
- in C3 plants at high temperatures rubisco combines with oxygen / photorespiration occurs
- there is less rubisco to combine with CO_2

In C4 plants:
- the mesophyll cells absorb CO_2
- CO_2 reacts with PEP
- forms oxaloacetate
- converted to malate
- malate passes to bundle sheath cells
- CO_2 released to combine with RuBP (in bundle sheath cells)
- this keeps rubisco away from oxygen
- avoids photorespiration
- allows Calvin cycle to continue
- enzymes involved have high optimum temperatures.

Revision checklist

Check that you know:

- [ ] an overview of photosynthesis
- [ ] the structure of a chloroplast
- [ ] the light-dependent reactions of photosynthesis
- [ ] the light-independent reactions of photosynthesis
- [ ] the role of chloroplast pigments
- [ ] the formation and uses of other products of photosynthesis
- [ ] absorption and action spectra of chloroplast pigments
- [ ] chromatography of chloroplast pigments

- [ ] limiting factors and their effects on the rate of photosynthesis
- [ ] how to use knowledge of limiting factors to increase crop yields
- [ ] how to investigate the effects of environmental factors on the rate of photosynthesis in an aquatic plant
- [ ] how to investigate the effects of light intensity and wavelength on the rate of photosynthesis in isolated chloroplasts
- [ ] adaptations of C4 plants.

Exam-style questions

1 Figure 13.16 is an electron micrograph of a chloroplast.

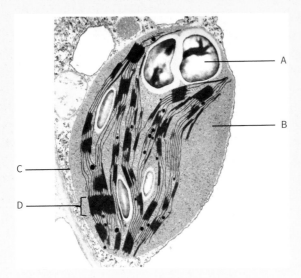

Figure 13.16

a Identify the parts of the chloroplast labelled A–D. [4]

b Indicate which of A, B, C or D:

   i   contains chloroplast pigments

   ii is the site of the light-independent reactions. [2]

c The rate of photosynthesis may be affected by light intensity, carbon dioxide concentration and temperature. These factors affect different stages of photosynthesis. Copy and complete Table 13.02 using a tick (✔) if the factor directly affects the stage of photosynthesis or a cross (✗) if it does not affect the stage. [3]

Total: 9

Factor	Stage	✔ or ✗
light intensity	photolysis	
	Calvin cycle	
carbon dioxide concentration	photolysis	
	Calvin cycle	
temperature	photolysis	
	Calvin cycle	

Table 13.02

2 The light-dependent stage of photosynthesis involves photolysis of water and photophosphorylation.

a Write a balanced equation for photolysis. [1]

b Explain the meaning of photophosphorylation. [2]

c Describe the role of accessory pigments in photophosphorylation. [2]

d Describe the roles of the following in the light-independent stage of photosynthesis:

   i   RuBP [2]

   ii reduced NADP [2]

   iii ATP. [2]

Total: 11

3 The apparatus shown in Figure 13.11 was used to investigate the effect of light intensity on photosynthesis in an aquatic plant. A bubble of gas from the plant was collected in the capillary tube. The distance moved by the bubble over a fixed period of time was used to calculate the rate of photosynthesis. The light intensity was varied by changing the distance of the lamp from the plant. A small amount of sodium hydrogencarbonate was added to the water in the test-tube. The results are given in Table 13.03

Light intensity / arbitrary units	Rate of photosynthesis / arbitrary units
0	0
5	16
10	33
15	49
20	56
25	60
30	60

Table 13.03

a Plot a graph to show the relationship between light intensity and the rate of photosynthesis. [3]

b With reference to limiting factors, explain the shape of the graph you have drawn. [3]

c Explain why sodium hydrogencarbonate was added to the water in the test-tube. [1]

Total: 7

4 a Describe an absorption spectrum of chloroplast pigments. [3]

   b Explain how an action spectrum differs from an absorption spectrum. [1]

Total: 4

Homeostasis

Learning outcomes

When you have finished this unit, you should be able to:

☐ understand the importance of homeostasis in mammals

☐ explain the principles of homeostasis in terms of internal and external stimuli, receptors, central control, coordination systems and effectors (muscles and glands)

☐ define the term negative feedback and explain how it is involved in homeostasis

☐ outline the roles of the nervous system and endocrine system in coordinating homeostatic mechanisms, including thermoregulation, osmoregulation and the control of blood glucose concentration

☐ describe the deamination of amino acids and outline the formation of urea in the urea cycle

☐ describe the structure of the kidney and the nephron, with its associated blood vessels

☐ describe the processes involved with the formation of urine in the nephron

☐ describe the roles of the hypothalamus, posterior pituitary, antidiuretic hormone and collecting ducts in osmoregulation

☐ explain how the blood glucose concentration is regulated, with reference to insulin and glucagon

☐ outline the role of cyclic AMP as a second messenger

☐ describe the three main steps of cell signalling in the control of blood glucose by adrenaline

☐ explain the principles of dip sticks and biosensors for the quantitative measurements of glucose in blood and urine

☐ explain how urine analysis is used in diagnosis with reference to glucose, protein and ketones

☐ explain that stomata have daily rhythms of opening and closing

☐ describe the structure and function of guard cells

☐ describe the role of abscisic acid in the closure of stomata in times of water stress, including the role of calcium ions.

14.01 Homeostasis in mammals

The term **homeostasis** refers to the regulation of the internal environment of an organism. In mammals, for example, a number of different factors are controlled so that they are kept within narrow limits. In humans, core body temperature is maintained between 36 and 37.5 °C, although the external temperature can vary widely. The term internal environment refers to the composition of blood and body fluids. Factors that are controlled by homeostatic mechanisms in mammals include:

- body temperature
- body water content
- blood pH
- blood glucose concentration

- metabolic waste products, such as urea

- the respiratory gases oxygen and carbon dioxide.

Homeostatic systems must be able to detect changes and to bring about an appropriate response. For example, in the regulation of body temperature, a rise in body temperature is detected and the appropriate response is made to counter the increase, bringing the temperature back to its set value. Homeostatic systems therefore require receptors that are capable of detecting internal or external stimuli, central control and coordination mechanisms, and **effectors** to bring about the appropriate response.

Homeostatic systems involve the principle of **negative feedback**, which means that they are self-correcting. They operate to return a factor to its set point, so if the factor increases, negative feedback brings about a change to decrease the factor. Similarly, if a factor decreases, negative feedback opposes the change and increases the factor. In this way, the factor does not stay exactly constant, but fluctuates between closely controlled values.

Homeostatic mechanisms are coordinated by the nervous system and nerve impulses, the endocrine system and hormones or a combination of both. As examples, changes in skin blood flow to adjust heat loss by radiation are brought about by nerve impulses; blood glucose concentration is controlled by several hormones, secreted by endocrine organs in the body. Body water content is controlled by **antidiuretic hormone (ADH)**, secreted by the posterior pituitary gland.

Progress check 14.01

Draw a flow diagram to show how negative feedback is involved in the regulation of body temperature in a mammal.

Excess amino acids, from the digestion of proteins, are not stored in the body, but undergo a process of deamination in the liver. This results in the formation of a keto acid and ammonia. The keto acid can be used as a source of energy, or converted to various other compounds including glycogen and fat.

Ammonia is highly toxic to cells and, in mammals, is immediately converted into urea, through a cycle of reactions, in the liver, known as the urea cycle.

You do not need to know the biochemical details of the urea cycle, but it involves combining ammonia with carbon dioxide, to form urea:

ammonia + carbon dioxide → urea + water

Urea is much less toxic than ammonia and is soluble in water. Urea is carried in the bloodstream from the liver and is filtered out of the blood in the kidneys and lost in the urine.

TIP

Be careful not to confuse urea and urine. They are not the same!

a The kidney

Each kidney, in section, can be seen to consist of an outer **cortex** and an inner **medulla** (Figure 14.01)

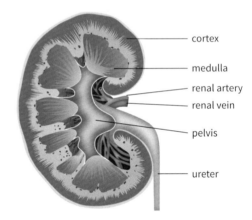

Figure 14.01 A mammalian kidney seen in section.

Each kidney is supplied with blood through the **renal artery**. The renal vein returns blood to the circulatory system. The **ureter** conveys urine, formed in the kidney, from the kidney to the bladder, where the urine is stored until the bladder is emptied.

The functional unit of the kidney is known as a **nephron**, a microscopic tubule and associated blood vessels. Each kidney contains many thousands of nephrons.

TIP

Be careful to distinguish between a nephron and a neurone.

Figure 14.02 shows the structure of a nephron.

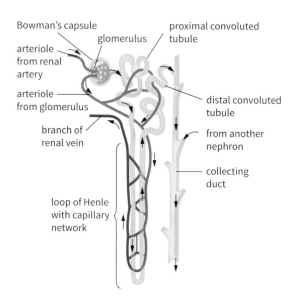

Bowman's capsule
glomerulus
proximal convoluted
tubule
arteriole
from renal
artery
arteriole
from glomerulus
distal convoluted
tubule
branch of
renal vein
from another
nephron
collecting
duct
loop of Henle
with capillary
network

Figure 14.02 The structure of a nephron.

The functions of each part of a nephron are summarised in Table 14.01.

b Osmoregulation

Regulation of body water content, or osmoregulation, is brought about by the action of ADH. **Osmoreceptors** (nerve endings sensitive to the water potential of blood) in the hypothalamus of the brain constantly monitor the water potential of blood. If the water potential decreases, nerve impulses stimulate the release of ADH by nerve endings in the posterior pituitary gland. ADH is an example of a neurosecretory hormone, as it is released directly by

nerve cells. ADH is transported around the body and affects the permeability of cells in the collecting ducts to water. An increase in the levels of ADH results in an increase in the permeability, through the action of protein water channels, known as aquaporins, in the cell membranes.

As more water is reabsorbed, less is lost in the urine so the volume of urine decreases.

Progress check 14.02

Outline the sequence of events if a person drinks 500 cm³ of water.

c Regulation of blood glucose

The concentration of glucose in the blood is maintained between 4.5 and 5.5 mmol dm^{-3}. Following a meal containing carbohydrates, the concentration of glucose in the blood starts to increase as glucose is absorbed. This increase is detected by cells in the pancreatic **islets of Langerhans**, known as β cells, which secrete the hormone **insulin**.

Insulin binds to receptors on the membranes of cells, such as liver and muscle cells, and brings about two responses:

- insulin increases the rate at which these cells take up glucose from the blood

Parts of nephron	Functions
Bowman's capsule	The process of **ultrafiltration** occurs here. Water and many solutes are forced out of the glomerular capillaries by blood pressure, forming the glomerular filtrate. Protein molecules are too large to pass through the basement membrane of the endothelial cells making up the capillaries and remain in the plasma. The glomerular filtrate contains water, glucose, urea, amino acids and inorganic ions such as Na$^+$, Cl$^-$ and K$^+$.
proximal convoluted tubule	The process of **selective reabsorption** occurs here. Sodium and chloride ions are reabsorbed, along with glucose, amino acids, vitamins and some urea. The reabsorption of solutes into the blood creates a water potential gradient and much of the water in the filtrate is reabsorbed by osmosis.
loop of Henle	Cells in the ascending limb of the loop of Henle actively pump sodium and chloride ions out of the filtrate into the surrounding tissue fluid. This sets up an osmotic gradient in the medulla of the kidney. Cells in the descending limb of the loop of Henle are permeable to water, which passes out of the descending limb, by osmosis. The loop of Henle functions as a **counter-current multiplier**, enabling the kidneys to produce concentrated urine.
distal convoluted tubule and collecting ducts	Sodium ions are actively pumped out of the filtrate, into the surrounding tissue fluid and potassium ions are actively pumped into the tubule. ADH affects the permeability of cells in the collecting duct to water. When the secretion of ADH increases, the permeability of cells to water increases and more water is reabsorbed. As a result, the volume of water lost in the urine decreases.

Table 14.01 The functions of parts of a nephron.

- insulin activates enzymes, including glycogen synthase, that catalyses the conversion of glucose to glycogen.

As a result, the concentration of glucose in the blood decreases and returns to the set concentration. This is another example of a negative feedback mechanism.

A decrease in blood glucose, which may occur as a result of fasting, is detected by α cells in the pancreatic islets. These cells secrete the hormone **glucagon**, which effectively has the opposite effect to insulin, bringing about changes resulting in an increase in blood glucose concentration.

Worked example 14.01

Question

The fasting concentration of glucose in a person was measured and found to be $5.0 \, \text{mmol dm}^{-3}$. Assuming a total blood volume of $5.0 \, \text{dm}^3$, calculate the total mass of glucose, in grams, in the blood.

Answer

You need to know that the relative molecular mass of glucose is 180. A solution of $5.0 \, \text{mmoles}$ of glucose contains:

$0.18 \times 5 = 0.9$ grams of glucose per dm^3

$5 \, \text{dm}^3$ of blood will therefore contain:

$0.9 \times 5 = 4.5$ grams of glucose

Glucagon attaches to a receptor on the liver cell membrane and brings about a sequence of events resulting in the formation of cyclic AMP. Cyclic AMP (cAMP) then triggers an enzyme cascade, finally activating glycogen phosphorylase, an enzyme that catalyses the breakdown of glycogen to glucose. Glucose then diffuses out of liver cells, through transporter proteins in the cell membrane, into the blood. As a result, the blood glucose concentration rises.

Insulin and glucagon act as a pair of antagonistic hormones, that is, they have opposite effects, maintaining the blood glucose concentration within set limits.

Progress check 14.03

Explain what is meant by the terms 'glucagon', 'glycogen' and 'glycolysis'.

Insulin and glucagon are not the only hormones involved in the regulation of blood glucose. **Adrenaline**, secreted by the adrenal glands in response to stimulation by the autonomic nervous system, brings about the rapid breakdown of glycogen to form glucose. Both adrenaline and glucagon bind to receptors on liver cell membranes and bring about an enzyme cascade, resulting in the breakdown of glycogen.

This is an example of cell signalling (see Unit 4) and can be illustrated by the flow diagram in Figure 14.03.

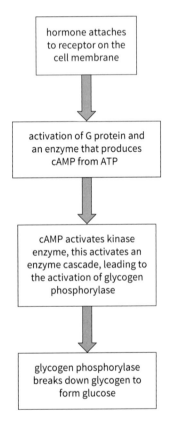

Figure 14.03 Main stages in cell signalling in the control of blood glucose by adrenaline.

d Dip sticks and biosensors

Dip sticks (Figure 14.04) and biosensors provide a rapid means of detecting and measuring the concentration of substances in blood and urine. For example, the presence of glucose in urine can be detected using a dip stick which changes colour if glucose is present (Figure 14.04).

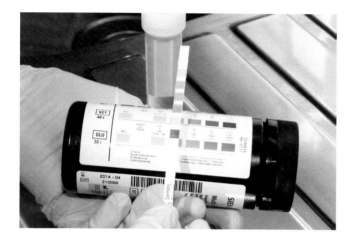

Figure14.04 Dip sticks used to detect glucose in urine.

These dip sticks have a pad at one end, which is impregnated with a number of chemicals to bring about a colour change in the presence of glucose. The pads contain glucose oxidase, and enzyme which oxidises glucose, forming hydrogen peroxide and gluconolactone. The pads also contain the enzyme peroxidase, which catalyses a reaction between the hydrogen peroxide and various colourless compounds resulting in a colour change. The colour is then matched to a colour chart; different colours can give a quantitative result.

Biosensors are electronic devices, which give rapid quantitative results. A biosensor for the detection of glucose also involves the enzyme glucose oxidase. This enzyme oxidises glucose and simultaneously reduces flavin adenine dinucleotide (FAD). The reduced FAD is oxidised by an electrode in the biosensor and this produces an electric current, proportional to the glucose concentration. The biosensor is accurately calibrated to give a quantitative reading of the glucose concentration in a small drop of blood.

Dip sticks and biosensors have a wide range of clinical applications, including the detection and measurement of glucose, protein and ketones in urine samples. The clinical significance of these is summarised in Table 14.02.

Compounds in urine	Clinical significance
glucose	glucose is not normally present in urine, but may be present in diabetes; further tests are needed to confirm the diagnosis
protein	protein is not normally present in urine; if protein is detected, it may indicate kidney disease causing increased permeability of the glomerular capillaries
ketones	uncontrolled diabetes causes fatty acids to be metabolised and for ketones to be excreted in the urine; this indicates the need to change insulin therapy

Table 14.02 Clinical significance of some compounds in urine.

Worked example 14.02

Question

The blood glucose concentration of a person at rest was measured and found to be 5.1 mmol dm^{-3}. Two hours after eating a meal containing carbohydrates, the blood glucose concentration rose to 7.2 mmol dm^{-3}. Calculate the percentage increase in blood glucose concentration.

Answer

Remember that to calculate a percentage change, we need to find the change in concentration, divide this by the original value and then multiply by 100.

So in this case the percentage change is:

$7.2 - 5.1 = 2.1$

$2.1 \div 5.1 = 0.41$

$0.41 \times 100 = 41\%$

14.02 Homeostasis in plants

Plants have homeostatic mechanisms to control their internal environment, such as maintaining a supply of carbon dioxide and controlling the loss of water vapour. Stomata allow carbon dioxide to diffuse into leaves and allow water vapour to diffuse (Figure 14.04).

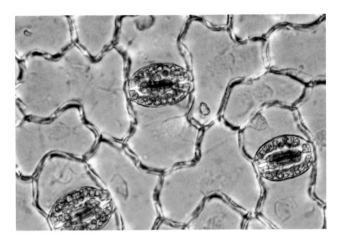

Figure 14.05 Three stomata on the lower epidermis of a leaf, as seen with a light microscope. magnification × 400.

Each stoma consists of two curved **guard cells**, surrounding a pore. Changes in the curvature of the guard cells alter the size of the pore. Stomata show a natural rhythm of opening and closing; they are typically open during the day and closed at night, a rhythm that persists even if a plant is kept in constant light or constant dark. Stomata will also close during the day if a plant is exposed to water stress. This reduces the loss of water vapour by transpiration.

Open and closing of stomata is brought about by changes in the turgor of the guard cells. When stomata open, proton pumps in the guard cell membranes actively transport protons out of the guard cells. This sets up an electrochemical gradient and potassium ions pass into the guard cells, lowering their water potential. Water then moves into the guard cells, by osmosis,

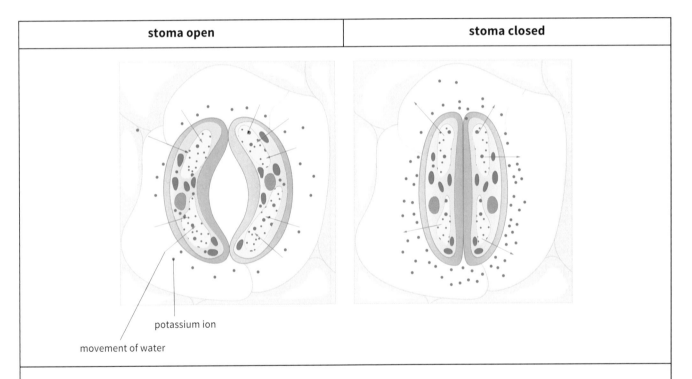

stoma open	stoma closed

potassium ion

movement of water

- proton pumps actively transport H$^+$ ions out of guard cells
- this causes potassium channels to open and K$^+$ ions enter the guard cells
- the increase in the concentration of potassium ions in the guard cells lowers the water potential
- water enters the guard cells, by osmosis, increasing the turgor of the guard cells
- because of differences in the cell wall thickness, the guard cells become curved, opening the stomatal pore

  When stomata close, these changes are essentially in the opposite direction; loss of water by the guard cells causes them to lose turgor.

Figure 14.06 The structure and function of guard cells.

down the water potential gradient. The increase in turgor of the guard cells causes the cells to move apart, increasing the stomatal aperture.

Closure of stomata in response to water stress involves **abscisic acid (ABA)**. ABA is secreted in large quantities in drought conditions, causing stomatal closure. The exact mechanism for this is not known, but it seems that ABA attaches to receptors on guard cell membranes. This has two main effects:

- inhibition of proton pumps

- stimulating the movement of calcium ions into the cell cytoplasm.

Calcium ions act as a second messenger and change the permeability of the guard cell membrane by activating membrane channel proteins. This allows ions to leave the guard cells, followed by the movement of water down the water potential gradient. As the guard cells lose water, they also lose turgor and the stomatal pore closes.

Progress check 14.04

Give four factors that result in closure of stomata.

Sample question 14.01

In an investigation, the transpiration rate of a sunflower plant was recorded at different times of the day. The results are shown in the table 14.03:

Time of day / 24 h clock	Transpiration rate / g water lost per 2 h
08:00	5
10:00	32
12:00	40
14:00	55
16:00	38
18:00	20

Table 14.03

Describe the changes in the rate of transpiration. Suggest reasons for the changes you have described. [5 marks]

[Mark points are shown in square brackets – to a maximum of 5 marks]

From 08:00 until 14:00 the rate of transpiration increases, reaching a maximum rate at 14:00. From 14:00 until 18:00 the rate of transpiration decreases **[2]**.

Reasons for the increase in transpiration include stomatal opening, an increase in temperature and an increase in wind speed **[2]**. Reasons for the decrease in the rate of transpiration may be because the stomata are closing, and the temperature and wind speed are decreasing **[2]**.

This answer correctly describes the changes in the rate of transpiration, with suitable references to the time periods. This is better than simply stating that 'the rate increases and then decreases'. You could support your description with a manipulated reference to the data in the table (e.g. by stating that the rate of transpiration increases from 08:00 until 14:00 'by 50 g of water per 2 hours'. Note that is not simply quoting figures directly from the table, but working out a difference in the rates of transpiration.

The factors affecting the rate of transpiration are correct; other factors could include changes in humidity or changes in the availability of water.

Revision checklist

Check that you know:

- ☐ the importance of homeostasis in mammals

- ☐ the principles of homeostasis in terms of internal and external stimuli, receptors, central control, coordination systems and effectors (muscles and glands)

- ☐ negative feedback and how it is involved in homeostasis

- ☐ the roles of the nervous system and endocrine system in coordinating homeostatic mechanisms, including thermoregulation, osmoregulation and the control of blood glucose concentration

- ☐ the deamination of amino acids and outline the formation of urea in the urea cycle

- ☐ the structure of the kidney and the nephron, with its associated blood vessels

- ☐ the processes involved with the formation of urine in the nephron

- ☐ the roles of the hypothalamus, posterior pituitary, ADH and collecting ducts in osmoregulation

- ☐ the regulation of blood glucose concentration, with reference to insulin and glucagon

- ☐ the role of cAMP as a second messenger

- ☐ the three main steps of cell signalling in the control of blood glucose by adrenaline

- ☐ the principles of dip sticks and biosensors for the quantitative measurements of glucose in blood and urine

- ☐ how urine analysis is used in diagnosis with reference to glucose, protein and ketones

- ☐ daily rhythms of opening and closing of stomata

- ☐ the structure and function of guard cells

- ☐ the role of abscisic acid in the closure of stomata in times of water stress, including the role of calcium ions.

Exam-style questions

1 a Prepare a table to compare the composition of plasma and glomerular filtrate. [6]

   b Explain how each of the following processes are involved in the formation of urine:

   i ultrafiltration [3]

   ii selective reabsorption. [4]

Total: 13

2 Explain the role of abscisic acid (ABA) in the closure of stomata. [8]

Total: 8

Control and coordination

15.01 The nervous and endocrine systems

The nervous and endocrine systems provide a means of coordinating the responses of an organism to changes in the external and the internal environment (see Unit 14). The nervous system coordinates responses by nerve impulses, conducted by specialised cells, called **neurones**. Neurones transmit impulses from receptors to effectors, usually resulting in rapid responses to stimuli. The impulse passes from one neurone to another across specialised gaps called synapses, in the form of chemical transmitter substances. The endocrine system consists of a number of glands that secrete **hormones**. Hormones act as 'chemical messengers' transported in the blood and affect the activity of other target organs in the body. Responses to nervous coordination are usually rapid; responses to hormones are usually slower. You have already met the hormones insulin and glucagon and their roles in the regulation of blood glucose concentrations; in this Unit you will learn about some other hormones and their roles in coordinating responses in mammals and plants.

Table 15.01 shows some examples of endocrine glands in humans and the hormones they secrete.

Endocrine organ	Hormones secreted
anterior pituitary gland	follicle stimulating hormone (FSH) luteinising hormone (LH)
posterior pituitary gland	antidiuretic hormone (ADH)
islets of Langerhans in the pancreas	insulin glucagon
adrenal gland	adrenaline
ovaries	oestrogen progesterone
testes	testosterone

Table 15.01 Some examples of endocrine glands in humans.

Coordination in plants is also brought about by electrical impulses and by chemical hormones. In plants, hormones are often referred to as plant growth substances, or plant growth regulators.

15.02 Neurones and the nerve impulse

The nervous system consists of specialised cells, known as neurones, which are adapted to conduct electrical impulses. The entire nervous system consists of the **central nervous system** (CNS) and the **peripheral nervous system** (PNS). The CNS consists of the brain and spinal cord; the PNS includes all the nerves that conduct impulses towards the CNS, or away from the CNS. A nerve consists of many individual neurones and their supporting cells.

Neurones are classified according to their structure and function. A **sensory neurone** conducts impulses from a receptor to the CNS, while a **motor neurone** conducts impulses from the CNS to an effector, such as a muscle, that brings about a response. A third type of neurone, known as an intermediate or **relay neurone**, forms links between sensory neurones and motor neurones. Relay neurones are found in the CNS only.

The combination of a sensory neurone, relay neurone and motor neurone acting together to respond immediately to a stimulus is called a **reflex arc**. Reflex arcs are used in reflex actions, such as pulling your hand away from a hot surface. The CNS is not required so the action is faster.

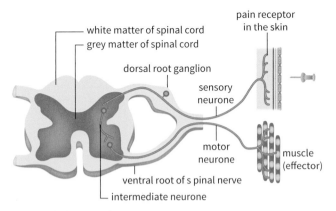

Figure 15.01 A reflex arc.

Figure 15.02 shows the structure of a typical neurone, consisting of a cell body and a long **axon**, for the conduction of the nerve impulses.

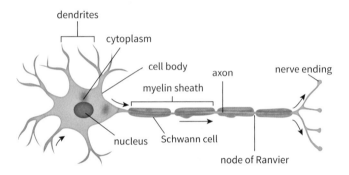

Figure 15.02 A motor neurone.

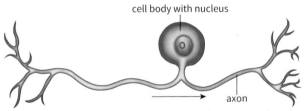

The arrow shows the direction of the nerve impulse

Figure 15.03 A sensory neurone

The cell body of a neurone contains the nucleus, many mitochondria and dense rough endoplasmic reticulum. Axons may be covered by a myelin sheath, formed by **Schwann cells**. The Schwann cells wrap around the axon, forming an insulating layer which is interrupted at intervals by the **nodes of Ranvier**. These types of axons are referred to as myelinated axons and, as you will read later, myelinated axons generally have a much faster speed of conduction of the impulse than non-myelinated axons.

Sensory neurones carry impulses from a receptor. Receptors detect and respond to specific stimuli and send an impulse towards the CNS. One example of a receptor is a taste bud, situated on the tongue, which functions as a chemoreceptor. Taste buds respond to specific chemical stimuli, such as the presence of sodium ions, giving rise to impulses in a sensory neurone and the sensation of a specific taste (salt, sour, sweet, bitter or savoury).

Progress check 15.01

Make a table to show five different receptors, the form in which energy is received by the receptor and the resulting sense.

When a neurone is not conducting an impulse, it is said to have a **resting potential**. This is due to differences in the concentrations of ions inside the axon, compared with the concentration of ions in the surrounding tissue fluid. The resting potential in an axon can be measured (in millivolts) and is found to be slightly negative compared with the outside, having a value typically between −60 mV and −70 mV.

The resting potential is maintained by the action of **sodium–potassium pumps** in the axon membrane. These pumps actively transport sodium ions (Na$^+$) out of the axon and potassium ions (K$^+$) into the axon. This is an example of active transport, described in Unit 4. These ion pumps remove three sodium ions for every two potassium ions brought in.

When conducting a nerve impulse, part of the axon membrane briefly becomes **depolarised** – the inside of the membrane becomes positively charged, changing from the resting potential of about −70 mV to a value of about +40 mV. This is brought about by a change in the permeability of the membrane to sodium ions and potassium ions, resulting in the formation of the positive **action potential**. You should remember that there is a greater concentration of sodium ions outside the axon than inside and a higher concentration of potassium ions inside the axon than outside. At the start of the action potential, the axon membrane becomes more permeable to sodium ions, as voltage-gated sodium ion channels open. This allows sodium ions into the axon, because there is a diffusion gradient inwards and they are attracted in by the negative charge inside the axon. Sodium ions are positively charged and this inwards movement of positively charged ions causes the

membrane potential to rise from the resting value to a positive action potential. This increase in permeability to sodium ions is followed by an increase in permeability to potassium ions, as voltage-gated potassium ion channels open. This allows potassium ions to leave the axon, restoring the resting potential.

Progress check 15.02

Make an annotated diagram of an action potential.

A nerve impulse is a propagated action potential, travelling along the axon at a constant speed, referred to as the conduction velocity. In a myelinated axon the action potential 'jumps' from one node of Ranvier to the next, which greatly increases the conduction velocity. As a general rule, myelinated axons have a much faster conduction velocity than non-myelinated axons. The conduction velocity also depends on the axon diameter and the conduction velocity increases as the axon diameter increases.

Progress check 15.03

Sketch a graph to show the relationship between conduction velocity and axon diameter in myelinated and non-myelinated axons. Some typical values for conduction velocities are given in table 15.02

Axon diameter / μm	Conduction velocity / m s^{-1}	
	Non-myelinated axon	Myelinated axon
2	1.2	12
3	1.4	18
4	1.6	24
5	1.8	30
6	2.0	36

Table 15.02

After the conduction of a nerve impulse, there is a short **refractory period** during which the axon cannot be stimulated to conduct another impulse.

15.03 The synapse

Individual neurones are not in direct contact with each other, instead there are minute gaps between one neurone and another. These gaps are referred to as synapses and the impulse is transmitted from one neurone to the next in the form of a chemical transmitter substance, such as **acetylcholine (ACh)**. A synapse that uses acetylcholine as the transmitter substance is referred to as a **cholinergic synapse**.

Figure 15.04 shows the structure of a typical synapse. Notice the vesicles in the **presynaptic neurone**, containing the transmitter substance.

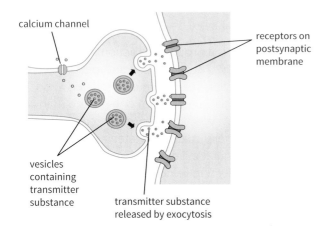

Figure 15.04 The structure of a typical synapse.

The function of a synapse can be summarised by the following sequence of events:

1 A nerve impulse arrives at the end of the presynaptic neurone.

2 This causes calcium ion channels to open and calcium ions enter the presynaptic neurone.

3 This stimulates some of the vesicles to move towards the presynaptic membrane, fuse with it and release the transmitter substance.

4 The transmitter substance rapidly diffuses across the synaptic cleft and binds with receptors on the postsynaptic membrane.

5 This causes a change in the permeability of the postsynaptic membrane. For example, it may become more permeable to sodium ions, which diffuse into the postsynaptic cell, resulting in depolarisation of the postsynaptic cell membrane.

6 The transmitter substance is broken down by enzymes. For example, acetylcholine is broken down by acetylcholine esterase and the products are recycled in the presynaptic neurone.

Synapses have four essential roles in the nervous system, as outlined below.

- they ensure one-way transmission of nerve impulses, because impulses can only pass from the presynaptic neurone to the postsynaptic neurone

- they enable integration of impulses because both excitatory and inhibitory synapses exist and the activity of the **postsynaptic neurone** depends on the number of excitatory and inhibitory stimuli it receives

- they allow complex interconnections between nerve pathways

- they are involved in learning and memory.

Nerve impulses to striated muscles in motor neurones are transmitted to the muscle itself across a type of synapse, referred to as the **neuromuscular junction**. This has a similar structure and function to a synapse between two neurones. The transmitter substance released is acetylcholine, which causes depolarisation of the muscle membrane and may result in contraction of the muscle.

15.04 The structure and function of muscle tissue

There are three types of muscle tissue:

- cardiac, which is found in the heart only

- smooth, which is found in the walls of structures including bronchioles, intestine and arteries

- striated, also known as voluntary muscle, which forms the muscles attached to the skeleton.

Here, we are going to focus on the structure and function of striated muscle.

Striated muscle consists of long fibres. The surface membrane of muscle fibres is referred to as the sarcolemma and this gives rise to many inholdings, forming the **transverse system tubules**, or **T-tubules**. The T-tubules are closely associated with the **sarcoplasmic reticulum**, the endoplasmic reticulum of muscle tissue, containing calcium ions. Muscle fibres also contain many mitochondria, generating the ATP, by aerobic respiration, required for muscle contraction.

Each fibre consists of many myofibrils, with a characteristic pattern of alternating light and dark bands. The light and dark bands can be seen using a light microscope, but an electron microscope is needed to see the detailed structure of individual myofibrils. Figure 15.05 shows a diagrammatic myofibril, based on the appearance using an electron microscope.

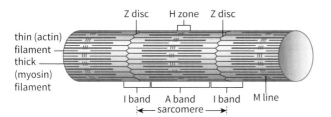

Figure 15.05 The structure of a myofibril.

Each myofibril consists of two main proteins, **actin** and **myosin**, arranged in a highly ordered way, giving rise to the regular pattern of light (I) and dark (A) bands. Actin makes up the thin filaments and myosin makes up the thick filaments. Two other proteins, **troponin** and **tropomyosin** are associated with actin. The individual unit of the structure of a myofibril is referred to as a **sarcomere**. The arrangement of actin and myosin within a sarcomere is shown in Figure 15.07.

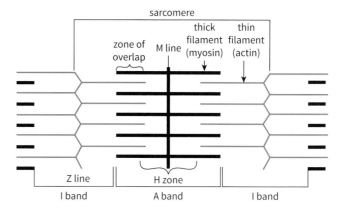

Figure 15.07 The structure of a sarcomere showing the arrangement of actin and myosin.

This arrangement of actin and myosin filaments gives rise to the way in which muscles contract and relax, as the filaments slide past each other. The mechanism for muscle contraction is known as the **sliding filament model**, as outlined below.

1 The nerve impulse arrives at the motor end plate and acetylcholine is released.

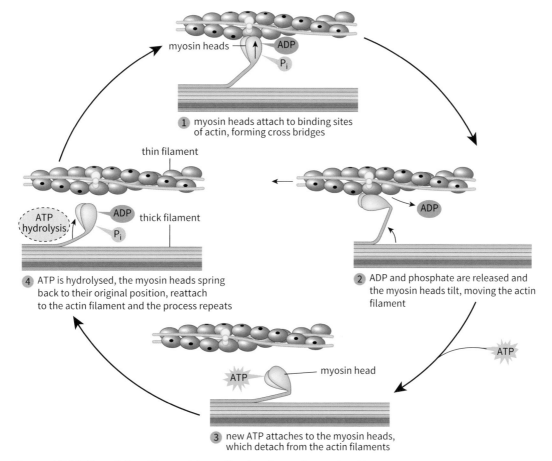

Figure 15.06 The sliding filament hypothesis of muscle contraction

2 Acetylcholine binds to a receptor on the muscle membrane (sarcolemma) resulting in depolarisation of the membrane.

3 An action potential sweeps along the membrane and down the T-tubules.

4 Calcium ions are released from the sarcoplasmic reticulum.

5 Calcium ions bind to troponin and tropomyosin moves to expose myosin binding sites on the actin filaments.

6 Myosin heads form cross bridges with actin.

7 The myosin heads tilt, moving the actin filaments towards centre of the sarcomere.

8 Hydrolysis of ATP causes the myosin heads to release from the actin and myosin heads return to their original position. The myosin heads then bind to actin further along the actin filament.

9 Steps 7 and 8 repeat, resulting in muscle contraction.

15.05 Hormones and the menstrual cycle

The menstrual cycle is controlled and coordinated by hormones. These hormones include follicle stimulating hormone (FSH), luteinising hormone (LH), oestrogen and progesterone.

FSH and LH are secreted by the anterior pituitary gland, at the base of the brain. Oestrogen and progesterone are secreted by cells within the ovaries.

The functions of these hormones in the menstrual cycle are summarised in Table 15.03.

Hormone	Functions
follicle stimulating hormone (FSH) and luteinising hormone (LH)	At the start of the menstrual cycle, the anterior pituitary secretes both FSH and LH. These hormones trigger the development of a follicle in the ovary. Cells surrounding the follicle secrete oestrogen. A later increase in the secretion of LH stimulates ovulation and the formation of a corpus luteum in the ovary.
oestrogen	Oestrogen stimulates repair and growth of the endometrium (the lining of the uterus) after menstruation.
progesterone	This hormone is secreted by the corpus luteum and, with oestrogen, is responsible for the maintenance of the corpus luteum. High levels of oestrogen and progesterone inhibit the secretion of FSH and LH in the second half of the menstrual cycle.

Table 15.03 Hormones and the menstrual cycle.

Figure 15.08 shows how the levels of these hormones change during the menstrual cycle.

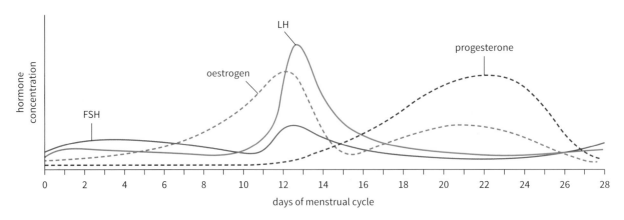

Figure 15.08 Changes in the levels of hormones during the menstrual cycle.

15.06 The biological basis of the contraceptive pill

Contraceptive 'birth control' pills were developed in the 1960s. The combined contraceptive pills contain synthetic oestrogen and progesterone; there are also contraceptive pills containing progesterone only. The oestrogen and progesterone mimic the effect of the natural hormones and inhibit the secretion of FSH and LH. As a result, development of follicles in the ovary and ovulation are prevented. In some cases, women take one of the pills daily for 21 days and then stop for 7 days, during which menstruation occurs. Progesterone-only contraceptive pills cause thickening of mucus in the cervix, preventing sperm from reaching the egg. Some types of progesterone-only contraceptive pills may also inhibit ovulation. When used correctly, contraceptive pills are over 99% effective in preventing pregnancy.

15.07 The Venus fly trap

The Venus fly trap is a species of carnivorous plant (Figure 15.09). The end of each leaf is modified to form a two-lobed trap. Each lobe of the trap has three small hair-like structures which, when simulated, cause the trap to close remarkably quickly. In this way, the plant is able to catch small insects and spiders, which are digested by enzymes secreted by the lobes. The edges of each lobe have longer hair-like structure that interlock when the trap closes, helping to prevent the escape of prey.

Figure 15.09 The Venus fly trap – a carnivorous plant.

When the sensory hairs in the traps are stimulated, for example by an insect, calcium ion channels open, resulting in the formation of a receptor potential. An electrical impulse, similar to an action potential, sweeps across the cells of the trap. Plants do not, of course, have a nervous system, but the impulse is conducted from cell to cell via the plasmodesmata (see Unit 1).

The precise mechanism for closure of the trap is not known, but it seems likely that it is due to a sudden change in the tension of cell walls in cells that cause the trap to close quickly. This is followed by further changes causing the edges of the trap to close completely, so that prey cannot escape. Digestive enzymes are secreted by the process of exocytosis by gland cells. The trap remains closed for about a week to allow digestion to take place, before the trap opens again.

15.08 Chemical coordination in plants

Plant hormones, or **plant growth regulators**, are responsible for most of the control and coordination of responses in plants to their environment. Unlike animal hormones, plant growth regulators are not produced in specialised tissues and move directly from cell to cell or are carried in the xylem or phloem sap. There are a number of different types of plant growth regulators, including:

- **auxins** (of which the principal one is indole acetic acid (**IAA**))

- **gibberellins**.

These are both involved in a number of responses in plants, some of which are summarised in Table 15.04.

Plant growth regulators	Roles
auxins	stimulate the growth of cell walls
gibberellins	stimulate enzyme synthesis in germinating cereal grains stimulate stem elongation

Table 15.04 Some roles of plant growth regulators.

Auxin is synthesised in the growing tips of roots and shoots. The effect of auxin in cell wall elongation is explained by the 'acid growth hypothesis'. Auxin attaches to receptors on the cell membrane and stimulates proton pumps which actively transport protons (H^+) out of the cytoplasm and into cell walls. The protons cause the pH in the cell wall to drop and this activates proteins called expansins. These proteins loosen bonds between cellulose microfibrils, allowing them to slide past each other, allowing the cell to expand.

Gibberellins, like auxin, have a number of different effects in plants. One effect is causing elongation of stems of genetically dwarf plants. Height in some plants is controlled by the allele **Le**. If the dominant allele is present, the plants grow tall. However, if the plant has the homozygous recessive genotype, **lele**, the plant remains short. The dominant allele, **Le**, regulates the synthesis of an active form of gibberellin known as GA_1. This form of gibberellin stimulates cell division and elongation of the stem. Plants with the genotype **lele** produce an inactive enzyme and the active form of gibberellin is not synthesised.

In germinating cereal grains, such as wheat and barley, the embryo synthesises gibberellins. The gibberellins diffuse to the aleurone layer, surrounding the endosperm. Gibberellins stimulate amylase synthesis by cells in the aleurone layer. In turn, amylase hydrolyses starch stored in the endosperm, converting starch to maltose, which is further broken down to glucose. The glucose provides an energy source for the developing embryo. Gibberellins regulate genes involved in the synthesis of amylase. You will read about this in Unit 16.

Sample question 15.01

In an investigation, the mean amylase activity of barley grains was determined each day for the first 8 days of germination. Table 15.05 shows the results of this investigation.

Time / days	Mean amylase activity / arbitrary units
0	0.2
1	0.2
2	0.5
3	1.2
4	2.0
5	3.1
6	4.2
7	7.8
8	8.6

Table 15.05

1 Explain the role of amylase in germinating cereal grains, such as barley.

2 Suggest an explanation for the changes in amylase activity as shown in the table.

[6 marks]

[Mark points are shown in square brackets – to a maximum of 6 marks]

1 Cereal grains contain starch stored in the endosperm. Starch is a polysaccharide and is broken down to simple sugars, such as maltose, by amylase. The simple sugars are then used as respiratory substrates during the early stages of growth [3].

This answer correctly outlines the role of amylase in germination of cereal grains. Starch is insoluble and so must first be mobilised, by breaking it down into soluble products, eventually forming glucose (remember that starch is a polymer of α-glucose). The glucose is used as a respiratory substrate and provides the energy for the early stages of germination and growth of the seedling.

2 From day 0 to day 8 there is an overall increase in amylase activity of 8.4 arbitrary units. During germination, gibberellin, a plant growth regulator, is secreted by the embryo and this diffuses to the aleurone layer. In response, cells in the aleurone layer synthesise amylase by an increase in the synthesis of mRNA coding for amylase **[3]**.

Amylases are just one group of enzymes that are involved with the mobilisation of food reserves in germinating seeds. Find out about other groups of hydrolases found in germinating seeds.

This answer initially refers to the considerable increase in amylase activity and describes the sequence of events to account for this change in amylase activity. The whole process starts as the barley grains take up water; this stimulates the embryo to secrete gibberellins.

Revision checklist

Check that you know:

- [ ] how to compare the nervous and endocrine systems in the coordination of responses in the changes to the internal and external environment
- [ ] the structure of a sensory neurone and a motor neurone
- [ ] the role of a receptor cell in the detection of a stimulus and transmission of a nerve impulse
- [ ] the functions of the neurones in a reflex arc
- [ ] how an action potential is transmitted in a neurone
- [ ] the importance of the myelin sheath and the refractory period
- [ ] the structure and function of a synapse

- [ ] the roles of synapses in the nervous system
- [ ] the role of neuromuscular junctions in stimulating the contraction of striated muscle
- [ ] the ultrastructure of striated muscle
- [ ] the sliding filament model of muscle contraction
- [ ] the roles of the hormones follicle stimulating hormone, luteinising hormone, oestrogen and progesterone in the human menstrual cycle
- [ ] the biological basis of contraceptive pills
- [ ] the rapid response of the Venus fly trap to stimulation of hairs on modified leaves
- [ ] the role of auxin in growth of a plant
- [ ] the role of gibberellin in the germination of a cereal grain
- [ ] the role of gibberellin in stem elongation.

Exam-style questions

1   a   Explain how a nerve impulse is transmitted along the axon of a neurone. [10]

     b   Explain how a nerve impulse is transmitted across a synapse. [5]

Total: 15

2   Explain how the menstrual cycle is coordinated by the action of hormones. [10]

Total: 10

Genetics

Genetics is the scientific study of inheritance. Genes determine the genetic make-up or **genotype** of an individual and whether a characteristic is shown or 'expressed' in its appearance or **phenotype**. **Meiosis** is the type of nuclear division that takes place in the sex organs and leads to the production of gametes. An understanding of meiosis is essential for interpreting the results of genetic crosses.

16.01 Meiosis

In a human body cell there are 22 matching pairs of chromosomes, called **homologous chromosomes**. There is also a non-homologous pair of sex chromosomes, X and Y (females have XX and males XY). An individual inherits one chromosome of each of the 23 pairs from their father and one from their mother. With two complete sets of chromosomes, body cells are said to be **diploid**, while gametes contain only one set and are **haploid**.

Before meiosis starts, replication of DNA takes place in the same way as in mitosis (see Unit 5). During meiosis two divisions of the nucleus take place, called meiosis I and meiosis II:

- In meiosis I, homologous chromosomes pair up and then separate into two daughter nuclei. Meiosis I is called the reduction division, because it reduces the chromosome number from diploid to haploid.

- In meiosis II, replicate copies of the chromosomes (chromatids) separate. The result is that four haploid gametes are formed from each parent cell.

When gametes fuse at fertilisation the diploid number is restored. The stages of meiosis are shown in Figure 16.01.

a Meiosis increases genetic variation

A homologous pair carries genes for the same characteristic at the same position on each chromosome. The forms (alleles) of a gene may be the same or different.

Meiosis produces new combinations of alleles in the gametes. This increases genetic variation, ensuring that offspring are different from their parents and

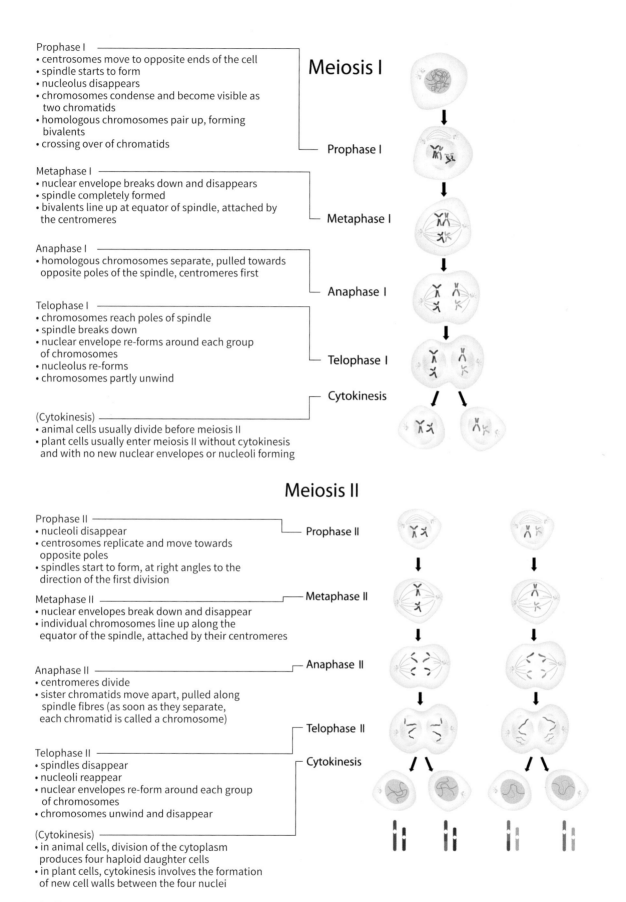

Meiosis I

Prophase I ———
• centrosomes move to opposite ends of the cell
• spindle starts to form
• nucleolus disappears
• chromosomes condense and become visible as
  two chromatids
• homologous chromosomes pair up, forming
  bivalents
• crossing over of chromatids

— Prophase I

Metaphase I ———
• nuclear envelope breaks down and disappears
• spindle completely formed
• bivalents line up at equator of spindle, attached by
  the centromeres

— Metaphase I

Anaphase I ———
• homologous chromosomes separate, pulled towards
  opposite poles of the spindle, centromeres first

— Anaphase I

Telophase I ———
• chromosomes reach poles of spindle
• spindle breaks down
• nuclear envelope re-forms around each group
  of chromosomes
• nucleolus re-forms
• chromosomes partly unwind

— Telophase I

— Cytokinesis

(Cytokinesis) ———
• animal cells usually divide before meiosis II
• plant cells usually enter meiosis II without cytokinesis
  and with no new nuclear envelopes or nucleoli forming

Meiosis II

Prophase II ———
• nucleoli disappear
• centrosomes replicate and move towards
  opposite poles
• spindles start to form, at right angles to the
  direction of the first division

— Prophase II

Metaphase II ———
• nuclear envelopes break down and disappear
• individual chromosomes line up along the
  equator of the spindle, attached by their centromeres

— Metaphase II

Anaphase II ———
• centromeres divide
• sister chromatids move apart, pulled along
  spindle fibres (as soon as they separate,
  each chromatid is called a chromosome)

— Anaphase II

Telophase II ———
• spindles disappear
• nucleoli reappear
• nuclear envelopes re-form around each group
  of chromosomes
• chromosomes unwind and disappear

— Telophase II

— Cytokinesis

(Cytokinesis) ———
• in animal cells, division of the cytoplasm
  produces four haploid daughter cells
• in plant cells, cytokinesis involves the formation
  of new cell walls between the four nuclei

Figure 16.01 The stages of meiosis in an animal cell. In order to make the process easier to understand, only two pairs of homologous chromosomes are shown. Note that cytokinesis is not part of meiosis.

each other. This variation comes about as a result of **crossing over** and **independent assortment** of chromosomes.

Crossing over happens during prophase 1. Chromosomes of a homologous pair link together at **chiasmata** (singular = **chiasma**), break and exchange portions of chromatids (Figure 16.02). Chiasmata may form once, more than once or not at all in each homologous pair.

chiasma

Figure 16.02 Chiasma formation and crossing over.

If a part of a chromatid becomes attached to a chromatid of the other chromosome, this produces a new combination of alleles. The altered chromosomes are called **recombinants**.

Independent assortment takes place during metaphase 1, when homologous pairs of chromosomes lie along the equator of the spindle. Each pair consists of a chromosome from the mother (maternal) and one from the father (paternal). The way round that each pair is orientated is completely random. With two pairs of chromosomes, this produces four different arrangements in the gametes (Figure 16.03).

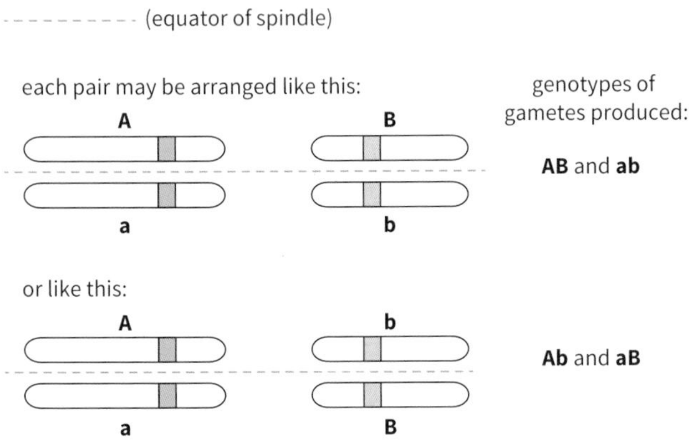

------------ (equator of spindle)

each pair may be arranged like this:

| A | B |

genotypes of gametes produced:

AB and **ab**

| a | b |

or like this:

| A | b |

Ab and **aB**

| a | B |

Figure 16.03 Independent assortment. For simplicity, sister chromatids of each homologous chromosome are not shown. The dashed line represents the equator of the spindle.

In a human cell there are 23 pairs of chromosomes. This means there are 2^{23} (over 8 million) possible combinations of maternal and paternal chromosomes in

the gametes – an enormous degree of genetic variation that will be passed to the offspring at fertilisation.

Fertilisation itself introduces yet more genetic variation, when the male and female gametes come together and form a zygote with new combinations of alleles from each parent. Occasionally recessive alleles that are rare in the population as a whole will be expressed when they come together by chance at fertilisation.

Progress check 16.01

State the stage of meiosis in which the following events take place:

1   Crossing over.

2   Independent assortment.

3   Separation of homologous chromosomes.

4   Separation of chromatids.

5   Formation of a nuclear membrane around a group of haploid chromosomes.

16.02 Gametogenesis

Gametogenesis is the formation of mature gametes in the reproductive organs. It involves meiosis and mitosis.

a Gametogenesis in humans

The formation of male gametes is called **spermatogenesis** and the formation of female gametes is **oogenesis** (Figure 16.04). Spermatogenesis occurs in the wall of the seminiferous tubules of the testes. In the periphery of the tubule are diploid, undifferentiated germ cells called spermatogonia, which go through stages of mitosis, meiosis and differentiation to form mature spermatozoa. Oogenesis begins in the tissues of the ovary and follows a similar sequence from oogonia to mature ovum.

Formation of gametes occurs in three stages:

*   a multiplication phase, where many diploid cells are formed by mitosis, so that eventually many gametes can be produced

*   a growth phase, where DNA replication occurs and more cytoplasm is formed

*   a maturation phase, during which the cells divide by meiosis – this produces haploid cells, which differentiate into gametes.

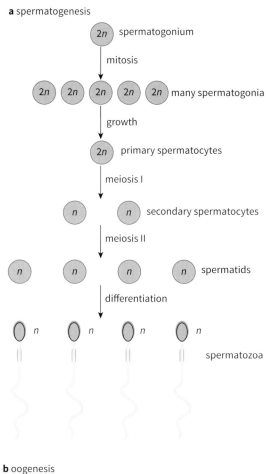

a spermatogenesis

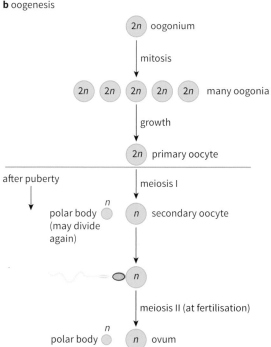

b oogenesis

Figure 16.04 Gametogenesis in humans.

There are a number of differences between spermatogenesis and oogenesis:

- Spermatogenesis takes place continuously in the testes from puberty onwards. Oogenesis begins in the ovary of the fetus – the ovaries of a baby girl contain about 400 000 primary oocytes. Development halts and then starts again at puberty, when one cell develops into a secondary oocyte every month.

- In spermatogenesis, each primary spermatocyte divides by meiosis to form four haploid spermatids, all of which develop into functional spermatozoa. In oogenesis the cytoplasm divides unequally during meiosis, forming one functional secondary oocyte and up to three polar bodies. The polar bodies are haploid cells but have no function beyond acting as a place to put half the chromosomes during the meiotic divisions.

- In oogenesis, the functional gamete (the egg cell or ovum) is only formed after the secondary oocyte has been fertilised by a sperm.

> **TIP**
>
> Note that the 'egg' released each month at ovulation is actually a secondary oocyte.

b Gametogenesis in flowering plants

Male gametes are produced in the anthers of a flower and female gametes in the ovules.

In an anther, diploid pollen mother cells divide by meiosis to form four haploid cells. The nucleus of each cell then divides by mitosis, but cytokinesis does not occur. This produces four cells, each containing two haploid nuclei. Each cell develops into a pollen grain. One nucleus becomes the **generative nucleus** and the other the **tube nucleus**. Following pollination, a pollen grain produces a pollen tube, which grows down through the tissues of the stigma and style of the flower and into the ovule. Growth of the tube is controlled by the tube nucleus. The generative nucleus divides by mitosis into two haploid nuclei, which are the male gametes (Figure 16.05).

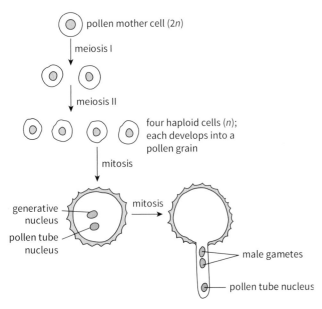

Figure 16.05 Development of male gametes within pollen grains.

In an ovule, a diploid spore mother cell develops. It divides by meiosis to produce four haploid cells. Three of these degenerate, and the fourth develops into an **embryo sac** (Figure 16.06).

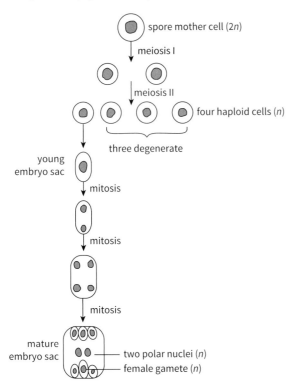

Figure 16.06 Development of the embryo sac.

The haploid nucleus divides by mitosis four times, producing eight haploid nuclei. One of these becomes the female gamete.

At pollination, the pollen tube enters the ovule. The tube nucleus degenerates and the two male gametes are released into the embryo sac. The first gamete fertilises the female gamete, producing a diploid zygote. The second fuses with the two polar nuclei, forming a triploid nucleus. The zygote goes on to develop into the embryo within the seed, while the triploid nucleus divides repeatedly by mitosis to become a food store within the seed. The other female nuclei degenerate. This is sometimes called a double fertilisation, although only the fusion of male and female gamete is true fertilisation.

16.03 Terms used in genetics

A **gene** is a length of DNA that codes for a particular protein or polypeptide. The **locus** (plural = loci) is the position of a gene on a particular chromosome. Different forms of a gene are called **alleles**.

At fertilisation, an individual normally inherits one allele of a gene from its female parent and one from its male parent. The two alleles may be the same, or different:

- a **homozygote** (adjective = **homozygous**) is an organism that has two identical alleles for a particular gene

- a **heterozygote** (adjective = **heterozygous**) is an organism that has two different alleles for a gene.

If the effect of an allele on the phenotype of the heterozygote is identical to its effect in the homozygote (i.e. only one copy of the allele is required for the gene to be expressed) the allele is said to be **dominant**. An allele that is only expressed if no dominant allele is present is called **recessive**. Sometimes two alleles of a gene are both expressed in the phenotype – they are known as **codominant**.

16.04 Monohybrid inheritance

Genetic diagrams are used to predict the outcome of crosses. In genetic diagrams, dominant alleles should be given a capital letter, recessive alleles a small (lower case) letter. The same letter should be used for alleles of one gene. The simplest case is a cross where only one gene is considered. This is known as **monohybrid inheritance**.

TIP

Avoid choosing letters where the capital and small letter have the same shape (e.g. **C** and **c**).

For example, in guinea pig coat colour, black is dominant to white. We could use **B** for the allele for black and **b** for the allele for white. The possible genotypes and phenotypes are:

Genotype	Symbols for genotype	Phenotype
dominant homozygote	**BB**	black
heterozygote	**Bb**	black
recessive homozygote	**bb**	white

If neither allele is dominant (i.e. they are codominant) the same letter is used for each allele, with a superscript to distinguish between the two. For example, snapdragon (*Antirrhinum*) flowers can be red, white or pink:

Genotype	Symbols for genotype	Phenotype
dominant homozygote	$C^R C^R$	red
heterozygote	$C^R C^W$	pink
recessive homozygote	$C^W C^W$	white

TIP

The existence of a third, intermediate phenotype shows this is a case of codominance.

Using the example of guinea pig coat colour, if two heterozygous black guinea pigs are crossed, the possible offspring can be worked out, as below. The diagram should be introduced and set out as shown, with gametes indicated by putting the symbols in circles.

Let **B** be the allele for black coat colour and **b** be the allele for white coat colour.

Genotypes of parents: **Bb**   ×   **Bb**

Genotypes of gametes: Ⓑⓑ   Ⓑⓑ

Genotypes and phenotypes of offspring:

TIP

It is a convention to draw circles around the genotypes of the gametes.

The offspring of the parents are called the F1 generation (the next generation is the F2 generation). The cross predicts a ratio of 3 black : 1 white offspring. There is an important point to note here. These are only the *expected* ratios, based on the laws of probability. What this means is that if the cross produces a *large number* of offspring, the probability is that their genotypes will be in the ratio 1 **BB** : 2 **Bb** : 1 **bb**, or their phenotypes 3 black : 1 white. With small numbers of offspring it is quite likely that all may be black or even all white. Even with large numbers it is still unlikely that the ratios will be exactly 3 : 1. The significance of differences between observed and expected numbers can be tested statistically using the chi-squared test (see below).

A cross between two snapdragon plants that are both heterozygous for flower colour can produce the following offspring:

Let C^R be the allele for red flower and C^W be the allele for white flower colour.

Genotypes of parents: $C^R C^W$ × $C^R C^W$

Genotypes of gametes:

Genotypes and phenotypes of offspring:

female gametes

	C^R	C^W
C^R	$C^R C^R$ red	$C^R C^W$ pink
C^W	$C^R C^W$ pink	$C^W C^W$ white

male gametes

The predicted ratio of genotypes is 1 $C^R C^R$: 2 $C^R C^W$: 1 $C^W C^W$ and phenotypes 1 red : 2 pink : 1 white.

a Test crosses

A test cross is a breeding experiment carried out to distinguish between an individual that is homozygous dominant and one that is heterozygous. For example, a black guinea pig could have the genotype **BB** or **Bb**. To find out which genotype it has, the animal is crossed with a homozygous recessive guinea pig. If any white offspring are produced in the F1, they must have inherited a **b** allele from the heterozygous parent. The possible genotypes and phenotypes from both crosses are shown below (in this example the female has the unknown genotype).

eggs

	B	**B**
b	**Bb** black	**Bb** black
b	**Bb** black	**Bb** black

sperm

Offspring all black

eggs

	B	**b**
b	**Bb** black	**bb** white
b	**Bb** black	**bb** white

sperm

Offspring 50% black and 50% white

b Multiple alleles

Many genes have more than two alleles. For example, the gene determining the antigens on red blood cells, which controls ABO blood groups in humans, has three alleles, I^A, I^B and I^O. The alleles I^A and I^B are codominant, but I^O is recessive to both I^A and I^B. The possible genotypes and phenotypes are shown in Table 16.01.

Genotype	Antigen on red blood cells	Blood group (phenotype)
$I^A I^A$ or $I^A I^O$	A	A
$I^B I^B$ or $I^B I^O$	B	B
$I^A I^B$	A and B	AB
$I^O I^O$	neither	O

Table 16.01 Genetics of ABO blood groups.

As I^O is recessive, there are two genotypes that produce blood group A ($I^A I^A$ and $I^A I^O$) and two producing group B ($I^B I^B$ and $I^B I^O$). I^A and I^B are codominant, so the heterozygote $I^A I^B$ shows a third phenotype – blood group AB. If neither I^A nor I^B is present ($I^O I^O$) the person is group O. A cross between a man who is heterozygous (group A) and a woman who is heterozygous (group B) can produce all four phenotypes:

eggs

	I^B	I^O
I^A	$I^A I^B$ group AB	$I^A I^O$ group A
I^O	$I^B I^O$ group B	$I^O I^O$ group O

sperm

c Sex linkage

In humans, females have two X chromosomes and males have an X and a Y. The X chromosome is larger than the Y and most of the genes present on the X are not present on the Y. These are called sex-linked genes. This means that for some genes, a male will only have one allele of a pair. This has important consequences if the allele causes a harmful condition.

One example of this is a gene that causes a blood disorder called **haemophilia**. When a healthy person's skin is cut a clot forms, which reduces blood loss and entry of bacteria. The commonest form of haemophilia is caused by a gene mutation that affects the production of a blood protein involved in the clotting process. Without this protein, the blood of a person with haemophilia does not clot (see the section on gene mutation later in this unit).

The condition is caused by a recessive allele on the X chromosome, given the symbol X^h. The dominant allele for normal production of the blood clotting factor is given the symbol X^H. There is no allele for the gene on the Y chromosome, so this is shown as Y. The possible genotypes and phenotypes are:

Genotype	Phenotype
X^HX^H	female with normal blood clotting ability
X^HX^h	female with normal blood clotting ability
X^hX^h	female with haemophilia
X^HY	male with normal blood clotting ability
X^hY	male with haemophilia

A woman who is heterozygous for the condition (X^HX^h) will not have the disease, but can pass the allele to her children, so she is called a **carrier**. Boys inherit the recessive allele from a carrier mother, so that two healthy parents can have a son with haemophilia:

eggs

	X^H	X^h
X^H	X^HX^H normal female	X^HX^h normal female (carrier)
Y	X^HY normal male	X^hY haemophiliac male

sperm

Since a woman has two X chromosomes, she would need to inherit a copy of the faulty allele from both her parents in order to have the genotype X^hX^h. This means that she would have to be the daughter of a haemophiliac father and a carrier mother. This is possible, but much less likely to happen. This means that haemophilia is much more common in boys than girls.

There are a number of other sex-linked genes that follow this pattern of inheritance, such as the gene causing red-green colour blindness.

Progress check 16.03

1 Explain the difference between genotype and phenotype.

2 Cystic fibrosis is a disorder caused by a recessive allele that is not sex-linked. What is the probability of two people who are carriers of the allele having a child who is:

   a affected by cystic fibrosis

   b a carrier of the cystic fibrosis allele ?

3 Coat colour in shorthorn cattle is controlled by a codominant gene. Pure-breeding red cattle (**RR**) crossed with pure-breeding white cattle (**WW**) produce offspring that are all pale brown, called 'roan'. Draw genetic diagrams to show the possible genotypes and phenotypes of offspring resulting from a cross between:

   a a red bull and a roan cow

   b a roan bull and a roan cow.

16.05 Dihybrid inheritance

It is possible to construct genetic diagrams to show the inheritance of two genes. This is called **dihybrid inheritance**. For example, pea plants can be tall or short, and have round or wrinkled seeds. These characteristics are genetically determined. The allele for tall plants (**T**) is dominant to the allele for short (**t**) and the allele for round seeds (**R**) is dominant to the allele for wrinkled seeds (**r**).

If a plant that is homozygous dominant for both height and shape of seeds (**TTRR**) is crossed with one that is homozygous recessive for both features (**ttrr**), all the offspring in the F1 generation will be heterozygous for both characteristics. They will all be tall with round seeds:

Genotypes of parents:	**TTRR**	×	**ttrr**
Genotypes of gametes:	all (TR)		all (tr)
Genotype of F1:		all **TtRr**	
Phenotype of F1:		all tall with round seeds	

TIP

Note that in a dihybrid cross, each gamete contains *two* alleles – one for each gene.

Note that either gametes could be dominant or recessive, here for simplicity the female gametes are shown carrying the recessive alleles.

Assuming the two genes are on *different chromosomes* (i.e. they are not *linked* – see 'Autosomal linkage' below) then four possible gametes can be produced from the F1 genotype, **TtRr**. These are **TR**, **Tr**, **tR** and **tr**. The four combinations of alleles are a consequence of independent assortment during meiosis.

If two F1 plants are crossed, the possible outcomes in the F2 are:

female gametes

		TR	Tr	tR	tr
		TTRR tall, round	**TTRr** tall, round	**TtRR** tall, round	**TtRr** tall, round
male gametes	TR				
	Tr	**TTRr** tall, round	**TTrr** tall, wrinkled	**TtRr** tall, round	**Ttrr** tall, wrinkled
	tR	**TtRR** tall, round	**TtRr** tall, round	**ttRR** short, round	**ttRr** short, round
	tr	**TtRr** tall, round	**Ttrr** tall, wrinkled	**ttRr** short, round	**ttrr** short, wrinkled

The expected ratio of phenotypes in the F2 is:

9 tall, round seeds : 3 tall, wrinkled seeds : 3 short, round seeds: 1 short, wrinkled seeds

9 : 3 : 3 : 1 is the usual ratio obtained with unlinked genes from a dihybrid cross between two double heterozygotes.

a Gene interactions

Two alleles of one gene can interact to produce a different phenotype, as in codominance. Two genes at different loci can also interact to affect the same characteristic.

One example involves two of the genes affecting coat colour in mice. Most wild mice have a grey coat colour called agouti. This results from individual hairs having a light band of pigment on a dark hair shaft. The allele for agouti (**A**) is dominant over the allele for 'solid' hair colour (**a**). A second gene determines whether any pigment is produced at all. The dominant allele (**M**) determines

the production of melanin, while the recessive allele (**m**) prevents the production of melanin, producing white (albino) mice. The possible genotypes and phenotypes are:

Genotype	Phenotype
AAMM, AAMm, AaMM, AaMm	agouti
aaMM, aaMm	black
aamm, Aamm, AAmm	albino

If two double heterozygous agouti mice (genotype **AaMm**) are crossed, the possible genotypes and phenotypes of the offspring are:

eggs

		AM	Am	aM	am
sperm	AM	**AAMM** agouti	**AAMm** agouti	**AaMM** agouti	**AaMm** agouti
	Am	**AAMm** agouti	**AAmm** albino	**AaMm** agouti	**Aamm** albino
	aM	**AaMM** agouti	**AaMm** agouti	**aaMM** black	**aaMm** black
	am	**AaMm** agouti	**Aamm** albino	**aaMm** black	**aamm** albino

The expected ratio of phenotypes in the F2 is 9 agouti : 3 black : 4 albino, which is a modified version of the 9 : 3 : 3 : 1 ratio.

Progress check 16.04

In tomato plants the allele for tall plants (**T**) is dominant to the allele for short plants (**t**) and the allele for red fruit (**R**) is dominant to the allele for yellow fruit (**r**). A cross was carried out between two tomato plants.

1 The possible genotypes of the gametes of the plant selected as the male parent were **TR**, **tR**, **Tr** and **tr**. What was the genotype and phenotype of this plant ?

2 The possible genotypes of the gametes of the plant selected as the female parent were **Tr** and **tr**. What was the genotype and phenotype of this plant ?

3 Construct a genetic diagram to show the offspring of this cross. What proportion of the offspring would you expect to have red fruit ?

Unit 16 Genetics

158

16.06 Autosomal linkage

If genes are located together on a non-sex chromosome (an autosome) this is known as **autosomal linkage**. Two or more genes on the same chromosome are said to be linked and all the genes on a single chromosome are called a linkage group.

With linked genes, two alleles on the same chromosome will tend to be inherited together. When the homologous chromosomes are separated during anaphase I of meiosis, both genes will go into the same daughter cell. In other words independent assortment does not apply to linked genes.

Imagine two genes **A** and **B**, with recessive alleles **a** and **b**. A double heterozygous individual has the genotype **AaBb**. If the genes are on different chromosomes, independent assortment means that gametes with four different genotypes can be formed. If they are on the same chromosome only two genotypes are possible (Figure 16.07).

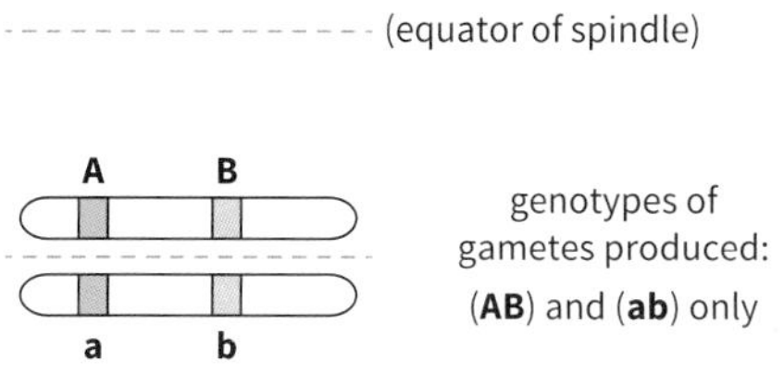

------------------------------ (equator of spindle)

A   B
genotypes of
gametes produced:
(**AB**) and (**ab**) only
a   b

Figure 16.07 Linked genes cannot show independent assortment. The dashed line represents the equator of the spindle.

In genetics diagrams, genes in linkage groups can be bracketed to show they are inherited together. For example, (**AB**)(**ab**) rather than **AaBb**. If two heterozygous individuals are crossed together, unlinked genes will produce offspring in a 9 : 3 : 3 : 1 ratio of genotypes, whereas linked genes will give a 3 : 1 ratio, like a monohybrid cross:

Genotypes of parents: (**AB**)(**ab**)   ×   (**AB**)(**ab**)

Genotypes of gametes: (**AB**) (**ab**)   (**AB**) (**ab**)

female gametes

	(**AB**)	(**ab**)
(**AB**)	(**AB**)(**AB**)	(**AB**)(**ab**)
(**ab**)	(**AB**)(**ab**)	(**ab**)(**ab**)

male gametes

It is possible for these alleles to be separated however, if *crossing over* occurs between the two gene loci during prophase I of meiosis (see Figure 16.01). In that case, some recombinants will result in gametes with genotypes **Ab** and **aB**. This is shown in the example in Sample question 16.01.

Sample question 16.01

Genetic crosses were carried out on the sweet pea plant *Lathyrus*. Plants that were homozygous for purple flowers and long pollen were crossed with plants that were homozygous for red flowers and round pollen. The F1 plants all had purple flowers and long pollen.

Read the whole question before you start.

1 State which of the phenotypes above are controlled by dominant alleles. Explain your choice. [2]

2 Using the letters A or a for flower colour and B or b for pollen shape, state the genotypes of:

   a The parent plants. [2]

   b The F1 plants. [1]

Plants from the F1 generation were allowed to self-pollinate. The results are shown in Table 16.02.

Phenotype	Numbers of plants with each phenotype
purple flowers, long pollen	234
purple flowers, round pollen	16
red flowers, long pollen	22
red flowers, round pollen	75

Table 16.02 Results of crosses between F1 plants.

3 Explain why the results in Table 16.02 indicate that the genes for flower colour and pollen shape are linked. [3]

4 Assuming the genes *are* linked, explain the process that results in the production of plants with purple flowers and long pollen. [3]

[Mark points are shown in square brackets – to a maximum of 11 marks]

1 Purple flowers and long pollen. [1] These are the only phenotypes appearing in the F1. [1]

2 a AABB and aabb [1]

   b AaBb. [1]

3 If the genes were not linked, a cross between two F1 plants with the double heterozygous genotype **AaBb** would be expected to produce a 9 : 3 : 3 : 1 ratio [1] (of phenotypes in the F2 generation:)

   9 purple flower, long pollen

   3 purple flower, round pollen

   3 red flower, long pollen

   1 red flower, round pollen [1] (*mark awarded for details of F2 phenotypic ratios*)

   Linkage means that (**AB**) and (**ab**) are inherited together, [1] so that most plants have purple flowers and long pollen or red flowers and round pollen, in [1] (approximately) a 3 : 1 ratio. [1] (Maximum 3 marks)

4 The process is crossing over [1] in prophase I of meiosis. [1] Formation of a chiasma between genes for flower colour and pollen shape [1] produces some gametes (**Ab**) and (**aB**) [1] which can result in recombinants such as **AAbb** and **Aabb**. [1] These genotypes produce plants with purple flowers and round pollen. [1] (Maximum 3 marks)

Alternatively, assuming the genes are linked, you could write the linked alleles in brackets: (**AB**)(**ab**).

16.07 The chi-squared (χ^2) test

It is clear just by looking at the numbers that the frequencies of phenotypes in Table 16.02 do not fit a 9 : 3 : 3 : 1 ratio. With some crosses however, the 'goodness of fit' may not be so clear. Imagine you find the ratio is 93 : 44 : 35 : 27. Is this observed ratio 'close enough' to a 9 : 3 : 3 : 1 ratio or not? In a situation like this it is possible to carry out a statistical test to find out whether the observed frequencies are significantly different from the expected frequencies. The test used is called the **chi-squared test** (chi is the Greek letter χ).

The test starts with a statement of the null hypothesis, which is 'the observed frequencies are not significantly different from the expected frequencies'. The chi-squared test gives a probability value, which tells us the probability of obtaining the differences by chance. If this is less than 1 in 20 (5%), we can reject the null hypothesis and accept the alternative, that the differences are significant.

Worked example 16.01

Question

In dogs, two unlinked genes interact to affect coat colour. The dominant allele **A** produces a white coat, while the recessive allele **a** allows the development of a coloured coat. Black coat colour is determined by a dominant allele **B** and brown coat colour by its recessive allele **b**. A cross between white dogs that are double heterozygous for coat colour (**AaBb**) produces the following possible genotypes and phenotypes:

eggs

	AB	**Ab**	**aB**	**ab**
AB	**AABB** white	**AABb** white	**AaBB** white	**AaBb** white
Ab	**AABb** white	**AAbb** white	**AaBb** white	**Aabb** white
aB	**AaBB** white	**AaBb** white	**aaBB** black	**aaBb** black
ab	**AaBb** white	**Aabb** white	**aaBb** black	**aabb** brown

sperm

The expected ratio is 12 white : 3 black : 1 brown. A series of crosses between double heterozygous white dogs produced 102 puppies, of which 67 were white, 25 were black and 10 were brown.

Carry out a chi-squared test to find out if the observed frequencies fit a 12 : 3 : 1 ratio.

Answer

Step 1:

State the null hypothesis: there is no significant difference between the observed and expected frequencies.

Step 2:

Calculate the expected frequencies (values rounded to one decimal place):

white $= \dfrac{12}{16} \times 102 = 76.5$

black $= \dfrac{3}{16} \times 102 = 19.1$

brown $= \dfrac{1}{16} \times 102 = 6.4$

Step 3:

Calculate χ^2:

$$\chi^2 = \Sigma \frac{(O-E)^2}{E}$$

where Σ means 'the sum of', O is the observed frequency and E is the expected frequency.

Phenotype	O	E	$O - E$	$(O - E)^2$	$(O - E)^2/E$
White	67	76.5	−9.5	90.25	1.18
Black	25	19.1	5.9	34.81	1.82
Brown	10	6.4	3.6	12.96	2.03
Totals	102	102		$\chi^2 =$	5.03

Step 4:

Find the 'degrees of freedom': this is the number of categories (in this case phenotypes) minus 1:

degrees of freedom $= (3 - 1) = 2$

Step 5:

Look up the probability of getting $\chi^2 = 5.03$. Table 16.03 shows the critical values of χ^2 with different degrees of freedom, for different probability levels. For 2 degrees of freedom, 5.03 falls between the values in italics in Table 16.03.

→

Degrees of freedom	Critical values of χ^2				
	P = 0.10	P = 0.05	P = 0.02	P = 0.01	P = 0.001
1	2.71	3.84	5.41	6.64	10.83
2	4.60	5.99	7.82	9.21	13.82
3	6.25	7.82	9.84	11.34	16.027
4	7.78	9.49	11.67	13.28	18.46

Table 16.03 Critical values of χ^2 with different degrees of freedom, for different probability (P) levels.

If the null hypothesis is correct, the probability of getting $\chi^2 = 5.03$ is between 0.05 and 0.10 (5 and 10%).

Step 6:

Draw a conclusion. The probability is greater than 0.05, so we can accept the null hypothesis – the observed frequencies are not significantly different from the expected ones. In other words the results do fit a 12 : 3 : 1 ratio.

16.08 Gene mutation

A **gene mutation** is a change in the base sequence of part of a DNA molecule. This may change the sequence of amino acids in a protein encoded by the DNA, which in turn may affect the three-dimensional structure of the protein and interfere with its proper function. Gene mutations are random events that occur during DNA replication, such as where an incorrect base is inserted into the new strand of DNA. There are enzymes in cells that identify and correct most mutations, although some are missed. Mutations that occur during meiosis are particularly important, since they may be passed to gametes and on to future generations.

Although mutations are random events, there are a number of environmental factors that increase the rate of mutation. These are called mutagens. They include:

- ionising radiation (alpha, beta and gamma radiation)

- ultraviolet radiation

- a wide range of chemicals, from simple molecules like nitrous acid to organic compounds such as benzene and nitrosamines found in tobacco smoke.

There are three types of gene mutation that alter the sequence of bases in DNA:

- *Substitution*, where a base is replaced by another. For example, the sequence GTG AAA CGG becomes GTG AA<u>T</u> CGG (adenine replaced by thymine in the second triplet).

- *Addition*, where a base is added. For example, GTG AAA CGG becomes GT<u>A</u> GAA ACG G (adenine added at third base position in the first triplet).

- *Deletion*, where a base is lost. For example, GTG AAA CGG becomes <u>GG</u>A AAC GG (thymine lost from the first triplet).

Additions and deletions usually have serious consequences, because they can change the whole sequence of the triplet codes 'downstream' of the mutation, in what is called a frame shift. This will change many amino acids in the protein the DNA codes for, so that it is unlikely to maintain its three-dimensional structure and function. Substitutions are less damaging to the genetic code, because they do not cause a frame shift. In addition, a substitution may have no effect at all. This is because the code is degenerate and a different triplet may still code for the same amino acid (e.g. the DNA triplets AAA and AAG both code for phenylalanine); however, some base substitutions can have a large effect (e.g. the triplet ATG if mutated to ATT becomes a 'stop' triplet, terminating protein synthesis).

16.09 Human conditions caused by gene mutations

Most mutations have no effect on the phenotype – they are neutral. Some mutations are beneficial in the long term, since mutations are the only source of new alleles, which add genetic variation to populations and allow natural selection and evolution to take place (see Unit 17). However some mutations are harmful. These mutations are unlikely to persist for more than one generation, because of the serious effects on the phenotype of individuals that carry the harmful gene.

a Haemophilia

You have already seen one example of a harmful human gene mutation – the gene that causes the blood disorder **haemophilia**. In fact there are several kinds of haemophilia. The two main types (A and B) are both sex-linked and more common in men. Haemophilia A is caused by mutation to gene F8, which codes for the production of a blood protein called coagulation factor VIII. Haemophilia B is caused by mutation to another gene F9, which codes for a related coagulation factor IX. The mutations reduce or eliminate the activities of these proteins, leading to continuous bleeding that is difficult to control. Haemophiliacs also suffer from prolonged internal bleeding after knocks, and spontaneous bleeding in the joints, intestine and other tissues.

b Huntington's disease

Most mutated alleles are recessive. **Huntington's disease** is unusual in that it is caused by a gene mutation that is inherited as a dominant allele. The condition normally develops during middle age, when nerve cells start to degenerate more rapidly than normal, resulting in involuntary muscular movements and progressive mental deterioration. The disease is always fatal, death usually occurring within 10 years of the first appearance of symptoms.

The mutation happens to a gene on chromosome 4 that codes for a protein called huntingtin. The part of the chromosome affected normally contains small numbers of repeats of the base triplet CAG. People with Huntington's disease have a larger number of these repeats, called a 'stutter'. It is most commonly inherited when one parent is heterozygous for the condition and the other person has the normal homozygous recessive genotype. They have a 50% chance of having a child with the Huntington allele (**H**). For example:

eggs

	H	**h**
h	**Hh** (affected)	hh (normal)
h	**Hh** (affected)	hh (normal)

sperm

(Note that the mutant allele **H** can be carried by the eggs or sperm.)

Since onset of the disease is in middle age, by the time someone is aware that they have the condition they may have already passed the gene to their children. Nowadays DNA testing can establish whether or not someone has the Huntington allele.

c Sickle cell anaemia

Sickle cell anaemia affects the gene that codes for the production of haemoglobin. People suffering from sickle cell anaemia produce abnormal haemoglobin in their red blood cells, which causes the cells to take on a distorted crescent or 'sickle' shape in low concentrations of oxygen (Figure 16.08).

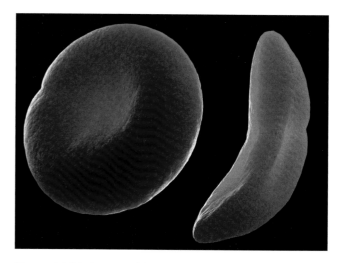

Figure 16.08 A normal biconcave disc-shaped red blood cell and a sickle-shaped cell.

The mutation occurs in the gene that codes for one of the polypeptides that make up haemoglobin. There are 438 bases in the gene. A single base substitution to one triplet (CTT) produces CAT, which codes for the amino acid valine instead of glutamic acid. This change to a single amino acid in the polypeptide is enough to alter the three-dimensional structure of the protein and affect its function. When the haemoglobin is combined with oxygen it retains its normal structure, but when it is deoxygenated it assumes a fibrous structure that is less soluble. The molecules stick together in the red blood cells, distorting their shape.

Sickling happens in tissues that are actively respiring and using up oxygen, such as muscles. There are two main consequences:

- Sickle cells carry less oxygen than normal cells. They are more delicate and easily burst. Sickle cells are also destroyed by the spleen at a faster rate than normal cells. These effects lead to anaemia, which gives the disease its name.

- The sickle cells stick together, blocking capillaries and causing severe pain, especially in the joints. This is called a 'sickle cell crisis'. Several of the body's organs may be affected. If the blood supply to the brain is reduced, this can lead to a stroke.

Sickle cell anaemia is a dangerous condition and results in a lowered life expectancy. People with the disease often die in childhood. There are treatments, including transfusions and bone marrow transplants. However these are expensive and unlikely to be available in less affluent countries.

The sickle cell allele (Hb^S) is codominant with the allele for normal haemoglobin (Hb^A). There are three possible genotypes: Hb^AHb^A, Hb^AHb^S and Hb^SHb^S. The phenotypes and effects of these three genotypes are shown in Table 16.04.

	Hb^AHb^A	Hb^AHb^S	Hb^SHb^S
Phenotype	normal haemoglobin and normal red blood cells	over 50% normal haemoglobin; few sickle-shaped red blood cells	many sickle-shaped red blood cells
Symptoms	none	normally no symptoms except slight anaemia	sickle cell anaemia with severe sickle cell crises

Table 16.04 Phenotypes and symptoms of the genotypes determining sickle cell anaemia.

To be fully affected by the mutation, a person must be homozygous for the mutant allele (Hb^SHb^S). The heterozygote Hb^AHb^S is intermediate in phenotype between the other two genotypes. The two alleles are codominant but do not show *equal* dominance – a person who is heterozygous shows few visible symptoms of the disease.

If two heterozygous individuals have children, there is a 25% chance that a child will have the disease:

eggs

	Hb^A	Hb^S
Hb^A	Hb^AHb^A (normal)	Hb^AHb^S (carrier)
Hb^S	Hb^AHb^S (carrier)	Hb^SHb^S (sickle cell)

sperm

Sickle cell anaemia is common in many tropical regions of the world, particularly sub-Saharan Africa, the Indian sub-continent and the Middle East. Three-quarters of all people with the disease live in Africa. In other countries such as the Caribbean and USA it affects people of African descent. The reason why the disease is common in these areas of the world is discussed in Unit 17.

d Albinism

Albinism is a condition where there is a lack of the dark pigment melanin in the body. People with albinism are very light skinned, with white hair. The irises of their eyes are pale blue or pink (Figure 16.09). Lacking the protection provided by melanin, their skin is easily damaged by ultraviolet light.

Figure 16.09 An albino child.

Albinism is a good example of the relationship between a gene, an enzyme and a phenotype. Common forms of albinism involve mutations to the TYR gene on chromosome 11. This gene codes for the production of an enzyme called tyrosinase. Tyrosinase is a copper-containing protein that controls the production of melanin from the amino acid tyrosine. It converts tyrosine into a substance called dopaquinone. This is followed by a series of reactions in which dopaquinone is converted into melanin in skin, hair follicles, the iris and the retina. Over 100 different mutations of the TYR gene have been identified. Some eliminate tyrosinase activity, while others reduce its activity. The mutated alleles are recessive and inherited from parents who are heterozygous for the condition.

Progress check 16.05

1   State whether or not each of the following gene mutations would result in a frame shift:

    a   deletion of 1 base

    b   deletion of 6 bases

    c   substitution of 1 base

    d   addition of 3 bases.

2   Briefly summarise how the **Hb^S** mutation affects the structure and function of haemoglobin in a person with the genotype **Hb^SHb^S**.

16.10 Control of gene expression

Gene expression involves using the information encoded in the DNA sequence of a gene to make messenger RNA and subsequently a protein (see Unit 6). Gene expression can be controlled at various points in this process. In both prokaryotes and eukaryotes, one method of control is carried out by proteins called **transcription factors**. They bind to a specific sequence of DNA and control the formation of mRNA.

Genes may be structural or regulatory:

* **structural genes** code for proteins such as enzymes, or proteins that form part of the cell itself, such as actin and myosin

* **regulatory genes** code for proteins that regulate the expression of other genes, such as transcription factors.

Another way that gene expression is controlled is by regulation of enzyme synthesis. Most enzymes in a cell (e.g. the enzymes involved in glycolysis or the Krebs cycle) are produced in approximately the same amounts regardless of the composition of their surroundings. Other enzymes are inducible or repressible:

* **Inducible enzymes** are produced in response to the presence of their substrate (i.e. they are only synthesised when needed).

* The synthesis of **repressible enzymes** is switched off or 'downregulated' by the presence of a substance, such as a product of the pathway in which the enzyme participates. In prokaryotes the synthesis of a repressible enzyme can be stopped by the binding of a repressor protein to a site on the bacterium's DNA.

a Control of gene expression in a prokaryote – the *lac* operon

An **operon** is a group of structural genes headed by a non-coding sequence of DNA called the **operator** and under the control of another sequence of DNA called the **promoter**. The promoter binds to RNA polymerase and initiates transcription of all the genes in the operon. Close to the promoter is a **regulatory gene**, which codes for a protein called a repressor. The repressor protein can bind to the operator and prevent it binding with RNA polymerase (Figure 16.10).

Operons were once thought to only exist in prokaryotes, but now many have been discovered in a range of eukaryotic cells. The first operon to be described was the *lac* operon in the bacterium *Escherichia coli*, which lives in the intestine of mammals and preferentially metabolises glucose. However if there is a high concentration of the sugar

Unit 16 Genetics

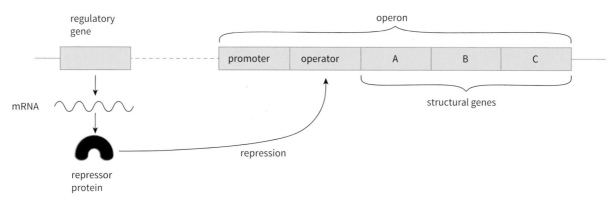

Figure 16.10 An operon.

165

lactose around the bacterium (e.g. in the gut of a young mammal that is feeding on milk) it can mobilise enzymes that enable it to use lactose instead. To do this, the bacterium needs to express genes for three enzymes:

- β-galactosidase (lactase), which hydrolyses the disaccharide lactose into glucose and galactose.
- β-galactoside permease, which allows lactose to enter the bacterial cell.
- β-galactoside transacetylase (the precise function of this enzyme in the *lac* operon is not known).

These enzymes are encoded in the *lac* operon by three structural genes called *lacZ*, *lacY* and *lacA*, respectively (at A, B and C in Figure 16.10).

If there is no lactose in the medium around the bacterium:

- The repressor protein binds to the operator. This prevents RNA polymerase binding with the DNA at the promoter and the structural genes cannot be transcribed.

When lactose is present in the medium:

- Lactose binds to the repressor protein, altering its shape and preventing it from binding to the operator. This allows RNA polymerase to bind with the promoter, 'switching on' transcription of the genes for the three enzymes.

Regulation of expression of the genes for metabolising lactose enables *E. coli* to avoid wasting energy and materials when there is no lactose available.

b Control of gene expression in eukaryotes

Cells of eukaryotes have been found to have a very large number of different protein transcription factors that bind to DNA and regulate transcription.

An example is involved in the actions of the plant hormone gibberellin. One role of gibberellin is to stimulate the production of amylase in germinating seeds. Starch is stored in many seeds such as wheat and barley. When a seed germinates, amylase hydrolyses starch, producing glucose for respiration. DELLA proteins are repressors of transcription of various genes in plant cells, including the gene coding for amylase (DELLA comes from single-letter abbreviations of the first five amino acids of these proteins). Gibberellin is known to increase the transcription of the gene for amylase, probably by causing the breakdown of a DELLA protein. Removal of the DELLA repressor allows a transcription factor to activate the gene's promoter.

Revision checklist

Check that you know:

- the stages of meiosis
- crossing over and independent assortment
- gametogenesis in humans
- gametogenesis in flowering plants
- terms used in genetics
- monohybrid inheritance
- codominance
- test crosses
- multiple alleles
- sex linkage
- dihybrid inheritance
- gene interactions
- autosomal linkage
- the chi-squared test
- gene mutation
- human conditions caused by gene mutations
- control of gene expression
- the *lac* operon.

Exam-style questions

1 Figure 16.11 shows chromosomes in cells at different stages of meiosis. The cells are from an organism that has two pairs of homologous chromosomes.

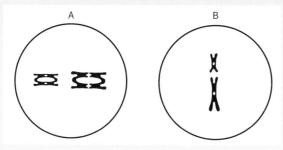

Figure 16.11

a Identify the stage of meiosis shown in cell A and cell B. [2]

b Independent assortment takes place during stage A. Explain how independent assortment leads to an increase in genetic variation. [3]

Total: 5

2 Spermatogenesis takes place in the seminiferous tubules of the testis. Figure 16.12 shows cells from part of a seminiferous tubule. Spermatogonia develop from primordial germ cells in the testis.

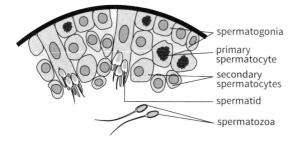

Figure 16.12

a State whether each of the cells labelled in Figure 16.12 is haploid or diploid. [2]

b Spermatogenesis involves mitosis, meiosis and a growth phase. State which of these processes is involved in the following steps of the process:

i primordial germ cells to spermatogonia

ii spermatogonia to primary spermatocytes

iii secondary spermatocytes to spermatids. [3]

c Describe two differences between the processes of spermatogenesis and oogenesis. [2]

Total: 7

3 Female cats have the genotype XX and male cats XY, as in humans. One gene for coat colour in cats is determined by a sex-linked gene that shows codominance. The allele X^o produces ginger fur, while the allele X^b produces black fur. Cats that are heterozygous for the alleles have black and ginger patches, called tortoiseshell.

a Explain what is meant by codominance. [1]

b Explain why it is not possible for a male cat to be tortoiseshell. [2]

c Construct a diagram to show the possible offspring of a cross between a black male cat and a female tortoiseshell cat. Show the genotypes and phenotypes on the diagram [2].

Total: 5

4 In fruit flies (*Drosophila*) the allele for grey body colour (**G**) is dominant to the allele for black body colour (**g**), and the allele for normal wings (**N**) is dominant to the allele for vestigial wings (**n**). A cross between a grey-bodied, normal-winged fly and a black-bodied, vestigial-winged fly produced offspring with the following phenotypes:

32 grey-bodied, normal-winged

22 grey-bodied, vestigial-winged

29 black-bodied, normal-winged

21 black-bodied, vestigial-winged.

a State the genotype of the grey-bodied, normal-winged parent. [1]

b State the genotypes of the gametes which could be produced by one of the grey-bodied, vestigial-winged offspring [1]

c A chi-squared test was carried out to find out if the flies in the F1 generation fitted an expected 1 : 1: 1 : 1 ratio. The calculated value of χ^2 was 3.31. Use Table 16.03 to interpret the results of the test, explaining your conclusions fully. [4]

Total: 6

5 Explain how the *lac* operon controls the metabolism of lactose in the bacterium *Escherichia coli*. [9]

Total: 9

Selection and evolution

Within any species there are differences between individuals. This biological variation means that some individuals are better adapted to their environment, increasing their chances of surviving to reproduce. This is 'survival of the fittest', or natural selection. Natural selection can lead to isolated groups within a population diverging so much that they become separate species. The process of change by natural selection, leading to speciation, is called **evolution**.

17.01 Continuous and discontinuous variation

Genetic variation within a species starts with mutations, and is increased by meiosis and fertilisation (see Unit 16). This produces differences in phenotype which can be either continuous or discontinuous. It is easier to consider discontinuous variation first.

Discontinuous variation is where a characteristic fits into a number of separate, distinct categories, with no intermediates. An example of this is the ABO blood group system. A person is either group A, B, AB or O and the frequencies of individuals in the population that fit into each group can be shown as a bar chart (Figure 17.01).

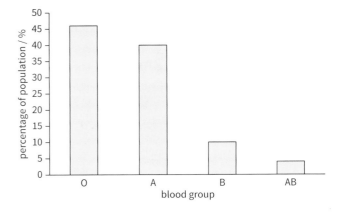

Figure 17.01 The four distinct blood groups in the ABO system is an example of discontinuous variation.

Features that show discontinuous variation are sometimes described as *qualitative*, since the feature is either present or absent. They are normally under the control of a single gene, or at most a few genes. ABO blood groups are determined by one gene with three alleles: I^A, I^B and I^O. The human conditions albinism, sickle cell anaemia, haemophilia and Huntington's disease (see Unit 16) are all examples of discontinuous variation. The genetic crosses shown in Unit 16 all result in discontinuous variation, since they involve monohybrid inheritance (one gene) or dihybrid inheritance (two genes).

Continuous variation is where a characteristic shows a complete range of measurements, without falling into separate categories. Human height and body mass are typical examples. A histogram of numbers of people against height forms a bell-shaped curve called a 'normal distribution' (Figure 17.02).

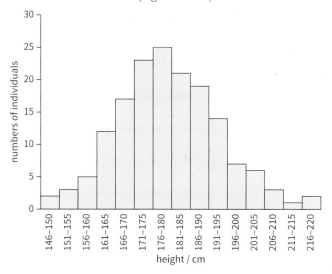

Figure 17.02 Human height is a continuous variable. It shows a complete gradation from short to tall, with the height of most individuals falling around the mean.

TIP

Note that 'normal distribution' is a technical term used in statistics, not an everyday expression.

Characteristics showing continuous variation are *quantitative*, meaning that they can be measured. They are dependent on the action of many genes – they are *polygenic*. Often, polygenic features are highly influenced by the environment. For example, a person's height depends on the actions of genes controlling metabolism, bone growth, muscle formation and synthesis of certain hormones. However, height also depends on a person's food intake and will be severely restricted if they do not eat a balanced diet, especially during childhood.

The environment may sometimes affect discontinuous variables. In the *lac* operon, the presence of lactose in the medium around a bacterium switches on the production of enzymes needed to digest lactose (see Unit 16). Here the environment directly affects the expression of a gene.

Another environmental effect is seen in Siamese cats. These cats are affected by a gene mutation affecting coat colour, which is a form of albinism (see Unit 16). The gene codes for an enzyme called tyrosinase, which is involved in the formation of melanin in the fur. This gene is sensitive to the surrounding temperature. In cooler parts of the body such as the paws, tail, face and ears, the gene brings about the production of dark hair. In the warmer, core parts of the body the cats have light hair (Figure 17.03).

Figure 17.03 A Siamese cat.

The environment can affect the phenotype of plants too. Hydrangea plants have flowers that may be pink or blue. Hydrangeas grown in alkaline or neutral soils have pink flowers, while plants grown in acid soils produce blue flowers. The difference is due to the concentration of aluminium in the soil, which differs in acid and alkaline conditions. Addition of aluminium sulfate to a soil will change hydrangea flowers from pink to blue, as a result of Al^{3+} ions binding to a pigment called anthocyanin in the flowers.

The green colour of plants is also dependent on the environment. Green plants that are kept in the dark exhibit chlorosis (yellowing of the leaves), since light is needed in order for a plant to make chlorophyll. A similar effect results from depriving plants of magnesium, since Mg^{2+} ions are required to make the chlorophyll molecule.

Progress check 17.01

1 State whether the following are examples of continuous or discontinuous variation.

   a Eye colour.

   b Heart rate.

   c Leaf length.

   d Height of tall and dwarf varieties of pea plant.

2 Is human skin colour a continuous or discontinuous variable? Is it affected by the environment? Explain your answers.

17.02 Using the *t*-test to compare the means of two groups

The **t-test** is a statistical test that can be used to find out if there is a significant difference between the means of two independent groups. The two groups each have to fit a normal distribution. For example, we could use the *t*-test to find out if the mean height of a group of plants treated with a fertiliser was different from the mean height of a control group.

The null hypothesis is that there is no difference between the means of the two groups (i.e. the means are equal). The alternative hypothesis is that the means are not equal. As with the chi-squared test (see Unit 16), we use a probability level (*P*) of 5% (5 in 100 or 0.05) that will allow us to reject or accept the null hypothesis. If our calculated value of *t* is greater than the critical value of *t* at *P* = 0.05, we

can reject the null hypothesis and say that the means are significantly different.

The formula for the *t* statistic is:

$$t = \frac{\overline{x}_1 - \overline{x}_2}{\sqrt{\dfrac{s_1^2}{n_1} + \dfrac{s_2^2}{n_2}}}$$

where $\overline{x}_1$ is the mean of sample 1, $\overline{x}_2$ is the mean of sample 2, s_1 is the standard deviation of sample 1, s_2 is the standard deviation of sample 2, n_1 is the number of measurements in sample 1 and n_2 is the number of measurements in sample 2

Worked example 17.01

Question

A student noticed that a species of plant growing in a wood seemed to have larger leaves than plants of same species growing in an open field. She measured the lengths of 10 leaves collected at random from plants in each of the two habitats. Her data is given in Table 17.01. Carry out a *t*-test on the data to find out if the mean leaf lengths are significantly different.

Answer

Step 1:
State the null hypothesis: there is no difference between the means of the leaves in the two habitats.

Step 2:
Calculate the differences between each observation and the mean for each sample $(x - \overline{x})$, the square of each of these values $(x - \overline{x})^2$ and the sum of squares $\sum (x - \overline{x})^2$.

Sample 1: Length of leaves in wood / cm	Sample 2: Length of leaves in field / cm
9.5	8.3
10.1	7.1
5.7	6.6
8.4	5.2
11.6	5.4
12.0	7.9
8.8	6.8
8.3	8.5
9.4	6.3
10.9	6.7
Mean $(\overline{x}_1)$ = 9.47	Mean $(\overline{x}_2)$ = 6.88

Table 17.01

(Use a reasonable number of significant figures in the intermediate calculations – only round up or down at the end, or you may introduce rounding errors that result in an inaccurate value of *t*.)

Sample 1			Sample 2		
x_1	$x_1 - \bar{x}_1$	$(x_1 - \bar{x}_1)^2$	x_2	$x_2 - \bar{x}_2$	$(x_2 - \bar{x}_2)^2$
9.5	0.03	0.0009	8.3	1.42	2.0164
10.1	0.63	0.3969	7.1	0.22	0.0484
5.7	−3.77	14.2129	6.6	−0.28	0.0784
8.4	−1.07	1.1449	5.2	−1.68	2.8224
11.6	2.13	4.5369	5.4	−1.48	2.1904
12.0	2.53	6.4009	7.9	1.02	1.0404
8.8	−0.67	0.4489	6.8	−0.08	0.0064
8.3	−1.17	1.3689	8.5	1.62	2.6244
9.4	−0.07	0.0049	6.3	−0.58	0.3364
10.9	1.43	2.0449	6.7	−0.18	0.0324
Sum of squares $\sum (x - \bar{x})^2 =$		30.561	Sum of squares $\sum (x_2 - \bar{x}_2)^2 =$		11.196

Step 3:

For Sample 1, divide the sum of squares by $(n_1 - 1)$, and for Sample 2, divide the sum of squares by $(n_2 - 1)$. (In this investigation both sample sizes =10, so $n - 1 = 9$ in both cases.)

Sample 1: $\dfrac{30.561}{9} = 3.396$

Sample 2: $\dfrac{11.196}{9} = 1.244$

Step 4:

Find the square root of each value from step 3. This gives you the values of s_1 and s_2, the standard deviations of each sample.

$s_1 = \sqrt{3.396} = 1.843$

$s_2 = \sqrt{1.244} = 1.115$

Step 5:

For each sample, square the standard deviation and divide by the number of observations in each sample. Add these values together and take the square root of this number:

$$\sqrt{\frac{s_1^2}{n_1} + \frac{s_2^2}{n_2}} = \sqrt{\frac{1.843^2}{10} + \frac{1.115^2}{10}} = 0.6812$$

Step 6:

Calculate the value of t. Divide the difference between the means of samples 1 and 2 by the value calculated in step 5:

$$\frac{\bar{x}_1 - \bar{x}_2}{0.6812} = \frac{9.47 - 6.88}{0.6812} = 3.80$$

Step 7:

Calculate the degrees of freedom (v) from:

$v = (n_1 - 1) + (n_2 - 1)$

$= (10 - 1) + (10 - 1) = 9 + 9 = 18$

(You are expected to remember the formula used to calculate the degrees of freedom.)

Step 8:

Look up the calculated t value on a table of critical values of t for different degrees of freedom. The table below shows the probabilities of obtaining different t values, for 18 degrees of freedom, if the null hypothesis (no difference between means) is correct.

Probability (P)	0.10 (10%)	0.05 (5%)	0.01 (1%)	0.001 (0.1%)
t value	1.73	2.10	2.88	3.92

Conclusion:

The calculated value of t is 3.80. If the null hypothesis is correct, the probability of getting a t value this big is between 0.01 and 0.001 (1% and 0.1%). This is less than 5%, so we can *reject* the null hypothesis – the means are significantly different.

If you use a computer program to calculate t, it will tell you the exact probability of getting the t value (in this example $P = 0.0013$).

Progress check 17.02

A *t*-test was used to compare the mean rate of growth of two groups of baby mice. Eight mice were fed on a high protein diet and a control group of nine mice were fed on a normal diet. The calculated value of *t* was 2.05.

1   State the null hypothesis.

2   What are the degrees of freedom?

3   For *P* = 0.05 (5%), the critical value of *t* for this number of degrees of freedom is 2.13. Can we reject or accept the null hypothesis? Explain your answer.

17.03 Natural selection

Natural selection is the mechanism that brings about the evolution of new species. The theory of evolution by natural selection was developed independently by Charles Darwin and Alfred Russel Wallace, who published their ideas jointly in 1858. The process of natural selection has been summarised as consisting of three observations and two deductions:

Observations

1   Organisms produce far more offspring than are needed to replace them. For example, in a year, a single pair of rabbits and their offspring are capable of breeding to produce 500 rabbits; a fish such as the cod can lay 5 million eggs in a year.

2   Despite this capacity for over-production, populations of organisms tend to remain a constant size over long periods of time.

3   All species show variation.

Deductions

1   Many offspring are produced, yet populations remain the same size. Therefore many offspring must not survive. They die because there is a competition for resources such as food, or because of adverse conditions, such as cold or disease. Darwin called this a 'struggle for existence'.

2   Individuals that are best adapted to their environment will be the ones that are most likely to survive. They will go on to reproduce, while the less well adapted will die. This has been called 'survival of the fittest'.

TIP

Note that 'fittest' does not mean 'strongest'. 'Fittest' organisms are *best adapted* to their environment, so that they *survive to reproduce*.

Take the example of the rabbits. A single pair could in theory produce 500 animals in a year. But in an actual rabbit population, after a year there will still be only two rabbits – most will have died through predation, disease, hunger, cold and other factors. These biological (**biotic**) and physical (**abiotic**) factors act to maintain the population at a constant level.

The key points of natural selection are in deduction 2. It is the *best-adapted* individuals that will be most likely to survive and these are the ones that can *go on to reproduce*. For example, if a particular rabbit is better camouflaged than others it is less likely to be seen and eaten by a predator. It is more likely that it will reproduce and pass on its genes for better camouflage.

In this way, over many generations, genes that give a 'selective advantage' are passed on to later generations. With each generation there will be more of the well-adapted individuals, and fewer of the less well-adapted ones. Natural selection means that the environment is 'selecting' which individuals pass on their genes.

a   Examples of natural selection

Species on the Earth today have evolved through the process of natural selection. Generally, this has happened over very long periods of time, sometimes millions of years. However, natural selection can be observed to happen in some living organisms if they have a high rate of reproduction. You have already seen one example of this in Unit 10 – antibiotic resistance in bacteria. If a particular antibiotic is in use, bacterial cells that acquire a gene mutation that gives them resistance to that antibiotic have a strong selective advantage compared with non-resistant bacteria. The resistant strains survive and reproduce, while the non-resistant strains are killed by the antibiotic. This is a simple example of natural selection in action, and happens quickly, because the generation time of bacteria is so short.

There are a number of different kinds of resistance that have developed in fast-reproducing organisms. These include:

*   *Insecticide resistance in species such as the malaria mosquito.* Over 500 species of insect pests have now been identified which show resistance to various insecticides.

- *Warfarin resistance in rats and mice.* Warfarin is a compound that was first used as a rat poison in 1952. Within 10 years rats and mice had developed resistance to the poison. In countries where warfarin was used, warfarin-resistant strains became common around the world. The same thing has happened with later generations of rodenticide.

- *Resistance to myxomatosis in rabbits.* Myxomatosis is a disease caused by a virus called myxoma. In the past it was deliberately introduced to kill rabbits in places where their populations were out of control, such as Australia in the 1950s. At first it was highly successful, but within a few years of its introduction, strains of rabbits appeared that were resistant and not killed by the disease.

- *Heavy metal tolerance in plants.* Mines where they extract ores of metals such as copper and lead are often surrounded by spoil heaps containing high concentrations of these metals. The soil is normally toxic to plants, but strains of grasses and other plants have developed tolerance to the metals and can grow on these polluted soils.

In all these examples the resistant organisms have arisen through gene mutations that have given the organisms a selective advantage when their environment changed.

b Sickle cell anaemia

Sickle cell anaemia is a genetic disorder that is common in many parts of the world (see Unit 16). It is a harmful condition and many children who are homozygous for the sickle cell allele (**Hb^{S}Hb^S**) die from the disease before they reach adulthood. If this is so, you may be wondering why natural selection does not act to eradicate the condition altogether. The answer is that people who are heterozygous 'carriers' for the condition (**Hb^{A}Hb^S**) have protection against another disease – malaria.

The parasite that causes malaria spends part of its life cycle inside red blood cells (see Unit 10). The red blood cells of carriers are mostly normal in appearance, but because they contain about 40% abnormal haemoglobin, they are more delicate than normal red blood cells, and are easily damaged. When the malaria parasite enters these cells they burst, and the parasite is killed before it can develop any further. This interrupts the life cycle of the parasite, so the person is less likely to develop the full signs and symptoms of malaria, and is less likely to die from the disease.

This gives heterozygotes a strong selective advantage in areas of the world where malaria is endemic. The places in the world where the sickle cell allele is most common correlate with the malaria zones (Figure 17.04) shows this in Africa.

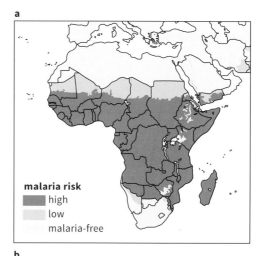

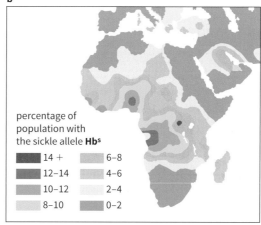

Figure 17.04 **a** Some parts of Africa and Southern Europe where malaria is found. **b** Incidence of sickle cell disease in the same areas.

Over many generations, natural selection has acted to maintain the sickle cell allele in these populations, because of the advantage shown by the heterozygote.

In some countries such as the USA there is a high incidence of the sickle cell allele, despite the fact that there is no malaria in that country. This is because most people in the USA who carry the gene mutation are of African descent. The allele is still present in the African-American population, although the occurrence of the disease is lower than in Africa, and is falling with each generation. There is selection pressure against the gene because of the change in the environment (i.e. the absence of malaria).

17.04 Stabilising, directional and disruptive selection

Natural selection can be stabilising, directional or disruptive. These can be shown as graphs (Figure 17.05).

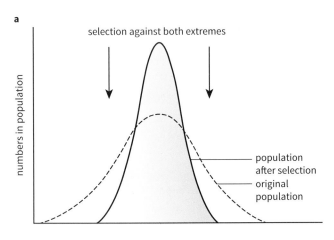

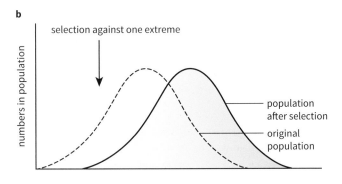

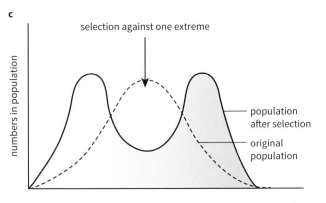

Figure 17.05 **a** Stabilising, **b** directional and **c** disruptive selection.

If organisms are well adapted to their environment and that environment does not change, natural selection acts against new phenotypes or against extremes of phenotype and acts in favour of the 'average' phenotype. This is called **stabilising selection**. In the case of sickle cell disease, stabilising selection can be thought of as favouring the intermediate (heterozygote) phenotype, while the two homozygote phenotypes are at a disadvantage, either through anaemia or malaria.

If organisms are well adapted but the environment changes, natural selection favours a new phenotype, or one at the extreme of a phenotypic range. This is called **directional selection**. With sickle cell disease, the African-American population of the USA is experiencing directional selection, which now favours the phenotype of the homozygote **HbᴬHbᴬ**. Directional selection is the cause of most cases of adaptive evolution, because it results in a phenotypic change that increases the fitness of the organism in a new environment. The different kinds of resistance described above are all examples of directional selection, brought about by a change in the environment.

Disruptive selection is the opposite of stabilising selection. It is when the extremes of phenotype are favoured over the intermediates. Over time the two extreme forms become more common and the intermediates decrease in number. Disruptive selection is thought to happen when there is more than one type of habitat within an area. Imagine a simple example – a population of snails living on a rockery. The snails vary in colour, from white, through grey, to black. The rockery is made up of pale-coloured, sunlit rocks, with deep shady gaps between the rocks. White snails are camouflaged from predators because they match the colour of the rocks, while black snails are well hidden in the shadowy cracks. Each type of snail has a selective advantage within its microhabitat. The intermediate grey snails have a selective disadvantage in each of the microhabitats. Disruptive selection is thought to bring about sympatric speciation (see below).

Progress check 17.03

Leaf insects of the family Phylliidae are herbivorous insects that show a remarkable degree of camouflage. They mimic the appearance of the leaves of their food plant (Figure 17.06). A female leaf insect can lay hundreds of eggs per year.

Figure 17.06 A leaf insect.

1   Using the ideas of natural selection, explain how leaf insects may have evolved.

2   Fossils of leaf insects show that these animals have changed little in appearance for 50 million years. What type of selection has been involved in their evolution since that time?

a Genetic drift and the founder effect

Natural selection is *not* a random process. Selection is a consequence of selection pressures, which direct changes in allele frequencies in a population.

However, allele frequencies can change by a random process, which is called **genetic drift**. Genetic drift happens entirely by chance, governed by the laws of probability. It is thought that genetic drift is only important in small populations, where a small proportion of the organisms are the only ones to reproduce and pass on their alleles to the next generation. In effect, the offspring from each generation contain a random sample of the alleles from their parents.

If you toss a coin 20 times, the laws of probability mean that the most likely outcome is that you will get 10 heads and 10 tails. However, it is quite likely that you would get 12 heads and 8 tails, or (less likely but still possible) 16 heads and 4 tails. If the head and tail represented two alleles of a gene, you can see that with a small population (20 tosses) an allele might increase in numbers entirely by chance. One allele could even become 'fixed' in the population (all 20 heads) and the other eliminated altogether. Genetic drift is thought to have been responsible for changes in allele frequency in many actual cases involving small, isolated populations of organisms.

At the point when a population becomes isolated, the numbers of each allele may not be equal (i.e. not the 10 heads : 10 tails in the coin tossing experiment). If a population *starts* with unequal numbers of alleles (e.g. 18 heads : 2 tails) genetic drift is more likely to happen. This special case of genetic drift is called the **founder effect**. There are a number of small, isolated human populations that have unusual allele frequencies that are thought to be due to the founder effect. For example, a medical condition called Ellis-van Creveld syndrome is found in human populations living on some small islands and in the Amish religious communities of the USA. People with this condition show a number of symptoms, including heart defects, a cleft palate, malformed bones and polydactyly (extra fingers and toes). Such communities have each grown from a few original founders, and tend to be culturally and reproductively isolated from the general population, so that the frequency of the harmful gene is maintained by inbreeding.

Sample question 17.01

The fruit fly Drosophila can have brown or red eyes, determined by a pair of alleles A (red eyes) and a (brown eyes). A laboratory experiment was carried out to simulate (model) genetic drift in fruit flies. Two small populations of Drosophila were set up, each consisting of eight males and eight females. Both populations started with 50% red eye alleles and 50% brown eye alleles. The flies were bred over 20 generations. Each generation produced a large number of offspring. From these, eight males and eight females were chosen at random to use as the parents for the next generation. Figure 17.07 shows how the frequencies of the red eye allele A changed over the course of the experiment.

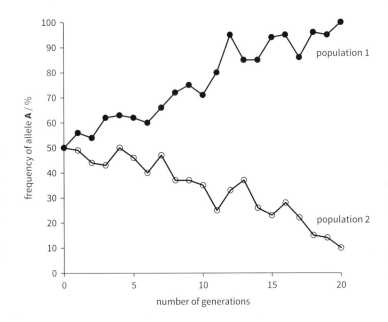

Figure 17.07 Changes in frequency of the red eye allele **A** in two small populations of *Drosophila* over 20 generations.

1 Describe the results shown in Figure 17.07. [3]

2 With reference to Figure 17.07, explain the meaning of *genetic drift*. [2]

3 Assuming the flies in populations 1 and 2 were kept under identical conditions, explain why natural selection cannot be involved in the change in frequency of allele A. [2]

4 How could you modify this experiment to simulate the *founder effect*? [2].

[Mark points are shown in square brackets-to a maximum of 9 marks]

1 *Both populations:*

The frequency of allele **A** fluctuates / goes up and down (between each generation). **[1]**

Population 1:

The trend shows an increase in frequency of allele **A**. **[1]**

The frequency of allele **A** is 100% by generation 20. **[1]**

Population 2:

The trend shows a decrease in frequency of the red eye allele. **[1]**

The frequency of the red eye allele is very low / 10% by generation 20. **[1]**

[Maximum 3 marks]

In the mark scheme, words in brackets are not essential to gain the mark, but they help to make your explanation clear.

If one allele or the other scores 100% it is referred to as 'fixed' in the population. This is an alternative to stating 100% in your answer.

2 Genetic drift is a <u>random</u> change in allele frequencies / occurs <u>by chance</u>. **[1]**

Occurs in small populations. **[1]**

(Caused by / modelled by) the experimenter choosing eight pairs of flies at random for breeding. **[1]**

Only some of the flies from each generation reproduce. **[1]**

[Maximum 2 marks]

Words that are underlined are essential in your answer (in this case 'random' and 'by chance' are alternatives).

3 Identical conditions, so any selection pressure would have the same effect on the frequency of allele **A** in both populations. **[1]**

Frequency of allele **A** in both populations would increase / decrease / stay the same. **[1]**

4 Start with different frequencies of alleles **A** and **a**. **[1]**

Any correct values (apart from 50/50). **[1]**

*For example, 80% **A** and 20% **a**.*

Unit 17 Selection and evolution

17.05 The Hardy–Weinberg principle

The **Hardy–Weinberg principle** states that in a diploid, sexually reproducing organism, allele and genotype frequencies remain constant from generation to generation, as long as certain conditions are met. These conditions are:

- the population is large (i.e. there is no genetic drift)

- matings are random

- there are no net mutations (e.g. mutation from allele '**A**' to allele '**a**' must equal mutation from '**a**' to '**A**')

- there is no migration into or out of the population

- there is no selection for or against an allele.

If any of these conditions do not exist (e.g. there is natural selection or an influx of new genes through migration), the Hardy-Weinberg principle does not apply. The principle is also known as the Hardy–Weinberg Law, or Hardy–Weinberg equilibrium.

In its simplest form, the principle deals with two alleles of a single gene, **A** and **a**. The frequency of each allele in the population is given as a proportion of the total, i.e. a decimal fraction out of 1. The frequency of allele **A** is given the symbol p and the frequency of allele **a** is given the symbol q.

Individuals with genotypes **AA**, **Aa** and **aa** will be present in the population, and will contribute their alleles to a large pool of gametes. For both sexes, the probability that any gamete contains allele **A** is p and the probability that any gamete contains allele **a** is q. Therefore the probabilities of getting each of the three genotypes is shown by:

	female gametes	
	A (p)	**a** (q)
A (p)	**AA** (p^2)	**Aa** (pq)
a (q)	**Aa** (pq)	**aa** (q^2)

male gametes

The probability of getting genotype **AA** is $p \times p = p^2$

The probability of getting genotype **aa** is $q \times q = q^2$

The probability of getting genotype **Aa** is $2 \times p \times q = 2pq$

A gamete must contain either allele **A** or allele **a**, so:

$p + q = 1$ (**Equation 1**)

Also, the sum of the genotypes is **AA** + 2**Aa** + **aa**, so:

$p^2 + 2pq + q^2 = 1$ (**Equation 2**)

This is the Hardy–Weinberg equation. It can be used to calculate the proportions of the alleles and the genotypes in a population.

17.06 Selective breeding

Selective breeding is used by humans to breed crop plants or domesticated animals that have desirable characteristics. It is also known as artificial selection. For example, cereal crops are bred for their yield of grain, or cattle for their yield of meat or milk.

a Milk yield in domestic cattle

Humans have been selectively breeding domestic cattle for thousands of years. The process starts by choosing which characteristics are important, then breeding from parent animals that show these characteristics. Some strains of cattle have been selected for their milk yield and quality. Obviously bulls do not produce milk, so the male calves from cows with a high yield are kept until they are mature and crossed with cows that also give a high yield. The female offspring are monitored for their milk production and the process repeated. It is not just the amount of milk that is important, but also its composition (e.g. its fat content).

Over many generations alleles for 'desirable' characteristics increase in frequency and those for undesirable characteristics decrease. This has led to dramatic increases in milk yield, with production per cow more than doubling over the last 50 years. However, breeding for a high yield has brought

---

Worked example 2

Question

The ability to taste the compound phenylthiocarbamide (PTC) is determined by a single gene. The allele for tasting (**T**) is dominant to the allele for non-tasting (**t**). In a large population sample, 29% of people were non-tasters. Calculate the proportions of people with the genotypes **TT**, **Tt** and **tt**.

Answer

Step 1:

Non-tasters can only have the genotype **tt** and thus the proportion with this genotype is 29%: Therefore:

$q^2 = 0.29$ and $q = \sqrt{0.29} = 0.54$

Step 2:

Using **Equation 1**:

$p = 1 - 0.54 = 0.46$

so

$p^2 = 0.46^2 = 0.21$

and

$2pq = 2 \times 0.46 \times 0.54 = 0.50$

(Alternatively, using **Equation 2**, $2pq = 1 - (0.29 + 0.21) = 0.50$.)

Conclusion:

- The proportions of the genotypes **TT** : **Tt** : **tt** in this population are 0.21 : 0.50 : 0.29; or, as percentages:

  TT = 21%

  Tt = 50%

  tt = 29%

problems. It often damages the health of the animals and leads to a decrease in their productive lifetime. Dairy cows have to give birth to calves in order to lactate (produce milk) and a cow may only be able to achieve three pregnancies and lactations before she has to be culled due to health problems or infertility.

b Improving crop plants

Crop plants have also been selectively bred by humans for thousands of years. Selective breeding is particularly important in cereals such as wheat, rice and maize, which form the staple foods of people around the world. Modern methods involve transferring pollen from the anther of one plant to the stigma of another (the second plant has its anthers removed so that it cannot self-pollinate). The seeds are collected and sown, and the plants allowed to grow to maturity. The offspring with the desired characteristics are then identified and the process repeated.

In recent years our understanding of the science of artificial selection, along with the increasing use of biotechnology, has allowed us to further improve the characteristics of these plants. Three examples are:

- *Disease-resistant varieties of wheat and rice.* Cereal plants are affected by diseases caused by bacteria and viruses, as well as a range of fungal infections such as smuts, rusts and mildews. Infected plants die or they may be unsuitable for sale, lowering the economic value of the crop. A great deal of research goes into identifying new varieties of plants that show resistance to disease and using these in selective breeding programmes. Often the resistant variety lacks other desirable characteristics such as large grain size or a short stem, so it needs to be crossed with another variety with these features in order to produce a strain with all the necessary phenotypic qualities. The genes that produce resistance to certain diseases have been identified, but at present no genetically modified disease-resistant strains of wheat or rice have been developed for commercial use.

- *Inbreeding and hybridisation in maize.* Farmers require crop plants that are genetically identical and show little phenotypic variation. This is achieved by inbreeding – crossing plants with other plants of the same genotype. A good example of this is maize (in some countries known as corn), which is inbred to produce plants that grow at the same

rate, are the same height, and have fruits and seeds that ripen at the same time. These features make it easier to harvest and sell the crop. The problem with inbred plants is that they become progressively smaller and weaker with each generation, and produce a lower yield. This is due to the accumulation of disadvantageous genes, and is known as **inbreeding depression**. To prevent this happening, inbred strains of maize that show desirable characteristics are crossed with other inbred strains having different advantageous features. This produces **F1 hybrids** with new combinations of genes from the parents (i.e. outbreeding). The new lines of maize plants are assessed for their qualities and the best strains selected for further breeding and commercial use. Thousands of new varieties are produced in this way in order to find ones that have the best combinations of growth, resistance to disease, and other features, without showing inbreeding depression.

- *Selection for rice plants with short stems.* In the 1960s the expansion of the world population was expected to produce a chronic food shortage. The International Rice Research Institute (IRRI) in the Philippines responded by setting up a programme of artificial selection which produced a new strain of rice called IR8. IR8 was a 'semi-dwarf' variety of rice with a short stem. Restricted growth of the stem meant that a greater proportion of the plant's energy went into making grain, producing a higher yield. In 2002 it was shown that the short stem length was determined by a mutation to a gene coding for an enzyme involved in the synthesis of the plant hormone gibberellin (see Unit 15). Development of IR8 was successful in averting the feared food shortage, but there were problems with IR8 plants. These were solved by crossing IR8 with other varieties of rice, eventually producing other semi-dwarf strains such as IR36 and IR72, which had all the desired characteristics – good grain quality, resistance to diseases and a rapid growth rate, which meant that two crops could be produced every year.

17.07 Speciation

Speciation means the formation of new species from an existing one. Although the species is a basic unit of classification, it is a difficult term to define and several definitions have been proposed. One that is widely used is: 'A species is a group of organisms that have similar morphological, physiological and biochemical features, and are capable of reproducing to produce fertile offspring'. It follows that for two groups of organisms to be *different* species, they must be unable to breed with each other - they must evolve to become **reproductively isolated** from each other. Reproductive isolation consists of biological barriers or 'mechanisms' that prevent gene flow between species.

There are a number of barriers that have evolved which bring about reproductive isolation. They are divided into two categories:

- **prezygotic** mechanisms prevent a zygote being formed; they may happen before or after mating

- **postzygotic** mechanisms prevent hybrids from passing on their genes; offspring may not be produced, or if they are produced they have reduced fitness.

Table 17.02 shows some examples of isolating mechanisms.

Prezygotic	Postzygotic
• *Ecological isolation* – populations breed in different habitats within the same general area, in different seasons, or at different times of day. In plants, populations may use different animal pollinators, or different body parts of the same pollinator.	• *Hybrid inviability* – a zygote is formed but it fails to develop.
• *Behavioural isolation* – (e.g. animals evolve different methods of courtship behaviour).	• *Hybrid sterility* – zygote is formed and develops, but hybrids are sterile (e.g. a cross between a female horse and a male donkey produces a mule, which cannot produce viable gametes by meiosis).
• *Mechanical isolation* – animals are physically unable to mate (e.g. due to the evolution of incompatible sexual organs).	• *Hybrid breakdown* – successive generations of hybrids have increasingly lowered fertility; eventually they are selected out of the population.
• *Gametic isolation* – (e.g. incompatibility of pollen and stigma in flowering plants, or inability of the male and female gametes to fuse).	

Table 17.02 Examples of prezygotic and postzygotic isolating mechanisms

a Allopatric and sympatric speciation

The evolution of most species is thought to have taken place as a result of **geographical isolation**. This happens when two populations of one species come to occupy two different environments. They become separated by a physical barrier, such as a mountain range or a river. Once isolated, the two populations may experience different selection pressures, so that natural selection leads to the evolution of different characteristics. In time this may result in reproductive isolation, so that two species are formed. Speciation resulting from geographical separation of populations is called **allopatric speciation** (allopatric means 'different places').

A well-known example of allopatric speciation is the way that many island species are thought to have evolved. You can imagine a situation where a species of bird colonises a group of islands, perhaps having been blown there by a storm. Once established on the islands, there might be little interbreeding between the bird populations on the different islands. Each population could experience different selection pressures, so that after a long period of time they might diverge enough to be reproductively isolated and constitute different species. Darwin recorded a number of species of finch on the different Galapagos Islands that he visited (Figure 17.08). It is now thought that they evolved from a common ancestor from the South American mainland.

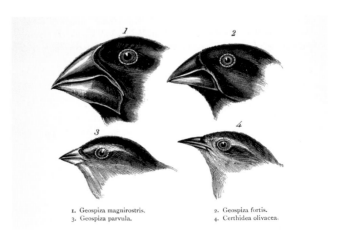

Figure 17.08 Drawings of four species of Galapagos Island finches in a book by Charles Darwin. The birds show adaptive variations, including the size and shape of their beaks. These adaptations allow them to exploit different food sources on the different islands.

The physical barrier that separates two populations does not have to be as large as a mountain range or a river. For a small, slow-moving animal such as a snail, the construction of a new road or an irrigation canal could act as a barrier, isolating two populations of snails and preventing gene flow between them.

Sympatric speciation occurs when two (or more) species are formed from a single ancestral species, each occupying the same geographical location (sympatric means 'same place'). It is much less common than allopatric speciation. The best understood method of sympatric speciation takes place by **polyploidy**. Polyploids are organisms with more than two complete sets of chromosomes in their cells ($3n$, $4n$, etc.). Polyploidy is rare in animals but common in plant species – many domesticated crops and ornamental flowering plants are polyploids. Polyploidy results from problems during meiosis, for example if the pairs of homologous chromosomes fail to separate, producing a gamete with two sets instead of one. If two gametes like this fuse, a tetraploid ($4n$) zygote is formed.

Crosses between polyploids and the original (diploid) plants often result in sterile hybrids. This means that there is immediate reproductive isolation of the two. Polyploidy was responsible for the evolution of new species of cord grass, a species inhabiting mudflats along the banks of estuaries (Figure 17.09).

Figure 17.09 Cord grass (*Spartina alterniflora*) growing on a mudflat.

In England before 1830 the native species of cord grass was *Spartina maritima*. After this date another species called *Spartina alterniflora* was accidentally introduced from America. By 1878 there were reports of a sterile hybrid of these two species, called *Spartina townsendii*. Spontaneous doubling of the chromosomes of the hybrid resulted in a new species called *Spartina anglica*. *Spartina anglica* is a tetraploid ($4n$). It has two sets of chromosomes from each of the parents, so it can undergo meiosis and is self-fertile, but it is unable to cross with either of the original parent species (Figure 17.10).

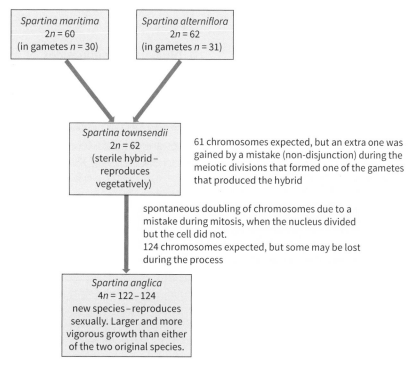

Figure 17.10 The evolution of a new species of cord grass.

Spartina anglica is a highly successful species, well adapted to living on estuarine mudflats, where it shows vigorous growth and an ability to withstand fluctuating levels of salinity. It has spread widely along the coast of Western Europe, out-competing and replacing the other species of cord grass. It is also found along the Pacific coast of the USA, and is an invasive species in New Zealand and Tasmania.

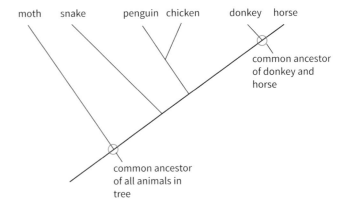

Figure 17.11 Relative positions of the animals in Table 17.03 on the branches of an evolutionary tree. Shorter branches indicate closer common ancestry (e.g. the penguin and the chicken evolved fairly recently from an ancestor of all modern birds).

Progress check 17.04

1   Explain why reproductive isolation is essential for speciation to take place.

2   Explain the difference between allopatric and sympatric speciation.

17.08 Molecular evidence for relationships between species

Species that are closely related are not just similar in appearance – they also have a similar biochemistry. The amino acid sequences of proteins and the nucleotide sequences of mitochondrial DNA are two pieces of molecular evidence that have been used to identify how closely related species are.

a Amino acid sequences of proteins

Proteins are coded for by DNA, so they reflect the genotype of an organism. If the primary structure of a particular protein is compared in two species, the number of amino acids that are different is a measure of the closeness of the relationship between the two. A protein that has been extensively investigated is cytochrome *c*, which is a part of the electron transfer chain in oxidative phosphorylation (see Unit 12). Cytochrome *c* contains just over 100 amino acids (104

in humans). Its structure is very similar in a wide range of animals, plants, fungi and bacteria. A comparison of cytochrome *c* between species shows how close they are in the evolutionary tree. A simple example is shown in Table 17.03 and Figure 17.11.

The fewer the differences between amino acid sequences, the more closely related the animals are. In the case of humans our nearest living relative is the chimpanzee, and there are no differences in the sequence of amino acids of cytochrome *c* in humans and chimpanzees. The rhesus monkey (a more distant relative) has one amino acid difference.

b Nucleotide sequences of mitochondrial DNA

Mitochondria contain circular loops of DNA – **mitochondrial DNA (mtDNA)**. Each loop contains a small number of genes (37 in humans, compared with over 20 000 in the nuclear genome). The 37 genes are essential to control all the functions of the mitochondrion. mtDNA is a major tool for use in

	Horse	**Donkey**	**Chicken**	**Penguin**	**Snake**	**Moth**
horse	0	1	11	13	21	29
donkey		0	10	12	20	28
chicken			0	3	18	29
penguin				0	17	27
snake					0	29
moth						0

Table 17.03 Number of amino acid differences in cytochrome *c* of various animals.

studying evolutionary relationships. There are three main reasons for this:

- mtDNA is highly *conserved* – it evolves slowly compared with nuclear DNA. Since mtDNA is in a loop it is unable to undergo crossing over, so that changes to its nucleotide sequence can only take place by mutation. Unlike nuclear DNA, mtDNA is not protected by histone proteins, so its rate of mutation is 10 times faster. However, the lack of crossing over means that overall the mtDNA changes much more slowly than nuclear DNA.

- In humans and most other animals, mtDNA is inherited solely from the mother. This is because any sperm mitochondria that enter the fertilised egg are destroyed by the embryo's cellular machinery.

- Materials such as bone, teeth or hair from very old or decomposed specimens contain little nuclear DNA, which is broken down by enzymes called exonucleases. Cells contain many copies of mtDNA, which is also less susceptible to degradation by exonucleases. This means that more mtDNA is available for analysis.

mtDNA is used to track human evolution. It allows us to compare nucleotide sequences in different populations of humans and has provided evidence that our species (*Homo sapiens*) originated once, in East Africa, about 100 000–200 000 years ago. It is thought that all modern races of humans are descended from one woman, called 'Mitochondrial Eve', whose descendants subsequently migrated around the world. The date is only approximate, because it is derived from the 'molecular clock' hypothesis, which assumes there has been a constant rate of mutation of mtDNA with time. (Note that 'Eve' was not the *only* woman alive at the time – it is just that her female contemporaries did not produce a direct unbroken line to any people alive on Earth today.)

Biologists have used the nucleotide sequences of mtDNA to build up evolutionary trees for many other species of animals. The commonest DNA sequence used is the gene coding for a protein in the electron transport chain called cytochrome *b*.

17.09 Extinctions

Extinction is the disappearance of species. It is not a new phenomenon. Evolution is a process of change, where new species are constantly appearing and older species die out. It is impossible to be precise, but one recent estimate is that there are about 10 million species of eukaryotes living on the planet, with tens of millions more if prokaryotes are included. What is certain is that these represent less than 1% of all the species that have existed since life began on Earth.

At some point during the existence of most species, their rate of mortality exceeds their rate of reproduction, so that they die out. However, the rate of this turnover has not been constant. Over the Earth's geological history there have been five 'mass extinctions' involving rapid (in geological terms) loss of species, with major reductions in biodiversity. A period of climate change 300 million years ago brought cooler, drier conditions that caused a global collapse of rainforests and a great loss of diversity, especially amongst amphibians. The last mass extinction was 65 million years ago, when whole groups of organisms became extinct, most famous of which were the dinosaurs. This event is thought to have been caused by a large asteroid hitting the Earth, resulting in a dust cloud that persisted in the Earth's atmosphere, along with severe changes to the global climate.

Between mass extinctions there have been lower rates of extinction, called 'background extinction'. These rates vary widely between different groups of organisms, but to give an example, the average species life span of most animals is about ten million years, and somewhat less (less than a million years) for mammals and birds. What is particularly worrying is that many biologists think that the rate of species extinction due to human activities is so high that it will have a greater effect on biodiversity than any of the previous five mass extinctions. These activities include practices that cause global warming and climate change, destruction of habitats, pollution, hunting and overfishing.

Revision checklist

Check that you know:

- ☐ continuous and discontinuous variation
- ☐ how the environment can affect phenotypes
- ☐ how to use the *t*-test
- ☐ the meaning of natural selection
- ☐ examples of natural selection
- ☐ stabilising, directional and disruptive selection
- ☐ genetic drift and the founder effect
- ☐ the Hardy–Weinberg principle
- ☐ selective breeding
- ☐ speciation
- ☐ prezygotic and postzygotic isolating mechanisms
- ☐ allopatric and sympatric speciation
- ☐ molecular evidence for the relationships between species
- ☐ extinctions

Exam-style questions

1 *Rhagoletis pomonella* is a species of 'maggot fly' native to North America. It is a major pest of fruits in the USA and Canada. The larva of the fly originally fed on the berries of hawthorn trees. From the 17th century onwards, apple trees were introduced to North America. In 1864 new populations of maggot flies were identified that infested apples (Figure 17.12).

There are now separate races of hawthorn maggot flies and apple maggot flies. Research has shown that:

- hawthorn maggot flies strongly prefer to mate on and lay eggs in hawthorn berries

- apple maggot flies strongly prefer to mate on and lay eggs in apples

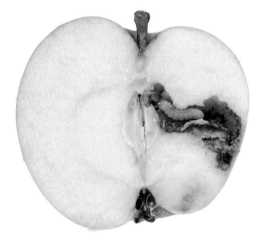

Figure 17.12 a Maggot fly larva feeding inside an apple. b Adult maggot fly.

- there is a 5% rate of hybridisation between hawthorn maggot flies and apple maggot flies; fertile offspring are produced

- hawthorn and apple maggot flies are identical in appearance but have different DNA profiles

- apples provide a number of advantages over hawthorn berries for the developing larvae, including a larger food supply and protection against parasitic wasps that kill the larvae.

a Explain why the hawthorn maggot fly and the apple maggot fly are not considered to be different species. [3]

b The existence of the two races of maggot flies is thought be an early stage of the evolution of a new species by sympatric speciation. Explain this statement. [3]

Hawthorn trees produce fruit over a number of weeks during late summer. Natural selection has acted on the time of hatching of hawthorn maggot flies so that the number of flies hatched coincides with the availability of hawthorn berries (Figure 17.13).

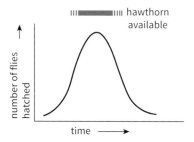

Figure 17.13

Lack of availability of fruit selects against flies with extremes of hatching time.

c What sort of variation is shown by the hatching time of hawthorn flies? [1]

d Name the type of natural selection that acts to maintain a narrow range of hatching time over many generations. [1]

Apple trees produce fruit earlier in the season than hawthorn trees. When both types of tree became available in a habitat, flies that hatched early and laid eggs in apples gained a selective advantage over those that hatched later. Over successive generations two peaks in hatching time developed (Figure 17.14).

e Name the type of selection acting to produce the two peaks in hatching time. [1]

f This type of selection may in time produce two species of maggot flies. Use the information given in the question to explain how this could happen [6].

Total: 8

2 The cheetah (*Acinonyx jubatus*) is a species of big cat. Its natural habitats are the plains of central Africa, where it is an endangered species. One reason for this is that natural populations of cheetahs show a very low degree of genetic variation. This is thought to be due to modern cheetah populations having evolved from a small ancestral group and the consequences of genetic drift. This low variability has relevance for the captive breeding of cheetahs in zoos, where artificial selection must be applied carefully, to avoid the inbreeding of undesirable characteristics.

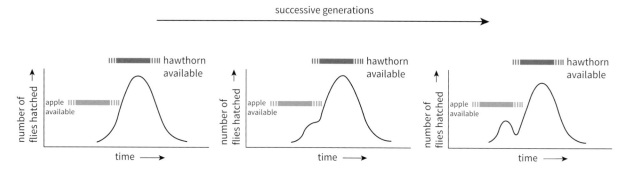

Figure 17.14

a What is 'genetic drift'? Explain why genetic drift may be important in small populations. [3]

b What is meant by 'artificial selection'? [3]

c Suggest how zoos might avoid 'inbreeding of undesirable characteristics'. [2]

Total: 8

3 The diploid number of chromosomes (2n) in the cells of a horse is 64, while the diploid number for a donkey is 62.

a Copy and complete the table below to show the number of chromosomes in a nucleus at different stages of cell division: [3]

Stage	Horse	Donkey
at the end of mitosis		
at the end of meiosis I		
at the end of meiosis II		

The offspring of a cross between a female horse and a male donkey is called a mule. Mules are infertile.

b What would be the diploid number for a mule? Explain your answer. [2]

c Explain why mules are infertile. [2]

d Explain why a horse and a donkey are considered to belong to different species. [1]

Total: 8

4 In a certain part of Africa, 9% of people are born with the severe form of sickle cell anaemia, as a result of having the genotype **Hb^{S}Hb^S**.

a Use the Hardy–Weinberg principle to calculate the percentage of this population that have the heterozygous genotype **Hb^{A}Hb^S**. [5]

b Explain how people with the heterozygous genotype are protected against malaria. [3]

Total: 8

Biodiversity, classification and conservation

Learning outcomes

When you have finished this unit, you should be able to:

- [ ] define the terms species, ecosystem and niche

- [ ] explain the meaning of biodiversity and its importance

- [ ] use Simpson's Index of Diversity to measure the diversity of a habitat

- [ ] explain the need to use random sampling to investigate the biodiversity of a habitat

- [ ] use suitable sampling methods to assess the distribution of organisms in a habitat

- [ ] use correlation coefficients to analyse the distribution of species

- [ ] explain how species are classified

- [ ] outline the characteristics of the three domains of organisms

- [ ] outline the characteristics of the four kingdoms of eukaryotic organisms

- [ ] outline the classification of viruses

- [ ] discuss the threats to biodiversity in aquatic and terrestrial ecosystems

- [ ] discuss methods of protecting endangered species

- [ ] discuss methods of assisted reproduction to conserve endangered mammals

- [ ] discuss the use of culling and contraceptive methods to prevent overpopulation of species

- [ ] explain the reasons for controlling alien species

- [ ] discuss the roles of non-governmental organisations in local and global conservation

- [ ] outline how degraded habitats may be restored.

Ecological fieldwork is essential for investigating biodiversity. Different methods can be used to sample the organisms present in a habitat, and the distribution and abundance of species analysed using statistical tests.

The biodiversity of the Earth is threatened by human activities. There are many reasons why it is important that biodiversity is maintained and actions taken at local, national and global levels to conserve species and ecosystems.

18.01 Some ecological terms

A **species** is a group of organisms that have similar morphological, physiological and biochemical features, and are capable of reproducing to produce fertile offspring. In other words a species is reproductively isolated (see Unit 17).

An **ecosystem** consists of all the organisms living in a defined area, together with their physical environment. The living organisms make up the **biotic** component

of the ecosystem and the physical environment is the **abiotic** component. An ecosystem can be as large as a tropical rainforest or as small as a freshwater pond. The total number of individuals of *one* species living in a particular ecosystem at one time is called a **population**. All the organisms of *different* species living in an ecosystem are known as the **community**.

TIP Note that 'community' is sometimes used to describe a sub-set of the total organisms (e.g. the 'plant community').

An ecological **niche** is the 'role' of an organism in an ecosystem. It is most commonly applied to animals, where it is determined by qualities such as the animal's trophic level, method of feeding, body size and type of locomotion. A niche may be filled by different species in different habitats. For example, the niche of a 'large terrestrial grazing herbivore' is filled by deer in Europe, antelope in Africa and kangaroos in Australia. However, in *one* habitat two different species cannot occupy exactly the same niche – one species will always out-compete the other, less well-adapted species.

18.02 Biodiversity

Biodiversity is not a very precise term, but it can be thought of as the amount of variation shown by organisms in an environment. Biodiversity can be considered at three levels:

- the amount of genetic variation within each species

- the number of species in an ecosystem and their relative abundance

- the diversity of habitats within an ecosystem.

The sum of all the genes in a population is known as the 'gene pool'. Individuals of one species all have the same genes, but they may have different alleles of those genes. The number of different alleles in the gene pool of a species is its **genetic diversity**. Genetic diversity is important to any species because it produces phenotypic variation, which is the raw material upon which natural selection acts. Without this variation a species may not be able to adapt to changes in its environment, which could lead to its extinction.

Species diversity is a combination of two measurements – the number of different species present in a community (called the **species richness**), along with the 'evenness' of numbers of each species. Take the example of the two communities shown in Table 18.01.

Species	Number of individuals of each species in community 1	Number of individuals of each species in community 2
A	10	1
B	10	1
C	10	1
D	10	1
E	10	46

Table 18.01 The composition of two communities of organisms.

Both communities contain the same number of species (5) and organisms (50) but community 2 is dominated by species E. Community 1 contains even numbers of each species, so it has a higher species diversity. Species diversity can be measured using **Simpson's Index of Diversity** (see below).

Some ecosystems (e.g. tropical rainforests or coral reefs) have a very high species diversity. Others are dominated by one species. For example, the commercial conifer plantations of northern Europe are dominated by trees that produce a very dense canopy (Figure 18.01). Lack of light severely restricts the growth of other tree species and ground-layer plants. In addition, the pine forest provides a limited variety of habitats for animals – it has a low **habitat diversity**.

Figure 18.01 A pine tree plantation.

Ecosystems with a high biodiversity tend to be more stable than ones with a low biodiversity. This is because an ecosystem that is dominated by one (or a few) species is more likely to be badly affected by any sort of disturbance. For example, if a new disease arose that wiped out the dominant tree species, this would have an impact on other species that relied on the tree for food, shelter and so on; in a more diverse ecosystem other tree species might supply these resources.

18.03 Simpson's Index of Diversity

Simpson's Index of Diversity (*D*) is a measure of diversity. It takes into account the species richness and the relative abundance of each species. One formula for calculating *D* is:

$$D = 1 - \sum \left(\frac{n}{N} \right)^2$$

where *N* is the total number of individuals of all species and *n* is the total number of individuals of a particular species.

You calculate $\dfrac{n}{N}$ for each species, square each of these numbers, and then sum (Σ) all the squares to find D. Values of D range from 0 to 1, where 0 represents a low diversity and 1 a high diversity.

If you have a community with more than just a few species it is easier to do the calculations in a table (or better still a spreadsheet).

Worked example I

Question

Calculate Simpson's Index of Diversity for both of the communities in Table 18.01.

Answer

For community 1.

Step 1:

Calculate $\dfrac{n}{N}$:

$N = 50$ and $n = 10$ for each of species A to E.

Therefore $\dfrac{n}{N} = \dfrac{10}{50}$ for each species

Step 2:

Calculate the squares of $\dfrac{n}{N}$ and sum these values:

$$\Sigma \left(\frac{n}{N}\right)^2 = \left(\frac{10}{50}\right)^2 + \left(\frac{10}{50}\right)^2 + \left(\frac{10}{50}\right)^2 + \left(\frac{10}{50}\right)^2 + \left(\frac{10}{50}\right)^2$$

$= 0.2^2 + 0.2^2 + 0.2^2 + 0.2^2 + 0.2^2$

$= 0.04 + 0.04 + 0.04 + 0.04 + 0.04$

$= 0.20$

Step 3:

Subtract this value from 1 to find D:

$D = (1 - 0.20) = 0.80$

This value is close to 1.0, showing that community 1 has a high biodiversity.

Repeating steps 2 and 3 for community 2 gives the following:

$$\Sigma \left(\frac{n}{N}\right)^2 = \left(\frac{1}{50}\right)^2 + \left(\frac{1}{50}\right)^2 + \left(\frac{1}{50}\right)^2 + \left(\frac{1}{50}\right)^2 + \left(\frac{46}{50}\right)^2$$

$= 0.02^2 + 0.02^2 + 0.02^2 + 0.02^2 + 0.92^2$

$= 0.0004 + 0.0004 + 0.0004 + 0.0004 + 0.8464$

$= 0.848$

$D = (1 - 0.848) = 0.152$

This value is closer to zero, showing that community 2 has a low biodiversity.

Note that Simpson's Index of Diversity is not a statistical test like the chi-squared or t-test. It does not tell you whether two communities are *significantly* different in their biodiversity.

Progress check 18.01

1 Explain the meaning of the following terms.

   a   Ecosystem.

   b   Community.

   c   Genetic diversity (of a species).

2 Community X contains these organisms:

Species	Number of individuals of each species in community X
A	5
B	15
C	2
D	21
E	7

Calculate Simpson's Index of Diversity for community X.

18.04 Sampling with quadrats

It is impossible to identify and count every organism living in an ecosystem, so samples must be taken. A sample should be representative of the area of study, so that the results can be scaled up to provide an estimate of the total numbers present.

Sampling of plants, or species of animals that do not move much (e.g. snails) can be carried out using a sampling frame called a **quadrat**. The size of quadrat depends on the size of the organisms being sampled. For example, to count plants growing in a field you could use a quadrat with sides 0.5 or 1 metre in length. Some quadrats have a wire grid of smaller squares to make it easier to count the organisms, or for estimating percentage cover (Figure 18.02).

Figure 18.02 Sampling using a gridded metre-square quadrat.

If you are trying to measure the biodiversity in an area where the organisms appear to be uniformly distributed, or if there is no clear pattern to their distribution, random sampling should be used.

Imagine you are sampling from a field, but for convenience you choose to place your quadrats next to a path. This would *not* be a random sample - it might give you results that were different from the rest of the field. The sample would be unrepresentative or *biased* by your choice of where to sample. If you use random sampling, it should give you a correct overall picture of the numbers of the different species present.

Random sampling can be carried out by placing quadrats at randomly selected coordinates within a marked out area (Figure 18.03). The coordinates can be produced using a random number generator on a calculator. The number of samples taken must be large enough to provide a reliable estimate of the biodiversity of the whole sampling area.

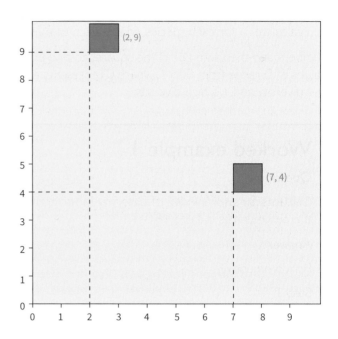

Figure 18.03 Placing quadrats using random coordinates in an area marked out by two 10-metre tapes.

Random sampling is a good way to sample from an area if the organisms are fairly evenly distributed, as with the plants in a field. However, in some habitats there is a gradual change in the habitat and the community over a distance. A good example of this is on a rocky seashore, where the habitat gradually changes from marine at the bottom of the shore to terrestrial at the top (Figure 18.04). As a result of the tides, the organisms living at the bottom of the shore will be under water for most of the day, while those living at the top of the shore will be on dry land for most of the day, with a gradient of tidal cover in between. This produces zones of animals and seaweeds as you go up the shore. This gradual change in the habitat over a distance is called an 'environmental gradient'.

Figure 18.04 A rocky seashore is an environmental gradient between marine and terrestrial ecosystems.

It would be wrong to use random sampling over the area covered by this environmental gradient, since it would not show the presence of the zones. Instead, samples would need to be taken at regular intervals up the shore. This type of sampling is called a **transect**. The simplest kind of transect is a *line transect*. A tape measure is placed in a straight line across the area to be sampled and all the species touching the tape recorded. A *belt transect* is similar, but instead a quadrat is placed alongside the tape, and samples taken from the areas inside the quadrats. If the quadrat is placed at intervals along the tape, this is called an *interrupted belt transect* (Figure 18.05).

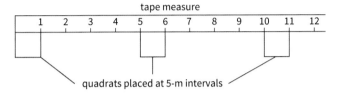

Figure 18.05 An interrupted belt transect.

Using transects is an example of *systematic* sampling – the quadrats are placed at selected intervals along the environmental gradient. Note however that it is still possible to sample randomly *at each interval*, by placing the quadrat at a random position along a line at right angles to the tape.

18.05 The mark–release–recapture method

Quadrats can be used to sample animals that do not move from place to place (e.g. barnacles) but are of no use in assessing the abundance of mobile animals. A way that can be used to estimate the population size of a mobile species is the **mark–release–recapture** method. It can only be used if the population lives in a well-defined area.

A sample of the population is caught and marked in a way that does not harm them. The animals are then released back into their habitat and left to mix with the rest of the population. After a suitable period of time, a second sample is taken and the numbers of marked and unmarked individuals are counted. The proportion of marked individuals in the second sample is used to estimate the size of the total population, using the formula:

$$\text{population size} = \frac{(\text{number in first sample} \times \text{total number in second sample})}{\text{number of marked individuals in second sample}}$$

Worked example 18.02

Question

A student wanted to find out the size of a population of snails living in a small enclosed garden. He carried out a 60-minute search of the garden and collected 65 snails. He marked each snail with a small spot of quick-drying non-toxic paint and returned the snails to their habitat, placing them evenly throughout the garden. After 3 days, he returned and carried out another timed search. In his second sample he collected 78 snails, 22 of which were marked ones from the first sample.

Calculate the total size of the snail population.

Answer

$$\text{Estimated population size} = \frac{65 \times 78}{22}$$

= 230.4 (or 230 to the nearest whole snail!)

The method of marking must not harm the animals. It must also not make them more visible (i.e. by predators) and the sampling method must not alter their habitat. There must also be no immigration or emigration from the habitat during the time between samples.

18.06 Correlation

A correlation is a relationship between two variables where they *co-vary*, or change in parallel. For example, a species of plant might increase in abundance with increasing light intensity (a positive correlation). Another species might decrease in biomass with increasing numbers of a herbivore (a negative correlation). Correlations between two variables can be shown as scatter graphs (Figure 18.06). If all the coordinates lie on a straight line, there is a *linear* correlation between the two variables.

It is important to realise that correlation does not imply that the change in one variable *causes* the change in the other. A scatter graph of arm length against leg length for 100 people will show a positive correlation, but one variable does not cause the other to vary – it is just that the two go together with increasing body size.

The degree of correlation between two variables can be found by calculating a **correlation coefficient** (*r*). The value of *r* varies from 0 (no correlation) to 1 (a complete correlation where all the points fit on a straight line).

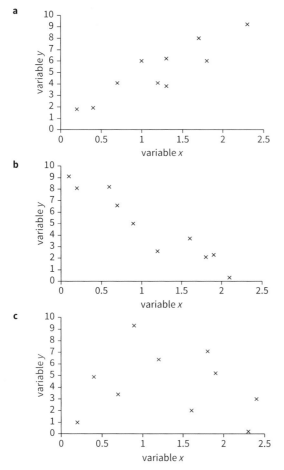

Figure 18.06 Three types of correlation: **a** a positive linear correlation, **b** a negative linear correlation and **c** no correlation.

a Pearson's correlation coefficient

Pearson's linear correlation is used to test for a linear correlation (positive or negative) between two variables. Both variables must be quantitative data such as length, mass or area, and should (approximately) fit a normal distribution. There should be no 'outliers' (outliers are coordinates that are far away from a best-fit line through the points).

One formula for Pearson's correlation coefficient (r) is:

$$r = \frac{\sum xy - n\bar{x}\,\bar{y}}{ns_x s_y}$$

Where x and y are the variables, n is the sample size, $\bar{x}$ is the mean of variable x, $\bar{y}$ is the mean of variable y, and s_x and s_y are the standard deviations of x and y. You can use this formula, or there are several equivalent versions of it. One is:

$$r = \frac{n(\Sigma xy) - (\Sigma x)(\Sigma y)}{\sqrt{[n\Sigma x^2 - (\Sigma x)^2][n\Sigma y^2 - (\Sigma y)^2]}}$$

This looks complicated, but it is easy to use when the data is put into a table.

Worked example 18.03

Question

Table 18.02 shows the data used to draw the scatter graph in Figure 18.06(a). Assume that variables x and y are normally distributed. Calculate Pearson's correlation coefficient for this data and comment on the result.

Answer

Step 1:
Draw a scatter diagram of the data (see Figure 18.06a – the points appear to show a linear correlation and there are no outliers).

Step 2:
State the null hypothesis: there is no correlation between variables x and y.

Step 3:
Complete a table showing the values of x^2, y^2 and xy. Sum the values in the columns and calculate the values of $(\Sigma x)^2$ and $(\Sigma y)^2$.

Variable x	Variable y
0.2	1.8
0.4	1.9
0.7	4.1
1.0	6.0
1.2	4.1
1.3	3.8
1.3	6.2
1.7	8.0
1.8	6.0
2.3	9.2

Table 18.02

x	y	x²	y²	xy
0.2	1.8	0.04	3.24	0.36
0.4	1.9	0.16	3.61	0.76
0.7	4.1	0.49	16.81	2.87
1.0	6.0	1.00	36.00	6.00
1.2	4.1	1.44	16.81	4.92
1.3	3.8	1.69	14.44	4.94
1.3	6.2	1.69	38.44	8.06
1.7	8.0	2.89	64.00	13.60
1.8	6.0	3.24	36.00	10.80
2.3	9.2	5.29	84.64	21.16
$\Sigma x = 11.9$	$\Sigma y = 51.1$	$\Sigma x^2 = 17.93$	$\Sigma y^2 = 313.99$	$\Sigma xy = 73.47$
$(\Sigma x)^2 = 141.61$	$(\Sigma y)^2 = 2611.21$			

Step 4:
The sample size (n) = 10. Substitute values from the table into the formula to find r.

$$r = \frac{n(\Sigma xy) - (\Sigma x)(\Sigma y)}{\sqrt{\left[n\Sigma x^2 - (\Sigma x)^2\right]\left[n\Sigma y^2 - (\Sigma y)^2\right]}}$$

$$= \frac{10(73.47) - (11.9 \times 51.1)}{\sqrt{\left[10(17.93) - 141.61\right]\left[10(313.99) - 2611.21\right]}}$$

$$= 0.897$$

Step 5:
Interpret the result. The table below shows the probabilities of obtaining different values of r, for 10 pairs of observations, if the null hypothesis is correct.

Probability (P)	0.10 (10%)	0.05 (5%)	0.01 (1%)	0.001 (0.1%)
Value of r	0.549	0.632	0.765	0.872

Conclusion:
If the null hypothesis is correct, the probability of getting $r = 0.897$ is $P < 0.001$. This is less than 0.05, so we can *reject* the null hypothesis. There is a positive correlation between variables x and y. (Note that if the value of r is negative it indicates a negative correlation.)

b Spearman's rank correlation coefficient

Spearman's rank correlation also tests whether there is a correlation between two variables, but the correlation does not need to be linear, and the variables do not need to be normally distributed. Spearman's test can also cope with the odd outlier amongst the data.

> **TIP**
> Spearman's test is very useful in analysing the results of ecological investigations, where the data rarely fits the constraints of Pearson's test.

Finding Spearman's rank correlation coefficient (r_s) involves ranking the data for each variable. For example, if your measurements of 10 leaves (in cm) were: 5.1, 6.0, 6.4, 7.1, 5.3, 5.2, 4.5, 5.2, 4.1 and 4.9, their rank order values would be:

Length /cm	5.1	6.0	6.4	7.1	5.3	5.2	4.5	5.2	4.1	4.9
Rank	4	8	9	10	7	5.5	2	5.5	1	3

Note that there are two leaves of length 5.2 cm. These are 'tied' values so they are given the same rank (the average of ranks 5 and 6).

Spearman's coefficient is calculated by applying exactly the same formula as is used to find Pearson's coefficient (see above) but using the rank values instead of the 'raw' data.

If there are *no tied ranks* for either variable a much simpler formula for Spearman's coefficient can be used:

$$r_s = 1 - \left(\frac{6 \times \sum D^2}{n^3 - n} \right)$$

where ΣD^2 is the sum of the differences between the ranks of the two variables and n is the sample size (number of pairs of observations). Unfortunately this formula does not give an accurate result if there are any tied ranks.

Take the example shown in Figure 18.07. Burrowing mayfly larvae live in mud at the bottom of streams. More mud accumulates in parts of a stream where there is a slow rate of water flow, so there tends to be a negative correlation between flow rate and number of burrowing mayfly larvae.

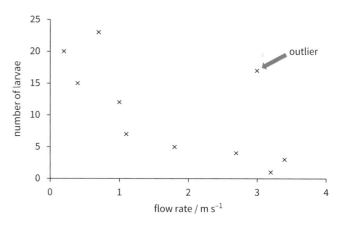

Figure 18.07 Correlation between numbers of burrowing mayfly larvae and water flow rates in 10 random samples from a stream.

Although there appears to be a negative correlation between the two variables in Figure 18.07, it is not linear. Instead it shows a curve of decreasing gradient. There is also an outlier in the data.

Worked example 18.04

Question

Table 18.03 shows the data used to draw the scatter graph in Figure 18.07. Calculate Spearman's rank correlation coefficient for these data and comment on the result.

Table 18.03

Variable *x* (flow rate / ms⁻¹)	Variable *y* (number of burrowing mayfly larvae)
0.2	20
1.0	12
1.8	5
2.7	4
0.4	15
3.0	17
1.1	7
3.4	3
0.7	23
3.2	1

Note that there are no tied ranks in either set of variables, so the simpler formula for r_s can be used.

Step 1:
Draw a scatter diagram of the data (see Figure 18.07).

Step 2:
State the null hypothesis: there is no correlation between flow rate and number of burrowing mayfly larvae.

Step 3:
Complete a table showing the ranked values of each variable, the differences between each pair of ranked values (*D*) and D^2. Sum the values in the last column to find ΣD^2.

Flow rate / ms^{-1}	Rank flow rate	Number of larvae	Rank number of larvae	Difference in rank D	D^2
0.2	1	20	9	−8	64
1.0	4	12	6	−2	4
1.8	6	5	4	2	4
2.7	7	4	2	5	25
0.4	2	15	7	−5	25
3.0	8	17	8	0	0
1.1	5	7	5	0	0
3.4	10	3	3	7	49
0.7	3	23	10	−7	49
3.2	9	1	1	8	64
					$\Sigma D^2 = 284$

Step 4:
Calculate Spearman's rank correlation coefficient.

$$r_s = 1 - \left(\frac{6 \times \sum D^2}{n^3 - n} \right)$$

$$= 1 - \left(\frac{6 \times 284}{10^3 - 10} \right)$$

$$= -0.721$$

Step 5:
Interpret the result. The table below shows the probabilities of obtaining different values of r_s, for 10 pairs of observations, if the null hypothesis is correct

(ignore the minus sign of the calculated r_s value).

Probability (P)	0.10 (10%)	0.05 (5%)	0.01 (1%)
Value of r_s	0.564	0.648	0.794

Conclusion
If the null hypothesis is correct, the probability of getting this value of r_s is between 0.05 and 0.01. Since this is less than 0.05 we can reject the null hypothesis and conclude that there is a significant correlation between flow rate and numbers of larvae. The negative value of r_s tells us that it is a negative correlation.

Progress check 18.02

1   Suggest a sampling method you could use to investigate the following:

   a   The species richness of plants in a field treated with fertiliser compared with that of a control field.

   b   The distribution of a species of grass across a large field containing marshy areas and dry areas.

   c   The size of a population of woodlice living under a log.

2   A student investigated whether the height of a plant species varied in different depths of soil. 10 pairs of observations produced an r_s value of 0.631. Use the probability table above to interpret the significance of this r_s value.

18.07 Classification

The scientific study of the classification of species is called taxonomy. Taxonomy aims to achieve a *natural* classification, which means that organisms are put into groups based on their evolutionary relationships. The groups are called **taxa** (singular = taxon) and are arranged in a hierarchy. At the base of the hierarchy is the **species**. Similar species are grouped into a **genus** (plural = genera), genera into a **family** and so on. Above the level of the family come the **order**, **class**, **phylum** and **kingdom**, with the **domain** at the top of the hierarchy. Look at the examples shown in Table 18.04.

Group (taxon)	Tiger	Wolf	Desert locust
domain	Eukarya	Eukarya	Eukarya
kingdom	Animalia	Animalia	Animalia
phylum	Chordata	Chordata	Arthropoda
class	Mammalia	Mammalia	Insecta
order	Carnivora	Carnivora	Orthoptera
family	Felidae	Canidae	Acrididae
genus	*Panthera*	*Canis*	*Schistocerca*
species	*Panthera tigris*	*Canis lupus*	*Schistocerca gregaria*

Table 18.04 The classification of three species of animal.

Note that all names in all groups start with a capital letter. A genus name is written in italics. The binomial (two part) name of a species name is also written in italics, starting with a capital letter for the genus and a lower case letter for the species.

Clearly the tiger and the wolf are more closely related to each other than either of them is to the locust. Tigers and wolves are both carnivorous mammals, and only differ at the level of the family and below – tigers belong to the cat family (Felidae) and wolves to the dog family (Canidae). The locust differs from both at the level of the phylum. Locusts and other insects belong to the phylum Arthropoda (animals with a hard external skeleton and jointed limbs). The classification indicates that tigers and wolves have a recent common ancestor - the first carnivores evolved about 42 million years ago, while the arthropods diverged from other animals much earlier in the evolutionary tree (about 500 million years ago).

a Domains

In Unit 1 you saw that organisms are divided into two groups based on their cell structure – prokaryotes and eukaryotes. All prokaryotes were once classified as bacteria. Since the 1980s, DNA analysis and other molecular evidence have shown that prokaryotes actually consist of two distinctly different groups of organisms. This led taxonomists to recognise that at the top of the hierarchy we should classify living organisms into three fundamental **domains** – Bacteria, Archaea and Eukarya. The first living cells probably evolved on Earth about 4000 million years ago and it is thought that the three domains diverged relatively shortly after this.

Bacteria are prokaryotic organisms with the following characteristics:

- they have no nucleus
- their DNA is in a circular 'chromosome' with no histone proteins
- they may contain small rings of DNA called plasmids
- they have no membrane-bound organelles (such as mitochondria and chloroplasts)
- they contain smaller (70S) ribosomes than eukaryotic cells
- all have a cell wall made of peptidoglycan (rather than cellulose)
- their cells divide by binary fission rather than mitosis
- they are mostly unicellular or consist of small groups of cells.

Archaea look very similar to bacteria (Figure 18.08) but they are fundamentally different in their cell chemistry and metabolism.

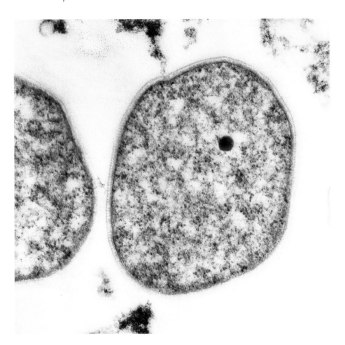

Figure 18.08 The archaean *Sulfolobus* sp. Archaea are similar to bacteria but have characteristics of eukaryotic cells, as well as some unique features such as the structure of their cell wall (yellow in this photomicrograph). *Sulfolobus* is an extremophile that lives in hot springs and thrives in acidic and sulfur-rich environments. Its optimum temperature for growth is 80 °C.

Like Bacteria, Archaea have no nucleus or membrane-bound organelles. They have a circular chromosome, divide by binary fission, and exist as unicellular organisms or as small groups of cells. Differences between Archaea and Bacteria include:

- Archaea always have a cell wall, but it is not made of peptidoglycan (or cellulose)

- Archaea have uniquely structured membrane lipids found in no other kinds of organism

- Archaea have a single circular chromosome, but it is sometimes associated with histone proteins

- Archaea have small ribosomes, but they have a structure similar to that of eukaryotic ribosomes

- the machinery for transcription and protein synthesis in Archaea is similar to that in eukaryotes.

Many Archaea live in extreme and harsh environments, such as acidic, near-boiling volcanic springs, salt lakes, and around volcanic vents at the bottom of the oceans ('black smokers'). However they have since been discovered in more 'normal' habitats, such as ordinary seawater and in the guts of animals. It is likely that they are much more widespread than was first thought.

In some ways Archaea have more in common with Eukarya than with Bacteria. It is thought that Archaea and Bacteria diverged early on in the evolution of life on Earth, and that Eukarya probably evolved from Archaea.

Eukarya include all the organisms that have eukaryotic cells – animals, plants, fungi and protoctists. Their characteristics include:

- cells with a nucleus and membrane-bound organelles

- DNA present in linear chromosomes with associated histone proteins

- large (80S) ribosomes (chloroplasts and mitochondria contain 70S ribosomes – it is likely that these organelles evolved from symbiotic bacteria)

- cell division by mitosis

- a great diversity of forms – unicellular, colonies of cells and multicellular.

b The four kingdoms of the Eukarya

The domain Eukarya is divided into four kingdoms: Animalia, Plantae, Fungi and Protoctista. Some characteristics are unique to one kingdom, but many species have features in common with members of other kingdoms.

TIP In each kingdom there are species that do not show all the characteristics listed below. There are always exceptions in biology!

The **Animalia** (animals) are members of a very diverse kingdom. They are all multicellular eukaryotes. Their other characteristics include:

- differentiation to form many different kinds of cells, tissues and organs

- heterotrophic nutrition, using a wide range of feeding methods – carnivorous, herbivorous, filter-feeding and so on

- store carbohydrates as glycogen

- a nervous system for coordination

- some cells have cilia or flagella

- no cell walls

- no chloroplasts and cannot photosynthesise

- during its early development the embryo of an animal forms a hollow ball of cells called a blastula.

Plantae (plants) are all complex multicellular eukaryotes. Examples include mosses, ferns, conifers and flowering plants. Some of their other characteristics are:

- differentiation to form different kinds of cells, tissues and organs

- autotrophic nutrition – some plant cells contain chloroplasts and carry out photosynthesis

- store carbohydrates as starch

- cell walls made of cellulose

- some cells contain large, permanent vacuoles

- growth takes place from special dividing tissues called meristems

- zygote develops into a diploid, multicellular embryo protected inside specialised tissues of the parent plant.

Unit 18 Biodiversity, classification and conservation

Fungi include mushrooms, moulds and yeasts. Some of their other characteristics are:

- cell walls made of materials other than cellulose (e.g. chitin)

- apart from the unicellular yeasts, they have bodies made of thread-like filaments called hyphae

- no chloroplasts and cannot photosynthesise

- heterotrophic nutrition, feeding on dead organic matter (saprobiontic nutrition) or as parasites

- store carbohydrates as glycogen

- reproduce by forming spores.

Protoctista (protoctists) are often called the 'dustbin kingdom', since they contain a wide range of unicellular and multicellular organisms that do not fit into any of the other three kingdoms. It is their wide range of simple body forms that characterises this group. They include unicellular 'animal-like' cells such as *Amoeba*, unicellular plant-like algae and multicellular algae ('seaweeds'). Some of their other characteristics are:

- most are unicellular but some species form colonies and others are multicellular

- algae have cell walls made of cellulose, other protoctists have no cell walls

- algae contain chlorophyll and can photosynthesise

- 'animal-like' species are heterotrophic.

c Viruses

The structure of viruses is described in Unit 1. They are not included in the system of classification described above, because they are not composed of living cells. In fact many biologists think that viruses should not be considered as being living organisms, since they do not show the usual 'characteristics of life' such as feeding, respiration, growth and excretion. The only life-like characteristic they show is the ability to reproduce, and they can only do this as parasites inside living cells. Viruses are not given a species name, and are classified using a different system, based on:

- the type of nucleic acid they contain (DNA or RNA)

- whether the nucleic acid is double-stranded or single-stranded (in cellular organisms DNA is double-stranded and RNA is single-stranded, but in viruses both types of nucleic acid can be either single- or double-stranded)

- the type of disease that they cause.

Progress check 18.03

Copy and complete Table 18.05.

Domain	Archaea	Bacteria	Eukarya			
Kingdom			**Animalia**	**Plantae**	**Fungi**	**Protoctista**
cell type	prokaryotic		eukaryotic	eukaryotic	eukaryotic	
number of cells		mostly unicellular		multicellular	unicellular and multicellular	mostly unicellular, some multicellular (algae)
method of feeding	autotrophic and heterotrophic					autotrophic and heterotrophic

Table 18.05

18.08 Threats to biodiversity

Biodiversity on Earth is threatened because species are being driven to extinction by habitat destruction, pollution and overexploitation of resources. This is becoming worse as the human population continues to increase exponentially. The main threats to biodiversity are a result of:

- loss of habitats and ecosystems (e.g. those caused by deforestation and conversion of land to agricultural use)

- pollution by the waste products of homes, industry and agriculture

- overexploitation of resources (e.g. over-fishing)

- climate change resulting from the production of carbon dioxide and other 'greenhouse gases', as well as deforestation

- the introduction of alien species and their harmful effects on native species.

a Why does biodiversity matter?

The arguments for maintaining biodiversity fall into four main categories – aesthetic, ethical, ecological and economic reasons:

- *Aesthetic reasons*. It is difficult not to appreciate the beauty of a tropical rainforest or the Great Barrier Reef (Figure 18.09). Most people would agree that natural ecosystems should be preserved for generations to come.

- *Ethical reasons*. Many people argue that destruction of ecosystems and loss of biodiversity is a simple ethical issue – we have no right to destroy the planet and drive species to extinction.

- *Ecological reasons*. Ecosystems with a high biodiversity tend to be more stable and able to resist disturbance. The extinction of any species in an ecosystem will have a knock-on effect on other species. This could be a result of disruption of food chains and food webs, or because a habitat is destroyed (e.g. trees for nesting). Some human activities may eventually threaten all life on Earth, the most obvious being the human-induced climate change.

- *Economic reasons*. Other living organisms (particularly rainforest plants) are a source of food, medicines and other resources for humans. Many of these organisms have yet to be discovered, and could provide new crop plants or new drugs, or act as a source of new

genes to increase the diversity of cultivated species. They will be lost if species become extinct.

Figure 18.09 The Great Barrier Reef off the eastern coast of Australia.

Conservation is the management of the Earth's resources to provide for the needs of humans at a sustainable level, while ensuring that resources are neither over-exploited nor destroyed. It is important that we conserve ecosystems, not just individual species. However, sometimes a particular species becomes endangered (threatened with extinction) so that action is needed to protect it.

18.09 Protecting endangered species

There a number of ways that endangered species can be protected. These include conservation areas, zoos and botanic gardens, 'frozen zoos' and seed banks.

a Conservation areas

The best place to protect endangered species is in their natural environment. Many countries have set up national parks and nature reserves that offer protection to the environment and its wildlife. Conservation areas generally limit access to the public and are governed by legislation that controls activities such as mining, building, hunting or farming.

Nature reserves are not just on land – there are also marine reserves. For example, the Galapagos Islands and the sea close to the islands have long been a national park, but in 1998 this was extended to form the Galapagos Marine Reserve, which covers the entire area within a 40-mile radius of the outer islands. In the islands, the land ecosystem needs the protection of the marine ecosystem, and there are interactions between the two (e.g. some bird species nest on land but feed in the sea).

There are always conflicts of interest in national parks. Primarily these are between the park authorities and the people who live in the area covered by the park, such as farmers. To address this problem, national parks often involve local people in the running of the park, providing employment or financial rewards for their cooperation with conservation activities. Visitors to the park also bring valuable income and tourism must be allowed to proceed at a level that does not have a detrimental effect on the environment.

b Zoos and botanic gardens

There are a number of ways that zoos can protect endangered species:

- *Education.* Zoos can educate the public about conservation issues. Entrance fees and donations can be used to help fund conservation programmes.

- *Research.* Animals in captivity can be studied to provide information about their breeding habits and other behaviour that will help us understand how they can be protected in the wild.

- *Captive breeding programmes.* Breeding programmes in zoos aim to increase genetic diversity of endangered species through outbreeding. This involves only allowing crosses between animals that are not closely related. Matings are arranged between animals from different zoos, or sperm frozen and transported long distances and used for artificial insemination or in vitro fertilisation (see below).

The ultimate aim of a breeding programme is to reintroduce the animals to their natural habitat. This has been successful with a number of species. For example, the scimitar-horned oryx has been reintroduced to Tunisia and the golden lion tamarin to protected rainforest reserves in Brazil.

Similar to the way in which zoos help protect endangered animals, botanic gardens can conserve plants by acting as a repository for endangered species.

c Frozen zoos

'Frozen zoos' are storage facilities for sperm, eggs, embryos and other living tissues from endangered species. These are kept frozen in liquid nitrogen until they might be needed. Since 1976, the San Diego zoo has amassed a collection of 8400 samples from over 800 species of animals and plants. The United Arab Emirates Breeding Centre for Endangered Arabian Wildlife has a collection of frozen embryos that include the highly endangered Gordon's wildcat and the Arabian leopard. There are relatively few frozen zoos at present, but more are being built.

d Seed banks

Seed banks are repositories for seeds of rare species and can be used to protect biodiversity. In particular they are used to store seeds from crop plants that are no longer grown commercially, in case they may be needed as a source of new genes in the future. Seeds are stored under conditions of low humidity (less than 5%) and low temperatures ($-18\,°C$ or below). The seeds are regularly planted and grown to check for their viability and to collect new seeds for storage. The largest seed bank in the world is the Millenium Seed Bank in Sussex, UK. It has facilities for storing billions of samples, and its ultimate aim is to store seeds from every plant species possible. It achieved 10% of this target in 2009 and is working towards 25% by 2020. There are about 1300 storage facilities for seeds and other plant tissues around the world.

18.10 Assisted reproduction

There are various methods of assisted reproduction that are used in the breeding of endangered mammals in zoos. They include artificial insemination, embryo transfer, surrogacy and in vitro fertilisation.

In **artificial insemination** (AI), semen is collected from a male and injected into the female's reproductive system using a catheter. This method can be used if animals refuse to mate in captivity. It is carried out while the female is ovulating naturally, or following hormone treatment to stimulate ovulation, and improves the chances of fertilisation taking place. Hormone treatment and AI may result in the production of multiple embryos. These can be washed out of the uterus at an early stage of their development and transferred to other females in a process of **embryo transfer**. The recipient females are prepared for pregnancy by giving them hormone injections. The embryos are then allowed to develop in these **surrogate** mothers. Sometimes related but non-endangered species are used as surrogates.

With **in vitro fertilisation** (IVF), hormone treatment is also given to a female mammal in order to stimulate the development of many mature follicles in the ovary. The follicles are removed using a needle and syringe and the secondary oocytes placed in a culture medium. Semen is added to the oocytes and fertilisation takes place. Any zygotes that are formed are allowed to develop into early embryos and transferred into the mother or into surrogates to complete their development.

Sperm, oocytes and embryos can all be stored for future use. They are frozen in liquid nitrogen at −196°C.

18.11 Preventing overpopulation

Sometimes the numbers of a species becomes too great for the carrying capacity of an ecosystem and can threaten its biodiversity. This can happen with both protected or non-protected species. As a result it may be necessary to reduce the size of a population. This can be done in two ways: culling and use of contraceptive methods.

Culling means reducing numbers by deliberately killing part of a population. The killing is often selective. It sometimes targets old or sick individuals, but in order to be most effective in reducing the size of a population it may have to target young, fit adults, which are the ones most likely to reproduce. Culling of natural populations is often a very controversial issue. For example, culling was used to reduce the population of African elephants in the Kruger National Park in South Africa by over 16 000 individuals between 1966 and 1994, until the practice was banned in 1995. Since that time the population has increased again and there have been calls for renewed culling.

Zoos also practise culling. Animals that are no longer useful for a breeding programme are culled and replaced with more desirable individuals. In 2014 a young male giraffe in Copenhagen zoo was culled. Although healthy, he was considered to be genetically unsuitable for breeding. His death caused an international outcry against the practice.

An alternative method of preventing overpopulation is the use of contraception. Although steroid hormones similar to the human 'pill' have been tried as a contraceptive in animal populations, a more successful method uses a failed human contraceptive called porcine zona pellucida (PZP). PZP is a vaccine made from a layer (zona pellucida) around the egg of a pig. It was first used in the 1980s to control populations of wild horses in the USA. If PZP is injected into a female horse, proteins in the PZP stimulate the horse to produce antibodies against them. The antibodies also bind to zona pellucida proteins surrounding the horse's own oocytes, preventing fertilisation by a sperm. Using PZP only 4% of vaccinated horses became pregnant, compared with 45% of unvaccinated animals. Since the ending of culling, PZP has since been used successfully with herds of African elephants, more than halving the pregnancy rate in the elephants of the Kruger National Park and completely preventing pregnancies in a smaller reserve.

18.12 Invasive alien species

Invasive alien species (IAS) are organisms that have spread from one ecosystem to another where they are not naturally present. There are IAS from all taxonomic groups – animals, plants, fungi and microorganisms. Most species transported to new environments do not survive to become invasive.

However, if a species' new habitat is similar to its native one, it may adapt, survive and reproduce. To become invasive it needs to thrive and out-compete native species. In time IAS can have severe negative impacts on an ecosystem, threatening its biodiversity.

IAS nearly always become established as a result of human activities. Some have been introduced deliberately, such as a food source or an ornamental plant, or in an attempt at biological control. In other cases they have been introduced accidentally, such as hidden amongst traded goods on ships. The effects of IAS are often most obvious on islands, such as Australia, New Zealand, the Galapagos Islands and Hawaii. This is because islands have been geographically isolated for a long time, allowing established species to evolve with few strong competitors and predators. IAS can have devastating effects on these ecosystems.

Hundreds of IAS have been identified. The following are just a few examples:

- Cane toads (*Bufo marinus*) are native to South and Central America. They were introduced to many islands of the Caribbean, Pacific and Australia as a method of biological pest control. They were first brought to Australia in 1935 to deal with insect pests of sugar cane (this is how the toad gets its name). The toad has few predators in Australia. It breeds very quickly, and has poison glands that make it and its tadpoles highly toxic. Cane toads have particularly harmful effects on native Australian species. They compete with other amphibians for food, eat chicks of ground-nesting birds, and are responsible for the deaths (by poisoning) of several species of predatory lizards, snakes and crocodiles as well as an endangered carnivorous marsupial called the northern quoll.

- The water hyacinth (*Eichhornia crassipes*) is one of the worst invasive species of aquatic plants in the world (Figure 18.10). This beautiful ornamental plant is native to the Amazon Basin. It is grown in garden ponds for its foliage and large, beautiful purple flowers. It has escaped into natural watercourses and is now found as an invasive species in over 50 countries. The plant grows quickly, spreading to cover lakes and rivers, where it blocks out sunlight and out-competes native plants, reducing biodiversity in aquatic ecosystems.

Figure 18.10 Water hyacinths blocking a waterway in California.

- The Western mosquitofish (*Gambusia affinis*) is a small species of fish native to the eastern and southern USA. It was introduced to many waterways around the world as a biological control for the larvae of mosquitoes that carry malaria. It has since been found to be no more effective in this role than local species

of fish, and is itself harmful to the ecosystems where it has been introduced, where it feeds on other native invertebrates and on the eggs of other species of fish. Despite the proven problems with this method of biological control, the fish is still being released in new habitats by mosquito-control agencies.

- The rosy wolf snail (*Euglandia rosea*) is a native of the south-eastern USA (Figure 18.11). It is a predatory species that was introduced to islands in the Pacific and Indian Oceans as a biological control for another alien species, the giant African snail. This snail was intended to be a food source for humans, but became an agricultural pest. The rosy wolf snails soon moved on to destroy populations of local species of snail, such as the Partulid tree snails, many of which now only exist in zoos. This alien species has caused a significant loss of biodiversity on the islands where it has been introduced.

Figure 18.11 The rosy wolf snail, a voracious predator of other snails.

The best way to prevent alien species becoming invasive is not to introduce them in the first place.

Deliberate introductions of species as biological control agents are often not successful, or cause other problems for the ecosystem, and the case for their use must be very carefully considered. Accidental introductions of species hidden in cargo must be prevented by customs checks and inspections of goods to make sure that there are no 'stowaways'. Eradication of alien species after they have become invasive is sometimes possible.

18.13 Conservation organisations

The World Wide Fund for Nature (WWF) is the largest international non-governmental conservation organisation. First set up in 1961, it now operates in 100 countries and has over 6 million members. The WWF lists six things it considers essential for the survival of the planet and its ecosystems, including humans:

- conservation of the world's forests

- maintaining healthy ocean ecosystems and marine livelihoods (e.g. fishing)

- ensuring secure sources of fresh water for people and nature

- protection of the world's endangered species

- doubling food production while freezing its 'footprint' (the area used for agriculture)

- creating a climate-resilient and zero-carbon world, powered by renewable energy.

The WWF participates in conservation at every level – from local to global. Around 85% of its income is spent on conservation projects and programmes, including publicity and education about environmental issues.

Another conservation organisation is CITES, which stands for the Convention on International Trade in Endangered Species of Wild Flora and Fauna. CITES is an agreement between governments that aims to ensure that international trade in wild animals and plants does not threaten their survival. It was established in 1973 at a meeting of 80 governments, and by 2016 had expanded to include 182 member states.

CITES does not just cover trade in living organisms, but also products such as skins, fur and ivory. The species covered by CITES are constantly reviewed and updated. They are placed into three categories called appendices:

- Appendix I: species threatened with extinction. Trade in these species is banned or only allowed in exceptional circumstances.

- Appendix II: species not threatened with extinction, but they are likely to be unless trade is controlled.

- Appendix III: species that is protected in a particular member country and that country has asked other CITES members for help in controlling the trade.

a Restoring degraded habitats

Habitat restoration aims to repair ecosystems that have been destroyed by activities such as agriculture, mining and logging, as well as those affected by natural disasters such as floods and earthquakes. Habitat restoration projects vary widely in scale, from small urban restorations such as 'wildlife gardening' and local tree planting schemes, through to large regional programmes.

The large-scale projects sometimes aim to counteract the impacts of 'habitat fragmentation' by joining up remaining areas of undamaged habitat into larger ecosystems that are more sustainable. Projects usually start by identifying a target species or group of species affected by the restoration (Figure 18.12). The requirements of the target species act as a guide to the process. Less commonly, restoration focuses on entire ecosystems. In both cases efforts must start with the protection and management of the remnant endangered areas before restoration of degraded habitats can be carried out.

Figure 18.12 The Sumatran orangutan (*Pongo abelii*) is critically endangered because of the loss of its habitat due to rainforest destruction. The WWF and other conservation agencies are helping to conserve 100 000 hectares of the remaining forest. The forest is the home of orangutans and other endangered species, including Sumatran tigers and elephants. Conservation will also involve habitat restoration.

Plants make up most of the community of any terrestrial ecosystem, so habitat restoration is generally focused on the reestablishment and management of plant species to historical levels of diversity. Re-establishing plants provides food and shelter for animals and allows the ecosystem to return to what it was. The most obvious example is the reforestation of areas of destroyed rainforest. Sometimes damaged forests are able to regenerate themselves naturally if enough trees remain nearby and seeds can be dispersed into the deforested areas via animals or wind. However, areas of forest which have been severely degraded may need to be replanted by hand using seedlings of native tree species (Figure 18.13).

Figure 18.13 A nursery in Brazil growing trees for reforestation.

Progress check 18.04

1   List four threats to the biodiversity of ecosystems.

2   Explain the meaning of:

    a   A frozen zoo.

    b   A seed bank.

    c   Culling.

3   Name an alien invasive species and explain how it is damaging an ecosystem to which it has been introduced.

Revision checklist

Check that you know:

- ◼ ecological terms
- ◼ biodiversity
- ◼ Simpson's Index of Diversity
- ◼ random sampling and transects
- ◼ the mark-release-recapture method
- ◼ how to use correlation coefficients
- ◼ classification

- ◼ the three domains of organisms, the four kingdoms of eukaryotes, and viruses
- ◼ threats to biodiversity
- ◼ methods of protecting endangered species
- ◼ methods of assisted reproduction
- ◼ methods of preventing overpopulation
- ◼ invasive alien species
- ◼ conservation organisations
- ◼ restoring degraded habitats.

Exam-style questions

1   A student investigated the numbers of five species of plant (A-E) by random sampling in a field, using 1-m² quadrats. Her results are shown in Table 18.06.

Species		Quadrat number							
		1	**2**	**3**	**4**	**5**	**6**	**7**	**8**
Species	**A**	14	6	9	12	2	5	5	1
	B	0	0	2	0	1	0	11	2
	C	16	35	4	14	4	8	43	10
	D	18	28	22	23	19	23	19	26
	E	6	5	1	12	20	15	11	8

Table 18.06

a   Explain how the student could have made sure that the quadrats were placed randomly in the field. [2]

b   What is the species richness in quadrat 1? [1]

c   Calculate the mean species density in numbers per square metre (m⁻²) for species C. Show your working. [2]

d   Copy and complete Table 18.07.

Species	Number of individuals of each species (n)	$\frac{n}{N}$	$\left(\frac{n}{N}\right)^2$
A			
B			
C			
D			
E			
Total (N) =			

Table 18.07

i   Find the total number of individuals (n) for each of the five species shown in Table 18.06 and enter your answers in the second column of Table 18.07. [1]

ii   Add up the total number of individuals of all the species (N). Enter your answer in the box indicated on your table. [1]

iii   Calculate Simpson's Index of Diversity (D) using the formula:

$$D = 1 - \sum \left(\frac{n}{N}\right)^2$$

Use the last two columns in Table 18.07 to help you with the calculations. [3]

iv   The value of D for plants in another field was found to be 0.399. Does this indicate a higher or lower species diversity than the value you have calculated in part **iii**? [1]

Total: 11

2   Table 18.08 shows the taxonomy (classification) of the king colobus monkey (*Colobus polykomos*). The table is incomplete.

Group (taxon)	
	Eukarya
Kingdom	
	Chordata
Class	Mammalia
	Primates
Family	Cercopithedae
Genus	
Species	*Colobus polykomos*

Table 18.08

a   Copy and complete Table 18.08. [2]

b   This system of classification is described as hierarchical. Explain what is meant by hierarchical. [1]

c   Which kingdoms of the Eukarya contain organisms that have the following:

i   cell walls

ii   hyphae

iii   autotrophic nutrition? [3]

Total: 6

3   The Millennium Seed Bank in the UK is the world's largest storage facility for seeds. It aims to store seeds from 25% of wild plant species by 2020.

a   Give three reasons why it is important to conserve endangered species of plants. [3]

b   State two conditions under which seeds are stored in order to keep them viable for future use. [2]

c   Every few years a sample is taken from each type of seed in the seed bank and the seeds allowed to germinate. Suggest why this is done. [2]

Total: 7

4   Corals are simple marine animals that live in colonies of thousands of individuals. 'Stony' corals construct skeletons made of calcium carbonate, which can form large coral reefs (Figure 18.14).

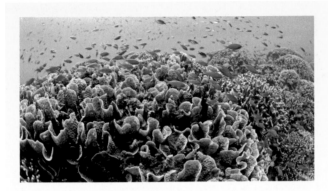

Figure 18.14 A coral reef.

Coral reefs have the highest biodiversity of any marine ecosystem, and are the home of over a quarter of all the Earth's fish species. The reefs are under threat from the activities of humans, including illegal collection of specimens for the aquarium trade. To help conserve coral reefs, all stony corals are listed in CITES Appendix II. (CITES stands for the Convention on International Trade in Endangered Species of Wild Flora and Fauna.)

a Explain the meaning of the terms:

    i   biodiversity [2]

    ii ecosystem. [2]

b What is the purpose of listing stony corals in CITES Appendix II? [2]

Total: 6

5 The kingdom Protoctista has been described as the 'dustbin kingdom', since it consists of a diverse group of organisms that do not fit into the other three kingdoms. Discuss the similarities and differences between the members of the Protoctista. [6]

Total: 6

Genetic technology

Learning outcomes

When you have finished this unit, you should be able to:

- [ ] define the term recombinant DNA

- [ ] explain that genetic engineering involves extracting genes from one organism, or the synthesis of genes, and then placing them in another organism such that the receiving organism expresses the gene product

- [ ] describe the principles of the polymerase chain reaction (PCR) to clone and amplify DNA, including the role of *Taq* polymerase

- [ ] explain how gel electrophoresis is used to analyse proteins and nucleic acids, and to distinguish between the alleles of a gene

- [ ] describe the properties of plasmids that allow them to be used in gene cloning

- [ ] explain why promoters and other sequences may have to be transferred with the desired gene

- [ ] explain the use of genes for fluorescent or easily stained substances as markers in gene technology

- [ ] explain the roles of restriction endonucleases, reverse transcriptase and ligases in gene technology

- [ ] outline how microarrays are used in the analysis of genomes and in detecting mRNA

- [ ] define the term bioinformatics

- [ ] outline the role of bioinformatics following the sequencing of genomes

- [ ] explain the advantages of producing human proteins by recombinant DNA techniques

- [ ] outline the advantages of screening for genetic conditions

- [ ] outline how genetic diseases can be treated with gene therapy

- [ ] discuss the social and ethical considerations of using gene testing and gene therapy in medicine

- [ ] outline the use of PCR and DNA testing in forensic medicine and criminal investigations

- [ ] explain the significance of genetic engineering in improving the quality and yield of crop plants and livestock

- [ ] outline the way in which the production of some crops may be increased

- [ ] discuss the ethical and social implications of using genetically modified organisms (GMOs) in food production.

19.01 Principles of genetic technology

Before you start on this unit, it will be helpful if you revise the structure of DNA and protein synthesis (see Unit 6). Genetic technology, sometimes also referred to as genetic engineering, involves the manipulation of DNA and naturally occurring processes such as protein synthesis for a wide range of applications, including the production of therapeutically important proteins, including insulin and the improvement of crop plants.

One aspect of genetic technology involves extracting a gene from one organism and transferring it to the DNA of another organism, of the same or another species. The DNA produced in this way is referred to as **recombinant DNA**, which may contain DNA from two different species, such as a human gene incorporated into the DNA of a fungus.

Progress check 19.01

Explain what is meant by the term 'recombinant DNA'.

To produce recombinant DNA, a gene is extracted from one organism and then transferred to another organism in which the gene is expressed and protein synthesis occurs. As an alternative to extraction of a gene, it is possible to use mRNA as a template for the synthesis of a strand of complementary DNA. This technique requires the use of the enzyme reverse transcriptase, described later in this unit.

The **polymerase chain reaction (PCR)**, developed in the early 1980s, is an important technique which is widely used in genetic technology. This technique makes it possible to make many millions of identical copies of just one strand or a few strands of DNA, in a relatively short time. PCR involves essentially the same principle as DNA replication, although it is carried out under precisely controlled conditions in a laboratory. The PCR takes place in a small plastic tube, placed in a machine which is programmed to repeat a series of steps and changes in temperature for DNA replication to occur. Each tube, in which the PCR occurs, contains the following:

- the original 'target' DNA sample

- a buffer solution to control the pH

- short DNA 'primers' – single strands of DNA that are complementary to the 3′ ends of the target DNA

- nucleotide triphosphates – these are the building blocks of the new DNA molecules

- a DNA polymerase enzyme.

One of the DNA polymerase enzymes used in the PCR is known as *Taq* polymerase. This enzyme is thermally stable and remains active at the high temperatures used (around 70 °C).

> **TIP**
>
> *Taq* polymerase is so-called because it was originally extracted from *Thermus aquaticus* – a species of bacterium adapted to live in hot springs. *Taq* polymerase has an usually high optimum temperature.

The PCR process has three essential stages:

1 The target DNA is heated to separate the two strands (denaturation).

2 Primers attach to the 3′ end of each DNA strand (annealing).

3 Each DNA strand is replicated by the DNA polymerase (elongation).

These three stages are repeated. The power of PCR is that for each cycle of the process, the number of DNA molecules doubles, so the number increases exponentially.

Worked example 19.01

Question

Calculate the number of DNA molecules produced from a single target molecule, in the PCR, after 20 cycles.

Answer

The number of DNA molecules increases exponentially (i.e. the number doubles with each cycle of the PCR.) After 20 doublings, the number of replicated DNA molecules will be 2 to the power 20 (2^{20}), which is a remarkable 1 048 576.

You could copy and complete table 19.01 below to show this exponential increase.

Cycles of PCR	Number of DNA molecules
start	1
1	2
2	4
3	8
4	16
5	32
6	
7	
8	
9	
10	
etc.	

Table 19.01

The PCR process requires a series of temperature changes, illustrated in Figure 19.01. These are controlled automatically by the PCR machine.

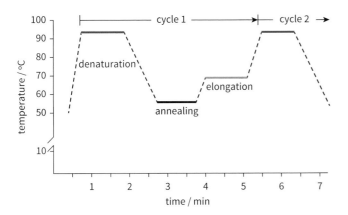

Figure 19.01 Temperature changes in the PCR.

The technique of **gel electrophoresis** is used to separate different proteins and nucleic acids. This technique relies on the principle that charged molecules will move in an electric field, through an agarose gel, containing a buffer solution. Agarose is a type of polysaccharide and forms a gel, similar to the agar gel used for culturing microorganisms. A sample containing the molecules to be separated is placed in a small well cut in the gel and an electric current is applied. Molecules with a negative charge (such as nucleic acids and many proteins) move towards the anode. This is illustrated in Figure 19.02.

Movement of molecules through the gel depends on several factors including:

- the overall charge on the molecule
- the size of the molecule (smaller molecules move faster than large molecules).

Before separation, a sample of DNA may be treated with a **restriction enzyme**, to cut the DNA into fragments.

After separation, the molecules form distinct bands in the gel. There are several different methods for visualising these bands, including the use of a fluorescent dye which can be seen in ultraviolet light, or the use of radioactive probes and X-ray film.

Gel electrophoresis is used to separate proteins and can be used to identify carriers of sickle cell anaemia (see Units 6 and 16), as both forms of haemoglobin (i.e. haemoglobin A and haemoglobin S) can be separated.

Progress check 19.02

Suggest the pattern of bands after electrophoresis of haemoglobin from people with the following three genotypes: **HbᴬHbᴬ**, **HbᴬHbˢ** and **HbˢHbˢ**.

The PCR and gel electrophoresis have important applications in diagnostic medicine and in forensic medicine and criminal investigations. You will read more about this later in the unit.

In the process of genetic engineering, various **vectors** are used to introduce DNA into host cells. Vectors include viruses, liposomes and **plasmids**. Plasmids are relatively small, circular loops of double-stranded DNA, found naturally in bacterial cells. Plasmids may contain genes which confer resistance to antibiotics to bacteria and are widely used as vectors in genetic engineering.

The process of introducing a gene into a host cell using plasmids is outlined below.

1 A gene is removed from DNA, using a restriction enzyme.

2 Plasmids are extracted from bacterial cells and 'cut open' using the same restriction enzyme.

3 The isolated gene and cut plasmid have complementary 'sticky ends' and the bases join by hydrogen bonding between pairs of complementary bases.

4 The enzyme DNA ligase is used to form covalent phosphodiester bonds so that the gene is now attached to the plasmid, forming recombinant DNA.

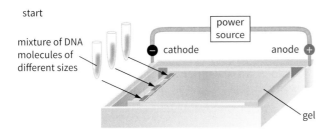
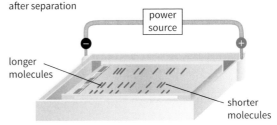

Figure 19.02 Gel electrophoresis.

5 Bacterial cells then take up the recombinant plasmids, forming transformed cells. This is encouraged by treating the cells with high concentrations of calcium ions or subjecting the cells to a temperature shock.

Not all of the bacterial cells will take up the recombinant plasmids and some cells will take up plasmids that have not been modified. There are various methods for identifying the transformed cells, including the use of marker genes, such as those for antibiotic resistance, the synthesis of green fluorescent protein (GFP), or the gene for the enzyme β-glucuronidase (GUS).

Inside the host bacterial cells, the plasmid replicates and when the cell divides, the daughter bacterial cells receive copies of the plasmid. Expression of the introduced gene results in the synthesis of a protein by the transformed cells. For example, bacteria which have been genetically modified to contain the gene for human insulin, synthesise insulin which is then extracted and purified.

In addition to the desired gene, it may also be necessary to transfer promoters and other control sequences to the plasmid. These allow RNA polymerase to bind and start the process of transcription of the desired gene, so that the required protein will be synthesised by the cell. The role of a promoter in 'gene switching' is described in Unit 16.

So far, we have outlined the use of several important enzymes used in genetic technology. These enzymes and their uses are summarised in Table 19.02.

Enzymes	Uses
DNA polymerase	The temperature-stable *Taq* polymerase is used to replicate DNA in the PCR
reverse transcriptase	This enzyme, found in retroviruses, uses RNA as a template to synthesise a complementary single strand of DNA; the enzyme DNA polymerase then synthesises a complementary DNA strand, forming double-stranded DNA
restriction endonucleases	These enzymes 'cut' DNA at specific recognition sites. Some restriction endonucleases, such as *Eco*RI and *Bam*HI, make a staggered cut across DNA, leaving a sequence of unpaired bases, forming sticky ends
DNA ligase	This enzyme forms covalent phosphodiester bonds in the sugar–phosphate backbone of DNA and is used to attach an introduced gene to a plasmid vector

Table 19.02 Enzymes used in genetic technology.

A **microarray** is used to investigate gene function. In a typical DNA microarray experiment, mRNA is hybridised with the DNA template from which it was synthesised. Many different DNA samples are used in the array and the amount of mRNA bound to each DNA sample gives an indication of the expression of various genes. Alternatively, DNA produced from mRNA using reverse transcriptase is hybridised with the DNA on the microarray. The extent of hybridisation of the two results in a colour change which is read with a laser scanner.

The microarray is a neat, systematic arrangement of thousands of tiny DNA samples on a solid material, such as a glass or plastic slide, typically 2 cm × 2 cm. Microarrays are used to help identify genes and their functions, in the diagnosis of disease with a genetic basis, drug discovery and development, and research into the toxic effects of substances on the genetic profile of a cell.

19.02 Genetic technology applied to medicine

Recent advances in molecular biology, including gene and protein sequencing, generate enormous quantities of data. The term **bioinformatics** refers to the use of computers to store and analyse this data, including the analysis and comparison of base sequences in DNA and amino acid sequences in proteins.

Bioinformatics has provided an essential tool in the genome sequencing of many different organisms. The first full DNA genome to be sequenced was that of a virus in the late 1970s. The Human Genome Project produced the first complete sequence of the human genome, with the first draft sequence being published in 2001. The genomes of thousands of different organisms have now been sequenced. Analysis of these genomes provides information about the structure and functions of genes, and provides a basis for the understanding of genetic disorders in humans. The genome of the malarial parasite, *Plasmodium*, has also been sequenced, which could provide essential information in the control of malaria.

Recombinant DNA technology is used to produce many proteins with applications in medicine. The first therapeutic protein to be produced in this way was human insulin, developed in the early 1980s. Insulin is used in the treatment of diabetes and was previously extracted from cells in the pancreas of animals. This had two major disadvantages:

- the supply of insulin was dependent on the supply of pancreatic tissue from animals

- insulin from animals has a slightly different structure from human insulin and, as a result, could cause allergic reactions in patients using this form of insulin.

Recombinant DNA technology to produce insulin and other proteins involves transferring the human gene for the protein to bacterial host cells. The human proteins are then synthesised by the transformed cells, extracted and purified. This technology has made it possible to produce many different proteins of therapeutic use on a large scale, without the need for supplies extracted from animal tissue.

Human proteins produced using the techniques of recombinant DNA technology include:

- insulin for the treatment of diabetes
- factor VIII for the treatment of haemophilia, a blood clotting disorder
- adenosine deaminase which is used in the treatment of severe combined immunodeficiency (SCID).

Sample question 19.01

Many proteins, used for therapeutic purposes in humans, are now produced using recombinant DNA technology.

1 Name one protein, used to treat patients, that is produced using recombinant DNA technology.

2 Give three advantages of producing proteins for therapeutic use by recombinant DNA technology.

[4 marks]

[Mark points are shown in square brackets – to a maximum of 4 marks]

1 Human insulin **[1]**.

2 Three advantages are:

 a the protein may be produced on a large scale, ensuring adequate and regular supplies

 b the protein is identical to the human protein

 c the protein does not need to be extracted from animal tissues, which raises ethical concerns **[3]**.

Human insulin (Humulin®) is a good example and was the first such therapeutic protein to be licensed for use. This is used for the treatment of diabetes. There are many other examples, including human growth hormone, blood clotting factor VIII and erythropoietin.

These are all suitable advantages of producing the proteins by recombinant DNA technology. Before these techniques were available, the proteins had to be extracted from animal (or, occasionally, from human) tissue. This limited their availability. For example, insulin was extracted from the pancreas of pigs and cows, but this was dependent on the supply of these pancreases. Insulin from pigs and cows has a slightly different structure from human insulin which alters its effectiveness. Production of therapeutic proteins from genetically modified microorganisms has the potential of an almost unlimited supply of these products.

Another advantage of their use is there is a reduced chance of contamination, particularly with infective agents. For example, there is a risk that insulin derived from cows could be infected with the agent that causes bovine spongiform encephalopathy (BSE), sometimes known as 'mad cow disease'.

Developments in genetic technology have also revolutionised the diagnosis and detection of diseases with a genetic basis. These techniques may involve the identification of a specific protein product, such as haemoglobin S in sickle cell anaemia, or the identification of a gene and its alleles. The identification of the haemoglobin S allele, for example, makes use of a restriction endonuclease, *MstII*, which produces DNA fragments of different sizes from the unaffected haemoglobin gene and from the haemoglobin S allele. The fragments are separated using gel electrophoresis.

Genetic screening may be used to detect genetic disorders or to identify couples who are at risk of passing on an inherited condition to their children. Screening may be carried out to recognise a wide range of genetic conditions and to identify specific genes, such as those associated with breast cancer (*BRCA1* and *BRCA2* genes). Screening programmes may also be carried out to identify genetic disorders including haemophilia, sickle cell anaemia, Huntington's disease, cystic fibrosis, thalassaemia and Tay–Sachs disease.

Progress check 19.03

Explain the genetic basis and inheritance of haemophilia and sickle cell anaemia.

Gene therapy offers the possibility of treatment of genetic disorders, by placing a 'normal' allele into the cells of a patient with a genetic disorder. This can be achieved with the use of a virus or a liposome as a vector for the gene, or by using 'naked' DNA. A liposome, illustrated in Figure 19.03, is a small spherical structure, surrounded by a lipid bilayer, similar to an artificial cell.

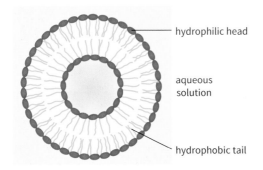

hydrophilic head

aqueous solution

hydrophobic tail

Figure 19.03 A liposome.

Insertion of a gene into body cells is referred to as **somatic cell** gene therapy. It would also be possible to insert a gene into **germ cells** (i.e. cells involved in

sexual reproduction or cells in an early embryo, but this is illegal in humans). In practice, gene therapy has proved to be difficult to carry out successfully, but some success has been achieved in the treatment of:

- a form of hereditary blindness

- thalassaemia

- haemophilia B

- SCID.

The choice of an appropriate vector is important to deliver the gene to the target cells and this has presented difficulties in gene therapy. For example, use of a virus as a vector may cause side-effects because of the virus itself. Delivery of a gene using liposomes may have only a limited effect if the target cells are short-lived.

Screening for genetic disorders and gene therapy raise a number of social and ethical concerns. As examples, when selecting people for genetic screening, the following points could be considered:

- Are the people to be screened able to give informed consent?

- What are the ethical and practical implications of a positive result?

- What will the testing cost and will the benefits justify the costs?

Selection of people to be screened also needs to be considered carefully. Where it may be impractical to screen everyone for genetic disorders, screening may be based on family history or the age of the mother. In other instances, where a genetic disorder has a higher incidence in certain ethnic groups, selection of people for the test needs to be done sensitively to avoid the risk of appearing to discriminate against certain groups of people.

Screening can be carried out on adults, particularly if they are identified as being at risk of a genetic disorder, on babies and children, or on material obtained in early pregnancy to screen a developing fetus for genetic disorders (prenatal diagnosis). Techniques for prenatal diagnosis of genetic disorders include amniocentesis and chorionic villus sampling (CVS). Both of these techniques are carried out in early pregnancy and may be used where parents are identified as being at risk of having a baby with a genetic disorder. The results of this diagnosis also raise ethical questions, such as where it is appropriate to have an abortion if the developing baby would be born with a serious, debilitating and incurable disorder. If so, parents may elect to have a therapeutic termination of pregnancy.

Preimplantation genetic diagnosis is also possible. Following in vitro fertilisation (IVF) and culture of an embryo, DNA analysis of a single cell can be carried out and an embryo free of a genetic disorder selected for implantation in the mother.

The techniques of PCR and gel electrophoresis to produce a DNA profile are now widely used in forensic medicine and in criminal investigations, to identify both victims and perpetrators of crimes. Minute samples of material containing DNA, including blood, semen and saliva, can be used for this purpose. There are also many less obvious sources of DNA which can be used in forensic analysis, including discarded chewing gum, cigarette ends, used cups, and used envelopes and stamps.

The DNA extracted from materials recovered from the scene of a crime is amplified using PCR and then separated using gel electrophoresis to produce a unique profile which can be compared with known profiles. In forensic DNA profiling, small regions of DNA referred to as short tandem repeats (also known as microsatellites or simple sequence repeats) are used, because these show very variable base sequences between different people. After amplification using PCR, the DNA is cut into fragments using restriction enzymes and the fragments separated by gel electrophoresis. The separate bands of DNA are then made visible using dyes or radioactive probes and X-ray film. The resulting pattern of bands forms the **DNA profile**, sometimes also referred to as a genetic fingerprint. Figure 19.04 shows an example of a DNA profile.

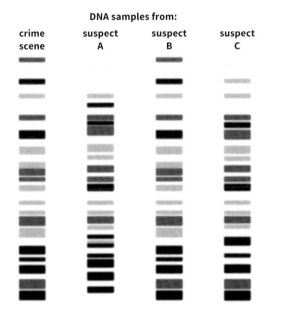

Figure 19.04 Profiles of DNA obtained from the scene of a crime and from three suspects.

19.03 Genetically modified organisms in agriculture

Genetic modification of livestock and crop plants, such as rice and maize, offers considerable benefits in terms of improvements in yield, pest and disease resistance, drought resistance and improvement in nutritional qualities. Table 19.03 gives some examples of genetically modified organisms (GMOs) in food production.

Organisms	Description
Bt maize	this is maize with a gene taken from a species of bacterium, *Bacillus thuringiensis*, which when expressed in the maize plants produces a toxin (Bt toxin) which kills insect pests but is harmless to other organisms
vitamin A enhanced rice (Golden Rice™)	genes for the synthesis of carotene have been transferred to rice plants; carotene is used in the synthesis of vitamin A and potentially this form of rice could help to avoid deficiencies of vitamin A in the diet and associated health problems, particularly in children
genetically modified salmon	Atlantic salmon have been genetically modified by inserting a gene which results in an increased growth rate so that these salmon reach a marketable size in about 18 months, rather than the 3 years of unmodified salmon

Table 19.03 Some examples of genetically modified organisms.

Crop plants, including maize, tobacco, cotton and oil seed rape, have been genetically modified to produce varieties that are resistant to insect pests or to certain herbicides. These varieties can result in increased yields, by reducing damage to the plants by insect pests, such as corn borers, or enabling effective weed control using herbicides in crops that are resistant to the herbicide used. While genetic modification of crop plants can increase yields, there are a number of concerns about the environmental impact, and ethical and social implications of cultivating these plants.

One particular environmental concern is the possibility that genes for herbicide resistance could spread to related wild species of plants, making them difficult to control using conventional methods. Also, it is possible that plants genetically modified to be resistant to insect pests could have harmful effects on non-target and possibly beneficial species.

Revision checklist

Check that you know:

- [ ] the term recombinant DNA

- [ ] genetic engineering involves extracting genes from one organism, or the synthesis of genes, and then placing them in another organism such that the receiving organism expresses the gene product

- [ ] the principles of the PCR to clone and amplify DNA, including the role of *Taq* polymerase

- [ ] how gel electrophoresis is used to analyse proteins and nucleic acids and to distinguish between the alleles of a gene

- [ ] the properties of plasmids that allow them to be used in gene cloning

- [ ] why promoters and other sequences may have to be transferred with the desired gene

- [ ] the use of genes for fluorescent or easily stained substances as markers in gene technology

- [ ] the roles of restriction endonucleases, reverse transcriptase and ligases in gene technology

- [ ] how microarrays are used in the analysis of genomes and in detecting mRNA

- [ ] the term bioinformatics

- [ ] the role of bioinformatics following the sequencing of genomes

- [ ] the advantages of producing human proteins by recombinant DNA techniques

- [ ] the advantages of screening for genetic conditions

- [ ] how genetic diseases can be treated with gene therapy

- [ ] the social and ethical considerations of using gene testing and gene therapy in medicine

- [ ] the use of PCR and DNA testing in forensic medicine and criminal investigations

- [ ] the significance of genetic engineering in improving the quality and yield of crop plants and livestock

- [ ] the way in which the production of some crops may be increased

- [ ] the ethical and social implications of using GMOs in food production.

Exam-style questions

1 a Explain the use of each of the following enzymes in gene technology.

    i   Restriction endonuclease. [2]

    ii Ligase. [2]

    iii Reverse transcriptase. [3]

  b Describe how bacteria can be screened for the presence of recombinant plasmids. [3]

Total: 10

2 a Explain what is meant by each of the following terms.

    i   Gene therapy. [2]

    ii Gel electrophoresis. [5]

  b Name <u>three</u> human therapeutic proteins produced by recombinant DNA technology. [3]

  c Crop plants have been successfully genetically modified to improved crop yields. Explain why many people are opposed to the cultivation of genetically modified crop plants. [4]

Total: 14

Planning, analysis and evaluation

Learning outcomes

When you have finished this unit, you should be able to:

(Planning)

- ☐ design an experimental method, given background information about a problem

- ☐ make a prediction as a written hypothesis or as a graph of the expected results

- ☐ identify the independent variable, dependent variable and the key variables to control

- ☐ describe how to change the independent variable, how to measure the dependent variable and how to control the other variables

(Analysis and evaluation)

- ☐ analyse, evaluate and make conclusions about experimental data presented as tables, graphs or written statements

- ☐ identify appropriate mathematical or statistical methods to process data

- ☐ answer questions on experiments that cannot easily be investigated in a school laboratory.

The experimental skills of planning, analysis and evaluation are tested in Paper 5. This is a written paper, *not* a 'hands-on' practical examination like Paper 3. It will test the practical skills you have developed during the A level course and builds on the skills tested in Paper 3. You will have to write extended answers, including appropriate diagrams and tables.

There are 30 marks available in Paper 5. Table P2.01 shows how the marks for Paper 3 are awarded.

Skill	Total marks	Breakdown of marks	
planning	15 marks	defining the problem	5 marks
		methods	10 marks
Analysis, conclusions and evaluation	15 marks	dealing with data	8 marks
		evaluation	4 marks
		conclusions	3 marks

Table P2.01 Skills and marks for Paper 5.

P2.01 Planning

At least one of the questions in Paper 5 will describe a particular situation and ask you to devise a hypothesis and a method to test that hypothesis. Often the question will tell you the apparatus to use. This may be something you have used in class or it may be completely new and you will have to apply your knowledge and understanding of similar investigations to the new task.

Planning will normally involve investigating the effect of one factor (the **independent variable**) on another factor (the **dependent variable**). You have read about these variables before, in Unit P1. The **hypothesis** is a prediction about how the independent variable affects the dependent variable.

| TIP | Here, the hypothesis refers to the biological hypothesis, not the null hypothesis used in statistical tests. |

a Defining the problem

This is easiest to explain by using a simple example. Imagine you are given some background information about an enzyme with an optimum temperature of 50 °C and an optimum pH of 8.0, and asked to plan an experiment to investigate the effect of temperature on the activity of the enzyme. In answering this you will have to state the variables and the hypothesis:

- The independent variable is temperature – the factor varied by the experimenter.

- The dependent variable is activity of the enzyme – the factor that is changing as a result of the change in temperature.

- Other key variables that need to be controlled are the concentrations of substrate and enzyme, pH (8.0) and the volumes of enzyme and substrate solutions.

- The hypothesis could be 'The activity of the enzyme will increase with temperature', or 'The activity of the enzyme will increase with temperature up to 50 °C, above which it will decrease. The hypothesis could be stated in words or as a graph of enzyme activity against temperature.

It is important to note that in some experiments it may not be possible to *directly* measure the dependent variable given in the hypothesis. For example, the activity of the enzyme might be found by measuring the rate of formation of a coloured product, using a colorimeter. In the actual experiment the dependent variable is the factor that is *measured directly* during the experiment – the absorbance reading in the colorimeter.

b Methods

The method should describe the steps in the procedure in a logical sequence, including how to use the apparatus to collect results. Depending on the question, the method may include some or all of the following points (those marked with an asterisk are not appropriate to all experiments):

- how to vary the independent variable and how to make sure its values are measured accurately

- how to measure the dependent variable

- how to standardise the other controlled variables

- how to prepare suitable volumes and concentrations of reagents*

- how to make proportional dilutions and serial dilutions from a stock solution*

- how to carry out a suitable control experiment*

- how to ensure results are precise, and a consideration of the need to calculate descriptive statistics such as standard deviation, standard error or 95% confidence interval

- a simple risk assessment and precautions to minimise risks.

Progress check P2.01

Lemna minor is a small flowering plant that grows on the surface of pond water. Each plant consists of a small leaf-like thallus and a single root. The plant reproduces asexually, forming buds that grow and split off to form separate plants. A student investigated the effect of nitrate ions on the growth of *Lemna minor*. She placed 10 plants in each of five beakers containing 200 cm³ of different concentrations of nitrate solution. After 10 days she counted the number of thalli produced.

1   State the independent and dependent variables in her investigation.

2   Identify two variables that the student controlled.

3   Suggest two other variables that could have been controlled.

Sample question P2.01

Blowfly larvae (maggots) are known to be more active in the light than in the dark. A student used the respirometer shown in Figure P2.01 to compare the rate of respiration in maggots kept in the light and in the dark.

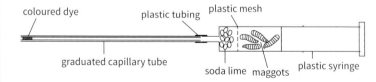

Figure P2.01

1 Suggest a hypothesis about the respiration of the maggots that the student could test using this apparatus. [1]

2 Identify the independent and dependent variables in this investigation. [2]

3 Describe a method that the student could use to compare the rates of respiration of the maggots under light and dark conditions, using the respirometer in Figure P2.01. Your method should be detailed enough for another person to use. [8]

[Mark points are shown in square brackets – to a maximum of 11 marks]

1 The rate of respiration of the maggots will be greater in the light than in the dark **[1]**.

There are various ways of answering this – the rates in the two conditions could be 'greater', 'different' or even 'the same' – they are all testable hypotheses.

2 Independent variable = light intensity (or light and dark) **[1]**.

Dependent variable = distance moved by the water in the capillary per unit time **[1]**.

Note this is the factor that is measured directly in the experiment.

3 Take a suitable number of maggots and weigh them on a balance to find their mass. Place the maggots in the syringe and assemble the respirometer, ensuring there are no air leaks. Immerse the respirometer in a thermostatically controlled water bath at a constant temperature of 20 °C. Turn off the lights in the laboratory and place a bench lamp with a 60 watt bulb above the respirometer at a fixed distance from the syringe, to provide a constant light intensity. Leave the respirometer set up for a suitable period of time to equilibrate to the new conditions. After equilibration, use the scale on the graduated capillary tube to measure the distance moved by the coloured dye over a measured time interval. The rate of movement will be equivalent to the rate of respiration of the maggots.

There is no one correct answer to a question like this, but this sample answer covers all the expected areas:
- *independent variable – how to control the light intensity in the light/dark conditions*
- *dependent variable – how to measure the distance moved by the water per unit time*
- *controlled variables – temperature, mass of maggots, mass of soda lime, airtight apparatus, equilibration*
- *control experiment*
- *safety – hazards*
- *reliability – replicates and means.*

Repeat the procedure as above but with the bench lamp switched off. Use a fresh batch of maggots of the same mass. Use the same mass of soda lime. This could be replaced to ensure there is enough to absorb all the CO_2 from the maggots.

Repeat the whole experiment to record six readings in the light and six in the dark and identify any anomalous results. Carry out a control experiment, replacing the maggots with the same mass of glass beads and measure any movement of the water in the light and in the dark. Calculate the mean rates of movement of the water in the light and in the dark.

Take necessary safety precautions during the investigation. When assembling the respirometer take care when inserting the graduated glass capillary tube into the plastic tubing. The tube could break and cause cuts. Soda lime is corrosive to the skin and eyes – wear gloves and goggles when handling it. **[8]**

The sample answer above does not use reagent solutions but other investigations may require you to explain how to make these up. The concentrations of solutions may be given in molar quantities, or as a percentage – mass of solute per volume of solvent (w/v). Normally in biology water is the solvent.

To make a 1 mol dm⁻³ solution you place 1 mole of the solute in a 1 dm³ flask and dissolve it in a volume of distilled water less than 1 dm³. When it is fully dissolved, you add more water to make the volume up to 1 dm³ and mix thoroughly.

To make a 1% solution you place 1 g of solute in a flask, dissolve it in a little water and then make the volume up to 100 cm³.

Given a stock solution, you should be able to make serial dilutions. These are described in Unit P1.

Progress check P2.02

The student in the investigation described in Progress Check P2.01 used sodium nitrate powder to make up solutions containing different concentrations of nitrate ions. The molar mass of sodium nitrate is 85.0 g mol⁻¹.

1   Describe how she could make 1 dm³ of a 0.1 mol dm⁻³ solution of sodium nitrate.

2   How could she make 0.5 dm³ of a 5% (w/v) solution of sodium nitrate?

P2.02 Analysis, conclusions and evaluation

At least one of the questions in Paper 5 will provide you with one or more sets of data to analyse. You will have to process the data (e.g. by carrying out calculations), evaluate the reliability of the data and draw conclusions about the experiments involved. These are largely skills you learnt during your AS studies and which were tested in Paper 3 (see Unit P1), but you will have developed these skills further during your A level work. One big difference is that Paper 5 examines your understanding of certain statistical tests.

a Dealing with data

When provided with data, you should be able to:

- recognise the different types of variable (qualitative and quantitative) and types of data (nominal, ordinal and continuous)

- decide which calculations and statistical tests are needed to draw conclusions

- identify key points from tables of data and graphs

- draw graphs correctly, including error bars

- find the mean, median, mode, range and interquartile range of a set of data

- carry out calculations such as percentage change, rate of change, Simpson's Index of Diversity and estimation of population size from the mark-release-recapture method

- use standard deviation and standard error values to judge whether means are significantly different

- select which statistical tests to use and apply these tests, choosing from:

  o t-test

  o chi-squared (χ^2) test

  o Pearson's linear correlation

  o Spearman's rank correlation.

Many of these points are dealt with in Unit P1 – additional information is covered here.

Qualitative variables can be observed and counted but not measured. Data is **nominal** if the variables can be sorted into a category, such as flower colour, species of tree or gender (nominal means 'named'). It is **ordinal** if the data can be placed into a rank order, such as depth of blue colour produced in a starch–iodine test.

Quantitative variables can be measured. Data is **continuous** if it can have any value within a particular range, such as length, mass, area, rate of reaction.

b Mean, median and mode

The mean, median and mode are different types of 'average' of a data set. For example, imagine you have taken a sample of 15 apples from a tree and found their masses to the nearest gram to be: 81, 87, 89, 91, 93, 93, 93, 94, 98, 101, 103, 106, 110, 110 and 111 g.

The **mean** is the sum of all the values divided by the total number of values:

$$\text{mean} = \frac{1460}{15} = 97.3 \text{ g}.$$

(Note that it is correct to give a mean value to the same number of significant figures as the data values, or to one more significant figure, as shown here.)

The **mode** is the most common value in the data set; in this example the mode is 93 g.

The **median** is the middle value of all the values in the data set; in this example the median is 94 g, since there are seven values below 94 g and seven above.

On a frequency histogram you can show the bars containing the median and mode. These are called the median class and the modal class (Figure P2.02).

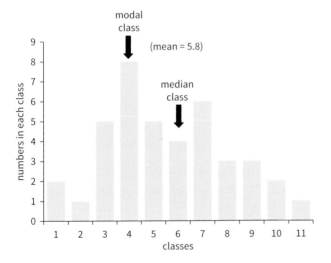

Figure P2.02 Frequency histogram showing the median class and modal class of a data set. If the data set is relatively symmetrical the mean and median will be close in value.

c Range and interquartile range

The **range** is the spread between the smallest and largest value in the data. Using the example of the apples given above:

81, 87, 89, 91, 93, 93, 93, 94, 98, 101, 103, 106, 110, 110 and 111 g

The range is 81 to 111 g.

The range can be divided into four quarters, containing equal numbers of values. The divisions are called quartiles. The median is the middle quartile (Figure P2.03). The range between the lower and upper quartiles is called the **interquartile range**. It is sometimes useful to compare the interquartile ranges of two sets of data, because it ignores values at the extreme ends of the range, called 'outliers'.

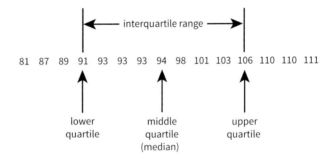

Figure P2.03 The interquartile range.

d Standard deviation, standard error and confidence intervals

The **standard deviation** (s) of a sample is a measure of the spread of the values in the sample around the mean. A larger value of the standard deviation shows a greater degree of variation. It is calculated from the formula:

$$s = \sqrt{\frac{\sum (x - \bar{x})^2}{n-1}}$$

where x represents the individual values in the sample, $\bar{x}$ is the mean, n is the sample size and Σ means 'the sum of'.

For example, seven specimens of a species of beetle were weighed. Their masses to the nearest 0.1 g were 5.7, 6.9, 5.5, 4.6, 5.8, 4.9 and 6.2 g. Table P2.02 shows a calculation to find the standard deviation of this data.

x	$x - \bar{x}$	$(x - \bar{x})^2$
5.7	0.04	0.0016
6.9	1.24	1.5376
5.5	−0.16	0.0256
4.6	−1.06	1.1236
5.8	0.14	0.0196
4.9	−0.76	0.5776
6.2	0.54	0.2916
$\Sigma x = 39.6$		$\Sigma (x - \bar{x})^2 = 3.5772$
$n = 7$		$s = \sqrt{\dfrac{\Sigma (x - \bar{x})^2}{n-1}}$
$\bar{x} = (39.6 \div 7) = 5.66$		$s = \sqrt{\dfrac{3.5772}{6}} = 0.7721$

Table P2.02 Calculation of the standard deviation.

The standard deviation is 0.77 (to two significant figures). For data that is 'normally distributed', about 68% of the data will be within ±1 standard deviation of the mean. In the above example this could be written as 5.66 ± 0.77 g. Two standard deviations either side of the mean include 95% of the data (Figure P2.04).

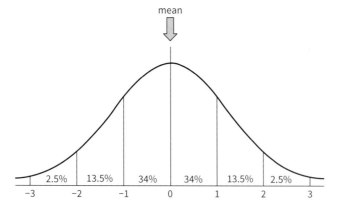

Figure P2.04 A normal distribution showing the range of values covered by different numbers of standard deviations; ±2 standard deviations either side of the mean includes about 95% of the data.

If you took another random sample of beetles you would probably find it had a slightly different mean and standard deviation. A third sample would give another pair of values and so on. How can you find the mean of the whole population from which the samples were taken? You cannot exactly, but you can get an estimate of it by calculating a statistic called the **standard error** (S_M). The standard error is the standard deviation of the sample means and is given by the formula:

$$S_M = \frac{s}{\sqrt{n}}$$

95% of sample means will be found within about ±2 standard errors of the population mean (this can be shown by a graph similar to Figure P2.04). There is therefore a 95% probability that the true population mean will lie between the sample mean ±2 standard errors, or $\bar{x} \pm (2 \times S_M)$. This is known as the 95% confidence interval for the sample. There is a 95% chance that this confidence interval contains the true population mean.

TIP

Here 'population' does not have the same meaning as in ecology. In statistics it refers to a set of numbers from which the sample is drawn.

With the beetle data in Table P2.02, the standard error is:

$$S_M = \frac{0.772}{\sqrt{7}} = 0.29$$

$(2 \times 0.29) = 0.58$, so there is a 95% probability that the range 5.66 ± 0.58 g contains the true population mean (i.e. from 5.08 to 6.24 g).

Note that for simplicity, the sample size in Table P2.02 is small ($n = 7$). You should really use larger sample sizes to calculate reliable confidence intervals. As the sample size increases, both S_M and the confidence interval get smaller.

The standard error can be used to draw error bars on a bar chart or graph (Figure P2.05). The error bars can help us decide whether there is a significant difference between two data points on the graph. If the error bars overlap, the difference between the values is not significant. If the error bars do not overlap, we cannot be *sure* that the difference is significant, although it may be (a statistical test would need to be carried out, such as the *t*-test).

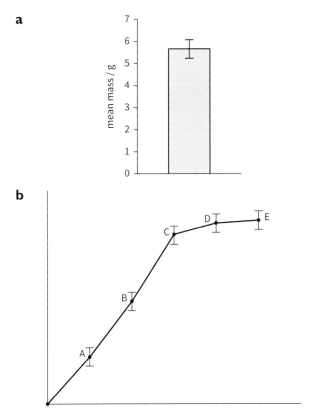

a

b

Figure P2.05 **a** The mean and standard error bars for the beetle data from Table P2.02. **b** A line graph with error bars. The data points are each mean values of a sample and each error bar is ± (2 × standard error) for that mean. Means C, D and E are not significantly different from each other, because the standard error bars overlap.

Progress check P2.03

1   State whether the following variables are qualitative nominal, qualitative ordinal or quantitative.

   a   The depth of red colour produced in a series of Benedict's tests for reducing sugars.

   b   The rate of transpiration of a plant, measured using a potometer.

   c   The numbers of *Drosophila* flies in a genetics cross having brown, red or white eyes.

2   The lengths of a sample of 20 leaves from a certain tree had a mean and standard deviation of 10.9 ± 0.2 cm. What does this standard deviation show about the data?

3   Explain the difference between the standard deviation and the standard error.

---

e Statistical tests

You need to be able to choose statistical tests appropriate to the type of data collected, justify the use of these tests, and apply them to the data. There are dozens of different statistical tests, but you only need to be familiar with four (these are described in other units of this book):

- The *t*-test is used to compare the means of two sets of continuous data to see if they are significantly different. See Unit 17.

- The chi-squared (χ^2) test is used to compare observed and expected frequencies to see if they are significantly different. The data consists of frequencies (counts) of observations in different categories, i.e. nominal data. A common application is to compare the numbers of different phenotypes from a genetic cross with an expected ratio (e.g. 3 : 1 or 9 : 3 : 3 : 1). See Unit 16.

- Pearson's linear correlation is a test for a linear (straight line) correlation between two paired sets of quantitative data (variables X and Y). Both data sets must approximately fit a normal distribution, as shown by scatter diagrams. It is not appropriate if variable X is a variable you manipulate (i.e. an independent variable). See Unit 18.

- Spearman's rank correlation is a test for correlation between two variables, but the correlation does not need to be linear, and the variables do not need to be normally distributed. As with Pearson's test, it is not appropriate if variable X is a variable you manipulate. See Unit 18.

f Other calculations

Calculation of Simpson's Index of Diversity and the mark–release–recapture method for estimating the population size of a mobile species of animal are both described in Unit 18.

g Evaluation

When provided with data, you will need to be able to assess its validity and how much confidence you can have in drawing conclusions from it and whether it can be trusted for testing the hypothesis. Evaluation is based on the following:

anomalous readings	• identify them in a table or graph • suggest reasons for them • suggest how to deal with them
replicates	• assess whether there are enough • explain why they are important • explain the practical limits on number of replicates
data range and intervals of the independent variable	• identify when the range is not good enough • identify when there are gaps in the range
measurement technique	• assess whether it is accurate and reliable enough
Controlled variables	• assess whether they are properly controlled

Anomalous values can be dealt with by repeating the experiment until results are consistent. They can only be ignored if there is a good scientific reason to do so.

There may be more appropriate measuring apparatus available, such as using a colorimeter instead of judging colour by eye, or using a pH meter instead of a pH indicator and colour chart.

h Conclusions

Your conclusions should include explanations based on knowledge and understanding gained from material in the AS and A level syllabus. You should be able to:

- summarise the key points from the data provided and any calculations or statistical tests, quoting any relevant figures

- decide whether a given hypothesis is supported or not and, if it is not fully supported, explain why

- give detailed scientific explanations of the data and your conclusions

- make predictions and hypotheses based on your conclusions

- suggest how an experiment could be modified to increase confidence in the results (e.g. by narrowing the range and decreasing the intervals of the independent variable to give a more accurate result).

Revision checklist

Check that you know how to:

- ☐ construct a testable hypothesis

- ☐ identify the independent variable, dependent variable and variables to control in an investigation

- ☐ describe how the independent variable would be altered, how the dependent variable would be measured and how the other variables would be controlled

- ☐ describe a control experiment for the investigation

- ☐ construct a logical sequence of steps in an investigation, including a risk assessment and ways to minimise risks

- ☐ describe how to make up solutions in molar quantities (mol dm^{-3}) or percentage (mass per volume)

- ☐ recognise different types of qualitative and quantitative variable

- ☐ find the mean, median and mode of a set of data, and identify the range and interquartile range

- ☐ calculate and use the standard deviation of a sample

- ☐ calculate standard error, use it to draw error bars on a graph and interpret whether data points are significantly different

- ☐ choose appropriate statistical tests to use with different data, justify their use, and apply the tests, selecting from:
  - the t-test
  - the chi-squared test
  - Pearson's linear correlation
  - Spearman's rank correlation

- ☐ evaluate data and whether the results are adequate to draw conclusions, give explanations for the results

- ☐ make further predictions and suggestions for modifications to the investigation.

Exam-style questions

1. The growing shoot of a germinating cereal seedling is covered by a sheath called a coleoptile. The coleoptile protects the leaves of the seedling as the shoot emerges through the soil (Figure P2.06).

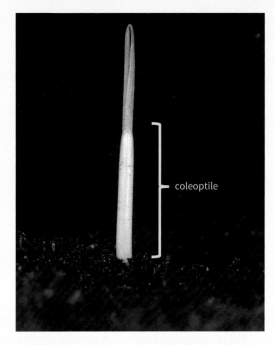

Figure P2.06 The first leaf of an oat seedling breaking through its protective coleoptile.

Auxin is a plant hormone that is known to stimulate the growth of coleoptiles. A student investigated the effect of different concentrations of auxin on the length of pieces of oat coleoptile. He prepared five beakers containing 100 cm³ of auxin solution, each containing different parts per million (ppm) of auxin. Each solution was made up in a 2% solution of sucrose. The student carefully removed coleoptiles from growing oat seedlings. He cut off the last 2.0 mm from the tip of each coleoptile, and then removed a 10.0 mm length and placed it in a dish. He repeated this until he had isolated 120 pieces of coleoptile, all 10.0 mm in length.

The student then placed 20 pieces of coleoptile in each of the beakers of auxin and 20 in another beaker, to act as a control. He covered the beakers and left them in the dark for 48 hours at a constant temperature of 20 °C. He then removed all the pieces of coleoptile and measured them.

a i Identify the independent and dependent variables in this investigation. [2]

   ii State two other variables that were standardised during the investigation. [1]

b Suggest the reason for:

   i removing 2.0 mm from the tip of each coleoptile [1]

   ii including 2% sucrose in the solutions of auxin. [1]

c Describe how, starting with a stock solution of 100 ppm auxin, the student could prepare the other dilutions of auxin solution. [2]

d Apart from the coleoptiles, what would the student have placed in the control beaker? [1]

Figure P2.07 shows the mean length of each group of coleoptiles after 48 hours in the auxin solutions. The error bars on Figure P2.07 are 2 standard error units above and below the mean.

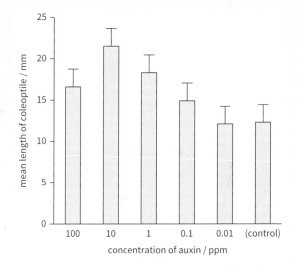

Figure P2.07 Mean lengths of coleoptiles after 48 hours treatment with different concentrations of auxin.

e Using evidence from Figure P2.07 state what these error bars show about the reliability of the data and the significance of differences between the mean values. [3]

f The mean coleoptile length in the 10 ppm solution of auxin is 21.5 mm. Calculate the mean percentage increase in length of these coleoptiles over the 48-hour period. Show your working. [2]

g A *t*-test was carried out to compare the mean lengths of coleoptiles in the 100 ppm auxin solution with those in the control. The difference was statistically significant at $P < 0.05$.

   i State a null hypothesis for the *t*-test. [1]

   ii Explain what is meant by 'statistically significant at $P < 0.05$'. [2]

h The student concluded that 'The results show that a concentration of 10 ppm auxin is most effective in stimulating the growth of coleoptiles in oat seedlings'. Discuss whether this statement is supported by his data. [2]

Total: 18

2 The common periwinkle *Littorina littorea* is a snail that lives on rocks at the seashore (Figure P2.08).

Figure P2.08 Common periwinkle (*Littorina littorea*).

Littorina is able to maintain its position on the rocks by suction between the opening (aperture) in the shell and the rock surface.

A study was carried out to establish whether there was a relationship between the mass of a snail and the force needed to pull it off a rock. Ten periwinkles of different sizes were collected and placed in a glass dish containing seawater. A piece of fine wire was wrapped around each snail, taking care to avoid obstructing the aperture of the shell. A small loop was made in the end of the wire. As soon as a snail emerged from its shell and began to move, the hook of a spring balance was slipped through the loop, and a force applied through the spring balance that was just enough to pull the snail off the surface of the dish. The size of the force was recorded in newtons (N). The wire was removed, the snail gently blotted to remove excess water, and its mass measured using a top-pan balance. The method was repeated with the other snails. A graph of the results is shown in Figure P2.09.

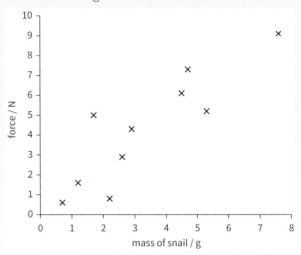

Figure 2.09

Mass of snail / g	5.3	2.6	1.2	2.2	2.9	7.6	4.7	1.7	0.7	4.5
Force / N	5.2	2.9	1.6	0.8	4.3	9.1	7.3	5.0	0.6	6.1

a What does the graph suggest about the relationship between the mass of snails and the force needed to pull them off the surface? [1]

This relationship was tested using Spearman's rank correlation. Table P2.03 shows the data table used to calculate the rank correlation coefficient (r_s).

Mass / g	Force / N	Rank (mass)	Rank (force)	D	D²
5.3	5.2	9	7	2	4
2.6	2.9	5	4	1	1
1.2	1.6	2	3	-1	1
2.2	0.8	4	2	2	4
2.9	4.3	6	5	1	1
7.6	9.1	10	10	0	0
4.7	7.3	8	9	-1	1
1.7	5.0	3	6	-3	9
0.7	0.6	1	1	0	0
4.5	6.1	7	8	-1	1

Table P2.03

The formula for Spearman's rank correlation coefficient is $r_s = 1 - \left(\dfrac{6 \times \sum D^2}{n^3 - n} \right)$.

b From the data in Table P2.03, calculate $\sum D^2$. [1]

c The number of pairs of observations (n) = 10. Calculate the value of r_s. [2]

d State the null hypothesis for the Spearman's rank correlation test when applied to this data. [1]

The table below shows the probabilities of obtaining different values of r_s for 10 pairs of observations, if the null hypothesis is correct:

Probability (P)	0.10 (10%)	0.05 (5%)	0.01 (1%)
Value of r_s	0.564	0.648	0.794

e From the value of r_s calculated in part **c**, what can you conclude about the relationship between the mass of snails and the force needed to pull them off the surface? Explain your answer. [3]

f Suggest three limitations of this study. [3]

Total: 11

Answers to Progress check questions

Unit 1

1.01

1 Nucleus, cytoplasm (also mitochondria, Golgi body if using a high-quality microscope).

2 Cell wall, chloroplasts, large permanent vacuole.

3 Stains are used to see structures more clearly and to colour particular substances, such as starch.

1.02

1 Each eyepiece division is equivalent to 2.5 μm. Therefore three divisions are equivalent to $3 \times 2.5 \, \mu m = 7.5 \, \mu m$.

2 a $7 \, \mu m = 7/1000$ of a mm, or $7 \times 10^{-3} \, mm$.

   b $7 \, \mu m = 7000 \, nm$, or $7 \times 10^{3} \, nm$.

1.03

1 The magnification of a microscope is a measure of how much larger the image is, compared with the size of the object. The resolution is the amount of 'detail' visible. It is the shortest distance between two points that can be distinguished as being separate.

2 a The nucleolus is located inside the nucleus. It synthesises ribosomal RNA and makes ribosomes.

   b Lysosomes are present in the cytoplasm. They contain digestive enzymes that break down unwanted materials and worn-out organelles.

   c Plasmodesmata are pores in plant cell walls. They contain fine strands of cytoplasm linking a plant cell with its neighbouring cells and allowing movement of materials between cells.

3 Ribosome, centriole, chloroplast, nucleus.

1.04

1 Prokaryotic cells are much smaller than eukaryotic cells. Prokaryotic cells lack many of the structures present in eukaryotic cells (e.g. they have no nucleus, no endoplasmic reticulum and no membrane-bound organelles, such as mitochondria and chloroplasts). Prokaryotic cells have smaller ribosomes than eukaryotic cells. The DNA of prokaryotic cells is circular and not associated with protein, unlike DNA in the chromosomes of eukaryotic cells. The cell wall of a prokaryotic cell is made of peptidoglycan, whereas the cell wall of a plant cell is made of cellulose.

2 Viruses are not cells. They have a very simple structure consisting of a protein coat surrounding their DNA or RNA. They can only reproduce parasitically inside a host cell. Therefore they have few features in common with living organisms.

Unit 2

2.01

Phospholipid molecules have a polar 'head' containing phosphate and non-polar hydrocarbon 'tails'. The polar heads are hydrophilic and the hydrocarbon tails are hydrophobic. The hydrophobic tails will associate with each other on the inside of the double layer and the hydrophilic heads will associate with the water on the outside of the membrane.

2.02

Statement	Starch	Cellulose	Triglyceride	Protein
contains the elements carbon, hydrogen and oxygen only	✓	✓	✓	✗
is a polymer of β-glucose	✗	✓	✗	✗
components are joined by ester bonds	✗	✗	✓	✗
contains the elements carbon, hydrogen, oxygen and nitrogen	✗	✗	✗	✓

Unit 3

3.01

1 There are thousands of different enzymes, each catalysing a different reaction. Each enzyme must have a different structure. Proteins are composed

of different combinations of 20 different amino acids, which can produce an almost infinite order of amino acids in the polypeptides and the variety of tertiary structures needed to produce the required specificity of different enzymes.

2   The lock and key hypothesis says that the shape of the active site of the enzyme is exactly complementary to that of the substrate. The induced fit hypothesis says that before the substrate enters, the active site is not a perfect fit for the substrate, but becomes so when an enzyme–substrate complex is formed.

3.02

1   Activation energy is the energy needed to break bonds in the reactants (shown as a 'hump' in a graph of energy changes during the course of a reaction).

2   The products of this reaction are reducing sugars, so you could measure the activity of invertase using the Benedict's test for reducing sugars (this could be done using a colorimeter to measure colour changes).

3.03

1   Heat breaks bonds between the R groups of the polypeptide chains of a protein. This damages the tertiary structure of the protein.

2   At high substrate concentrations, the concentration of the enzyme becomes limiting – at this point the substrate is in excess and the rate of reaction will not increase if more substrate is added.

3.04

1   A competitive inhibitor reduces the affinity of the enzyme for its substrate.

2   K_m is increased.

3   V_{max} is not affected by a competitive inhibitor.

Unit 4

4.01

Shape	Surface area / cm²	Volume / cm³
a cube with sides measuring 3 cm	54	27
a sphere with a radius of 4 cm	201	268

4.02

1   If red blood cells are placed in 1.0% sodium chloride solution, the cells will lose water and shrink. This is because 1.0% sodium chloride solution has a lower water potential that the cell contents (which have a water potential equivalent to 0.9% sodium chloride 'normal saline'). Water therefore moves out of the cells, by osmosis.

2   Red blood cells swell and burst, or lyse, if placed in distilled water. Water enters the cells and they swell slightly, but the membrane is unable to resist much increase in volume. Remember that animal cells, unlike plant cells, do not have a cell wall to resist increases in volume.

Unit 5

5.01

1   A chromosome is a thread-like structure in the nucleus, composed of DNA and protein. Each chromosome is made up of two identical chromatids, with identical copies of the DNA.

2   A centromere is the region along the chromosome where the two chromatids are joined. A telomere is a region of special DNA at the end of a chromatid, which prevents loss of DNA during replication.

5.02

A = interphase. The chromosomes are not visible, just the mass of chromatin in the nucleus, so the cell is not in mitosis.

B = prophase. Chromosomes have condensed and become visible but have not aligned at the equator yet.

C = metaphase. Chromosomes are lined up along the equator of the cell.

D = anaphase. Chromatids have separated (and are therefore chromosomes now) and are being pulled towards the poles of the cell.

E = telophase. Chromosomes have reached the poles and are starting to de-condense to form daughter nuclei.

F = interphase. Two daughter cells have formed, each with its own (smaller) nucleus.

5.03

1 Vegetative propagation is a type of asexual reproduction found in plants. It does not involve the formation of gametes or fertilisation. Part of the parent plant breaks off and forms new individuals.

2 A stem cell is a cell that retains the ability to divide many times by mitosis while remaining undifferentiated, but following this can differentiate into specialised cells.

3 A carcinogen is a factor that can increase the probability of a person developing cancer, such as ionising radiation or certain chemicals.

Unit 6

6.01

1 The monomers in proteins are amino acids and the monomers in polysaccharides are monosaccharides. Amino acids are joined by the formation of peptide bonds. Monosaccharides join by the formation of glycosidic bonds.

2 Statement D is incorrect. Adenosine consists of adenine joined to <u>ribose</u>, not deoxyribose.

6.02

1 Having a genetic code using triplets of four different bases gives 64 different codons, because this is 4 × 4 × 4 = 64 different possibilities. This is more than enough to code for the 20 different amino acids that occur in proteins and to include 'start' and 'stop' codons'. A genetic code based on pairs of bases would give only 16 possibilities.

2

Each sequence of three bases codes for one amino acid. This part of DNA therefore codes for three amino acids.

Unit 7

7.01

1 Transpiration is the loss of water vapour from the leaves. This produces a suction force called transpiration pull, which moves water through the plant from roots to leaves. This movement is the transpiration stream.

2 Plants must carry out photosynthesis. For photosynthesis to take place, the stomata must be open to exchange carbon dioxide and oxygen. If the stomata are open, transpiration will inevitably take place.

3 Water moves from root hair cells across the root and into the xylem down a water potential gradient. The gradient is maintained by osmotic uptake of water at the root hairs and movement of water into the xylem.

7.02

1 Any four adaptations from:

cells arranged end-to-end to form tubes for transport

no end walls, which allows free flow of water

no cytoplasm, which allows free flow of water

lignified walls to withstand negative pressure without collapsing

lignified walls are waterproof

pits to allow lateral movement of water

narrow lumen increases adhesion of water molecules to wall

cellulose lining is hydrophilic.

2 The pathway is via cortex cells and endodermis. The symplast pathway is through the cytoplasm and plasmodesmata, and vacuoles. The apoplast pathway passes along cell walls. The Casparian strip of the endodermis contains suberin, which is impermeable to water. This diverts the water through the symplast pathway.

7.03

1 If the air around the leaves is humid, this reduces the gradient of water potential between the air spaces in the leaf and the outside of the leaf, so the rate of diffusion of water vapour out of the stomata is lowered.

2 The rate at night will be lower than the rate during the day. Stomata close at night when there is no photosynthesis and open during daylight to allow gas exchange for photosynthesis.

3 Any three adaptations from:

curled / rolled leaf

few stomata

stomata in pits

thick waxy cuticle

hairs.

Unit 8

8.01

Blood cell	Essential structural features
red blood cell	• 'biconcave disc' shaped, with no nucleus
neutrophil	• this cell has an irregular, lobed nucleus • the number of lobes varies between 2 and 5 • the cytoplasm contains fine granules
lymphocyte	• has a round nucleus • the nucleus is large in relation to the size of the cell, often surrounded by a thin ring of cytoplasm
monocyte	• relatively large cells with clear cytoplasm • the nucleus is indented or 'horseshoe' shaped

8.02

Description	Type of blood vessel
small vessels (usually about the same diameter as a red blood cell) with a wall consisting of one layer of flattened endothelial cells	capillaries
relatively thick-walled vessels which transport blood away from the heart	arteries
thin-walled vessels, often containing valves, that transport blood back to the heart	veins

8.03

Carbon dioxide is transported in three ways:

- in simple solution, as carbon dioxide dissolved in the plasma

- attached to haemoglobin, in the form of carbaminohaemoglobin

- in the form of hydrogencarbonate (HCO_3^-) ions.

Unit 9

9.01

1 Cartilage is present in the trachea in C-shaped rings. It supports the trachea wall and prevents its collapse during inhalation.

2 Goblet cells secrete mucus, which traps particles of dust and bacteria. The mucus is removed by the action of cilia, preventing these impurities from entering the lungs.

3 The elastic fibres stretch during inhalation, allowing the alveoli to expand. During exhalation they recoil, helping to decrease the volume of the alveoli and push the air out of the lungs.

9.02

1 Nicotine is a colourless, odourless chemical that is the addictive substance present in smoke. Tar is an oily brown substance that contains toxic chemicals, including carcinogens.

2 Nicotine binds to receptors on neurones in the brain and other parts of the nervous system. It stimulates the release of the hormone adrenaline from the adrenal gland. Adrenaline increases the heart rate. Nicotine also causes arterioles in the body to constrict. This causes an increase in the resistance to blood flow. Increased heart rate and increased resistance to blood flow through the arteries results in high blood pressure.

3 Tar contains carcinogens, which can cause mutations to the genes that control cell division, resulting in cancer.

Unit 10

10.01

Infectious disease	Type of causative organism
HIV/AIDS	virus
cholera	bacterium
smallpox	virus
malaria	protoctist
TB	bacterium
measles	virus

10.02

Infectious disease	How the disease is transmitted
HIV/AIDS	contaminated blood, semen or across the placenta
cholera	food and water contaminated with the bacteria
malaria	bite of an infected female *Anopheles* mosquito
TB	inhalation of infected droplets and can also be spread to humans by drinking milk from infected cows
measles	infected droplets via the respiratory system

10.03

Ways of reducing the spread of malaria include:

- use of insecticides to control mosquito populations

- reducing areas of stagnant water needed for reproduction of mosquitoes

- stocking ponds with fish that eat mosquito larvae (a form of biological control)

- use of screening to prevent mosquitoes from entering homes

- use of bed netting, which may be impregnated with an insecticide, to prevent mosquitoes from biting a person while sleeping

- use of insect repellents

- drug treatment of patients with malaria.

10.04

Some of the differences between the structure of a bacterial cell and the structure of a mammalian cell are shown in the table.

Bacterial cell	Mammalian cell
no nucleus present	has a nucleus
small membrane-bound organelles, such as mitochondria and lysosomes	membrane-bound organelles present
has small (70S) ribosomes	has larger (80S) ribosomes
has a cell wall, made of murein (peptidoglycan)	no cell wall
no endoplasmic reticulum	endoplasmic reticulum present

Unit 11

11.01

1 The neutrophil engulfs the bacterium by endocytosis, taking it into a vacuole called a phagosome. Lysosomes fuse with the phagosome, releasing digestive enzymes such as proteases. These break down the bacterium.

2 Antigens are chemical 'markers' on the surface of cells, usually proteins, glycoproteins or polysaccharides. If they are present on a normal cell in a person's body, the person's immune system recognises them as 'self' antigens. If they are on a pathogen such as a bacterium or virus they are recognised as 'non-self'.

11.02

1 T cells are produced in the bone marrow before birth and mature in the thymus gland.

2 The body contains many thousands of different types of B cells. Each has specific receptor sites on its surface, whose shape matches the shape of a particular antigen. When receptors on a B cell bind with an antigen, the B cell is activated and starts to divide rapidly by mitosis to produce a clone of plasma cells. Plasma cells secrete antibodies against the antigen.

3 Memory B cells provide immunity to a disease. They remain in the blood for many years. If the person becomes re-infected by a pathogen, the memory B cells start to divide and produce more antibodies. This secondary immune response is faster, longer lasting and more effective than the first (primary) response, so that the pathogen is killed before it has time to multiply and cause symptoms of the disease.

4 Helper T cells and killer T cells.

11.03

1 Any three reasons

infections by a pathogen such as a bacterium or virus

injured tissues such as a broken bone or burn

inflammatory disorders such as rheumatoid arthritis

leukaemia / cancer of the white blood cells.

2 Active immunity occurs when the body produces its own antibodies in response to exposure to an antigen. Passive immunity is when a person receives antibodies from an outside source, such as by a baby in its mother's milk, or by injection.

3 A person is given a preparation of antigens from a pathogen, either by injection or by mouth. This stimulates the primary immune response and the production of memory cells. The memory cells provide immunity against the pathogen, so that a second exposure should result in the person not developing symptoms of the disease.

4 The protoctist that causes malaria mutates and frequently changes its surface antigens, so that it is difficult to develop a vaccine that will continue to provide protection against the disease.

11.04

1 An antigen is injected into a mouse. The mouse B cells respond by producing antibody-forming plasma cells. Spleen cells are taken from the mouse and fused with cancer cells, forming hybridoma cells. Single hybridoma cells are selected and grown into clones. The clone secreting the required antibody is identified by assaying for its ability to bind with the antigen. Once isolated, the clone divides indefinitely to produce the antibody, which is extracted and purified.

2 The antibody against antigens on the pathogen is 'labelled', so that it shows the presence of the pathogen. This is done in various ways, such as by binding the antibody to a coloured dye, to a fluorescent substance or to a radioactive chemical. Some methods use an enzyme attached to the antibody.

3 If the monoclonal antibody is raised in mice and introduced into humans, it will be recognised as non-self and cause an immune response. The patient develops human anti-mouse antibodies (HAMAs), which destroy the monoclonal antibody.

Unit P1

P1.01

1 The independent variable is the pH value and the dependent variable is the activity of amylase.

2 Control variables are:

temperature

volume of substrate solution

concentration of the substrate

volume of the enzyme solution

concentration of the enzyme.

3 Sample table of results:

pH	Activity of amylase / arbitrary units			
	Reading 1	Reading 2	Reading 3	Mean
6.0	0	0	0	0
6.5	4	2	3	3
7.0	13	12	14	13
7.5	18	20	22	20
8.0	14	16	15	15
8.5	11	10	12	11

P1.02

1 A line graph. The blood glucose concentration is plotted on the *y*-axis and time on the *x*-axis.

2 A line graph, plotting the number of flowers on the *y*-axis and the height on the *x*-axis. This may give a scatter of points. If there is a clear relationship, it is possible to draw a line of best fit through the points.

3 A bar chart is appropriate for these results. You would plot a series of bars, one for each species of tree, where the height of each bar represents the number of species of insects.

4 A histogram, if the data are grouped into categories. The histogram will show the number of leaves in each category (e.g. 1–9 mm, 10–19 mm, 20–29 mm, 30–39 mm and so on).

5 A bar chart, with one bar for each mean value.

6 A line graph, with the rate of transpiration on the *y*-axis and the wind speed on the *x*-axis.

Unit 12

12.01

One molecule of pyruvate contains three carbon atoms and one molecule of glucose contains six carbon atoms. Therefore two molecules of glucose yield <u>four</u> molecules of pyruvate in glycolysis.

12.02

The lactate produced in anaerobic respiration is transported in the blood from muscles to the liver. In liver cells, lactate is converted back to pyruvate and some of this is fully oxidised to form water and carbon dioxide. The remainder of the pyruvate is converted to glycogen.

12.03

Adaptations of rice plants to waterlogged conditions include:

- the presence of aerenchyma – spongy tissue to allow diffusion of oxygen

- leaves with access to oxygen in the atmosphere

- high levels of the enzyme alcohol dehydrogenase

- tissues that are relatively tolerant to ethanol.

Unit 13

13.01

1 The light-dependent stage and the light-independent stage.

2 a On the thylakoids / grana.

  b In the stroma.

13.02

1

$$2H_2O \xrightarrow{\text{light}} O_2 + 4H^+ + 4e^-$$

2 The synthesis of ATP from ADP and inorganic phosphate, using light energy.

3 a ATP and reduced NADP.

  b ATP.

13.03

The enzyme rubisco catalyses the fixation of <u>carbon dioxide</u> by ribulose bisphosphate (RuBP). The resulting 6-carbon compound immediately breaks down into two molecules of <u>glycerate 3-phosphate</u>. This compound is converted into triose phosphate using <u>ATP</u> and <u>reduced NADP</u> produced by the light dependent stage of photosynthesis. Some triose phosphate is used to regenerate ribulose bisphosphate so that the Calvin cycle can continue. The remaining triose phosphate is used to synthesise other compounds, including <u>acetyl coenzyme A</u> which can pass directly into the Krebs cycle.

13.04

1 Chlorophyll *a*.

2 They absorb different wavelengths of light and transfer energy to chlorophyll *a* in the photosystems.

3 An absorption spectrum is a graph showing the wavelengths of light absorbed by different chloroplast pigments. An action spectrum is a graph showing the rate of photosynthesis at different wavelengths.

13.05

1 The concentration of carbon dioxide in the air.

2 Using artificial lighting to increase light intensity.

  Heating to increase the temperature.

  Burning fossil fuels to increase the CO_2 concentration in the air.

3 a DCPIP / dichlorophenolindophenol (or any other suitable redox indicator).

  b DCPIP is blue when oxidised, colourless when reduced.

Unit 14

14.01

Your flow charts could be similar to those shown below.

Responses to an increase in temperature

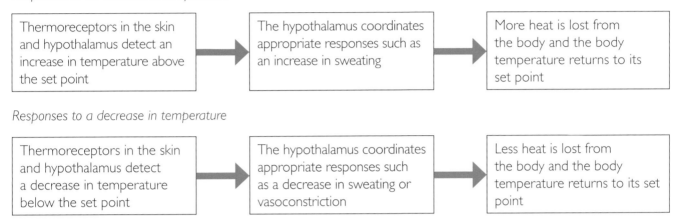

| Thermoreceptors in the skin and hypothalamus detect an increase in temperature above the set point | → | The hypothalamus coordinates appropriate responses such as an increase in sweating | → | More heat is lost from the body and the body temperature returns to its set point |

Responses to a decrease in temperature

| Thermoreceptors in the skin and hypothalamus detect a decrease in temperature below the set point | → | The hypothalamus coordinates appropriate responses such as a decrease in sweating or vasoconstriction | → | Less heat is lost from the body and the body temperature returns to its set point |

Notice that in both cases negative feedback operates to return body temperature to its set point.

14.02

The water will be absorbed into the bloodstream, making the water potential of the blood less negative. This change in water potential is detected by osmoreceptors in the hypothalamus and, as a result, less antidiuretic hormone is secreted. Consequently, less water is reabsorbed in the kidneys and the volume of urine produced will rise. This is an example of negative feedback, compensating for the increase in body water.

14.03

- Glucagon is a hormone involved in the regulation of blood glucose. Glucagon has the effect of increasing the concentration of blood glucose.

- Glycogen is a storage polysaccharide, consisting of many monomers of α-glucose, joined by both 1,4 and 1,6 glycosidic bonds.

- Glycolysis is the first stage in respiration, in which glucose is converted into pyruvate.

14.04

Factors that result in closure of stomata include:

- darkness

- low humidity

- high temperatures

- water stress and high rates of transpiration

- high concentrations of carbon dioxide in the air spaces inside the leaf.

Unit 15

15.01

Your table could include five of the following examples:

Receptor	The form in which energy is received	Resulting sense
hair cells in the cochlea	sound	hearing
stretch receptors in muscles	movement of a limb	position of a limb, muscle stretching
rods or cones in the retina	light	sight
taste buds on the tongue	chemical	taste
olfactory cells in the nose	chemical	smell
Pacinian corpuscles in the skin	pressure	movement and pressure on skin
Meissner's corpuscles in the skin	pressure	movement and pressure on skin

Note that there are other types of receptors, apart from those listed in the table. Find out about baroreceptors, chemoreceptors, thermoreceptors and osmoreceptors.

15.02

Your diagram should show the changes in potential of the neurone membrane, rising from a resting potential of about − 70 mV to a peak of about +40 mV, before returning to the resting potential. The x-axis is a time scale, in milliseconds.

You should note that the depolarisation of the membrane, as the potential rises, is due to the movement of sodium in and the subsequent repolarisation of the membrane is due to the movement of potassium ions out of the axon.

15.03

Your graph should show conduction velocity, measured in metres per second, on the y-axis, plotted against axon diameter measured in μm, on the x-axis. There will be two curves, one for each type of axon with the myelinated axon showing a faster conduction velocity than the non-myelinated axon, for a given axon diameter.

15.04

This is because oestrogen is a steroid hormone and is therefore able to pass through the phospholipid bilayer. Once inside the cytoplasm, oestrogen attaches to a receptor.

15.05

Stimulation of a single hair in the trap is insufficient to cause the trap to close and gaps between the larger hairs around the outside of the trap allow very small insects to escape.

Unit 16

16.01

1 Prophase I.

2 Metaphase I.

3 Anaphase I.

4 Anaphase II.

5 Telophase II.

16.02

1 Diploid.

2 Diploid.

3 Haploid.

4 Haploid.

5 Haploid.

6 Diploid.

16.03

1 The genotype is the genetic make-up of an individual, whereas the phenotype is the appearance of the genotype, or how it is expressed.

2 a ¼, 0.25 or 25%.

  b ½, 0.5 or 50%.

3 a

sperm	eggs	
	R	W
R	RR red	RW roan
R	RR red	RW roan

b

sperm	eggs	
	R	W
R	RR red	RW roan
W	RW roan	WW white

16.04

1 **TtRr** – tall with red fruit

2 **Ttrr** – tall with yellow fruit

3

		male gametes			
		TR	Tr	tR	tr
female gametes	Tr	TTRr tall red fruit	TTrr tall yellow fruit	TtRr tall red fruit	Ttrr tall yellow fruit
	tr	TtRr tall red fruit	Ttrr tall yellow fruit	ttRr short red fruit	ttrr short yellow fruit

50% have red fruit.

16.05

1 a Yes

   b No.

   c No.

   d No.

2 In the Hb^S mutation, a single base substitution to one triplet (CTT) produces CAT, which codes for the amino acid valine instead of glutamic acid in a polypeptide of haemoglobin. This changes the three-dimensional structure of the protein and affects its function. When the haemoglobin is combined with oxygen it retains its normal structure, but when it is deoxygenated it assumes a fibrous structure that is less soluble. The molecules stick together in the red blood cells, distorting them into a sickle shape. The sickle cells are able to carry less oxygen than normal cells, and stick together, blocking blood vessels.

Unit 17

17.01

1 a Discontinuous.

   b Continuous.

   c Continuous.

   d *Within* each category (tall or dwarf) height is a continuous variable. *Between* each category it is discontinuous – plants are either tall or dwarf (under the control of a single gene).

2 Continuous (it is controlled by many genes). Exposure to UV light causes an increase in the amount of melanin (darkening) so it is also affected by the environment.

17.02

1 There is no difference between the mean growth rate in the two groups of mice.

2 $v = (n_1 - 1) + (n_2 - 1)$

   $= (8 - 1) + (9 - 1) = 7 + 8 = 15$ degrees of freedom

3 We can accept the null hypothesis. The difference between the means is not significant, since the probability of getting the t value of 2.05 is greater than 0.05 (or the calculated t value is less than the critical value at $P = 0.05$).

17.03

1 Leaf insects mimic leaves, which protects them from predators. The ancestors of leaf insects would have looked less like leaves but would have shown variation. They produce many offspring but most would not survive. Any with leaf-like features would have been more likely to survive, reproduce and pass on their alleles for these features, while those that were less leaf-like would be more likely to be eaten and not pass on their disadvantageous alleles. Over many generations alleles for a leaf-like appearance accumulated.

2 Stabilising selection.

17.04

1 By definition, members of a species are able to interbreed with each other. Therefore to be different species they must become reproductively isolated (i.e. unable to interbreed).

2 Allopatric speciation results when two populations become geographically separated and experience different selection pressures, so that natural selection leads to the evolution of different characteristics and eventually they form different species. Sympatric speciation occurs when two (or more) species are formed from a single ancestral species, each occupying the same geographical location.

Unit 18

18.01

1 a An ecosystem consists of all the organisms living in a defined area, together with their physical environment.

   b A community consists of all the organisms of different species living in an ecosystem.

   c The genetic diversity of a species is the number of different alleles in its gene pool.

2 $\sum \left(\dfrac{n}{N}\right)^2 = \left(\dfrac{5}{50}\right)^2 + \left(\dfrac{15}{50}\right)^2 + \left(\dfrac{2}{50}\right)^2 + \left(\dfrac{21}{50}\right)^2 + \left(\dfrac{7}{50}\right)^2$

   $= 0.1^2 + 0.3^2 + 0.04^2 + 0.42^2 + 0.14^2$

   $= 0.01 + 0.09 + 0.0016 + 0.1764 + 0.0196$

   $= 0.2976$

   $D = (1 - 0.2976) = 0.7024$ (0.70 to two significant figures)

18.02

1 a   Random sampling using quadrats.

  b   The field is large, so an interrupted belt transect may be most suitable, although any transect could be used.

  c   Mark-release-recapture.

2 If the null hypothesis is correct, the probability of getting this value of r_s is between 5% and 10% (or $P > 0.05$). Therefore we cannot reject the null hypothesis, so there is no significant correlation between height of plants and depth of soil.

18.03

Only the missing information in Table 18.05 is shown

Domain Kingdom	Archaea	Bacteria
cell type		prokaryotic
number of cells	mostly unicellular	
method of feeding		autotrophic and heterotrophic

Eukarya			
Animalia	Plantae	Fungi	Protoctista
			eukaryotic
multicellular			
heterotrophic	autotrophic	heterotrophic	

18.04

1 Any four suitable threats, such as loss of habitats, pollution, overexploitation of resources, climate change, alien species (or named examples, e.g. deforestation, over-fishing).

2 a   Frozen zoos are storage facilities for sperm, eggs, embryos and other living tissues from endangered species.

  b   Seed banks are repositories for seeds of rare species of plants.

  c   Culling means reducing numbers by deliberately killing part of a population.

3 Any suitable alien species and its effects (e.g. water hyacinth – blocks waterways).

Unit 19

19.01

Recombinant DNA is DNA containing a gene from another organism. This is usually produced artificially, using techniques of genetic engineering. Bacterial DNA containing a human gene is an example of recombinant DNA.

19.02

Electrophoresis of haemoglobin from a person with the genotype **Hb^{A}Hb^A** (homozygous for haemoglobin A) will show one band corresponding to haemoglobin A. There will also be only one band from haemoglobin of a person with the genotype **Hb^{S}Hb^S**, but this band of haemoglobin S will be in a different position from the band for haemoglobin A. There will be two bands from the haemoglobin of a person with the genotype **Hb^{A}Hb^S**, corresponding to both haemoglobin A and haemoglobin S.

19.03

Haemophilia is an example of a sex-linked condition. The allele is carried on the X chromosome. The dominant allele **H** results in the production of a blood clotting factor (factor VIII) and the recessive allele **h** results in a lack of this clotting factor.

There is no corresponding locus on the Y chromosome. This means that males who inherit the recessive allele **h** will be affected by haemophilia and have the genotype **X^{h}Y**. A woman who is a carrier for haemophilia has the genotype **X^{H}X^h**.

People who are heterozygous for sickle cell anaemia have the genotype **Hb^{A}Hb^S**. The allele **A** results in the synthesis of normal haemoglobin A and the allele **S** results in the synthesis of haemoglobin S. People with the homozygous genotype **Hb^{S}Hb^S** synthesise haemoglobin S only and will have sickle cell anaemia.

You can read more about the inheritance of these two conditions in Unit 16.

Unit P2

P2.01

1 Independent variable = concentration of nitrate (ions). Dependent variable = number of thalli.

2 Number of plants placed in each beaker, volume of nitrate solution, time plants were in the solutions (any two).

3 Light intensity, temperature.

P2.02

1 Place 85.0 g of sodium nitrate in a 1 dm^3 flask and dissolve it in a volume of distilled water less than 1 dm^3. When it is fully dissolved, add more water to make the volume up to 1 dm^3 and mix thoroughly.

2 A 5% solution is 5 g in 100 cm^3 of solution. Therefore there needs to be 25 g in 500 cm^3 (0.5 dm^3) of solution. Place 25 g of solute in a 0.5 dm^3 flask and dissolve in a volume of distilled water less than 0.5 dm^3. When it is fully dissolved, add more water to make the volume up to 0.5 dm^3 and mix thoroughly.

P2.03

1 a   Qualitative ordinal.

  b   Quantitative.

  c   Qualitative nominal.

2 The standard deviation shows the spread of the values in the sample around the mean. The small size of the standard deviation suggests that the values show a low degree of variation.

3 The standard deviation shows the spread of the values in the sample around the mean. The standard error is a measure of the spread of sample means around the true population mean.

Answers to Exam-style questions

Unit 1

The exam-style questions and sample answers in this title were written by the author and have not been produced by Cambridge International Examinations.

1 a The oblique stroke (/) means that these are alternative answers – the question only requires <u>one</u> correct function per named organelle.

	Name of organelle	Function
A	smooth endoplasmic reticulum	synthesises and transports lipid molecules
B	rough endoplasmic reticulum	transports proteins synthesised on the ribosomes (through membrane-enclosed sacs)
C	Golgi body	chemically modifies proteins / synthesises glycoproteins / packages proteins for export from the cell
D	mitochondrion	produces ATP by aerobic respiration
E	nucleolus	synthesises ribosomal RNA / makes ribosomes
F	cell surface membrane	controls the movement of substances into and out of the cell / allows cells to interact with each other / allows cells to respond to external signals

Table 1.03

[6] – 1 mark per correct row (name and function).

b The electron micrograph shows greater resolution [1].

Resolution is the shortest distance between two points that can be distinguished as being separate [1].

c Cell wall, chloroplasts, large / permanent vacuole [3].

2

Feature	Animal cell	Plant cell	Bacterial cell
cell wall made of cellulose	✗	✓	✗
cell surface membrane	✓	✓	✓
rough endoplasmic reticulum	✓	✓	✗
ribosomes	✓	✓	✓
cytoskeleton	✓	✓	✗
Golgi apparatus	✓	✓	✗
chloroplasts	✗	✓	✗
mitochondria	✓	✓	✗

Table 1.04

[8] – 1 mark per correct row.

3 a A virus particle consists of a protein coat / capsid [1] made of protein molecules called capsomeres [1].

The protein coat surrounds the genetic material / DNA / RNA [1].

Some viruses have an outer membrane / envelope derived from their host cell [1].

[Maximum 3 marks]

b Viruses are not free-living [1].

They can only reproduce inside a host cell [1].

Unit 2

1 a Cellulose is a polysaccharide consisting of many β-glucose molecules, joined by 1,4 glycosidic bonds. The polysaccharide chains are straight and unbranched, forming parallel bundles held together by hydrogen bonds between adjacent –OH groups. [3]

b Cellulose consists of straight chains and 70–80 of these pack together forming microfibrils. Hydrogen bonding holds the chains together and many microfibrils pack together to form cellulose fibres. These are arranged in a criss-cross pattern in plant cell walls, giving the cell wall high tensile strength. [3]

2 a i The term primary structure of a protein refers to the precise order, or sequence, of amino acids in which they are joined together by peptide bonds. **[2]**

ii Secondary structure refers to the formation of either an α-helix, or a β-pleated sheet, by the polypeptide chain. The secondary structure is held in shape by hydrogen bonding (i.e. by weak forces of attraction between –NH– and –C=O groups in the polypeptide chain). **[2]**

b The table shows some of the differences between the structure of haemoglobin and the structure of collagen. Note that the question asks for differences in *structure*, so differences in *function* of these two proteins is not required here.

Haemoglobin	Collagen
a globular protein	a fibrous protein
each haemoglobin molecule consists of four polypeptide sub units, two α chains and two β chains	each molecule of collagen consists of three polypeptide chains forming a triple helix
each haemoglobin molecule has a precise number of amino acids, a total of 574 (141 in each α chain and 146 in each β chain)	collagen molecules have a variable length with repeating sequences of amino acids (often with glycine and proline)
each haemoglobin molecule is associated with four prosthetic haem groups, containing iron	collagen molecules are not associated with haem groups

[Maximum 3 marks]

Unit 3

1 A **[1]**.

2 a Use buffer (solutions) **[1]**.

b Optimum is at pH 5 **[1]**.

Activity increases between pH 1 and pH 5 / up to pH 5 **[1]**.

Activity decreases between pH 5 and pH 9 / above pH 5 **[1]**.

Enzyme is active over a wide range of pH values **[1]**.

[Maximum 2 marks]

c Low pH = high concentration of hydrogen ions / H^+ **[1]**.

Hydrogen ions disrupt / break, ionic bonds / hydrogen bonds **[1]**.

Changes shape of active site / active site no longer complementary to substrate **[1]**.

Fewer enzyme–substrate complexes formed / fewer effective collisions between enzyme and substrate molecules **[1]**.

Some denaturing of enzyme **[1]**.

[Maximum 3 marks]

3 a In uncut tissues the catechol and catechol oxidase are in separate parts of the cell / the catechol is in the vacuole and the catechol oxidase is in the cytoplasm / they are separated by a membrane / they are separated by the tonoplast; OR reverse of these arguments (e.g. cutting mixes enzyme with substrate) **[1]**.

Cutting exposes the cells to oxygen (in the air) **[1]**.

b Use a colorimeter to show the development of the brown colour **[1]**.

c Sketch graph with curve approximating to a straight line at low concentrations of substrate, levelling off at high concentrations **[1]**.

(At low concentrations):

Substrate (concentration) is limiting **[1]**.

Enzyme / active sites are in excess **[1]**.

(So) fewer collisions between enzyme and substrate / active sites **[1]**.

With increased substrate concentration, rate increases as more enzyme–substrate complexes form **[1]**.

(At high concentrations):

Active sites become saturated **[1]**.

(So) rate becomes constant / V_{max} reached **[1]**.

Enzyme (concentration) becomes limiting **[1]**.

[Maximum 6 marks]

d   Curve similar shape to that without inhibitor, but always lower [1].

Curve crosses that with no inhibitor at high concentrations of substrate [1].

Inhibitor is similar shape to substrate [1].

Binds to active site [1].

Prevents substrate entering [1].

Reduces rate of reaction [1].

V_{max} still reached at high substrate concentrations [1].

[Maximum 4 marks]

Unit 4

1 a   The concentrations of both ions is much greater in the vacuole than in fresh water [1].

For potassium ions, the concentration is 760 times higher and for chloride ions, the concentration is 130 times higher in the vacuole than it is in fresh water [1].

b   The ions must be taken up by active transport, because they are accumulated in the vacuole against their concentration gradient [1].

This requires energy [1].

c   A metabolic inhibitor stops the production of ATP [1].

With no ATP available, ion pumps will be unable to maintain the concentration difference [1].

There will be a diffusion gradient and ions will pass out of the cells, into fresh water, down the concentration gradient [1].

2 a   Phospholipids have a polar 'head' and a non-polar 'tail' [1].

The polar head of the molecule is hydrophilic, in other words it will attract water molecules [1].

The tails are hydrophobic and orientate themselves away from water [1].

In water, phospholipids spontaneously form a double layer, with the polar heads on the outside and the non-polar tails on the inside [1].

b   These drugs should be relatively small molecules [1].

They should also be lipid soluble, or non-polar, so that they are able to pass directly through the membrane [1].

Unit 5

1 a   i G_2 phase (of interphase) [1].

ii   S phase (of interphase) [1].

iii   Anaphase (of mitosis) [1].

b   i   20 units [1].

ii   20 units [1].

iii   10 units [1].

2 a   The tip is a meristem / a region where cells are dividing [1].

b   Acetic orcein [1].

c   More cells would be seen in metaphase than in anaphase [1].

d   To hold the chromatids together as they move to the equator [1].

To attach the chromosomes to the spindle fibres [1].

3 a   Telomeres are 'caps' of specialised DNA at the ends of the chromatids [1].

(During DNA replication) the enzyme that copies the DNA cannot continue all the way to the end of the DNA molecule [1].

Each time a cell divides, the end of the chromosome becomes shorter [1].

Without the telomeres, the genes at the end of the coding DNA would be lost [1].

To prevent this happening, part of the telomere is used up instead [1].

(This) allows the cells to divide without losing genes [1].

When the telomeres become too short, genes are activated which prevent the cell dividing any more [1].

[Maximum 4 marks]

b   Mitosis / cell division are under the control of genes [1].

(These) genes may mutate [1].

Cells do not respond to control signals / may divide over and over again [1].

Producing a mass of cells / a tumour [1].

Tumour cells spread around the body / formation of secondary tumours [1].

[Maximum 3 marks]

Unit 6

1 a A gene is a section of a DNA molecule [1] which codes for a particular polypeptide [1].

b Transcription is the process in which part of a DNA molecule unwinds and the two strands separate [1].

One of the strands acts as a template for the synthesis of a complementary strand of RNA, following the rules of complementary base pairing [1].

c Translation is the process in which the genetic code carried by a molecule of mRNA is converted into a sequence of amino acids [1].

This occurs on ribosomes [1].

Molecules of tRNA have complementary anticodons to the codons on mRNA and bring the correct amino acids, as specified by the codons [1].

The amino acids are joined together by the formation of peptide bonds, building up a polypeptide with the correct sequence of amino acids [1].

2 a DNA is a double-stranded molecule, RNA is single-stranded [1].

DNA contains the 5-carbon sugar deoxyribose, RNA contains the 5-carbon sugar ribose [1].

DNA contains the bases adenine (A), thymine (T), guanine (G) and cytosine (C), RNA contains the bases adenine (A), uracil (U), guanine (G) and cytosine (C) [1].

b One example of such a mutation is sickle cell anaemia in which one of the codons in the gene for the β chain of haemoglobin is altered, from CTT to CAT. This mutation results in the substitution of the amino acid valine for glutamic acid in the sixth position in the β chain

of the haemoglobin molecule and the synthesis of haemoglobin S. This small change alters the properties of haemoglobin, making it less soluble and causing red blood cells to form an unusual 'sickle' shape. [5]

Unit 7

1 a Cells / elements arranged one on top of each other [1].

Cell walls contain / lined with cellulose [1].

Lignified / wall contains lignin [1].

No end walls / continuous tubes [1].

Hollow / empty / no cytoplasm [1].

Pits / pitted walls [1].

[Maximum 4 marks]

b Movement of water out of xylem creates tension [1].

Pulls up column of water / transpiration pull [1].

Cohesion of water molecules / explanation in terms of hydrogen bonding [1].

Adhesion of water molecules to (cellulose) lining of vessels [1].

Water potential gradient from root to leaf [1].

Passive / does not require energy [1].

[Maximum 3 marks]

c Water moves down a water potential gradient [1].

Water leaves ends of xylem vessels through pits [1].

Symplast pathway described (through cytoplasm or vacuoles and plasmodesmata) [1].

Apoplast pathway described (along cell walls) [1].

Evaporation from walls of mesophyll cells [1].

Into air spaces [1].

Water vapour diffuses out [1].

Through stomata [1].

[Maximum 5 marks]

2 a Potometer [1].

b Attach rubber tubing / cut shoot / assemble potometer, under water [1].

To remove air / prevent entry of air [1].

Cut shoot at angle [1].

To prevent entry of air / make it easier to insert shoot into rubber tube [1].

Seal joints with grease / petroleum jelly [1].

Dry (before taking measurements) [1].

Allow plant to equilibrate to conditions (before taking measurements) [1].

[Maximum 4 marks]

c Transpiration is water loss from leaves [1].

Not all water taken up is lost in transpiration [1].

(Some) water is used for photosynthesis / maintaining turgidity [1].

[Maximum 2 marks]

d

Factor	Increase or decrease in rate	Explanation
high temperature	increase [1]	
high humidity	decrease [1]	reduces the water potential gradient between the air spaces in the leaf and the outside of the leaf, so the rate of diffusion of water vapour out of the stomata is lower [1]
high light intensity		stomata open in the light to allow gas exchange for photosynthesis, so more water vapour is lost [1]
high wind speed	increase [1]	removes any water vapour from around the surface of the leaves, maintains the water potential gradient between the air spaces in the leaf and the outside of the leaf. [1]

Table 7.02

[Maximum 6 marks]

3 a Amino acids [1].

b Occurs against a concentration gradient [1].

Proton pumps in surface membrane of companion cells [1].

Transport protons / hydrogen ions / H^+ out of cell [1].

Generates a proton gradient / high [H^+] outside cell [1].

(Gradient) drives sucrose uptake [1].

Cotransport [1].

Sucrose diffuses (from companion cell) into sieve tube element (down concentration gradient) [1].

[Maximum 3 marks]

c Assimilates / sucrose (entering sieve tubes) lowers water potential [1].

Water enters by osmosis [1].

Increases hydrostatic pressure [1].

Assimilates / sucrose leave at a sink / named sink [1].

Lowers hydrostatic pressure at sink [1].

(Produces) hydrostatic pressure gradient [1].

Mass flow [1].

[Maximum 4 marks]

Unit 8

1 a Carbonic anhydrase is an enzyme that catalyses the reaction between water and carbon dioxide. In actively respiring tissues, where the partial pressure of carbon dioxide is high, carbonic anhydrase combines carbon dioxide with water, forming carbonic acid. Carbonic acid dissociates, forming hydrogencarbonate ions and protons. In the lungs, where the partial pressure of carbon dioxide is lower, carbonic anhydrase catalyses the reverse reaction, releasing carbon dioxide. [3]

b The Bohr effect refers to the movement of the oxygen dissociation curve to the right, in response to an increase in the partial pressure of carbon dioxide. The importance of this is that for a given partial pressure of oxygen, the affinity of haemoglobin for oxygen is reduced, meaning that oxygen will be readily released. **[3]**

c   In the alveolar capillaries, carbon dioxide diffuses from the blood into the alveoli. This is because the partial pressure of carbon dioxide in the alveolar capillaries is higher than it is in the alveoli, so carbon dioxide moves down the diffusion gradient. Most of the carbon dioxide transported in the blood is in the form of hydrogencarbonate ions. These diffuse into red blood cells and combine with protons, released from haemoglobinic acid, forming carbonic acid. This is rapidly converted back into water and carbon dioxide by the enzyme carbonic anhydrase. Carbon dioxide then diffuses out of the capillaries and into the alveoli. **[4]**

2   a   The percentage change in the number of red blood cells is calculated by working out the difference in numbers, dividing this by the original number and multiplying by 100. The percentage change is, therefore:

$6.0 - 5.1 = 0.9$

$0.9 \div 5.1 = 0.176$

$0.176 \times 100 = 17.6\%$ **[2]**

b   At high altitudes, the partial pressure of oxygen in air is relatively low. The percentage increase in the numbers of red blood cells is a response to the decrease in the partial pressure of oxygen and increases the carrying capacity of blood for oxygen. The helps to overcome the breathlessness often experienced at high altitudes. By ascending the mountain slowly, it gives time for the mountaineers to acclimatise to the conditions. **[3]**

3   a   Myogenic means that heart muscle contacts and relaxes on its own, without the need for nervous stimulation. **[2]**

b   The sinoatrial node acts as a natural pacemaker. The sinoatrial node sends out a wave of electrical excitation across the atria, causing them to contract. The electrical excitation is picked up by the atrioventricular node and, after a brief delay, the excitation is carried by the bundle of His, through the septum between the left and right ventricles. The excitation then spreads through the walls of both ventricles, via Purkyne tissue, causing the ventricles to contact from the apex upwards. **[6]**

Unit 9

1   a   Goblet cells and ciliated (epithelial) cells **[2]**.

b   Goblet cells produce mucus **[1]**.

Mucus traps bacteria / pathogens **[1]**.

Mucus traps dust **[1]**.

Cilia waft / move mucus away from lungs / towards mouth / to be swallowed **[1]**.

Prevents dust / bacteria entering lungs **[1]**.

Bacteria (that are swallowed) destroyed by acid in the stomach **[1]**.

[Maximum 3 marks]

c   Cartilage **[1]**.

d   Supports the (wall of the) trachea **[1]**.

Prevents collapse during inhalation **[1]**.

2   a   Many alveoli **[1]**.

Large surface area **[1]**.

Many capillaries / network of capillaries **[1]**.

(Blood flow through capillaries) maintains diffusion gradients **[1]**.

Thin epithelium / squamous epithelium / thin alveolus wall / wall one cell thick **[1]**.

(So) short distance for diffusion **[1]**.

Elastic fibres (in alveolus wall) **[1]**.

(Elastic fibres) allow alveoli to expand / recoil **[1]**.

[Maximum 4 marks]

b   (Smoke) destroys cilia **[1]**.

Causes cilia to beat less strongly **[1]**.

Causes over-production of mucus **[1]**.

(Mucus and) bacteria enter lungs / not prevented from entering lungs **[1]**.

[Maximum 3 marks]

c   Breakdown of elastic tissue (in wall of alveoli) **[1]**.

Alveoli burst / damaged (by coughing) **[1]**.

Decreased surface area (for gas exchange) **[1]**.

[Maximum 2 marks]

3

	Trachea	Bronchus	Bronchiole	Alveoli
ciliated epithelium	✓	✓	✓	✗
squamous epithelium	✗	✗	✗	✓
cartilage	✓	✓	✓ (larger bronchioles)	✗
elastic fibres	✓	✓	✓	✓
smooth muscle	✓	✓	✓	✗

Table 9.01

[5] – I mark per correct row.

Unit 10

1 a i A pathogen is an organism that can cause disease; pathogens include bacteria and viruses [1].

ii An antibiotic is a substance that kills or inhibits the growth of bacteria, without harming the cells of the host organism [2].

b Penicillin is an antibiotic that inhibits cell wall synthesis in bacteria. The cell walls become weaker and the cells eventually lyse, resulting in death of the bacteria. Viruses do not have cell walls and are therefore unaffected by penicillin. [3]

c Steps that can be taken to reduce the impact of antibiotic resistance include:

Hand-washing and avoiding contact with infected people [1].

Using antibiotics only when properly prescribed by health-care professionals [1].

Completing the full course of antibiotic treatment [1].

Never sharing antibiotics with other people [1].

Avoiding the use of broad-spectrum antibiotics [1].

Prescribing antibiotics only when they are needed and not for viral infections [1].

[Maximum 3 marks]

2 a i *Vibrio cholerae* (a bacterium) [1].

ii *Plasmodium* sp. (a protoctist) [1].

iii *Mycobacterium tuberculosis* (a bacterium) [1].

b Malaria is spread by the bite of an infected female mosquito, genus *Anopheles*. This injects the infectious form of *Plasmodium* into a person's bloodstream. In very rare cases, malaria may be spread by unscreened blood transfusion. [2]

c This may be due to public health measures, including the use of insecticides to control mosquito populations. Diagnosis and treatment are also important, but require the presence of health-care professionals, who are able to give quick and effective treatment. [3]

Unit 11

1 Macrophages recognise non-self / foreign antigens on the bacterium [1].

Receptors on macrophages bind to antigens on the bacterium [1].

Phagocytosis / engulfing of bacterium [1].

Phagosome / vacuole / vesicle forms [1].

Bacterium broken down by digestive enzymes / hydrolytic enzymes / named enzyme (e.g. protease) [1].

Bacterium destroyed / killed [1].

[Maximum 4 marks]

2 a Quaternary [1].

Molecule contains more than one polypeptide chain / four polypeptide chains [1].

b (Answer should include name and function, although for P the function is clear from the name.)

P = antigen binding site / variable region to bind with antigen [1].

Q = disulfide bonds. Hold polypeptide chains together / maintain tertiary structure / maintain quaternary structure [1].

R = heavy chain / heavy polypeptide / constant region. Binds to receptor / phagocyte / macrophage [1].

c Antibodies secreted by plasma cells must be soluble in water / plasma (hence hydrophilic) [1].

Region R is anchored in plasma membrane / phospholipid bilayer (of B-lymphocytes) [1].

Reference to hydrophobic core (of membrane) / fatty acid tails of phospholipids hydrophobic [1].

Interaction between region R and hydrophobic core allows anchorage [1].

[Maximum 2 marks]

d   Hybridoma (cell) [1].

3 a   Foreign [1].

Protein / glycoprotein / polysaccharide [1].

Stimulates immune response / production of antibodies [1].

[Maximum 2 marks]

b   (B-lymphocytes have) antibodies on cell surface / cell surface membrane [1].

(Which act as) receptors [1].

Bind to antigens [1].

Shape specific to antigens / complementary to antigens [1].

[Maximum 2 marks]

c   Remain in the blood [1].

Give fast(er) response when exposed again to the same pathogen / same antigen [1].

Longer lasting response [1].

Faster cell division / faster formation of clone [1].

To form plasma cells (and more memory cells) [1].

More antibodies produced / higher concentration of antibodies [1].

Prevents person developing symptoms / becoming ill [1].

[Maximum 3 marks]

4 a

Source of antigen	Type of immunity
non-self antigen is present on a pathogen that invades the body	natural, active [1]
non-self antigen is given by vaccination	artificial, active [1]
antibody enters the body of a baby in breast milk	natural, passive [1]
antibody enters the body by injection	artificial, passive [1]

Table 11.03

b   Smallpox virus was genetically stable / did not mutate / did not change its surface antigens [1].

(So) same vaccine could be used throughout the programme / vaccine did not need to be changed [1].

Vaccine was live so gave a strong immune response [1].

One dose gave immunity for life / no boosters needed [1].

Simple to administer using steel / bifurcated / reusable needle [1].

No intermediate host [1].

No animal reservoir / only found in humans [1].

No symptomless carriers [1].

Infected people easy to identify [1].

(So) infected people can be isolated to prevent spread [1].

[Maximum 4 marks]

c   Existing lymphocytes / B cells / T cells no longer recognise the antigen / no longer activated [1].

Reference to specificity (of lymphocytes) [1].

Existing plasma cells do not produce suitable antibody [1].

Existing memory cells no longer activated [1].

New immune response needed [1].

[Maximum 2 marks]

Unit P1

1 a   Independent variable – wind speed [1].

Dependent variable – rate of transpiration [1].

b   Variables other than wind speed that affect the rate of transpiration include:

Temperature [1].

Humidity [1].

Light intensity [1].

Leaf surface area [1].

Stomatal aperture (degree of opening of stomata) [1].

[Maximum 2 marks]

c First, calculate the volume of the cylinder. Remember that 2.5 cm = 25 mm. The diameter of the capillary tube is 0.5 mm, so the radius is 0.25 mm.

$V = \pi r^2 \times d$

$= \pi (0.25)^2 \times 25$

$= 3.14 \times 0.0625 \times 25$

$= 4.9 \, \text{mm}^3$

This is the total volume of water taken up in 20 minutes, so the mean rate of uptake per minute will be 4.9 ÷ 20 = 0.25 mm^3 min^{-1} [3].

2 a Independent variable – temperature [1].

Dependent variable – activity of dehydrogenases [1].

b Your answer should contain references to the following:

Place a measured volume (e.g. 10 cm^3) of yeast suspension in a test-tube and stand this in a water bath at a suitable temperature (e.g. 20 °C).

Place a measured volume (e.g. 1 cm^3) of methylene blue solution in another test-tube and stand this in the same water bath as the yeast suspension.

Leave both tubes to reach the same temperature before mixing.

As soon as the yeast suspension and the methylene blue solution are mixed, start a stop clock and record the time taken for the blue colour to disappear (the end-point of the reaction).

Repeat this process at a range of temperatures (a minimum of five different temperatures in total) e.g. 10 °C, 20 °C, 30 °C, 40 °C and 50 °C. It would not be sensible to use temperatures that are very close together, such as 20 °C,

21 °C, 22 °C and so on. It is essential to use the same volumes of yeast suspension and methylene blue each time.

The experiment should also be repeated at each temperature to obtain a minimum of three sets of results at each temperature.

[6]

c The results of this experiment should be tabulated neatly, as shown in the table:

Temperature /°C	Time taken to reach the end-point / s			
	Result 1	Result 2	Result 3	Mean
10				
20				
30				
40				
50				

Notice how the results are presented in this table, with the independent variable in the first column, followed by the experimental results (the dependent variable) in the other columns. The units are given in the column headings and are not repeated in each column.

The table includes the replicate results and the mean values are included.

You could convert the time taken to reach the end-point to a relative *rate* of reaction at each temperature, by calculating the reciprocal of each time (i.e. 1 ÷ time).

The results could then be presented as a line graph, with the temperature (independent variable) on the *x*-axis and the relative rate of reaction (dependent variable) on the *y*-axis. Remember that if you sketch a graph to show how the results are to be presented, to label both axes fully, including the units.

[6]

3 a Your graph should look like the following example:

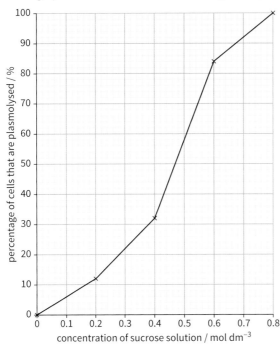

x-axis: concentration of sucrose solution / mol dm⁻³
y-axis: percentage of cells that are plasmolysed / %

Marks are awarded for:
having the axes the right way round with a
suitable linear scale **[1]**
labelling the axes fully **[1]**
plotting the points accurately **[1]**
joining the points as instructed with ruled lines **[1]**.

b To read this value from the graph, draw lines as
shown:

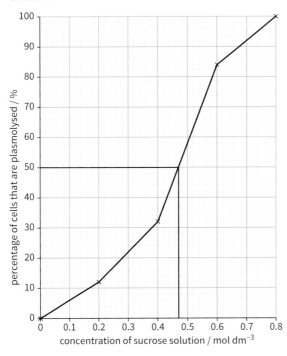

x-axis: concentration of sucrose solution / mol dm⁻³
y-axis: percentage of cells that are plasmolysed / %

This gives a value for the sucrose concentration
between 0.46 and 0.48 mol dm⁻³ **[1]**

c To improve the reliability of this investigation,
the student should repeat the counts at each
concentration of sucrose (e.g. by examining
at least three separate fields of view with
the microscope) or using different pieces of
epidermis at each concentration of sucrose
solution **[1]**.

The replicate counts can then be used to
calculate a mean value for each sucrose
concentration **[1]**.

4 a A: upper (adaxial) epidermis **[1]**.

B: palisade mesophyll **[1]**.

C: spongy mesophyll **[1]**.

b **i** Thickness = 19 mm **[1]**.

ii Magnification = 19 ÷ 0.95 = ×20 **[2]**.

c Marks are awarded for:

drawing a suitable size and with no shading **[1]**

no cells shown **[1]**

proportions correct **[1]**

four tissue layers shown in the lamina **[1]**

details of midrib (collenchyma, vascular bundle
and parenchyma) **[1]**.

Example low power plan:

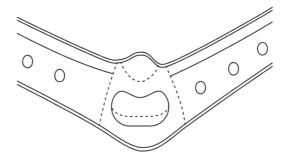

Unit 12

1 To make a valid comparison between the respiration
rates of these two, it is essential that the experiment
is carried out at the same temperature, because
temperature affects the rate of respiration.

- Set up a respirometer, containing a carbon dioxide
absorber such as potassium hydroxide, with a
known mass of germinating barley grains and leave
the respirometer in a water bath at a constant
temperature of 25 °C (for example).

- Leave the taps on the respirometer open and allow the apparatus to equilibrate.

- Close the taps and record the movement of the coloured liquid in the capillary tube for a given time.

- If the capillary tube is calibrated, the volume of oxygen used can be calculated.

- Several readings should be taken to calculate a mean rate of respiration (volume of oxygen used per minute).

- Repeat the experiment, at the same temperature, using a known mass of germinating peas.

- The respiration rates should be expressed as the volume of oxygen used per unit time per unit mass of material (at a given temperature).

[10 marks]

2 a   Decarboxylation means the removal of carbon dioxide from a substrate. In the link reaction, this occurs when pyruvate, a three-carbon compound, is converted to acetate, which contains two carbon atoms. **[3]**

b   Dehydrogenation means the removal of hydrogen from a substrate. In the link reaction, two atoms of hydrogen are removed from pyruvate and these are transferred to NAD, forming reduced NAD. **[3]**

3 a   The respiratory quotient (RQ) is the volume of carbon dioxide produced in respiration divided by the volume of oxygen **[1]**.

b   i   Cytoplasm **[1]**.

ii   Matrix of mitochondrion **[1]**.

iii   Matrix of mitochondrion **[1]**.

iv   Inner membrane (cristae) of mitochondrion **[1]**.

v   Cytoplasm **[1]**.

Unit 13

1 a   A = starch grain, B = stroma, C = envelope, D = granum **[4]**.

b   i   D **[1]**.

ii   B **[1]**.

c

Factor	Stage	✓ or ✗
light intensity	photolysis	✓
	Calvin cycle	✗
carbon dioxide concentration	photolysis	✗
	Calvin cycle	✓
temperature	photolysis	✗
	Calvin cycle	✓

Table 13.02

[3]

2 a $2H_2O \rightarrow O_2 + 4H^+ + 4e^-$

or

$H_2O \rightarrow \frac{1}{2}O_2 + 2H^+ + 2e^-$ **[1]**

b   The synthesis of ATP from ADP and inorganic phosphate **[1]** using light energy **[1]**.

c   They absorb different wavelengths of light **[1]** and transfer energy to chlorophyll *a* **[1]**.

d   i   Fixation of carbon dioxide **[1]**.

   Production of glycerate 3-phosphate **[1]**.

ii   Reduction of glycerate 3-phosphate / donates H to glycerate 3-phosphate **[1]**.

   Converts glycerate 3-phosphate to triose phosphate **[1]**.

iii   Supplies energy **[1]**.

   To convert glycerate 3-phosphate to triose phosphate **[1]**.

   To regenerate RuBP **[1]**.

[Maximum 2 marks]

3 a   Rate of photosynthesis on *y*-axis and light intensity on *x*-axis **[1]**.

All points plotted accurately **[1]**.

Line of best fit drawn **[1]**.

b   At low light intensity light is the limiting factor so rate increases (with increased light intensity) **[1]**.

At high light intensity other factor becomes limiting so rate levels off **[1]**.

Such as temperature (allow carbon dioxide) **[1]**.

c   To provide CO_2 / so that CO_2 is not a limiting factor **[1]**.

4 a Graph showing the wavelengths of light absorbed by different chloroplast pigments / diagram of absorption spectrum [1].

Chlorophyll absorbs light in the red and blue / violet part of the spectrum [1].

Carotenoids absorb light in the blue / violet part of the spectrum [1].

Reference to absorption spectrum peaks [1].

[Maximum 3 marks]

b Action spectrum shows the rate of photosynthesis (at different wavelengths) [1].

Unit 14

1 a

Component	Plasma	Glomerular filtrate
water	present	present
proteins	present	almost none
glucose	present	present
urea and creatinine	present	present
inorganic ions such as sodium and chloride	present	present
amino acids	present	present

[6]

b i Ultrafiltration is the process by which water and many solutes, including glucose and inorganic ions, are forced out of the glomerular capillaries, in Bowman's capsule, by blood pressure. This process forms the initial filtrate, which then passes through the rest of the nephron. [3]

ii Selective reabsorption takes place in the proximal convoluted tubule, loop of Henle, distal convoluted tubule and collecting duct. Normally, all of the glucose, some ions, amino acids, some urea and much of the water in the filtrate are reabsorbed back into the capillaries surrounding the nephron. This changes the composition of the urine that is formed and reduces the volume of water lost. [4]

2 Abscisic acid (ABA) is secreted in conditions of water stress. ABA attaches to receptors on plant cell membranes, causing inhibition of proton pumps and stimulating the movement of calcium ions into the cell cytoplasm. This in turn alters the permeability of the guard cell membrane to certain ions, which leave the cells, followed by movement of water, by osmosis, down the water potential gradient. The consequent decrease in turgor of the guard cells results in closure of the stomatal pores and a reduction in transpiration. [8]

Unit 15

1 a When it is not transmitting an impulse, the axon has a resting potential of about $-70\,mV$. During the conduction of an impulse, this potential is briefly reversed, rising to an action potential of about $+40\,mV$.

This is due to a sequence of changes in the permeability of the axon membrane to sodium ions and potassium ions. When stimulated, the axon briefly becomes permeable to sodium ions, due to the opening of voltage-gated sodium channels in the axon membrane. Sodium ions enter the axon, moving down their diffusion gradient and changing the internal potential of the axon from negative to positive.

This is followed by an increase in permeability of the membrane to potassium ions, as voltage-gated potassium channels open, allowing potassium ions to leave and return the membrane potential to its resting value.

This sequence of changes occurs along the axon membrane, generating a propagated action potential, or nerve impulse. Following the action potential, there is a brief refractory period, during which the axon does not respond to further stimuli. [10]

b When the action potential arrives at the membrane of the presynaptic neurone, the membrane becomes more permeable to calcium ions, which enter the neurone. This causes vesicles, containing a transmitter substance, to move towards the presynaptic membrane. Some of these vesicles fuse with the membrane and release their transmitter substance, by exocytosis, into the synaptic cleft.

The transmitter substance diffuses across the cleft and attaches to receptors on the postsynaptic membrane. This results in a change in permeability of the postsynaptic membrane and the generation of a postsynaptic potential. [5]

2 The menstrual cycle is controlled and coordinated by hormones released by the anterior pituitary gland (follicle stimulating hormone (FSH) and luteinising hormone (LH)) and by hormones secreted by the ovaries (oestrogen and progesterone).

At the start of the cycle, the anterior pituitary secretes FSH and LH, which start the development of follicles in the ovary and stimulate the secretion of oestrogen from the ovary. Oestrogen exerts negative feedback on the secretion of FSH and LH. Oestrogen stimulates the repair and thickening of the endometrium (lining of the uterus) which becomes more vascular due to the development of many blood capillaries.

When oestrogen reaches a high level, it stimulates secretion of FSH and LH, which trigger ovulation and the development of a corpus luteum from the remains of the follicle. The corpus luteum secretes oestrogen and progesterone during the second half of the cycle. These hormones maintain the endometrium so that it is ready for implantation of a blastocyst (early embryo), should fertilisation occur.

If fertilisation does not occur, the corpus luteum degenerates towards the end of the cycle and the levels of oestrogen and progesterone drop. This removes the inhibition of the anterior pituitary, FSH and LH are secreted again and the cycle repeats. **[10]**

Unit 16

1 a A = metaphase I, B = metaphase II **[2]**.

b Each pair of homologous chromosomes **[1]** lines up independently of the other pairs **[1]** on the (spindle) equator **[1]**. This results in gametes that are genetically different / unique **[1]**.

[Maximum 3 marks]

2 a Spermatogonia = diploid
primary spermatocytes = diploid
secondary spermatocytes = haploid
spermatids = haploid
spermatozoa = haploid

[All correct = 2, three or four correct = 1].

b i Mitosis **[1]**.

ii Mitosis **[1]**.

iii Meiosis **[1]**.

c Spermatogenesis begins at puberty; oogenesis begins in the ovary of the fetus **[1]**.

Spermatogenesis forms four functional gametes / spermatids / spermatozoa; oogenesis forms one functional gamete / secondary oocyte / forms polar bodies **[1]**.

In oogenesis, the functional gamete / ovum is only formed after the secondary oocyte has been fertilised (gamete formed before fertilisation in spermatogenesis) **[1]**.

[Maximum 2 marks]

3 a Codominance is when both alleles of a gene are expressed in the phenotype of the heterozygote. **[1]**.

b Male cats only have one X chromosome **[1]** so only have one allele for this gene / only have X^o or X^b **[1]**.

c Genotypes of parents: X^bY × X^bX^o

black male tortoiseshell female

Genotypes and phenotypes of offspring:

	eggs	
	X^b	X^o
sperm X^b	X^bX^b black. female	X^bX^o tortoiseshell female
Y	X^bY black male	X^oY ginger male

[1 for four correct genotypes, 1 for four correct phenotypes]

4 a GgNn **[1]**.

b Gn, gn **[1]**.

c There are 3 degrees of freedom **[1]**.

Probability of getting a χ^2 value of 3.31 is greater than 0.10 / greater than 10% **[1]**.

χ^2 value is greater than the critical value at $P = 0.05$ / 5% **[1]**.

Difference between expected and observed numbers is not significant / is due to chance / null hypothesis can be accepted / null hypothesis cannot be rejected **[1]**.

Numbers do fit a 1 : 1 : 1 : 1 ratio **[1]**.

[Maximum 4 marks]

5 Regulatory gene codes for a repressor protein [1].

   (With no lactose)

   Repressor protein binds to the operator [1].

   Repressor protein blocks promoter [1].

   (With lactose present)

   Lactose binds to repressor protein, which changes shape [1].

   Repressor protein stops binding to the operator [1].

   Promoter becomes unblocked [1].

   RNA polymerase binds to promoter [1].

   Structural genes transcribed [1].

   Structural genes translated into proteins [1].

   Enzymes formed [1].

   Reference to lactose permease / one enzyme allows uptake of lactose [1].

   β-galactosidase breaks down / hydrolyses lactose [1].

   Into glucose and galactose [1].

   [Maximum 9 marks]

Unit 17

1 a The two races of fly are identical in appearance [1] and can reproduce to form fertile offspring [1]. To be different species they must be reproductively isolated [1].

   b Sympatric speciation means two species are formed [1] in the same geographical location [1]. The two races of flies are genetically different [1] but they are not yet reproductively isolated [1].

      [Maximum 3 marks]

   c Continuous variation [1].

   d Stabilising selection [1].

   e Disruptive selection [1].

   f (Disruptive) selection happens when there is more than one type of habitat in an area [1].

      (Disruptive) selection acts against intermediate varieties / in favour of extremes [1].

The two habitats are hawthorn fruits and apples [1].

Mates selected by preference for hawthorn fruits or apples [1].

(And) by different times of mating [1].

(An Example of) ecological isolating mechanism / behavioural isolating mechanism [1].

No / reduced gene flow between the two fly populations [1].

Few intermediates mate [1].

Alleles for extreme phenotypes (more likely to be) passed on [1].

Different selection pressures in the two populations [1].

Example of selection pressure – parasitic wasps / size of food supply [1].

Eventually reproductive isolation / no longer interbreed [1].

[Maximum 6 marks]

2 a Change in the characteristics / proportion of alleles in a population [1].

      Due to random events / as a result of chance [1].

      Most likely to happen in small (isolated) populations [1].

      Reference to founder effect [1].

      [Maximum 3 marks]

   b When humans choose / select animals or plants [1].

      To breed from [1].

      Over several generations [1].

      In order to improve their characteristics [1].

      [Maximum 3 marks]

   c Do not breed from animals with undesirable characteristics [1].

      Only use animals for breeding if they show good characteristics [1].

      Do not allow matings between closely related animals [1].

      [Maximum 2 marks]

3 a **[3]** – 1 mark per correct row.

Stage	Horse	Donkey
at the end of mitosis	64	62
at the end of meiosis I	32	31
at the end of meiosis II	32	31

b 63 **[1]**.

32 chromosomes from the horse and 31 from the donkey **[1]**.

c The odd number of chromosomes will prevent homologous pairing **[1]**.

In prophase I of meiosis **[1]**.

d A species consists of organisms that can breed to produce fertile offspring **[1]**.

(Horses and donkeys can breed but) the offspring / mule is infertile **[1]**.

[Maximum 1 mark]

4 a The proportion of the population with the genotype **Hb^{S}Hb^S** = q^2 = 9% or 0.09 **[1]**.

Therefore $q = \sqrt{0.09} = 0.3$ **[1]**.

(First method)

Using the Hardy–Weinberg equation $p + q = 1$:

$p = (1 - 0.3) = 0.7$ **[1]**

The proportion of the population with the genotype **Hb^{A}Hb^S** = $2pq$ **[1]**.

$2pq = (2 \times 0.7 \times 0.3) = 0.42$, or 42% **[1]**.

(Alternative method)

Using the Hardy–Weinberg equation $p^2 + 2pq + q^2 = 1$:

$p = (1 - 0.3) = 0.7$ **[1]**.

$p^2 = 0.7^2 = 0.49$ **[1]**.

$2pq = 1 - (0.49 + 0.09) = 0.42$, or 42% **[1]**.

[Marks awarded for either method]

b The parasite that causes malaria spends part of its life cycle inside red blood cells **[1]**.

These red blood cells contain abnormal / **Hb^S** haemoglobin **[1]**.

When the malaria parasite enters these cells they burst **[1]**.

The parasite is killed / the life cycle of the parasite is interrupted **[1]**.

The person is less likely to develop (signs and symptoms of) malaria **[1]**.

[Maximum 3 marks]

Unit 18

1 a Use coordinates **[1]**.

In marked out area / grid **[1]**.

Reference to random number generator / tables **[1]**.

[Maximum 2 marks]

b 4 **[1]**.

c Total numbers of species C in 8 quadrats = 134 **[1]**.

(Total area of quadrats = 8 m^2)

Species density $= \dfrac{134}{8} = 16.75$ m^{-2} **[1]**.

d

Species	Number of individuals of each species (n)	$\dfrac{n}{N}$	$\left(\dfrac{n}{N}\right)^2$
A	54	0.117	0.0137
B	16	0.035	0.0012
C	134	0.291	0.0847
D	178	0.387	0.1498
E	78	0.170	0.0289
Total (N) =	460		

Table 18.07

i See Table 18.07 – mark for correct values in second column of Table 18.07 **[1]**.

ii See Table 18.07 – mark for correct value of N **[1]**.

iii Correct values in last two columns of Table 18.07 **[2]**.

$D = 1 - 0.2783 = 0.7217$ (or 0.722 to 3 significant figures) **[1]**.

iv Lower **[1]**.

2 a Answers in bold [2] – all five correct – 2 marks, three or four correct – 1 mark].

Group (taxon)	
Domain	Eukarya
Kingdom	**Animalia**
Phylum	Chordata
Class	Mammalia
Order	Primates
Family	Cercopithedae
Genus	**Colobus**
Species	*Colobus polykomos*

Table 18.08

b Different levels of classification / large groups divided into smaller groups (or words to that effect) [1].

c i Plantae, Fungi and Protoctista [1].

ii Fungi [1].

iii Plantae and Protoctista [1].

3 a Maintain biodiversity / genetic diversity / maintain gene pool [1].

Maintain stability in ecosystems / prevent damage to food chains [1].

Source of food [1].

Source of medicines / drugs [1].

Other uses for humans (e.g. wood / fuel / fibres for clothing) [1].

Aesthetic reasons [1].

[Maximum 3 marks]

b Low temperature [1].

Low humidity / dry [1].

c To check seeds are still viable [1].

To grow new plants as source of new seeds [1].

To check conditions needed to break dormancy [1].

[Maximum 2 marks]

4 a i Variation shown by organisms [1].
Genetic (diversity / variation) [1].
Species (diversity / variation) [1].
Habitat (diversity / variation) [1].

[Maximum 2 marks]

ii Organisms / biotic components / living components [1].

Abiotic / non-living components / physical environment [1].

b Controls trade of these species [1].

Species not threatened with extinction [1].

But could become extinct if trade not controlled [1].

[Maximum 2 marks]

5 *Similarities*

Eukaryotic (cells) [1].

Nucleus / linear DNA / linear chromosomes / chromosomes associated with histones [1].

Membrane-bound organelles / named example [1].

80S ribosomes [1].

Differences

Unicellular or multicellular [1].

Autotrophic or heterotrophic [1].

Chloroplasts or no chloroplasts [1].

Cell wall or no cell wall [1].

(Large, permanent) vacuole or no vacuole [1].

[Maximum 6 marks]

Unit 19

1 a i Restriction endonucleases are enzymes that cut DNA at specific recognition sites [1].

Some types of restriction endonucleases produce a staggered cut, leaving short sequences of unpaired bases known as sticky ends [1].

ii Ligase forms covalent phosphodiester bonds in the DNA sugar–phosphate backbone [1].

It is used to join pieces of DNA together (e.g. to attach a gene to a plasmid vector to form recombinant DNA) [1].

iii Reverse transcriptase is an enzyme that uses mRNA as a template to synthesise a complementary strand of DNA [1].

This provides a method of synthesising a gene using mRNA [1].

DNA polymerase is then used to produce double-stranded DNA from the single strand of complementary DNA [1].

b This depends on 'marker genes' on the plasmid [1].

Marker genes may confer resistance to antibiotics so that transformed bacteria can be selected by growing them on media containing antibiotics [1].

Other marker genes may result in the synthesis of green fluorescent protein (GFP) or an enzyme that results in a colour change [1].

2 a i Gene therapy is a technique by which a patient can be treated for a genetic disorder by inserting a functioning gene into the patient's DNA [2].

ii Gel electrophoresis is a technique used to separate and identify nucleic acids and proteins [1].

An electric charge is applied to a layer of gel containing a buffer and negatively charged molecules move towards the anode [1].

Smaller (or more negatively charged) molecules move faster than larger molecules and so become separated, forming a series of bands in the gel [1].

The bands are made visible using a dye or radioactive markers [1].

When applied to DNA, the pattern of bands produced is referred to as a genetic profile [1].

b Many different human therapeutic proteins are produced using recombinant DNA technology, including:

- insulin
- factor VIII
- human growth hormone (HGH)
- erythropoietin
- follicle stimulating hormone (FSH)
- α-antitrypsin.

Note: this is not a definitive list, so it is possible that you may have included another acceptable answer.

[Maximum 3 marks]

c People may have concerns about the cultivation of genetically modified crop plants for a number of reasons including:

- the possibility that a gene for herbicide resistance could spread to related plants, including weeds, making them difficult to control and having unforeseen environmental effects
- crops genetically modified to produce insecticides could have toxic effects on non-target insects, which may be beneficial (e.g. pollinating insects), or have effects on food chains or food webs
- genetically modified crops or their products could be harmful to human health
- herbicides used on herbicide resistant-crops could leave toxic residues
- seeds of genetically modified crops are expensive and some small-scale farmers may be unable to afford these.

[Maximum 4 marks]

Unit P2

1 a i Independent variable = concentration of auxin [1].

Dependent variable = length of coleoptile <u>after treatment</u> (with auxin) [1].

ii <u>Two</u> other variables from: volume of auxin solutions / concentration of sucrose / length removed from tip of coleoptile / initial length of pieces of coleoptile / time in auxin solutions / temperature (of treatment in auxin) / darkness (during treatment) [1].

b i To remove the natural source of auxin [1].

ii Provides an energy source / substrate for respiration (for growth) [1].

c ×10 dilution of stock solution with <u>2% sucrose</u> to give 10 ppm auxin [1].

Details of method, such as take 10 cm³ of 100 ppm auxin and add 90 cm³ of 2% sucrose solution (or other appropriate volumes) [1].

Repeat to give lower concentrations / serial dilutions [1].

[Maximum 2 marks]

d   100 cm³ of 2% sucrose solution [1].

e   Wide / long error bars indicate results are less reliable [1].

Reference to data, such as results for 10 ppm less reliable than results for 0.01 ppm [1].

Overlapping error bars indicate means are not significantly different [1].

Reference to data, such as mean for 100 ppm not significantly different from mean for 0.1 ppm / mean for 0.01 ppm not significantly different from mean for control [1].

[Maximum 3 marks – at least one piece of evidence from the data shown in Figure P2.07 must be given for full marks]

f $Increase = \dfrac{(21.5 - 10.0)\ mm}{10.0\ mm} \times 100\ \%$ [1]
(1 mark for any correct working).

$= 115\%$ [1].

g   i   There is no significant difference between the mean lengths of coleoptiles (in 100 ppm auxin and the control) [1].

ii   Statistically significant – the difference is not due to chance / is caused by the treatment [1].

$P < 0.05$ – less than 5% (or less than 0.05) probability of obtaining the results by chance [1].

h   The statement is not / is not fully supported by the data [1].

10 ppm is most effective in stimulating growth of pieces of coleoptile [1].

The statement is describing the effect on coleoptiles in (intact) seedlings [1].

[Maximum 2 marks]

2   a   There is a positive correlation between the mass of snail and force needed to pull it off the surface. [1].

b $\Sigma D^2 = 22$ [1].

c $r_s = 1 - \left(\dfrac{6 \times \sum D^2}{n^3 - n} \right)$

$= 1 - \left(\dfrac{6 \times 22}{10^3 - 10} \right)$

$= 1 - \left(\dfrac{132}{990} \right)$

$= 1 - 0.133$

$= 0.867$ [2].

[1 mark for correct answer, 1 mark for any correct working]

d   There is no correlation between mass of snail and the force needed to pull the snail off the surface. [1].

e   (If the null hypothesis is correct) the probability of getting this value of r_s is less than 0.05 / less than 0.01 [1].

Therefore we can reject the null hypothesis [1].

There is a strong / significant / positive correlation between mass of snail and force needed [1].

f   Small sample size [1].

No replicate measurements with each snail [1].

Laboratory experiment may not reflect conditions in the field (e.g. surface is a glass dish rather than rocks) [1].

Glossary

abscisic acid (ABA) an inhibitory plant growth regulator that causes closure of stomata in dry conditions

absorption spectrum graph that shows the wavelengths of light absorbed by photosynthetic pigments

accessory pigments photosynthetic pigments that absorb light of different wavelengths and pass the energy to chlorophyll *a*

acetylcholine (ACh) transmitter substance; can be found in the presynaptic neurone at neuromuscular junctions

actin protein that makes up the thin filaments in striated muscle

action potential brief change in the potential difference across cell surface membranes of neurones and muscle cells; caused by the inward movement of sodium ions followed by the outward movement of potassium ions

action spectrum graph that shows the rate of photosynthesis against wavelength of light

activation energy energy required to start a chemical reaction; enzymes reduce the activation energy

active immunity occurs when the body produces its own antibodies to a particular antigen; either as a result of an infection or a vaccination

active site area on the surface of an enzyme molecule where the substrate binds and the enzyme-catalysed reaction takes place

adenosine triphosphate (ATP) chemical made by respiration; acts as the energy 'currency' of cells; phosphorylated nucleotide consisting of adenine and ribose, joined to three phosphate groups

adult stem cell type of stem cell found in various tissues in adults, such as bone marrow, skin and the lining of the intestine

aerobic respiration respiration in the presence of oxygen

albinism condition caused by a gene mutation where there is a lack of the dark pigment melanin in the skin, hair, iris etc.

alcoholic fermentation anaerobic respiration when glucose is converted to ethanol and carbon dioxide

alleles different forms of a gene

allopatric speciation speciation that takes place as a result of two populations living in different places and having no contact with each other

amino acid monomer that is the building block of all proteins

amylopectin consists of α-glucose monomers but it is a branched molecule, as a result of the formation of 1,6 glycosidic bonds

amylose α-glucose monomers joined by 1,4 glycosidic bonds only

Animalia animals - members of a very diverse kingdom; all multicellular eukaryotes with heterotrophic nutrition

antibiotics drugs that kill or inhibit the growth of bacteria, without harming the cells of an infected organism

antibody glycoprotein (immunoglobulin) made by plasma cells derived from B-lymphocytes, secreted in response to an antigen

anticodon region with three exposed bases on the tRNA

antidiuretic hormone (ADH) hormone secreted from the pituitary gland; it increases water reabsorption in the kidneys, therefore reducing water loss in urine

antigen chemical foreign to the body which stimulates an immune response

apoplast pathway route by which water crosses the root along cell walls of the root cortex cells

Archaea domain in taxonomy; prokaryotic organisms looking very similar to bacteria but have fundamental differences in their cell chemistry and metabolism

arteries blood vessels that carry blood away from the heart; the walls are relatively thick

artificial insemination (AI) collection of semen from a male animal and transfer into the female's reproductive system using a catheter

assimilates substances made by a plant during photosynthesis

atrioventricular node (AVN) patch of tissue in the septum of the heart; a wave of electrical excitation is passed from the atria to the Purkyne tissue through the AVN

autoimmune disease type of disease caused by a mistaken immune response leading to the production of antibodies and the destruction of body tissues

autosomal linkage genes are located together on a non-sex chromosome (autosome)

auxin plant growth regulator or plant hormone that stimulates cell elongation

axon long cytoplasmic process of a neurone, transmits the impulse away from the cell body

Bacteria domain in taxonomy; prokaryotic organisms

bacterial chromosome bacterial DNA, which is loose in the cytoplasm, forming a single circular loop

biodiversity amount of variation shown by organisms in an environment

bioinformatics use of computers to store and analyse data, including the analysis and comparison of base sequences in DNA and amino acid sequences in proteins

B-lymphocyte type of lymphocyte that produces plasma cells and secretes antibodies

Bohr effect decrease in affinity of haemoglobin for oxygen that occurs when carbon dioxide is present

buffer solutions solutions of salts that resist changes in pH

Calvin cycle cyclical series of reactions in photosynthesis during which carbon dioxide is fixed into carbohydrate

capillaries smallest type of blood vessel; capillary walls are made up of a single layer of squamous epithelium

capsid protein coat of a virus

capsomeres protein molecules that make up a capsid of a virus

carbon monoxide a colourless, odourless gas that is highly toxic; present in tobacco smoke

carbonic anhydrase enzyme in red blood cells which rapidly combines carbon dioxide with water, forming carbonic acid

carcinogens chemicals that cause mutations that affect the genes that control cell division; they can cause cancer

cardiac cycle cycle of events that take place during one heart beat

carrier person infected with a pathogen, or in possession of a mutation, but does not show any symptoms of the disease related to the pathogen or mutation

cell basic 'unit' of living organisms

cellulose polymer of β-glucose, joined by 1,4 glycosidic bonds

central nervous system (CNS) part of the mammalian nervous system consisting of the brain and the spinal cord

centromere region of a chromosome where two chromatids are joined

chiasma point at which crossing over of homologous chromosomes occurs during meiosis

chi-squared test statistical test to find out whether observed frequencies of observations are significantly different from expected frequencies

chlorophyll green photosynthetic pigment

chloroplast organelle containing chlorophyll; the site of photosynthesis

chromatid one of two structures making up a chromosome; each chromatid contains identical copies of the DNA

chromatin loosely coiled material formed by chromosomes between cell divisions

chromatography a method of separating a mixture of substances on the basis of their solubility in a solvent

chromosomes bodies within the nucleus that contain the hereditary material (DNA)

cilia hair-like structures on the surface of certain cells, which beat back and forth to move materials; found in epithelial lining of the trachea and bronchi

ciliated epithelium single layer of cells covered with cilia; present in the lining of organs such as the trachea and bronchi

cisternae stack of flattened membranes enclosing hollow sacs found in the Golgi body

codominant two alleles of a gene are both expressed in the phenotype

codon sequence of three bases (e.g. CGA)

coenzymes a non-protein molecule that is essential for the activity of some enzymes; coenzyme A, NAD, FAD and NADP are coenzymes

cohesion–tension theory mechanism suggested to explain water movement through the xylem, involving forces between the water molecules and between the molecules and the walls of the xylem vessels

community all the organisms of different species living in an ecosystem

companion cells cell of the phloem which lies alongside a sieve tube element and controls its activities

compartmentalisation function carried out by membranes in isolating the chemical reactions going on within organelles

competitive inhibitors molecules that have a shape that is similar to that of the substrate and can bind to the active site, inhibiting an enzyme-catalysed reaction

condensation reaction chemical reaction involving the joining together of two molecules by removal of a water molecule

conservation management of the Earth's resources to provide for the needs of humans at a sustainable level, while ensuring that resources are neither over-exploited nor destroyed

continuous (data) data that has any value within a particular range, e.g. length, mass, area, rate of reaction

continuous variation property where a characteristic shows a complete range of measurements, without falling into separate categories

correlation coefficient (r) numerical value that describes the degree of correlation between two variables; ranges from 0 (no correlation) to 1 (complete correlation)

counter-current multiplier the way in which the loop of Henle operates to build up a concentration gradient; filtrate flows in opposite directions in the descending limb and the ascending limb

cristae shelf-like structure formed by the folding of the inner membrane of the mitochondrion; oxidative phosphorylation takes place on the inner membrane

crossing over process that occurs between homologous chromosomes during meiosis, where chromatids of each pair exchange genetic material

culling reducing numbers by deliberately killing part of a population

cytokines substances that stimulate B cells to divide into a clone of antibody-producing plasma cells and memory cells; some cytokines stimulate macrophages to carry out phagocytosis, others activate killer T cells

cytokinesis stage of the cell cycle when division of the cytoplasm occurs, forming two daughter cells

cytoskeleton protein tubules and filaments running throughout the cytoplasm of a cell; involved in movement of organelles

degenerate genetic code is said to be degenerate, as it is possible for several different codons to specify the same amino acid

denaturation breakdown of structure of proteins (especially enzymes) caused by high temperatures or extremes of pH

deoxyribonucleic acid (DNA) a double-stranded polynucleotide with hydrogen bonding between pairs of complementary bases, forming a double helix

deoxyribose a 5-carbon (pentose) sugar found in DNA

dependent variable variable that changes as a result of changing the independent variable and are the results you might take during an experiment

depolarised the reversal of the potential across a neurone or muscle cell membrane, changing from the negative resting potential to a positive value

diastole stage in the cardiac cycle in which the heart muscle is relaxed and the chambers of the heart start to fill with blood

dihybrid inheritance inheritance of two genes

diploid cell containing two sets of chromosomes (both members of each homologous pair)

directional selection natural selection favouring a new phenotype, or a phenotype at one end of the phenotypic range

discontinuous variation property where a characteristic fits into a number of separate, distinct categories, with no intermediates

disease type of disorder of an organism which is characterised by particular symptoms

disruptive selection natural selection favouring both extremes of the phenotypic range over the intermediates

DNA profile the result of separation of DNA fragments by electrophoresis, also known as a DNA fingerprint

domain highest group in the classification of living organisms; Bacteria, Archaea or Eukarya

dominant allele that is expressed in the phenotype of the heterozygote

ecosystem all the organisms living in a defined area, together with their physical environment

elastic fibres fibres present in the walls of various organs such as arteries and the trachea; elastic to allow stretching and recoil

electron transport chain present in the inner mitochondrial membrane, a system of carriers that transport electrons to oxygen, the final acceptor in aerobic respiration

embryo transfer removing embryos from a female mammal and transferring them to a surrogate mother to complete their development

embryonic stem cell type of stem cell found in an early stage of development of the embryo, called a blastocyst

endodermis innermost layer of cells of the cortex of a root

enzymes protein molecules that act as biological catalysts

Eukarya domain in taxonomy; all organisms that have eukaryotic cells – animals, plants, fungi and protoctists

eukaryotic cells with a true nucleus and membrane-bound organelles

evolution process of change by natural selection, leading to speciation

exocytosis vesicles fuse with the cell membrane, releasing their contents out of the cell

F1 hybrids the offspring of a cross between an organism with a homozygous dominant genotype and an organism with a homozygous recessive genotype (e.g. RR x rr)

fluid mosaic model proposes that the cell surface membrane consists of a double layer of phospholipids, known as a bilayer, in which there are other components, including proteins, glycoproteins, glycolipids and cholesterol

founder effect special case of genetic drift that occurs when a new, small population is established; the new population may by chance be genetically different from the parent population; differences may then be increased by genetic drift

Fungi kingdom that includes mushrooms, moulds and yeasts

gel electrophoresis this technique relies on the principle that charged molecules will move in an electric field, though an agarose gel, containing a buffer solution; it is used to separate different proteins and nucleic acids

gene a length of DNA that codes for a specific polypeptide or protein

gene mutation change in the base sequence of part of a DNA molecule

gene therapy placing a 'normal' allele into the cells of a patient with a genetic disorder

generative nucleus one of two haploid nuclei in a pollen grain; divides by mitosis to produce two gametes

genetic diversity number of different alleles in the gene pool of a species

genetic drift process of random change in frequencies of alleles in a population

genotype genetic make-up of an individual

geographical isolation two populations of one species become separated by a geographical barrier such as a river or mountain range, which can lead to divergence and allopatric speciation

germ cells cells involved in sexual reproduction or cells in an early embryo

gibberellins a group of plant growth regulators that can increase stem growth and stimulate enzyme synthesis in germinating cereal grains

globular protein a protein with a roughly spherical three-dimensional shape; globular proteins are water-soluble

glucagon hormone which effectively has the opposite effect to insulin, bringing about changes resulting in an increase in blood glucose concentration

glycogen similar in structure to amylopectin, but is more highly branched because the 1,6 glycosidic bonds between the α-glucose monomers form more frequently

glycoprotein protein with carbohydrate attached

goblet cells cells of the lining of the trachea and bronchi (and other organs) secrete mucus to trap particles of dust and bacteria

Golgi body organelle that synthesises glycoproteins and packages proteins for export from the cell

grana stacks of thylakoids

guard cells a pair of cells that surround each stoma; can change shape to open and close the stoma

haemophilia blood disorder resulting in inability of the blood to clot

haploid cells (gametes) containing one set of chromosomes (one member of each homologous pair)

Hardy-Weinberg principle in a diploid, sexually reproducing organism, allele and genotype frequencies remain constant from generation to generation, as long as certain conditions are met

helper T cells type of white blood cell (lymphocyte) that releases chemicals called cytokines

heterozygote organism that has two different alleles of a gene

high latent heat of vapourisation takes a relatively large amount of energy to break the hydrogen bonds and to change water from a liquid to a gas

high power drawing type of drawing that shows the details of individual cells

high specific heat capacity relatively large amount of energy is required to increase the temperature of water and the temperature of water tends to remain about the same if the environmental temperature changes

histogram a type of graph to show the frequency of a numerical independent variable, with continuous data; sometimes called a frequency diagram

histones proteins associated with DNA, forming nucleosomes

homeostasis regulation of the internal environment of an organism

homologous chromosomes matching pairs of chromosomes in body cells

homozygote organism that has two identical alleles of a gene

hormones act as 'chemical messengers' transported in the blood and affect the activity of other target organs in the body

Huntington's disease disease caused by a gene mutation inherited as a dominant allele; results in degeneration of nerve cells, involuntary muscular movements and progressive mental deterioration

hybridoma cell formed by fusing together an antibody-producing plasma cell with a cancer cell

hydrogen bonding attraction forces between water molecules; caused by the slight positive charge of the hydrogen and the slight negative charge of the oxygen

hydrolysis a chemical reaction in which a complex molecule is broken down into simpler ones, by the addition of water

hypothesis prediction about the outcome of an experiment, e.g. how the independent variable will affect the dependent variable

immobilised enzyme enzyme molecules attached to, or trapped within, an insoluble material; used in commercial processes

immune response reaction of the body to 'foreign' substances, especially disease-causing microorganisms

immunoglobulins group of plasma proteins also known as antibodies

in vitro fertilisation (IVF) fertilisation of a secondary oocyte outside of the body of a mammal ('in vitro' = 'in glass', i.e. in a test tube or dish); viable embryos allowed to develop in a surrogate mother

inbreeding depression accumulation of disadvantageous genes as a result of breeding between closely-related individuals; results in poor quality offspring (e.g. crop plants or domesticated animals)

independent assortment process happening during metaphase I of meiosis, when chromosomes of each homologous pair align themselves along the equator at random

independent variable factor that you might change in an experiment

induced fit hypothesis model of enzyme action where the substrate does not fit the active site perfectly until it actually enters the active site

inducible enzymes enzymes that are only produced in response to the presence of their substrate

insulin a polypeptide hormone involved in the regulation of blood glucose concentrations, insulin has the effect of reducing blood glucose by promoting its uptake

interphase phase of the cell cycle between nuclear divisions

interquartile range range between the lower and upper quartiles

invasive alien species (IAS) organisms that have spread from one ecosystem to another where they are not naturally present

islets of Langerhans groups of endocrine cells situated in the pancreas; includes cells that secrete insulin and glucagon

killer T cells lymphocytes which roam the body searching for virus-infected cells, tumour cells or cells that are damaged in some other way; they attach to infected cells and destroy them, killing the host cell and the pathogen

Krebs cycle a sequence of reactions that occurs in the mitochondrial matrix, resulting in the formation of carbon dioxide, reduced hydrogen carriers and ATP

leukaemia cancer of the white blood cells

light-dependent reactions reactions of the first stage of photosynthesis, which use light energy to split water molecules into hydrogen and oxygen, producing reduced NADP and ATP

light-independent reactions reactions of the second stage of photosynthesis, where reduced NADP and ATP from the light-dependent reactions are used to reduce carbon dioxide to carbohydrate

lignin strong, waterproof material present in the walls of xylem vessels

limiting factor factor which limits or 'holds back' the rate of a reaction

link reaction occurs in the mitochondrial matrix and links glycolysis to the Krebs cycle; puruvate is converted to acetyl CoA, with the formation of carbon dioxide and reduced NAD

lipids consist of the elements carbon, hydrogen and oxygen; lipids include a variety of different compounds, such as fats, oils, steroids and phospholipids which all have the property of insolubility in water, but they are soluble in organic solvents such as ethanol

lock and key hypothesis model of enzyme action where the substrate (key) fits into the shape of the active site (lock)

locus position of a gene on a particular chromosome

low power plan type of drawing used to show the distribution of tissues, such as in a transverse section through a plant stem or a leaf

lymph similar in composition to tissue fluid, but lymph contains proteins, derived from the lymphatic system; eventually returned to the blood stream, via ducts which connect the lymphatic system to veins near the neck

lymphocyte type of white blood cell (leucocyte) that includes both B and T cells

macromolecules very large molecules such as starch, cellulose, proteins and nucleic acids

macrophages phagocytic cells that are derived from monocytes and form antigen-presenting cells

magnification number of times larger a drawing or photomicrograph is, when compared with the actual size of the specimen

mark-release-recapture ecological method of estimating the population size of a mobile species in a well-defined area

matrix fluid-filled space in the middle of a mitochondrion where the Krebs cycle takes place

mean sum of all the values divided by the total number of values

median middle value of all the values in the data set

meiosis type of nuclear division leading to production of gametes, reduces number of chromosomes from diploid to haploid and introduces genetic variation

memory cells B lymphocytes that remain in the blood and are able to divide and produce antibodies on second exposure to a pathogen, producing a secondary immune response

mesophyll cells cells of the middle part of a leaf; made up of spongy and palisade mesophyll

messenger RNA (mRNA) a type of RNA that carries the genetic code from DNA to a ribosome where the code is translated in the process of protein synthesis

Michaelis–Menten constant (Km) in an enzyme-catalysed reaction, the value of the substrate concentration [S] at which the reaction rate is equal to half that of Vmax

microarray a slide with thousands of DNA probes, used in the analysis of DNA

mitochondria organelles that produce adenosine triphosphate (ATP) by aerobic respiration

mitochondrial DNA (mtDNA) circular loops of DNA found in the mitochondria

mitosis type of nuclear division that produces two daughter nuclei that are genetically identical

mitral (or bicuspid) valve the left atrioventricular valve, between the left atrium and the left ventricle

mode most common value in a data set

monoclonal antibodies antibodies that are made on a large scale in the laboratory; they are prepared from a single clone of cells, so that each is specific to a particular antigen

monocyte type of phagocytic white blood cell that form macrophages in body tissues

monomer relatively simple molecule used as a basic building block for the synthesis of a polymer, usually joined by condensation reactions

monosaccharides single molecules, or simple sugars, including glucose, fructose and galactose; each have six carbon atoms in their structure

motor neurone a neurone that conducts nerve impulses from the central nervous system (CNS) to an effector, such as a muscle

mucous glands glands that secrete mucus; found below the epithelium of the trachea and bronchus

myasthenia gravis (MG) autoimmune disease that causes weakness in the voluntary muscles of the body

myosin protein forming the thick filaments in muscle structure

negative feedback self-correcting mechanism in which a change brings about a corrective process to return to the 'set value'

nephron microscopic tubule and associated blood vessels in the kidneys

neuromuscular junction a type of synapse formed between a motor neurone and a muscle fibre

neurones specialised cells in the nervous system that conduct nerve impulses

neutrophil the most common type of white blood cell (leucocyte); these cells are phagocytic and have a multi-lobed nucleus

niche 'role' of an organism in an ecosystem

nicotine colourless, odourless chemical that is the addictive component of tobacco smoke

nodes of Ranvier small gaps between adjacent Schwann cells in myelinated neurones

nominal (data) data that can be sorted into categories, e.g. flower colour or tree species; nominal means 'named'

non-competitive inhibitor enzyme inhibitor that has a shape different from that of the substrate; binds to the enzyme away from the active site

nuclear envelope double membrane around the nucleus

nuclear pores 'holes' in the nuclear envelope that allow movement of materials between the nucleus and the cytoplasm

nucleotides consist of a 5-carbon sugar, a nitrogen-containing organic base and an inorganic phosphate group

nucleus organelle that contains the chromosomes; surrounded by a double membrane called the nuclear envelope

oogenesis formation of female gametes (in humans)

operator non-coding sequence of DNA heading a group of structural genes in an operon; binds to a repressor protein to stop RNA polymerase binding with the DNA at the promoter

operon group of structural genes headed by a non-coding sequence of DNA called the operator and under the control of another sequence of DNA called the promoter

ordinal (data) data can be placed into a rank order, e.g. depth of blue colour produced in a starch–iodine test

osmoreceptors nerve endings sensitive to the water potential of blood; found in the hypothalamus of the brain and constantly monitor the water potential of blood

oxidative phosphorylation production of ATP associated with the oxidation of reduced hydrogen carriers via the electron transport chain in mitochondria

passive immunity occurs when the body does not make its own antibodies but receives them from somewhere else, either to a baby in the mother's milk or across the placenta to the foetus

pathogen organism that can cause disease. These include viruses, bacteria, fungi and protoctists

Pearson's linear correlation statistical test for a linear correlation (positive or negative) between two variables

pentose a sugar containing five carbon atoms

peptide bonds covalent bonds formed by condensation reactions between adjacent amino acids in the formation of polypeptides

peptidoglycan chemical forming the cell wall of a bacterium; polysaccharide with some amino acid groups

peripheral nervous system (PNS) a system of paired nerves, including sensory and motor nerves, that arise from the central nervous system

phagocyte white blood cell produced by mitotic division of stem cells in the bone marrow

phagocytosis process where a cell engulfs solid particles to form a vacuole called a phagosome; the phagosome fuses with lysosomes containing digestive enzymes such as proteases; these digest and destroy the pathogen

phenotype how the genotype of an individual is expressed; its appearance

phloem plant tissue that carries products of photosynthesis from the leaves to other parts of the plant

phospholipid special type of lipid in which one of the fatty acids is replaced with a phosphate group

photolysis splitting of water into oxygen, hydrogen ions and electrons, using light energy

photophosphorylation production of ATP in the light-dependent reactions of photosynthesis, using light energy

photorespiration process occurring in chloroplasts at high temperatures and high light intensity, where rubisco binds oxygen to RuBP in place of carbon dioxide; RuBP is broken down into carbon dioxide and water and less carbon dioxide is fixed

photosynthesis conversion of carbon dioxide and water into organic compounds and oxygen using light energy

photosystems chloroplast pigments and associated proteins in the lamellae of chloroplasts; the site of the light-dependent reactions

plant growth regulators also known as plant hormones, these are substances produced by plants, such as auxin and gibberellin, that affect their growth and development

Plantae plants - complex multicellular eukaryotes; most carry out photosynthesis; examples include mosses, ferns, conifers and flowering plants

plasma a solution of many different solutes, including proteins and ions, in which blood cells are suspended

plasma cells blood cells produced by division of B-lymphocytes that have been activated by exposure to an antigen; secrete antibodies against the antigen

plasmids small loops of DNA in the cytoplasm of a bacterium

polymer large molecule made of repeating units of monomers

polymerase chain reaction (PCR) this technique makes it possible to make many millions of identical copies of just one strand or a few strands of DNA, in a relatively short time; the same principle as DNA replication, although it is carried out under precisely controlled conditions in a laboratory

polyploidy organisms with more than two sets of chromosomes in their cells (3n, 4n etc.)

population total number of individuals of one species living in a particular ecosystem at one time

postsynaptic neurone the neurone at a synapse to which the transmitter substance diffuses and attaches to receptors on the membrane of the postsynaptic neurone

postzygotic isolating mechanisms barriers that bring about reproductive isolation after a zygote has been formed, such as hybrid unviability or sterility

presynaptic neurone the neurone at a synapse at which the action potential arrives; this neurone releases the transmitter substance

prezygotic isolating mechanisms barriers that bring about reproductive isolation before a zygote has been formed, such as ecological, behavioural or mechanical mechanisms

primary pigment chlorophyll a

primary structure the precise sequence of amino acids in the structure of a polypeptide chain

prokaryotic cells lacking a true nucleus and membrane-bound organelles; e.g. bacteria

promoter non-coding sequence of DNA in an operon that binds with RNA polymerase to initiate transcription

Protoctista kingdom that contains a wide range of unicellular and multicellular organisms that do not fit into any of the other three kingdoms

proton pumps protein pumps in cell membranes that actively transport hydrogen ions into or out of a cell

pulmonary circulation circulation of blood from the heart, to the lungs and back to the heart

purines nitrogenous bases found in the structure of nucleotides; adenine (A) and guanine (G) are purines

Purkyne tissue modified cardiac muscle tissue in the septum of the heart that conducts the electrical excitation from the AV node to the ventricle walls

pyrimidines nitrogenous bases found in the structure of nucleotides; cytosine (C), thymine (T) and uracil (U) are pyrimidines

pyruvate a three-carbon compound formed as the end-product of glycolysis

quadrat frame used for the sampling of plants, or animals that do not move a great deal

qualitative variables variables that can be observed and counted but not measured

quantitative variables variables that can be measured

quaternary structure the final three-dimensional structure of a protein that consists of more than one polypeptide chain

random errors errors that arise as a result of difficulties in controlling variables or in measurement of the dependent variable

range spread between the smallest and largest value in the data

recessive allele that is only expressed if no dominant allele is present

recombinant DNA one aspect of genetic technology involves extracting a gene from one organism and transferring it to the DNA of another organism, of the same or another species; DNA produced in this way is referred to as recombinant DNA

recombinants chromosomes with new combinations of genes as a result of crossing over during meiosis

refractory period a brief recovery time in a neurone following the generation of an action potential, in which the neurone will not respond to a second stimulus

regulatory genes genes that code for proteins that regulate the expression of other genes, such as transcription factors

relay neurone a neurone that joins a sensory neurone to a motor neurone within the central nervous system, for example, in a reflex arc

renal artery supplies each kidney with blood

repressible enzymes enzymes that are switched off or downregulated by the presence of a substance such as a product of the pathway in which the enzyme participates

reproductively isolated populations of a species that are prevented from reproducing; necessary for speciation to occur

resolution in a microscope image, the shortest distance between two points that can be distinguished as being separate

respiration the overall breakdown of organic molecules, by enzymes, with the release of energy

respiratory quotient (RQ) ratio of the volume of carbon dioxide produced to the volume of oxygen used, in a given time, in respiration

resting potential the difference in the electrical potential across the membrane of a neurone when it is not conducting an impulse; the resting potential is about -70 mV and is maintained by sodium-potassium pumps

restriction enzyme enzyme that cuts DNA into fragments

Rf value in chromatography, the distance moved by the separated substances relative to the distance moved by the solvent front

ribose a 5-carbon (pentose) sugar found in the structure of RNA and ATP

ribosome organelle that is the site of protein synthesis

ribulose bisphosphate (RuBP) 5-carbon compound that combines with carbon dioxide in the light-independent reactions of photosynthesis

RNA polymerase enzyme that joins free nucleotides to form complementary mRNA

rough endoplasmic reticulum organelle consisting of an interconnected network of flattened, membrane-enclosed sacs covered with ribosomes; transports proteins synthesised on the ribosomes

rubisco ribulose bisphosphate carboxylase; enzyme that catalyses the fixation of carbon dioxide by RuBP

sarcomere the repeating structural unit of a myofibril of striated muscle extending from one Z line to the next Z line

sarcoplasmic reticulum a system of tubules within muscle tissue similar to the endoplasmic reticulum

Schwann cells specialised cells associated with neurones that form the myelin sheath by wrapping around the axon

secondary structure structural feature of a protein, either an alpha helix or a beta pleated sheet, held by hydrogen bonding

selective breeding technique used by humans to breed crop plants or domesticated animals that have desirable characteristics; also known as artificial selection

selective reabsorption process occurring in the nephron in which certain solutes, such as glucose and some ions, are removed from the filtrate and returned to the blood

semiconservative replication the process by which DNA forms identical copies; each daughter molecule consists of one original strand and one complementary newly-synthesised strand

sensory neurone a neurone that conducts nerve impulses from a receptor, such as a touch receptor in the skin, to the central nervous system

sickle cell anaemia disease caused by a mutation in the gene that codes for the production of haemoglobin; abnormal haemoglobin causes red blood cells to become distorted and affects transport of oxygen

sieve tube elements cells present in phloem that form continuous tubes for translocation

Simpson's Index of Diversity (D) mathematical measure of diversity that takes into account the species richness and the relative abundance of each species

sink any plant organ that is a net consumer of sucrose, such as roots, buds, flowers, young leaves, stems and fruits

sinoatrial node (SAN) the natural 'pacemaker' of the heart situated in the wall of the right atrium, it sends out regular electrical impulses that control and coordinate the heart beat

sliding filament model a mechanism to explain how muscles contract by the sarcomeres getting shorter as actin and myosin filaments slide past each other and the Z discs get closer together

smooth endoplasmic reticulum organelle consisting of an interconnected network of flattened, membrane-enclosed sacs; similar to rough ER but lacks ribosomes; synthesises and transports lipid molecules

smooth muscle tissue formed of specialised muscle cells that undergo slow, rhythmic contractions for extended periods without tiring; found in various organs such as the blood vessels and trachea

sodium–potassium pumps protein pumps situated in cell membranes that actively exchange sodium ions and potassium ions, using ATP as an energy source

somatic cell body cell, i.e. cells other than gametes

source part of the plant that is a net producer of sucrose

Spearman's rank correlation statistical test for a correlation (positive or negative) between two variables using the ranked values of the data

speciation process of formation of a new species

species group of organisms that have similar morphological, physiological and biochemical features, and are capable of reproducing to produce fertile offspring

species diversity measure of the number of different species present in a community and the 'evenness' of each species

species richness number of different species present in a community

spermatogenesis formation of male gametes (in humans)

squamous epithelium epithelium consisting of a single layer of flat cells, e.g. the alveolus

stabilising selection natural selection acting against new phenotypes or against extremes of phenotype and in favour of intermediates

standard deviation a measure of the spread of the values in the sample around the mean

standard error standard deviation of sample means

stem cell cell that retains the ability to divide many times by mitosis while remaining undifferentiated, but following this can differentiate into specialised cells such as muscle or nerve cells

stem cell therapy medical use of adult stem cells to regenerate tissues damaged by disease or injury

stomata pores in the leaf through which water is lost

structural genes genes that code for proteins such as enzymes, or proteins that form part of the cell itself, such as actin and myosin

substrate substance upon which an enzyme acts in an enzyme-catalysed reaction

substrate level phosphorylation the process by which ATP is synthesised directly, without involving the electron transport chain and a proton gradient; substrate level phosphorylation occurs in glycolysis and in the Krebs cycle

surrogate (mother) female mammal that carries an embryo from another individual implanted in its uterus

sympatric speciation two (or more) species are formed from a single ancestral species, each occupying the same geographical location (sympatric means 'same place')

symplast pathway route by which water crosses the root through the cytoplasm or vacuoles of the cells

systematic errors errors that arise if a measuring instrument is incorrectly calibrated

systemic circulation circulation of blood from the heart, around the body and back to the heart

systole a stage of the cardiac cycle in which the heart muscle is contracting

T cells lymphocytes that mature in the thymus gland; have various roles such as releasing cytokines and destroying infected cells and tumour cells

tar oily brown substance deposited in the filter of a smoked cigarette and in a smoker's lungs; contains a number of harmful chemicals, including many known to cause cancer

taxa groups used in classification of species

telomeres DNA found at the ends of chromatids; act as 'caps' on the end of the chromosomes, preventing loss of DNA during DNA replication

tertiary structure the three-dimensional structure of a protein, involving bonding between the R-groups of amino acids

thylakoids complex internal system of membranes found in chloroplasts

tonoplast partially permeable membrane surrounding the plant cell vacuole

transcription stage of protein synthesis when a molecule of messenger RNA (mRNA) is synthesised with a complementary base sequence to the template DNA strand

transfer RNA (tRNA) folded, single-stranded RNA molecule that carries an amino acid to a ribosome for protein synthesis

translation stage of protein synthesis when the sequence of bases on the mRNA molecule is used to specify the order in which amino acids are joined together to form a polypeptide

translocation movement of sugars and other products of photosynthesis through the phloem

transmission spread of a pathogen from one person to another

transmission electron microscope microscope that sends a beam of electrons through a very thin specimen. The image is formed from electrons that pass through the specimen and hit a fluorescent screen or photographic film.

transpiration loss of water from the leaves of a plant

triglyceride molecule that consists of glycerol (a type of alcohol) joined to three fatty acids ('tri' means three)

tropomyosin fibrous protein that is part of the thin filaments in myofibrils in striated muscle

troponin calcium-binding protein that is part of the thin filaments in myofibrils in striated muscle

t-test statistical test used to find out if there is a significant difference between the means of two independent groups

tumour mass of cells caused by uncontrolled cell division

ureter conveys urine, formed in the kidney, from the kidney to the bladder

vaccine preparation of antigens from a pathogen, which is given to a person in order to stimulate the primary immune response and the production of memory cells

vascular bundles strands of xylem and phloem found in young, non-woody stems; located around the periphery of the stem

vector method of delivering genes into a cell; also refers to organisms that transmit agents of infection

vein blood vessel that carries blood to the heart

xerophytes plants that are adapted to live in conditions of low water availability

xylem plant tissue that carries water and minerals from the roots to the leaves

xylem vessel elements dead, empty cells in the xylem; lacking end walls and forming continuous tubes

Index

Index